THE ENCYCLOPAEDIA OF DUBLIN
REVISED & EXPANDED

THE
ENCYCLOPAEDIA
OF
DUBLIN

REVISED & EXPANDED

Douglas Bennett

GILL & MACMILLAN

Gill & Macmillan Ltd
Hume Avenue, Park West, Dublin 12
with associated companies throughout the world
www.gillmacmillan.ie
First published in hard cover 1991
First published in paperback 1994
© Douglas Bennett, 1991, 1994, 2005
0 7171 3684 1
Index compiled by Helen Litton
Design and print origination by O'K Graphic Design, Dublin

Printed by MPG Books, Cornwall

The paper used in this book is made from the wood pulp of managed forests. For every tree felled, at least one tree is planted, thereby renewing natural resources.

A catalogue record for this book is available from the British Library.

1 3 5 4 2

CONTENTS

Illustration Credits

ACKNOWLEDGMENTS

This encyclopaedia has been compiled with the generous assistance of many individuals, official bodies and organisations. I would like to thank them all most sincerely for their support and help. I have tried to include as broad a spectrum as possible across a great variety of fields but I am only too aware that there are obvious omissions. In the twenty-first century, Dublin is evolving at an extraordinarily fast rate, much of it due to the tax incentives of the Designated Areas Scheme formalised in the Finance Act of 1986. It is impossible to include all the modern architecture, as new buildings appear to be rising out of the ground right up to the date of publication. It creates the usual problem when a work of this kind tries to be as up-to-date as possible. If greater emphasis appears to be on the past rather than the present this is due to two factors: one, that it is a short history of one of the great historic capitals of the world and two, it is written so that my fellow citizens might be made more aware of their heritage in an ever-changing environment. The debt to previous writers is prodigious. In particular, I wish to express my gratitude to the following people who gave permission to quote from material compiled by them and who offered advice:

The Dublin City Manager, Mr John Fitzgerald and Mr Matt Twomey, Assistant City Manager, for the use of material obtained from so many Dublin City Council Departments and for permission to reproduce the Arms of Dublin City Council. I trust that the kindly persons involved in these offices will accept this blanket acknowledgment: Michael Phillips, City Engineer, Batty White, Tom Leahy and Brian Smyth, Deputy City Engineers; Mr Philip Maguire, Assistant City Manager and Mary Clark, Archivist, Dublin City Library and Archive, for her untiring help; the late Clair Sweeney supplied information on the underground rivers of Dublin; Deirdre Ellis-King, Dublin City Librarian, and Dr Maire Kennedy, Divisional Librarian, for their help; David V. Craig, Director, National Archives; Aideen Ireland, Senior Archivist, National Archives, who was continually dipping into boxes and producing new material; Dr Muriel McCarthy, Keeper, Marsh's Library—so many hours were spent working with her in that wonderful environment and I am indebted to the Governors and Guardians of the library; Peter Coyne, chief executive, Dublin Docklands Development Authority; Maurice Craig, author of numerous publications including *Dublin 1660–1860*—I thank him for his kindly advice; David Griffin and the staff of the Irish Architectural Archive; the Council of the Old Dublin Society for giving me access to the Dublin historical records and for allowing me to extract information; the late Patrick Healy allowed me to reproduce his map of Dublin gates, towers and town walls and to publish extracts from 'The Tower Walls of Dublin'; Rev. E. E. O'Donnell SJ, author of *The Annals of Dublin*; the Very Rev. V. G. Griffin, former Dean and Ordinary St Patrick's Cathedral; Frederick O'Dwyer, for allowing me to use his book *Lost Dublin* as a source in principal—the sections on the Crampton Memorial, Jammet's Restaurant and Tara Street are gleaned from this work; Peter Costello's book, *Dublin*

Churches, was a good starting point for tracing many buildings in obscure places; the staff of the Dublin Civic Museum; Eugene Fitzgerald now retired, Valuation General of Ireland, for advice on city boundaries and for supplying maps; the statues of Dublin and the Dublin penny post are taken from manuscripts of the late F. E. Dixon and are reproduced by permission of his widow, Beatrice; Royal Society of Antiquaries of Ireland; Royal Irish Academy; Manuscripts Department, Trinity College Dublin; Brendan Doyle, for so much expert and time-consuming photographic work; and Eileen Davis for very helpful advice on the Huguenots. My thanks to Gill & Macmillan, especially Fergal Tobin, publishing director, who suggested a second edition and who gently nudged me along, and Patricia Hannon for the difficult task of slotting in new material. I am particularly indebted to my editor Deirdre Rennison Kunz for her careful close criticism of the entire typescript.

Scores of people have been left out, so many people answered queries—I hope they will understand and know that I am grateful to them all.

Finally no acknowledgment could be complete without mentioning Sandra, my wife, who typed and retyped so many of the entries and gave invaluable help in a variety of ways.

Author's Note

During the period 1582–1752 there was a discrepancy of ten or eleven days between the calendar used in Ireland and England and that used over a large area of continental Europe. This was corrected by an Act of Parliament of 1751 when Great Britain and the dominions of the crown adopted the Gregorian calendar. The act prescribed that 2 September 1752 should be followed by 14 September, and that the beginning of the year should be 1 January instead of 25 March. This explains why certain entries record two dates e.g. 25 December 1670–71. There is an inconsistency also in the dating of streets. An explicit date usually refers to the commencement and laying out of a particular area which, unless stated otherwise, was completed within a short period. When dealing with medieval thoroughfares the earliest known date is mentioned and the absence of a date is often because the development of that region continued over a long period—this is invariably explained in the text.

Introduction to the Revised Edition

The 1991 edition of the *Encyclopaedia of Dublin*, like its author, had begun to show its age. So there was a need for a new transformed edition to cover the enormous expansion of the city in the past fifteen years and which has now exceeded a population of one million. The following introduction is taken from the original edition but with suitable inclusions and updates as the compiling of an encyclopaedia encourages curiosity and new facts are continually emerging, creating an enormity of labour. I have not deliberately excluded information, so if your favourite place is missing, do not become vituperative, as sometimes space and the length of a volume determine its content. Today I send it home to my publisher with a sense of relief, having once again alleviated the solitary life of authorship, but also with a feeling of privation.

D. B.

2005

Asterisks* throughout the text indicate a separate entry for the subject thus marked.

Introduction to the First Edition

Just what has made Dublin into one of the great historic capitals of the world? What kind of people did it and how did they do it? These are the questions that this encyclopaedia intends to answer. A capital city includes almost by definition every imaginable form of architecture and every conceivable human type. Artists, architects, landscapers and developers have managed to formulate all shape and design supposedly possible in an ever-changing environment. Every street and square, every lane and alleyway was walked and noted with compass and rule before being included in this work. Also included in the phantomatic streetscape is the ghost of something that has gone forever: the story of Dublin as it used to be, the capital of Ireland with a geographical position of 53°23' north and 6°9' west, situated on the River Liffey which flows eastwards into a natural harbour on which a ford was built which gave the region its name Áth Cliath, the ford of the hurdles.

With the coming of the Vikings in the ninth century the area around Dubhlinn, the black pool, was developed into a large trading centre, which was to become the Norse kingdom of Dublin. Recent excavations at High Street and then at Wood Quay show how extensive was this commercial enterprise. It is not known for certain when the city was enclosed but by the time of the Norman invasion, in 1170, Dublin was a walled city. Two years later, Henry II granted to his men of Bristol his city of Dublin with all liberties and free usages which they have at Bristol and throughout the land. This is the first of one hundred and two charters granted to the city.

By the thirteenth century, the city was expanding; Dublin Castle, the seat of Anglo-Irish rule, was completed, as were the two cathedrals. In 1229, the first Mayor was elected under a charter of Henry III. The city continued to expand in the fourteenth century as far as the river. From earliest times, the River Poddle was the main supplier of water, then, in 1244, the River Dodder was diverted and a city watercourse linked the two rivers. This supply was extended in 1308, along Thomas Street and High Street to a common cistern outside St Audoen's Church. From 1361 to 1394, administration was moved from Dublin to Carlow; then because of unrest among the natives it was moved back to Dublin. The fourteenth century saw the annual election of a Mayor and bailiffs together with twenty-four aldermen, forty-eight sheriffs, peers and ninety-six common councillors. This structure was to remain until the Municipal Elections Act in 1841. Adjoining the area under the jurisdiction of the Mayor were several exempt jurisdictions of which the most important were the Liberty of St Sepulchre under the archbishop of Dublin, the Liberties of Thomas Court and Donore, belonging to the abbey of St Thomas, as well as the Liberty of St Patrick's. Towards the end of the fourteenth century, a general decline appears to have set in but this was arrested in the fifteenth century when many houses of wood were constructed.

In 1537, there came the suppression of the monasteries by Henry VIII, and the lands from these religious houses were divided. In 1592, Trinity College was founded and given the lands of the Priory of All Hallows. An important charter of 1547 allowed for the appointment of a Sheriff and legally released the city from the County Sheriff. In 1560, the first public clocks appeared at Dublin Castle, the Tholsel and St Patrick's Cathedral. In 1596, one hundred and twenty people were killed when the spark from a horseshoe accidentally set off a gunpowder explosion. The city continued to expand in the seventeenth century and, in 1610, John Speed published the first map of the city of Dublin. In 1616, the first record of public lighting appears when the Corporation ordered that every fifth house should have lantern and candlelight set forth from six o'clock to nine o'clock every dark night from Hallow-tide until after Christmas. Michael Cole, in 1697, was the first person to obtain a contract for lighting the city. A postal service that had commenced in 1562 was extended in 1638 with the opening of a General Post Office in Castle Street. In 1649, Oliver Cromwell arrived at Ringsend with 12,000 troops and stabled his horses in St Patrick's Cathedral. He introduced cabbages to Ireland for the first time and the Cabbage Patch is now a public park. The Commonwealth Government intensified attempts to impose a rigid and narrow Protestantism by a mixture of persecution, encouragement and settlement.

After the restoration of the monarchy in 1660, the city began to develop. The North Quays were built and Sir Humphrey Jervis laid out a street system on part of the lands of St Mary's Abbey. From 1630 onwards, there are records of Huguenots settling in Ireland but the two greatest influxes were in 1662 and 1686, causing a large industrial area in the Liberties of Thomas Court and Donore. Dutch immigrants brought a new style of frontgabled house called Dutch Billies.

The Wide Streets Commission was set up in 1757 when an act was passed for making a wide and convenient way, street or passage from Essex (now Grattan) Bridge to the Castle of Dublin. On the eastern side of the bridge and of Capel Street, and north of the river were fashionable areas like Henrietta Street and Sackville Street laid out by Luke Gardiner. The Commission had wide powers of compulsory purchase and of control over planning. South of the river, Parliament House and Trinity College were being laid out. It was a city of narrow streets, and fashionable squares like Merrion and Rutland (now Parnell) did not exist until 1760, and Mountjoy Square and Fitzwilliam Square were later still. Parliament Street was opened in 1762. The sum of £5,000 was granted in 1777 for the widening of Dame Street at the west end. This was commenced in 1782. The first stone of the new Custom House was laid in 1781–82.

Towards the end of the century, Westmoreland Street and D'Olier Street were opened up and, in 1790, £21,500 was spent on completing Dame Street. In 1792, Mountjoy Square was laid out and plans for Gardiner Street, leading to the square and thence to the Custom House, were prepared in the 1790s. Plans for Upper and Lower Mount Street were approved in 1791 together with those for Harcourt Street and Hatch Street. The area around Christ Church Cathedral down to St Patrick's Cathedral was improved on for the visit of George IV in 1821, and the roadways along the Quays were laid out for the same visit. The street pattern the Commissioners created has largely survived to the present day, and Dublin as we know it between the canals is thanks to them. The powers and duties of the Wide Streets Commissioners were taken over by Dublin Corporation in 1851. The Grand Canal Company (1772) and the Royal Canal Company (1789) were set up to link the port of Dublin with its hinterland. By the beginning of the nineteenth century, the city had spread to these boundaries and, by 1821, the population census showed 186,000 living within these territories. The disastrous Act of Union in 1801 removed the Dublin Parliament to Westminster and, in spite of the fact that the city continued to expand, the continuity of patronage was lost as many people left their town houses and removed to England. After the famine of 1840, country people moved into the empty Georgian houses which had turned into slums, and it is estimated that one third of the population living between the canals was housed in slum conditions.

The Catholic Emancipation Act of 1829 resulted in the building of a large number of Roman Catholic churches.

The majority of the Guild systems were abolished in 1841 with the Municipal Corporations (Ireland) Act, and Council members were elected by the rate payers of the city. The boundary of the city was fixed between the two circular roads and the two canals. The Iveagh Trust, founded in 1904, did much to alleviate the hardship of the poor, with the building of red-brick flats around the Nicholas Street area. O'Connell Street was badly damaged in 1916 and again in 1922, together with other streets, the Four Courts, the Custom House and the Public Records Office. With the administration of the Irish Free State, Dublin became the capital of the Free State in 1922.

After this, Dublin appears to have become a shabby city and increasingly brutalised with buildings being demolished and never rebuilt. There was an emphasis on moving to the suburbs, leaving Dublin a dead city at night. It was not until the 1960s, that new building in the form of office blocks began to take shape. In the late 1960s Dubliners became aware of the fact that hundreds of good houses were being demolished to make way for office blocks. The property market collapsed in 1974 with huge cutbacks in all aspects of construction, affecting architects to labourers, but this was arrested and rejuvenated with the introduction of the Section 23 tax incentive, when new apartment blocks were built, encouraging people to live in the inner city. One of the largest projects in recent years was the refurbishment of the Temple Bar area, one of the last fragments of the central area which gives a picture of the city before the Wide Streets Commissioners replaced its medieval street pattern. The Dublin Docklands Development Act 1997 produced a master plan to guide the durable economic and physical development of the area. This resulted in the complete redevelopment of a derelict space where people can avail of urban living in an attractive setting. The International Financial Services Centre was a project undertaken by the Irish Government in 1987, and today there are over 380 business firms employing more than 14,000 people. The city celebrated its dubious millennium in 1988 and was designated European City of Culture for 1991. Dublin is evolving at an extraordinarily fast rate, large numbers of hotels have opened and open-top sightseeing buses enjoy an all-year-round season, taking visitors around the sights. The city is again alive and well in the evenings with late-night shopping and restaurants and pubs doing a lively trade.

Under a new Local Government Act, Dublin Corporation changed its name to Dublin City Council. This was ratified by the Council in March 2002. Any entries in the encyclopaedia prior to this date refer to Dublin Corporation and any entries after March 2002 use the new title of Dublin City Council.

A

Abattoir

North Circular Road

The Corporation was concerned about the number of unhygienic slaughter houses operating throughout the city. A new abattoir, opened in 1882, was designed by Park Neville. It stood on ten acres outside the NCR and was divided by the Cattle Market. As it was outside the city boundary, the Corporation could not compel the butchers to use it, with the result that it ran at a financial loss. It closed after a few years.

Abbey Green. *See* Green Street.

Abbey Road. *See* Prussia Street.

Abbey Street Lower

From O'Connell Street to Beresford Place

Name comes from St Mary's Abbey.*

In 1971, Irish Life bought the old Brooks Thomas warehouse and timber yard and within three months had three acres stretching back as far as Talbot Street. The Irish Life Centre includes their headquarters, a large shopping mall and fifty apartments; its main piazza has a large sculpture by Oisín Kelly, 'Chariot of Life'. During the course of this work, the sculptor suffered a massive heart attack but managed to finish the plasterwork for the foundry. Wynn's Hotel at 35–39 is a mid-nineteenth century protected structure. A popular landmark especially with visitors from rural areas, it was extended to the rere in 2004.

Abbey Street Upper and Middle

From Capel Street to Lower O'Connell Street

Name comes from St Mary's Abbey, on the grounds of the suppressed Abbey.

With the opening of the new music hall at Fishamble Street in 1741, Mr Handel was in attendance in his house in Abbey Street from nine o'clock in the morning till three o'clock in the afternoon in order to receive subscription money. In the 1930s, the Grand National Sweepstake draw was held in nos. 99–101. At no. 6 stood the Presbyterian Church and at no. 84 The Dublin Central Mission and Methodist Church, also the Metropolitan Hall and Dublin Savings Bank; at no. 13 is the Salvation Army.* The Royal Hibernian Academy* was at no. 34. Eason's the well-known booksellers were at 81 and 82 Middle Abbey Street. A busy shopping area with cinemas, hotels, shops and general offices. Also the home of the Abbey Theatre,* opened 27 December 1904. Following a fire this was demolished in 1961. The new theatre was opened in 1966 at a cost of £725,000.

Abbey Theatre

27 Lower Abbey Street and 2 Marlborough Street

In 1904, the Irish Literary Theatre Society and the National Dramatic Company merged to form the Irish National Theatre Company. William Fay, who with his brother Frank owned the National Dramatic Company, suggested to a Manchester heiress, Miss Annie Frederica Horniman, that she should buy the Mechanics Institute. It was one of the few places in Dublin where people could learn the Irish language and O'Donovan Rossa gave classes there for a time. The building also served as the city morgue and as a music hall. Miss Horniman provided £1,500 to refit the building as the Abbey Theatre. She also gave an annual subsidy of £850 until 1908. It was not until 1924 that the Free State government allocated an annual grant of the same amount, making it the first state-subsidised theatre in these islands. The first productions in the new theatre, which opened on 27 December 1904, were a play by W. B. Yeats, *On Baile's Strand*, and Lady Gregory's *Spreading the News*.

Born out of the Celtic revival, the Abbey Theatre was perhaps the most important cultural foundation of the period. In the following years, productions there included plays by Shaw, Synge, Lennox Robinson, Padraic Colum, O'Casey and many others, as well as the classics. Among the distinguished Abbey players were Sarah Allgood, May Craig, Maureen Delaney, Eileen Crowe, Siobhán McKenna, Barry Fitzgerald and Cyril Cusack. The remodelling of the theatre was supervised by the architect Joseph Holloway (1861–1944) and the Company employed important members of the arts and crafts movement to decorate the building using stained glass from An Túr Gloine and, according to *The Irish Builder*, copper mirror frames from the new metal works at Youghal.

In 1925, the Peacock Theatre was constructed adjoining the Abbey. It staged experimental theatre that was usually performed by pupils of the Abbey School of Acting.

The auditorium and stage were badly damaged by fire on the night of 17–18 July 1951 but the main entrance and vestibule escaped. The Irish Academy of Letters continued meeting there. When the building was being demolished in 1961, the late Daithí P. Hanly had the granite masonry of the two-storey front wall on Marlborough Street (which included the main entrance and the corresponding wall in the adjoining lane with the stage door) carefully removed to his garden in Dalkey. The builder had been ordered to dump

everything. At the same time, Mr Hanly got the canopy over the main entrance, the doors and windows (except the stained-glass windows in the vestibule). He also salvaged the railings and the bell boards. It is hoped that one day these may be erected as part of a theatre museum, possibly on the Custom House site. Already some 16,000 items, scripts, stage directions, set designs, costumes and other theatrical objects have been collected.

After the fire, the Abbey players moved to the Queen's Theatre, and a new Abbey Theatre, designed by Michael Scott and built at a cost of £725,000, opened on a larger site in 1966 and included the Peacock Theatre, used for smaller and more intimate productions. In 2004, one hundred years after its founding, the Minister for the Arts, Mr John O'Donoghue announced on 20 October that the theatre will move from its current location. The Office of Public Works has short-listed three Dublin city locations.

Abercorn Road (1868)
North Lotts

Abercorn Terrace (1869)
North Circular Road
Named after James Hamilton, Marquis of Abercorn, Lord Lieutenant 1866–68, 1874–76.

Aberdeen Street (1886)
Infirmary Road

Aberdeen Terrace (1888)
Named after Earl of Aberdeen, Lord Lieutenant who opened a red-brick complex of houses built by the Dublin Artisans Dwellings Company.*
See **Infirmary Road.**

Adelaide Road (Old Circular Road) (1833)
From Harcourt Road to Wilton Terrace
Named after Queen Adelaide (1792–1849), wife of William IV.
Buildings include a Presbyterian church founded in 1840 in the form of a painted

Adelaide Road. The Royal Victoria Eye and Ear Hospital designed by Carroll and Batchelor in 1901.

porticoed building with a high podium. The Royal Victoria Eye and Ear Hospital was founded in 1897 with the amalgamation of the National Eye and Ear Infirmary, Molesworth Street, and St Mark's Ophthalmic and Aural Hospital, Lincoln Place. The large red-brick complex was designed by Carroll and Batchelor in 1901 and took twenty-six years to complete. The brick synagogue in the Eastern-Romanesque style of architecture was designed by J. J. O'Callaghan to seat 300 in the body and 150 in the galleries and was built to replace the building in Mary's Abbey, now at a distance from the Jewish homes of Dublin, which were situated along and off the South Circular Road. The former Dublin Hebrew Congregation schools opened as Adelaide Road National Schools on 10 November 1893 and closed in 1921. The new Adelaide Road Synagogue was consecrated on 4 December 1892 by the Chief Rabbi of Britain and Ireland, Rabbi Hermann Adler, who on the

previous day had preached a valedictory sermon at the concluding service in Mary's Abbey. The Adelaide Road Synagogue was closed in 1999 and is now part of an office block with a preservation order on the original brick front. The congregation amalgamated with the Terenure Hebrew congregation who in 2004 were granted permission to demolish their existing synagogue at Leoville, Rathfarnham Road, and replace it with a 292-seat synagogue and 35 residential apartments over a basement car park. The Jewish population has fallen to about 1,000 persons. A small granite church built by E. T. Owens in 1863 for the Catholic Apostolic Church, a high Anglo-Catholic order, was handed over to the Church of Ireland in 1939, who in turn leased it to the Lutheran Church who named it St Finian's. Some terraced houses remain together with a variety of modern office blocks. Davitt House, no. 65A, houses the office of the Minister for Labour Affairs, Employment Rights Legislation and Administration, also the Employment Appeals Tribunal. The houses between Leeson Street Bridge and the Jewish synagogue were originally called Earlsfort Place. It was at no. 4 (now 63 Adelaide Road) that Samuel Beckett (1906–90), poet, playwright and Nobel prize winner attended Earlsfort House School, having left a private kindergarten in Foxrock.

Aldborough House
Portland Row, Amiens Street/North Strand
Erected in 1796 as a private residence for Viscount Amiens, created Earl of Aldborough (1777). It cost £40,000 and was the last of the great eighteenth-century houses to be built. In the early nineteenth century, it became a boarding school run by a teacher from Luxembourg. Several silver medals are extant made by William Mossop junior, which bear the inscription 'Institutum Feinaighlianum Luxemburgi'. It then became a barracks, a store for Telecom Éireann and, in 1999, the Irish Music Rights Organisation paid €3.81 million for the house and spent €952,303 on conservation reports and planning permission for the construction of a new wing. They sold it in 2004.

Alfred Chester Beatty Library
Dublin Castle
Born in New York on 7 February 1875, Alfred Chester Beatty became a mining engineer and had extensive mining interests in Africa, Russia and Yugoslavia.

Over his lifetime, Beatty collected oriental art, manuscripts and rare books. He became a British citizen in 1933 and was given a knighthood in 1954 for his work in cancer research. In 1950, he bought a house on Ailesbury Road and brought 35 tons of art treasures to Dublin. He donated a large quantity of French nineteenth-century paintings to the National Gallery in 1953, and weapons and armour to the Military Museum at the Curragh. The Freedom of the City was conferred on him in 1956 and the following year he was made the first honorary Irish citizen.

He bought two acres of land at 20 Shrewsbury Road and built the library and a small gallery with a curator's house. The library was opened in 1954 and in 1958 was extended when an additional gallery was added. He died in 1968 in Monte Carlo, was given a state funeral in St Patrick's Cathedral and was buried at Glasnevin Cemetery. The library contains Babylonian clay tablets, Egyptian and Greek papyri, early vellum manuscripts, together with Russian and Armenian texts. There are over 250 Qur'ans and Persian manuscripts and miniatures. A large Indian collection includes manuscripts and paintings. The Chinese and Islamic cultures are also extensively represented.

In 2000, the library moved to the newly restored and greatly extended Clock Tower building in Dublin Castle and, in 2002, received the European Museum of the Year award.

Aldborough House, Portland Row. Built for Viscount Amiens in 1796.

All Saints (C OF I)
Phibsborough Road, Grangegorman

The parish of Grangegorman was formed from parts of those of St Michan, St Paul and St George about 1828 when the present church was built. The chancel was added in 1856, the north aisle in 1867 and the baptistry at the west end in 1889. In the mid-nineteenth century, Grangegorman became a stronghold of Puseyism (the High Church tenets of the Oxford School). A monument in the church commemorates the Monck family, Earls of Rathdowne, the local landlords.

ALONE
1 Willie Bermingham Place, Kilmainham Lane

An organisation founded in 1977 by a Dublin fireman, Willie Bermingham, in response to the discovery of many old people dying or a long time dead, in sub-human conditions. ALONE's main aim is to expose and to help remedy the appalling conditions in which many isolated old people are trapped and to encourage direct intervention by neighbours and relatives where the forgotten old suffer distress. The organisation has no paid staff or major overheads and does not receive or request any state funding. It never set out to become a housing group but the generosity of thousands who forwarded unsolicited donations has enabled ALONE to accumulate a building and refurbishment fund, the results of which may be seen in ALONE Walk in Artane and Synnott Row (off NCR). Their motto is, 'Don't let old people die alone'.

See also **Millennium Plot.**

Amiens Street
From Memorial Road to the North Strand

In 1728, this thoroughfare was known as The Strand. In 1800, it was renamed Amiens Street after Viscount Amiens, created Earl of Aldborough in 1777. In 1800, only the eastern end was so named. In 1829, the new name was given to the entire street.

The terminus of the Dublin and Drogheda railway, later the Great Northern Line, was built 1844–46 to a design by William Dean Butler. The much plainer proposal by John Kelly was rejected in favour of the more impressive campanile over the main entrance. The foundation stone was laid by the Lord Lieutenant, Earl de Gray, on 24 May 1844. The cast-iron Doric double colonnade that carried the line across Sheriff Street was designed by Courtney, Stephens and Bailey. This firm also built the loop-line bridge between Amiens Street and Westland Row, opened on 1 May 1891. A large cab ramp stretching to Store Street was added in 1875 but was removed in 2003 to make way for a station on the Luas. The station was renamed Connolly after James Connolly (1868–1916), Commandant in the General Post Office during the Easter Rising. Sentenced to death, he was shot on 9 May 1916.

City Morgue at nos. 2, 3 and 4. Entrance together with Coroner's Court at Store Street. At the junction of Portland Row stands a familiar landmark in the form of the Five Lamps erected to the memory of General Henry Hall who served with the British Army in India.

See **Aldborough House.**

Anglesea Street
From College Green to Temple Bar

Arthur Annesley was born in Fishamble Street in 1614. He was chief of the party to whom the Duke of Ormonde surrendered Dublin in 1647. As President of the new Council of State, he was influential in bringing about the restoration of the monarchy, for which he was given the title of Earl of Anglesea in 1661. He acquired three leases from the Corporation, dated 1657, 1658 and 1662: 'all that part of the strand unto land watermark which abutteth and meareth unto several houses and gardens belonging to Arthur Annesley esq., situate on the College Green, in the suburbs of the city and adjoining to the seaside there.'

The Anglesea estate together with the Temple estate covers the rectilinear network of streets between Dame Street and the river that were developed from about 1658. Their layout survives to the present day but they were completely rebuilt in the eighteenth century. Blooms Hotel sides onto the street, together with general office and trading accommodation. At no. 6 lived Thomas Perry who died in 1818, musical instrument maker, a master violin maker, who was described as the Irish Stradivarius. The Dublin Stock Exchange, founded in 1799, occupies nos. 24–28.

Anne Street North
From King Street North to George's Hill
St Michan's Church built 1817 with a new front onto Halston Street, redesigned 1891. Generally a rundown area.
See Halston Street and George's Hill.

Anne Street South
From Grafton Street to Dawson Street
Named from its proximity facing St Ann's Church* in Dawson Street.

Apothecaries' Hall
Efforts to separate pharmacy from the practice of medicine began early in the seventeenth century. In 1735, an Act of Parliament was passed for the purpose of safeguarding the quality of drugs and medicines sold and for preventing frauds and deceits committed in making unsound drugs in the city of Dublin and suburbs. Anyone selling drugs had to register with the College of Physicians who had the authority under the act to certify the drugs used. The Guild* or Corporation of Apothecaries was given a Royal Charter in 1747 and, as was typical of the Guild system, apothecaries had to serve a five-year apprenticeship, a rule that they had practised since 1735. In 1791, the apothecaries were incorporated by an act for regulating the provision of pharmacy in Ireland with a strict preliminary examination before issuing a licence. A hall was established in Mary Street where simple and compound medicines were chosen and prepared under inspection of a sworn Court of Directors. Membership was open to all apothecaries on payment of £100.

Because of differences of opinions over many years between apothecaries, chemists and druggists, and physicians, the Pharmaceutical Society of Ireland was founded in 1875 by the Pharmacy Act (Ireland), which made the pharmaceutical chemist and the licentiate apothecary the only persons allowed to compound and dispense prescriptions. In 1962, a further act abolished the right of apothecaries to register as pharmaceutical chemists, their interests being protected under the 1791 Act.
See Pharmaceutical Society of Ireland *and* Crow Street.

Appian Way
From Leeson Street to Leeson Park
Probably from the Roman road; the name was changed from Tivoli Avenue about 1845. Originally a street of fine Victorian houses. In 1964, a block of nineteenth-century houses was demolished to build two lots of flats designed by Alan Hope. Fitzwilliam Lawn Tennis Club gave up its premises in Wilton Place in 1969 and moved to a four-and-a-half acre site bounded by Winton Road and Appian Way. Four nineteenth-century houses were demolished to make way for a club house, seven hard courts and four grass courts, together with indoor seating for 1,800 spectators, a large car park and many other facilities.

Arbour Hill
From Brunswick Street North to Montpelier Hill
An area partially owned by Christ Church Cathedral in the Middle Ages and used for the storage of corn. The name is derived from the Irish *cnoc an arbhair* (corn hill). At the top of the hill stood a gallows where crowds would gather to witness a hanging. The Royal Barracks (Collins Barracks) borders the street (*see* Benburb Street). St Bricin's Military Hospital nearby is on the site of the old Prevost prison where Wolfe Tone died in 1798. In 1845, work commenced on the building of the military prison and church where many soldiers

were detained during the Fenian troubles, including John Boyle O'Reilly, the Fenian poet and writer who was transported to Australia in 1867. He wrote 'The Moondyne' (1880) and 'Statues in the Block' (1881). A large memorial to him stands in the small graveyard at Dowth, Co. Meath, where he was born. He escaped to America in 1869 and died in Massachusetts in 1890. In a plot behind the church is a cemetery mostly for the British military and their families. The headstones now stand against a boundary wall. In another section there is a Garden of Remembrance which contains the remains of the fourteen executed leaders of the 1916 Rising, which were removed from Kilmainham Gaol on 3 May 1916. In April 1966, President Eamon de Valera unveiled a plaque with the names of those interred.

Ardee Street
From the Coombe to Mill Street
Named after Sir Edward Brabazon, created Baron Ardee in the County of Louth by privy seal at Newmarket in 1613–14 and by patent in Dublin 1616. His son, the 2nd Baron, became Earl of Meath on 28 March 1627 and by patent at Dublin on 16 April.
This street, formerly known as Crooked Staff, became part of the Earl of Meath's Liberties. A run-down area; the old James Weir nurses' home, at one time connected with the Coombe Hospital, still stands.

Armorials of the City
A certificate in the Corporation archives describes the arms as follows: 'To all and singular to whom these presents shall come, I Sir Arthur Edward Vicars, D.S.A., Ulster King of Arms and Principal Herald of All Ireland, Registrar and Knight Attendant on the most illustrious Order of St. Patrick, do hereby certify and declare that the Armorial Bearings above depicted, that is to say Azure, three castles, Argent Flamment proper, for supporters, on the Dexter, a female figure proper, representing law, vested gules doubled, or holding in the dexter hand a sword erect and in the sinister an olive branch all proper, on the

sinister, a female figure proper, representing justice, vested gules doubled Or, holding in the dexter hand an olive branch proper, and in the sinister a pair of scales, Or, and for motto OBEDIANTIA CIVIUM URBIS FELICITAS do of right belong and appertain unto the Right Honourable the Lord Mayor, Aldermen, and the citizens of the City of Dublin and to their successors forever according to the Law of Arms, as appears by the records of my office and more especially by the visitation of the City of Dublin by Daniel Molyneux, Esquire, Ulster King of Arms and Principal Herald of All Ireland in the year of our Lord, one thousand and six hundred and seven. AS WITNESS my hand and seal this twenty fifth day of May in the year of our Lord, one thousand eight hundred and ninety nine. Arthur E. Vicars, Ulster.'
N.B. In the 1607 explanation, the supporters hold laurel rather than olive branches.
The local Government Act 2001 required that from 1 January 2002 the term Dublin City Council be used instead of Dublin Corporation. This was ratified by the Council in March 2002. A new logo was adopted, using a version of the three castles, which have been used since 1229

Armorials. Arms of the City with supporters, above the Fish and Fruit market.

when they first appeared on the City Seal.*
The castles have been used since 1324 and
were confirmed and entered as the official
arms of the city in 1607.
See **Civic Plate, Civic Regalia, City Charters**
and City Seal.
See also **Dublin City Council.**

Arran Street East
From Ormond Quay to Little Green Street
Named after Charles Butler, Earl of Arran
1693, brother of James II, Duke of
Ormonde, Lord Lieutenant 1703–07,
1711–13.
Street of tenements and entrance to the fish
and fruit markets.*

Artane
An area in the Clontarf West Ward
boundary on the Malahide Road in the
Coolock barony three miles north from the
General Post Office. Anciently called *Ard*
Aidhin. From the fourteenth century
formed part of the estate of the de
Hollywoods, an Anglo Norman family.
They lived in Artane Castle where it is
alleged that, in July 1534, John Allen,
Archbishop of Dublin, was murdered by
the followers of Silken Thomas because he
was considered an enemy of the
Geraldines. In 1825, the ruins of the Castle
were taken down by Matthew Boyle, a
linen merchant of Mary Street, who
erected a new residence also named Artane
Castle. In 1870, the Christian Brothers
spent a lot of money expanding the
building. It was the first school to be
established under the Industrial Schools
Act and taught a wide range of trades. Its
boys' band was a familiar sight at Croke
Park.* It closed in 1969. The area is
now mainly a housing and industrial
development.

Artichoke Road
See **Shelbourne Road** *and* **Grand Canal Street**
Upper.

Artisans' Dwellings Company
See **Dublin Artisans' Dwellings Company.**

Assay Office, Dublin Castle
The only assay office in Ireland authorised
for the testing and hallmarking of precious
metals is the assay office of the Company of
Goldsmiths of Dublin, situated at Dublin
Castle. Hallmarks are a series of marks,
collectively known as such, authorised by
Royal Charter of Charles I in 1637 and by
enactment of Dáil Éireann, to be stamped
on articles manufactured from gold, silver
and platinum, after the articles have been
tested and found to be of the legal standard
of purity before they are offered for sale. By
law, the composition of all articles made
from gold, silver or platinum must be
ascertained by assaying. The legal standard
of purity having been established, the
articles are stamped with a series of
hallmarks in the assay office. From 1
October 2002, the European Commission
changed national legislation regarding
standards. For silver there are four
standards: 999, 958.4, 925, 800 parts in
each 1,000. There are eight standards for
gold: 999, 990, 916, 833, 750, 585, 417, 375
parts in each 1,000 and four standards for
platinum: 999, 950, 900, 850 parts in each
1,000.
From that date, the Irish Hallmark
comprises a minimum of three compulsory
symbols: 1, maker or sponsor's mark
(person's initials); 2, assay office mark (the
figure of Hibernia); 3, metal and fineness
(purity) mark (any of the above numerals
in assorted surrounds). Prior to 2002, the
fineness mark was the Harp Crowned, and
a date letter denoted the year of assaying,
enabling one to determine the age of an
item. The date letter may still be used on
request but is not part of the hallmark, and
the Harp Crowned has been terminated.
The body responsible for the assay office is
the Company of Goldsmiths of Dublin,
being the Guild* of All Saints, founded on
22 December 1637 by Royal Charter of
Charles I, when the assay office was put on
a solid foundation, and many of the orders
set forth in the charter document are
applicable to the present day. The company
was set up to prevent certain abuses and
deceits which were daily being committed

through lack of a recognised mark or standard for precious metals. To correct this omission, a perpetual body, which understood the art and mysteries of the trade, was set up. The body was to be incorporate of itself and have perpetual succession. Every goldsmith and silver-smith in Ireland was to be bound by the rules of the charter. The Company of Goldsmiths is the only surviving one of twenty-five guilds.*

Aughrim Street

From North Circular Road to Manor Street (formerly Blackhorse Lane)

Named to mark the centenary of the Battle of Aughrim, which was fought in 1691. Residential Street. RC Church of the Holy Family was originally part of the parish of St Paul's, Arran Quay, until it became a separate unit in 1893. Built in 1876 and designed by J. S. Butler with additions over the years by Doolin, Butler and Donnelly. It was designed to accommodate an expanding congregation following the erection from 1870 onwards of large red-brick houses on the North Circular Road.

Marlborough Barracks (now McKee Barracks), built in 1888–92 for the cavalry regiment, now houses offices for the Department of Defence, including the Director of Communications and Information Services Corps.

Aungier Street

Shown on Speed's map of 1610 as St Stephen Street (c. 1455). Named after Sir Francis Aungier, Master of the Rolls, the Baron Aungier 1621. In the late seventeenth century, two churches stood there, side by side, one the chapel of St Stephen's* leper hospital from which the Green is named and the other the Church of St Peter Del Hille.*

The street bordered the lands of the White Friars, and Sir Francis Aungier used the abbey as a town house. A descendant, Francis Aungier, created Earl of Longford in 1677, became a developer, laying out Aungier Street, Longford Street and Cuffe Street. Thomas Moore (1779–1852), the poet and author of Moore's Melodies, was born at no. 12.

Later copy of Speed's Map of 1610.

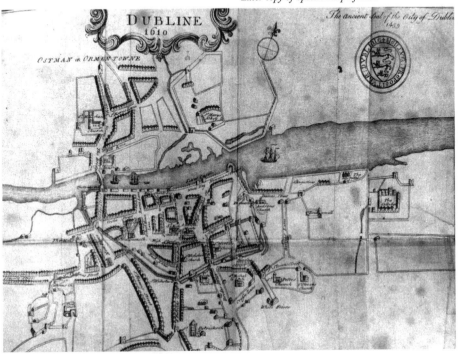

B

Back Lane

From Nicholas Street to the Cornmarket

So called from its position at the back of the High Street. Prior to the reign of Elizabeth I, it was called Rochell Street, Rochel Lane. During the reign of Charles I, a chapel and Roman Catholic university were established by the Jesuits; these were sequestrated by the government in 1630 and transferred to Trinity College. In 1583–84 the tailors built a Guild Hall in the lane and the present Tailors' Hall* was commenced in 1703, possibly on the site of the old university. The old James Winstanley shoe factory, built in 1875, was converted in 1988 to house the Christ Church festival market and Mother Redcap's Tavern (named after a hostelry founded in 1760 by Robert Burrell).

Baggot Rath

From Robert, Lord Bagod who was granted the Manor of Rath in the thirteenth century. Narrow portion at St Stephen's Green named Merrion Row 1776. Rocque's Map of 1756 calls it 'the road to Ball's Bridge'. After the execution of Charles I in January 1649, the Duke of Ormonde continued as Lord Lieutenant. Having surrendered Dublin to Cromwell's Parliament forces in 1647, he attempted to recover it in August 1649 but was defeated by Colonel Michael Jones and his Roundheads at the Battle of Baggot Rath, thus clearing the way for Oliver Cromwell who arrived in Dublin on 15 August 1649. Baggot-Rath Castle stood where Waterloo Road now meets Baggot Street.
See **Baggot Street.**

Baggot Street (1772)

From Merrion Row to Pembroke Road Lower (1839) Upper (1891)

Name comes from Robert, Lord Bagot. Red-brick houses in the Georgian style, private and commercial use. In 1831, a group of professors from the College of Surgeons bought a row of houses, 'for the purpose of affording additional hospital relief to the sick and poor of the metropolis'. A special wing for the treatment of fevers and contagious diseases was added in 1868. In 1893, The Royal City of Dublin Hospital was rebuilt and a new façade of red Ruabon brick and buff terracotta was added to a design of Albert E. Murray (1849–1924). The hospital closed on 20 November 1987 and was transferred to the Eastern Health Board on 1 January 1988. It was incorporated into Community Care Services providing elderly patient and a wide range of public health services.

In 1972, the Bank of Ireland opened its new headquarters in Lower Baggot Street. It was the largest bronze-walled building in Europe and cost £4.6 million. The Bank bought a further six Georgian houses in 1973, and in 1977 completed block three of its headquarters. The buildings were designed by Ronald Tallon. The street has greatly altered over the years with several office blocks including the glass-fronted building designed by Sam Stephenson originally for Bord na Móna and which won an award in 1984, and the headquarters of Bord Fáilte, designed by Michael Scott and Partners on Baggot Street Bridge.
See **Baggot Rath.**

Bagnio Slip
From Temple Bar to Wellington Quay. Now lower part of Fownes Street
Probably named after a 'bagnio' (brothel). The area housed characters connected with the river. In 1559, the Council agreed that, 'Thomas Simon Fitzmichell should have all the slyppes of the Merchants Quay from Usshers Ground; called Carle's Inns to the watering slyppe of the lane called the Bagnio, where Nicholas Seyntleger dwelled'. There was also a ferry station here to Aston Quay.

Baile Átha Cliath
Towards the end of the fourteenth century, the word *baile* or town was added to the old Irish name of the city which refers to hurdles anchored to the bed of the Liffey by heavy stones. Its actual location is not known but may have been near Church Street where the river was shallow and people and animals could wade across the river bed. There was probably a settlement or small community there.
See **Dubhlinn.**

Bailey Tavern
2 Duke Street
In 1837, John Bailey opened the Shellfish Tavern and, in 1856, Nicholas Bailey bought the next-door premises and renamed the established business Bailey's Tavern. It attracts a literary set as well as intellectuals and is the meeting place of many of Dublin's personalities. Oliver St John Gogarty observed that it had the best whiskey and beefsteak in Dublin. James Joyce was a frequent visitor and in *Ulysses* refers to it as Burton's. The door of no. 7 Eccles Street* immortalised by Joyce as the home of Leopold Bloom may be seen in the vestibule of the Bailey. Other artefacts include Brendan Behan's tankard and Michael Collins' revolver.
In 1971, the Brown Thomas stores bought the premises and in 1989 leased it to Murtagh Properties, a subsidiary of the Guinness Group. Murtagh Properties also own The Sheaf O' Wheat, The Cherry Tree and The Clonsilla Inn.

Baldoyle
Seven miles N.E. of Dublin, it is situated upon a small inlet of the Irish Sea to the north of the isthmus that connects the promontory of Howth with the mainland. The Vikings used it as a harbour base and the name is possibly derived from Baile Dubh Gall (the town of dark strangers) because of these settlers. The monks of the priory of All Hallows farmed a large area here until the disestablishment of the monasteries in 1536 when the farms became the property of the Corporation of Dublin. In 1369, Sir William de Windsor, the then Lord Deputy, convened a parliament here for the purpose of levying subsidies for the crown on the Anglo Normans. The RC church is a handsome structure with a portico of four Tuscan pillars, above which is a turret supporting a dome and a cross. Throughout the nineteenth century, there was a fishing fleet and coal boats also unloaded their cargoes. The racecourse, which had existed for over a hundred years, closed in 1972. Baldoyle is a rapidly expanding area with extensive housing developments, and a large industrial estate. The Old Farm or Grange name is perpetuated in the titles of many of the new housing developments and the Ward boundaries are divided into Grange A to E.

Balfe Street
From Chatham Street to Harry Street
From Michael William Balfe (1808–70), composer and violinist, who wrote *The Bohemian Girl, The Sicilian Bride* and other operas including *The Siege of Rochelle*. A portrait bust signed and dated T. Farrell R.H.A. Dublin 1878 (Thomas Farrell 1827–1900) was commissioned by the Balfe Memorial committee who presented it to the National Gallery of Ireland in 1879. Originally Pitt Street, when Balfe was born at no. 10, from William Pitt (1759–1806), son of the first Earl of Chatham. Rocque's map of 1756 includes this as part of Harry Street.
See **St Ann's (C of I)** *and* **St Patrick's Cathedral.**

Ballast Board

In 1708, Dublin Corporation through parliament set up a committee known as the Ballast Board. This in turn was succeeded in 1786 by the Corporation for Preserving and Improving the Port of Dublin. The Merchant Shipping Act of 1854 divided the Ballast Board into two distinct corporate bodies, identical in personnel and constitution, namely the Corporation for preserving and improving the Port of Dublin for Dublin Port and the Port of Dublin Corporation for lighthouses, light ships, buoys and beacons around the coast of Ireland.

The severance began in 1854 and was completed by the Dublin Port Act of 1867. The Corporation for Preserving and Improving the Port of Dublin became the Dublin Port and Docks Board, which was seen to represent more fully the shipping and trading interests, and the Port of Dublin Corporation became the Commissioners of Irish Lights who were responsible for the erection and maintenance of lighthouses and light ships etc. around the Irish coast. The Ballast Office at 21 Westmoreland Street, built in 1802, was remodelled in 1864, and in 1866, following a fire at the next-door premises, it was extended to take in numbers 19 and 20. The clock, which was installed in 1870, was connected to a time signal for mariners and regulated from Dunsink Observatory, the principal astronomical observatory in Ireland. Situated near Blanchardstown, 7 km from the city, it was founded by Trinity College in 1783. It ceased functioning in 1922 and, in 1947, reopened as part of the School of Physics of the Dublin Institute of Advanced Studies. The observatory organises public viewings at night of the galaxies twice a month during winter. A letter in the *Sunday Independent* of 1910 asks, 'Is the Port and Docks clock really reliable as giving the exact Irish time? In recent years I am informed there were some strange discrepancies, consequent upon interference with the Ballast Office clock wire by the Post Office Telegraphic Department, who have charge of it. The result was a serious discordance between the properly regulated clock and the Westmoreland timepiece' etc. Another letter addressed to Dr Whittaker, The Observatory, Dunsink, from Hopkins and Hopkins the jewellers, O'Connell Street, dated 19 April 1910: 'We are rating ship chronometers by the time ball on top of the Ballast Office and noted on the 17th inst. an irregularity, and we would like to know if you could explain what was the cause of it and how much was the variation etc'. A reply dated 20 April 1910 from Dunsink Observatory states, 'The Ballast Office clock was in agreement with the Dunsink clock on Saturday. On Monday morning the Ballast clock was 15 seconds fast on the Dunsink clock. My assistant telephoned this information to the Port and Docks Board officials when the daily comparison was made. The fall of the ball is regulated by the Ballast Office clock and therefore shares in its errors. The Ballast Office clock is connected by wire with the Dunsink clock, but the wire is so frequently interrupted by the Post Office Telegraphs Department, who have charge of it, that there is often a serious discordance between the two clocks. The wire was interrupted on Sunday and this caused discordance which was noted on Monday.' etc. 'Believe me, yours faithfully E. T. Whittaker, Royal Astronomer of Ireland.'

The Ballast Office building was demolished in 1979. The Port and Docks Board had vacated the premises in 1974, having sold it to the Royal Liver Insurance for £0.25 million.

See **Dublin Port, Dublin Docklands Development Authority, International Financial Services Centre.**

Ballast Office

See **Westmoreland Street.**

Ballsbridge

From the bridge spanning the River Dodder on the Merrion / Dublin Road Named after Mr Ball whose house once stood near the pond in what is now Herbert Park. The bridge was constructed in 1751 and replaced a ford. It was rebuilt in 1791 and again in 1835 and 1905. The Pembroke Township, founded in 1863, included Ballsbridge, and Pembroke Town Hall was built on the corner of Anglesea Road and Merrion Road in 1880. The township was incorporated into Dublin City in 1932 when the building became the headquarters of the City of Dublin VEC. In 1903, the Earl of Pembroke offered a site to the Pembroke UDC for a public park, and the Irish International Exhibition* was held there in 1907 on a site of 52 acres. Herbert Park, named after Sydney Herbert, a former owner of the Fitzwilliam Estate* and father of the Earl of Pembroke, was opened in 1911.

Fine nineteenth-century suburb built and laid out between 1830 and 1860. Ailesbury Road, Lansdowne Road after the fourth Marquis of Lansdowne who died in 1866, Mespil Road, Morehampton Road, Pembroke Road after the seventh Viscount Fitzwilliam who inherited the estates of the eleventh Earl of Pembroke. Waterloo Road, Raglan Road, Clyde Road, Elgin Road and Wellington Road are all named after British military heroes. On Merrion Road are the premises of The Royal Dublin Society.* The area contains many embassies and diplomatic offices including the American Embassy, a circular building designed by John McL. Johansen, on the corner of Elgin Road and Pembroke Road and opened in 1964. St Bartholomew's Church, built during the Oxford movement, has extremely elaborate frescoes and some fine stained glass.

Ballymun

Baile Muin. Town of the shrubland
A satellite town built on part of the grounds of the Albert Agricultural College (see Dublin City University). An English architect, Arthur Swift, acting on behalf of the National Building Agency and Dublin Corporation Planning Department, designed seven 14-storey towers together with eight- and four- storey blocks, creating a four-arm spiral with a central roundabout having a pedestrian underpass

for crossing a new dual carriageway. The pre-cast structural building complex was opened in 1967 by the Minister for Local Government, Neil Blaney. Built at a cost of over £12 million, the scheme had been much criticised for its design and layout, which created social problems. In the early years of this century, the Ballymun Tower Blocks were demolished and replaced with new housing models that would regenerate the area and retain the values of the community. A vibrant new quarter was created in 2004 called the New Town Centre, with apartments having an open-air plaza, a civic theatre, a technology park plus a leisure centre and swimming pool. A new one-kilometre-long main street stretching from Collins Avenue to Santry Avenue was created, with a large Civic Centre at one end. New apartments under section 23 tax-break scheme were commenced in 2004. These included two high-level blocks of one- and two-bedroom apartments and 20-ground floor shops. The overall cost of the new-image Ballymun will be in the region of €2.5 billion. The original shopping centre will be developed into a technology park.

Bang Bang

Tommy Dudley, known lovingly as Bang Bang. He lived in Bridgefoot Street and with great agility would spring, grinning and glitter-eyed, on and off moving buses, holding the central bar at the rear and shooting the enemy all around him with his large, iron door key. His roars of bang bang could be heard several streets away. He died on 12 January 1981, his latter years having been spent in Clonturk House for the Adult Blind.

Bank of Ireland

College Green
On 24 February 1780, several bankers and merchants petitioned the Irish House of Commons for the erection of a public national bank. The petition was favourably received and the following resolution passed '. . . that the erecting of a public bank upon a solid foundation under

proper regulations and restrictions, is at this time highly necessary and will contribute to the establishment of public credit and the support of trade and manufactures of the Kingdom'. An act of 1782 authorised the capital of the bank at £600,000 to be paid into the Treasury; in return, the government agreed to pay as interest £24,000 in turn to be paid by the bank to its stock-holders. Six members of the La Touche family were among the first subscribers, four of them subscribing the maximum allowed of £10,000 each. As a result, the newly formed Bank of Ireland was given a charter dated 15 May 1783, and the Rt Hon. David La Touche was elected first governor of the bank—a position which he held for nine years.

The bank's first premises were at 12 Mary's Abbey and nineteen people were employed on 20 May 1783. The bank opened its doors to the public on 25 June 1783. The premises were purchased outright in 1784 for £850 and, by 1790, the bank occupied four houses at the corner of Mary's Abbey. After 16 years, the existing premises were becoming too small for the expanding business and the governors tried un-successfully to acquire the site of the old Customs House on Essex Quay. They then took an option on a site from the Wide Streets Commissioners of a piece of land that was bounded by College Street, D'Olier Street and Westmoreland Street. John Soane, the architect of the Bank of England, was instructed to draw up suitable plans for the new building. These were completed in 1799, but with the passing of the Act of Union in 1800, the Parliament House became available and the bank entered into negotiations for its purchase. These negotiations were com-pleted in 1803 when the premises were acquired for a consideration of £40,000. Francis Johnston produced a design that adapted the premises to banking use and the building was reopened in June 1808. The premises remained the head office of the bank into the mid-1960s and are now its main Dublin branch.

In 1971, a programme of cleaning and restoring the outside of the building was begun, and damaged stones were replaced. The heads of Edward Smyth's statues of Fidelity, Hibernia and Commerce were newly carved by Paddy Roe of Sandyford. *See* **Parliament House,** *also* **David La Touche and Son,** *and* **Chichester House.**

Barnardo's
Christchurch Square

Thomas John Barnardo (1845–1905), born 4 July 1845 at Cork Hill next to City Hall, the ninth son of John Barnardo, born in Hamburg, who spent several years travelling before becoming a successful merchant in Dublin. His mother belonged to an English Quaker family which had settled in Ireland. At 17 years of age, during a religious revival, he was converted to Christ. As a result of a visit to Dublin by Dr Hudson Taylor of the China Inland Mission, he volunteered for missionary work in China. At age 20, he arrived in London and, instead of becoming a missionary, he remained in these islands.

In 1866, during the outbreak of cholera in London, he noticed the miseries of the poor and the need of thousands of homeless children in the East End and, in that year, boarded out the first group of children. The first Dr Barnardo's Home was established in 1870—the same year that he married Syrie Louise Elmslie. The work grew and so did the support. His principle was 'No destitute child ever refused admission'. Before 1900 there were 8,000 children in daily care. Great crowds lined the streets of London to pay tribute to the 'Father of Nobody's Children' when he died on 19 September 1905. His work continues to the present day in Britain, Ireland, Australia and New Zealand. *See* **Peace Garden.**

Barrack Street
See **Benburb Street.**

BARRACKS
Royal Barracks now Collins Barracks, Benburb Street

The central portion, Royal Square, was laid

down in 1701 with further work continuing until 1706. In 1735, it was described as the most commodious of its kind in Europe, with four battalions of infantry and one horse, approximately 5,000 men. Building recommenced in 1760 with the addition of further squares; the architect was Colonel Thomas Burgh. On 17 December 1922, the Royal Barracks was handed over to the National Army to General R. Mulcahy and Sean McMahon, and renamed Collins Barracks, after Michael Collins (1890–1922), the revolutionary leader. In 1997, it was completely restored and redesigned and opened as the Museum of Decorative Arts and History (*see* National Museum of Ireland).

Island Bridge Barracks now Clancy Barracks

The *Dublin Journal* of December 1797 reported 'that a piece of ground contiguous to the Royal Invalid Hospital at Kilmainham is preparing as a general Park or Repository of Artillery in the manner of Woolich Warren in England' It was built by convicts from Dublin jails including the Bridewell, Kilmainham and Richmond. During the first half of the nineteenth century a lower barracks was completed and called the Islandbridge Cavalry Barracks. On 15 December 1922, the Islandbridge barracks was taken over by the National Army. It was renamed Clancy Barracks on 21 November 1942, after Peadar Clancy (1894–1920), Republican Deputy Commandant of the Dublin Brigade.

Richmond Barracks, Inchicore (Keogh Barracks)

Built in 1807 and named after Charles Lennox, Duke of Richmond, Lord Lieutenant. A contemporary account records that it had two fronts with extensive courts open to the north and south and connected by a row of light and elegant houses 500 yards in length. The barracks was designed to accommodate seventy-six officers and 1,600 other ranks. There was also stabling for twenty-five

horses and a hospital for 100 patients. It was built to house the 91st Foot Regiment and the 92nd Highland Regiment. These were replaced with other foot regiments over the years. Under Commandant Coughlan the barracks was taken over by the Irish Free State troops on 15 December 1922. It was renamed Keogh Barracks after Commandant General Tom Keogh, a veteran of the War of Independence. It ceased to be used as a barracks in 1925 and (as Keogh Square) was used by Dublin Corporation to house poor families. Following years of protest from various church and social groups concerned about the squalid conditions, it was demolished in 1969. New Corporation flats now occupy the site.

Portobello Barracks, Rathmines (Cathal Brugha Barracks)

A large cavalry barracks built between 1810 and 1815. The district derives its name from Porto Bello where Sir Francis Drake succumbed to fever on 28 January 1596 while his expedition was fighting the Spaniards, and possibly named Porto Bello to mark his centenary also Admiral Vernon's capture of the town from the Spaniards in 1739. A garrison church and canteen were added in 1868 (*see* Harold's Cross). The barracks was handed over to General O'Duffy and Comdt General Ennis on 18 May 1922 and renamed Cathal Brugha Barracks after the revolutionary, born 1874 and died July 1922 from wounds received in the Civil War. Archives of the Department of Defence, the Defence Forces and the Bureau of Military History are held in the Military Archives.

Beggars Bush Barracks, Haddington Road

Built in 1827 as a recruit depot to supply trained soldiers to Portobello, Richmond and Royal Barracks. The barracks was handed over to Comdt General Paddy Daly on 31 January 1922. The Labour Court and Labour Relations Commission are housed in Tom Johnson House, named after Thomas Johnson (1872–1963), first parliamentary leader of the Labour Party. Archives of the Geological Survey are held at the offices of the Geological Survey, Beggars Bush.

Wellington Barracks (Griffith Barracks, South Circular Road)

Built in 1813 as a remand prison and penitentiary. The prison became Wellington Barracks in 1891 after Arthur Wellesley, First Duke of Wellington (1769–1852), and was taken over by the National Army on 14 April 1922 and renamed Griffith Barracks after Arthur Griffith (1871–1922), the political leader. It was vacated in 1987. It is now home to an educational college.

Marlborough Barracks now McKee Barracks

Built between 1888 and 1892 and first known as Grangegorman Barracks, then after the Duke of Marlborough. On Thursday, 15 October 1891, it became the headquarters of the 10th Hussars. It was renamed McKee Barracks after Dick McKee (1893–1920), officer commanding the Dublin Brigade.

Ship Street Barracks

In 1805, Robert Woodgate, the architect to the Board of Works, converted the early and mid-eighteenth-century houses on the south end of the street for use as accommodation for the military. In 1808, Francis Johnston designed the Quarter Master General's building now known as Block M. Houses on the north end of the terrace were replaced during the first half of the nineteenth century by new buildings for the military. During the 1990s, a complete refurbishment of all the buildings on the street was carried out by the Office of Public Works, and these now house government departments.

Beaumont Hospital

Beaumont Road

The hospital was planned, commissioned and built in the period from 1978 to 1984. The design is almost an exact replica of

Cork University College hospital (Wilton). It cost over £50 million to build and opened on 29 November 1987, following the closure of two city centre hospitals, the Charitable Infirmary,* Jervis Street, and St Lawrence's, the Richmond. It has 620 beds and is the principal undergraduate and postgraduate medical training centre attached to the Royal College of Surgeons in Ireland. Under the Eastern Regional Health Authority it is one of the largest major general hospitals providing acute hospital care.

Beaux Walk

See St Stephen's Green.

Bedford Square

Shown in a map dated 1753: 'Design for opening proper Streets or Avenues to His Majesty's Royal Palace in Dublin'. Facing the new Parliament Street* where the City Hall now stands. Named after the Duke of Bedford, then Lord Lieutenant. On Rocque's map of 1756 the statue of George I by John Van Nost Senior which was removed from the old Essex Bridge,* is shown erected in the centre of the new square.

See Royal Exchange, also Equestrian Statue George I.

Bell (The)

A literary journal founded by Sean O'Faolain in 1940 with contributions from many of the leading authors of the time, including Patrick Kavanagh, Oliver St John Gogarty and Flann O'Brien. It ceased publication in 1948 but was resurrected in 1950 and closed down permanently in 1955.

Belvedere House

Great Denmark Street at the head of North Great George's Street

Built by Michael Stapleton on a site taken from Nicholas Archdall, it was completed and occupied in 1786 by George Augustus Rochfort (1738–1814) 2nd Earl of Belvedere. In 1815, Rochfort's second wife married Abraham Boyd, and her son George Augustus Boyd sold the house to

Belvedere House. Built by Michael Stapleton and completed in 1786.

the Society of Jesus in 1841 when it became Belvedere College. The house built in brick has a wide flight of steps leading to the door which is flanked with high Doric columns and entablature. Some fine stucco plasterwork ceilings adorn the main rooms. James Joyce attended the school (1893–98).

Benburb Street
From Parkgate Street to Blackhall Place
Originally Barrack Street from its proximity to the Royal Barracks erected in 1701 to a design of Thomas Burgh. Renamed Collins Barracks after the revolutionary leader Michael Collins (1890–1922), it was the oldest inhabited barracks in Europe. In 1997, the newly restored and redesigned building opened as the Museum of Decorative Arts and History. A monument erected in 1985 marks the spot where some executed rebels of the 1798 rebellion are buried in Croppies' Acre* a plot in front of the barracks. Barrack Street and Tighe Street were joined in 1890 to make Benburb Street.
See **National Museum of Ireland** *and* **Barracks.**

Beresford Place
Part of the crescent in front of the Custom House. From Custom House Quay to Memorial Road
Approved on 26 November 1790 as part of the Wide Street Commissioners' axial planning in the north-east quarter of the city terminating in the long vista along Gardiner Street from Mountjoy Square.
The Rt Hon. John Beresford (1738–1805), Chief Commissioner of the Revenue, was one of the people responsible for bringing James Gandon to Ireland to design and build the neighbouring Custom House. The houses designed by Gandon have a unified palatial façade. Four of the five original red-brick houses remain; no. 5 on the corner is a replacement building following fire damage in 1928. A recent addition is Beresford Court, an office complex designed by A. and D. Wejchert

Bethesda, Lock Penitentiary and Work House
Dorset Street
Opened on 19 March 1794 for the reception and employment of women leaving the Lock Hospital. It was endowed by William Smith, Granby Row, with a chapel and other buildings.

Bird Market
See **Canon Street.**

Bishop Street
From Wexford Street to Bride Street
Name comes from its proximity to St Sepulchre's, the residence of the Archbishop of Dublin until c. 1815.
In 1852, W. and R. Jacob, a Quaker family of biscuit manufacturers, moved from Waterford and purchased no. 5 St Peter's Row from coach makers Thomas Palmer and Sons. Other Quaker families joined William and Robert, including Samuel Bewley and Charles Pim. The business would eventually extend to cover the entire block bounded by Bishop Street, Peter's Row, Peter Street and Bride Street. Jacobs merged with Bolands in 1966 to become Irish Biscuits, and moved to Tallaght on 17

November 1975. The property was left vacant and became vandalised. In 1981, it was put up for sale and was sold for £750,000. Six months later, in 1982, St Kevin's Vocational Educational College purchased a large part of the property for £1.25 million and, in 1994, a new college of the Dublin Institute of Technology, with faculties of business and applied arts, opened, incorporating the granite arches of the old loading bays carved with the Jacob name. In 1991, the National Archives,* formerly at the Four Courts, and the State Paper Office, formerly at Dublin Castle, moved to the remaining part of Jacobs' site in Bishop Street. Opposite are Dublin Corporation flats and a large branch office of the D epartment of Social Welfare which opened in 2003.

Black Church
See **St Mary's Chapel of Ease.**

Blackhall Place and Street
From Stoneybatter to Hendrick Street
Named after Sir Thomas Blackhall, Lord Mayor 1769. On the site of Oxmantown Green.*
The area together with Blackhall Street was laid out by Thomas Ivory (1720–86) who designed the King's Hospital* on the west side, with carving by Simon Vierpyl and plasterwork by Charles Thorpe Senior. The building was commenced in 1773. The chapel has a window by Evie Hone, depicting the resurrection. Between 1773 and 1800, large four-storey red-brick houses were built on the new Blackhall Street; all of these have been demolished.

Blackhorse Lane
See **Aughrim Street.**

Blackpitts
From Clarence Mangan Road to Ward's Hill
An area used by tanners and skinners. The name probably derives from the large black vats used in curing the hides. The area was also frequented by weavers who worked in three-storey houses with garrets, having large windows for cloth inspection, usually with Dutch gables and some having winches to raise and lower bales of cloth. In the early 1900s, the residents of the small cottages bred fighting cocks and brindle terriers.

Blackrock and Monkstown
Formed into a township by the Blackrock Township Act of 1863, embracing Monkstown, Williamstown and Booterstown. It was constituted an urban district under the Local Government Act 1898 and is now part of the Dún Laoghaire –Rathdown County Council. Raymond Carew, an Anglo-Norman landowner, gave some of the land to the Cistercian monks who farmed there until the suppression of the monasteries in 1536, when the lands were given to Sir John Travers, Master of Ordnance. At the beginning of the seventeenth century, the lands passed to John Cheevers, a Roman Catholic who married Katherine, daughter of Sir John Travers, a descendant of the original occupier. For a period under Cromwell, Cheevers lost the lands. His daughter married John Byrne and the area became known as Newtown Byrne; Newtown Avenue is on part of the estate.
The area of Blackrock became a popular holiday resort, and swimming baths were built adjoining the railway station and at Seapoint. There is also a public park containing fourteen acres. Frescati House was built by Hely Hutchinson in 1762 and occupied by Emily, Dowager Duchess of Leinster, from 1766 until 1802. Sir Henry Cavendish occupied it for a short time; then it passed to Mr Craig's School for Boys and was extended. The wings, which had become private houses were demolished in 1981. Amid much protest the house was levelled in October 1983 to make way for Roches Stores' large supermarket. A plaque on the new block reminds people that Lord Edward Fitzgerald lived there. Another house, Maretimo, was built in 1774 by Sir Nicholas Lawless. Valentine Lawless persuaded the Dublin and Kingstown Railway Company* to build the baths at the station. The house was

demolished in the 1970s and replaced by a block of flats.

Recently many new office blocks have been erected and Blackrock's village atmosphere has been lost through the construction of a bypass road. The first train to run through Blackrock did so on 17 December 1834. The area is now served by the DART network. Blackrock College was founded in 1860 by the Holy Ghost Fathers in the house and grounds of Castle Dawson at Williamstown. Eamon de Valera attended as a pupil.

The Church of St John the Baptist (RC) was designed by Patrick Byrne and was based on Pugin's drawings of the church of Stanton St John, Oxfordshire; it was dedicated in 1845 and has been extended over the years. There are windows by Evie Hone and Harry Clarke. Sources would indicate that the land was donated by Lord Cloncurry who was living at Maretimo, already mentioned. However, a local resident maintains that Cloncurry owned only the land to the Back Road River, now gone, and states that in 1920/30 his father bought from Alan Brook the ground rent of the 3 Tun public house and the ground rent of the RC church. There was a charge of £2 to the church, which has now lapsed as it has not been collected for some time. All Saints Church (C of I) was built about 1880, facing onto Proby Square, in rustic granite with a tower and spire. It is a typical design of the Ecclesiastical Commissioners. Charles Haliday (1789–1866) author of *The Scandinavian Kingdom of Dublin*, whose book collection is now in the Royal Irish Academy, lived in Fairy Hill in 1834 and in the 1840s moved to Monkstown Park where he died.

Facing the Dublin Road is Monkstown Church (C of I), a most distinctive structure designed by John Semple, with Moorish-style corner towers, battlements and a central tower. It has been a parish since 1789 when a simple church was erected, replaced by the present one in 1833. The Cistercian monks gave the townland its name. St Patrick's Church (RC) on Carrickbrennan Road, built to a design of

George Ashlin and consecrated in 1864, is in the high-vaulted Victorian Gothic, taste with a large rose window and a square tower supporting a spire. The Salthill Hotel at Monkstown was a private house until 1834 when the railway opened with a station at Salthill, when it was converted into a hotel with John Skipton Mulvany as architect. It had extensive grounds and, over the years, additions were made to the main structure. It closed in the early 1970s. The first block of a new apartment development on the site was completed early in 1991.

The area around Temple Hill and Seapoint Avenue started to develop in the 1920s when twenty houses were offered for sale on 18 February 1924, which was followed by people buying plots of land to build their own houses.

Blind Quay
See **Exchange Street Lower.**

Blue Coat School
See **King's Hospital.**

Board Walk
See **Quays, North Side, Bachelor's Walk.**

Body Snatching
By the time that the Royal College of Surgeons* had moved to St Stephen's Green in 1810, there were eighteen private medical schools in the city as well as the School of Physic in Trinity College and Sir Patrick Dun's teaching hospital. There was a shortage of corpses for the study of anatomy as the law allowed only the bodies of criminals executed for murder to be released for this purpose. The practice of stealing the newly buried grew. St Andrew's* churchyard was a favourite spot, where students and teachers paid the grave diggers up to a guinea per body that had been interred the same day. Sometimes, if the corpse had a good set of teeth, extra was allowed for this as teeth were fitted to plates similar to our modern dentures. One of the worst areas for the removal of corpses was Bully's Acre,* adjoining the Royal

Hospital* at Kilmainham, where there was an area reserved for paupers with unmarked graves. In fact, the practice became so widespread that 'A humane society of St John was founded to guard the remains of our poor fellow citizens who will be interred in the Hospital fields Burial grounds'. The burial ground closed in 1832 because of congestion following the cholera epidemic. By this time, the value of a corpse had risen to six or eight guineas. After the opening in February 1832 of Glasnevin* (Prospect) Cemetery with its high walls, the practice began to die out, and, in the same year, the Anatomy Act allowed bodies unclaimed in public institutions to be given to anatomy schools.

Bolton Street
From King Street North to Dorset Street
Together with Stoneybatter and North King Street, Bolton Street formed part of an old highway going north out of Dublin towards Drumcondra. It was originally known as Drumcondra Lane, until the area began to develop with the building of Henrietta Street. It was renamed about 1724 after the Duke of Bolton, Lord Lieutenant (1717–21). Much of the east side of the street is occupied by the College of Technology built in 1911, being the first new building in Ireland designed for vocational education by C. J. McCarthy, the City Architect. It was extended in 1961 to Hooper and Mayne's drawings, assisted by Donal O'Dwyer. A further addition was completed in 1987 in the form of an inner courtyard designed by Desmond McMahon.

Boot Lane
Named after an inn of that name. Now part of Arran Street East.

Booterstown
Four miles S.E. from the General Post Office situated on the south shore of Dublin Bay. With the opening of the Dublin–Kingstown railway, the company advertised that 'ample accommodation is afforded for sea bathing by the railway company'. The railway embankment, however, removed what had for years been a popular sandy beach. A marsh area now serves as a bird sanctuary.

In the townland there is a convent of the Sisters of Mercy, an order founded by Catherine McAuley in 1831. St Andrew's Protestant school, founded at St Stephen's Green in 1894, moved to Donnybrook in 1938 and to Booterstown in 1973. The Church of the Assumption (RC) is a large early nineteenth-century structure backing onto Booterstown Avenue, with an interesting interior. A plaque inside the building commemorates, 'Mrs Barbara Verschole who departed this life on the 25 January 1837 in the eighty fifth year of her age. She was the chief means of this sacred edifice being erected by the liberality of her attached friend and patron the last Richard Lord Viscount Fitzwilliam for the accommodation of his Roman Catholic tenants on this part of his estate.' The church must predate 1816 as the Fitzwilliam estates passed to the Earls of Pembroke on the Viscount's death. It has been extended over the years. The Church of St Philip and St James (C of I) is off Cross Avenue where Eamon de Valera spent many years of his life. The church has pinnacles supporting a parapet and square tower with a narrow spire. It was opened for worship in 1824 and extended in 1867 and 1876, the ground being given by the Pembroke Estate. Dr Richard Robert Madden (1798–1886) author of *The United Irishmen, their Lives and Times*, died at no. 3 Vernon Terrace. He was responsible for erecting the monument over the grave of Anne Devlin, the friend of Robert Emmet,* at Glasnevin Cemetery.

Bors Court (Borris, Burrowes)
Schoolhouse Lane West
From Christian and John Bor, gentlemen of Lower Germany who in 1618 were granted a patent 'that they be freed from the yoke of servitude of the German or Irish nation and enjoy all the rights and privileges of English subjects for the sum of £1–6–8.' They were merchants trading

mostly with Holland. In 1674, they leased the free school in Schoolhouse Lane.

Botanic Gardens
Glasnevin

Founded by the Dublin Society in 1795 in order to assist Irish agriculture and horticulture by experiments with plants most suitable to the climate.

In 1794, the distinguished botanists, Robert Perceval, Walter Wade and Edward Hill, were invited to a conference at which various sites were examined, after which Major Thomas Tickell's estate at Glasnevin was finally decided upon. An existing tenancy was bought and, in 1804, Major Tickell assigned all his interest in the ground for £1,800. Dr Walter Wade, author of *Flora Dubliniensis*, was appointed first professor and lecturer in botany to the Society and John Underwood was made head gardener.

From the beginning, the gardens benefited by gifts of plants from all over the world. Large sums of money were spent on plants and the maintenance of the grounds, and £1,500 was voted by Parliament in 1800 for the support of the Botanic Gardens, which were among the largest and most beautiful in Europe. In 1814, Thomas Pleasants, the great benefactor, paid for the lodge at the entrance to the gardens at a cost of £700.

In 1843, the government granted £4,000 and the Royal Dublin Society £1,000 towards the erection of new greenhouses that stand to this day. A new palm house, recently restored in 2004, was built in 1833 and the orchid house in 1854. Originally the gardens were open only a few days each week, but government pressure forced the Society to open on Sundays from 18 August 1861. In that month, 78,000 people visited the gardens and, on one Sunday that month, 15,000 visitors passed through the turnstiles. The Botanic Gardens came under state control in 1878. Near the main entrance is the Thomas Moore rose–raised from a cutting of the tree which inspired 'The Last Rose of Summer'.

Prior to the opening of the gardens, the Society had a botanic garden adjoining its premises in Mecklenburgh Street since 1733 (now Railway Street).

The curvilinear-range glass house was created by the noted Victorian designer, Richard Turner, in the 1840s using a cast-iron framework and glazing elements. Because of its architectural significance a full restoration was commenced in 1989 as rust had caused much of the original metal to crumble away.

Boyne Street
From Cumberland Street South to Erne Street

A street of tenements and small dwellings much depleted with the decline in population of St Andrew's (RC) parish. In the 1900s, Anderson, Stanford and Ridgeway had their carpet cleaning works at no. 29.

See **Westland Row.**

Boys' Brigade

Formed in England in 1883 by William A. Smith, later knighted for his work among boys. First Dublin company founded February 1891. Objective: 'The advancement of Christ's Kingdom among boys, and the promotion of habits of obedience, reverence, discipline, self-respect and all that tends towards a true Christian manliness.' Headquarters Dawson Street.

Bradogue Lane
See **Green Street Little.**

Braithwaite Street (1756)
Pimlico

Appears to have been a poor street inhabited by artisans connected with the weaving industry. Rev. James Whitelaw, on his visiting it in 1798 for the purpose of his census, found that in the thirty-one houses there were in all 367 inhabitants.

A survey carried out in 1816 showed that the labouring poor of the Liberties crowded together from two to four families in each apartment. Number 6 had 103 souls, while in the thirty-two adjoining houses there were 917 inhabitants.

See **Pimlico.**

Brazen Head Hotel, Bridge Street.

Brazen Head
Bridge Street
The oldest tavern in the country with references to it as far back as 1613 and it is likely that it was in existence sixty years prior to this. The first licensing laws in Ireland came into effect in 1635 but ale houses were known to exist in Dublin in 1185. The inn sign over the door of the Brazen Head maintains that it was founded in 1198. In 1703, it was described as 'a large timber house containing 35 ft. 6 ins. in front, 49 ft. in rere and 168 ft. in depth with all outhouses, stables, yards, rent £4–10–0'. It would appear that the present building was erected in 1754 when new houses were built in the street. The United Irishmen held some meetings there after a raid on Oliver Bond's house when the assembled delegates were arrested. Robert Emmet frequently used the inn, and his desk is preserved in the house. James Joyce mentions the inn and Brendan Behan, together with many of the literary community, met there. Recently a new castellated gateway was erected to the courtyard in front of the building which is still a popular Dublin pub.
See **Bridge Street.**

Bride Street, New Bride Street
From Werburgh Street to Heytesbury Street
Mentioned in 1465 as Synt Bryd Street from the parish church of St Bride,* rebuilt in 1684 and demolished in 1898 as part of the Iveagh scheme for laying out Bull Alley.* In 1941, the chapel of the Molyneux home was sold to Jacobs, the biscuit manufacturers, and, in 1974, a new front was constructed for Stephenson and Gibney, the architects, and a courtyard with a fountain added. A new Corporation inner-city housing development adjoins the building. Opposite is St Patrick's Park.*

Bridge Street Lower and Upper
From Corn Market to Merchant's Quay
In the seventeenth century, the street was a residential area for the gentry. It contained a house belonging to Mr Plunkett which

was seized by the government and handed over to Trinity College as it was 'a place whereunto the priests resort for mass'. By the beginning of the eighteenth century, the street had become a commercial centre for the textile and hardware trades. In 1754, new houses were built on a piece of ground beside the Brazen Head Inn.*

By 1895, James Doherty had opened a hotel at no. 19 and he opened another at no. 21 in 1900. Persons visiting the Brazen Head at no. 20 Lower Bridge Street had to pass under an arch between the two buildings. Part of a park laid out by Dublin Corporation sides onto the upper part, and Audoen House, a block of Corporation flats, occupies the lower part, together with some commercial properties, a pub and the Brazen Head Inn. St Audoen's House and Oliver Bond House, another block of Corporation flats, were built between 1936 and 1940, to the design of H. G. Simms. St Audoen's was named after the nearby church and Oliver Bond House after Oliver Bond (1760–98), a United Irishman who was sentenced to be hanged but died in prison. He is buried in St Michan's graveyard.

BRIDGES SPANNING THE RIVER LIFFEY

Sarah Bridge
(Islandbridge) between extended South Circular Road and Conyngham Road
Named after Sarah Fane, the wife of John Fane, 10th Earl of Westmoreland (Lord Lieutenant), who opened an iron-frame humpback bridge in 1794. Architect Alexander Stephens.

Heuston Bridge
From Victoria Quay to Parkgate Street
Named after Sean Heuston (1891–1916), Commandant in charge of the volunteers in the Mendicity Institute on Usher's Island. He was one of sixteen leaders executed after the rising in 1916. Opened in 1828 and called King's Bridge (George IV), it no longer carries heavy traffic to the Lucan Road since the opening of the Frank Sherwin Bridge.

Frank Sherwin Memorial Bridge
From St John's Road West to Wolfe Tone Quay
Frank Sherwin, a popular city councillor, died Christmas 1981. It was agreed to name the new bridge after him. The bridge was opened on 28 August 1982 below King's Bridge (Sean Heuston), to take the increasing flow of traffic, and afforded the facility of reversing the traffic flows on the North and South Quays.

It was designed by Dublin Corporation Road Section and built by Irishenco at a cost of £1.5 million.

James Joyce Bridge
From Usher's Island to Queen Street
On 16 June 2003, the Lord Mayor of Dublin, Cllr Dermot Lacey, opened a new bridge within sight of no. 15 Usher's Island where James Joyce set his story, 'The Dead'. Designed by Santiago Calatrava and built by Mowlem/Irishenco, it cost in the region of €8.4 million. The steel work was manufactured by Harland and Wolfe Heavy Industries, Belfast. It takes four lanes of traffic and two cycle tracks. There are seating areas on the wide pedestrian paths at either side of the bridge.

Rory O'More Bridge
From Watling Street to Ellis Quay
Named after one of the ring leaders of a plot to capture Dublin in October 1641. The participants were betrayed and O'More escaped by rowing upriver to Islandbridge. Made of cast iron with granite abutments and costing £13,700, it was opened in 1861 and called Queen Victoria Bridge to commemorate her visit to the city. The name was changed to Emancipation Bridge in 1929 and to Rory O'More Bridge in 1939. It spans the site of Barrack Bridge, a wooden structure built in 1674, which was the second bridge to be built across the Liffey. This was found to interfere with the interests of a ferry which had previously plied in the same locality, and a number of apprentices tried to destroy the new construction; twenty-one of them were seized and committed to the Castle. When they were being transferred

James Joyce Bridge opened on 16 June 2003 within the sight of no. 15 Usher's Island where James Joyce set his story, 'The Dead'. Designed by Santiago Calatrava.

to the Bridewell, they were rescued, but four of them were killed in the fray and, as a result of this, the bridge was always known as Bloody Bridge.

Mellows Bridge
Between Bridgefoot Street and Queen Street
Named after Lieut-General Liam Mellows, Republican (1892–1922) in 1942. Originally Queen Maeve Bridge after the Queen of Connaught who brought her whole army into Ulster to seize a bull that was better looking than the one her husband had in his possession. Built in 1764 and opened in 1768, this is the oldest bridge spanning the river. Originally named Queen's Bridge after Charlotte of Mecklenburgh, wife of George III, this replaced a former structure named Bridewell Bridge, built in 1683.

Father Mathew Bridge
Between Bridge Street and Church Street
Named after Father Theobald Mathew (1790–1856), the Capuchin apostle of temperance. The present bridge, opened in 1818, was originally named after Charles Earl of Whitworth, the Lord Lieutenant who laid the foundation stone on 16 October 1816. There is mention of a bridge

on this part of the river in 1014 and one of the public city officers cursed by Archbishop Lorcán Ó Tuathail in 1162 is recorded as falling to his death from the bridge. In 1210, the Normans built a new bridge here, and King John, on 23 August 1214, informed Archbishop Henry de Loundres that he had given the citizens permission to erect a new bridge across the Liffey and to take down the former one should they desire. This collapsed in 1385 and was rebuilt by the Dominicans in 1428. The Whitworth bridge was built on the foundations of this old bridge which had four arches and was described as 'remaining a long time mouldering in decay; a blemish amidst so many fine portal edifices'. Until 1674, no other bridge crossed the Liffey.

Arran Bridge
Between Essex Bridge and the old bridge near the present O'Donovan Rossa Bridge
Lord Arran succeeded his father, the Duke of Ormonde, after his recall in 1685, but died suddenly in 1686. Opened in 1683, the bridge named after Lord Arran was swept away by a flood in 1806 and replaced by the Richmond Bridge (O'Donovan Rossa) 1813–16.

O'Donovan Rossa Bridge
Between Winetavern Street and Chancery Place
Takes its name from Jeremiah O'Donovan Rossa (1831–1915), a republican who attacked British imperialism through his paper, *United Ireland*. Although in later years alienated from his republican colleagues, he epitomised the spirit of Fenianism to a younger generation. The bridge which was built in 1813 and opened in 1816 was named Richmond Bridge after the Viceroy Richmond. When the foundation of the south abutment was being sunk opposite Winetavern Street, several German, Spanish and British coins were found, including those of Philip and Mary and Elizabeth, also cannon balls and pike heads. When the north abutment was being sunk, two 18-foot-long wooden boats were found, in one of which was a skeleton.

Grattan Bridge
Between Parliament Street and Capel Street
Opened in 1874 and named after Henry Grattan (1746–1820) the patriot MP and orator who voted against the Act of Union and later devoted his life to the cause of Catholic emancipation. The original bridge on the site was built in 1676 and named Essex Bridge after Arthur Capel, Earl of Essex, then Lord Lieutenant (1672–77). It was the work of Sir Humphrey Jervis, one of the first of the city's developers. In 1687, there was severe flooding on the Liffey and part of the bridge was swept away. It was repaired and strengthened and a statue of George I was erected in 1722. This was removed when

the bridge was completely rebuilt in 1753. Rocque's map of 1756 shows a design for the new bridge. The statue was to be removed and erected in the centre of Bedford Square.*
See **Statues, Equestrian**.

Millennium Bridge
Between Wellington Quay and Ormond Quay
In 2000, The Rt Hon. Lord Mayor, Cllr Mary Freehill, opened a new pedestrian footbridge designed by Howley Harrington Architects and constructed by Price and Myers Engineers.

Halfpenny Bridge
See **Wellington Bridge**.

Wellington Bridge
Between Merchant's Arch and Liffey Street
Commonly called the Halfpenny Bridge after the toll exacted. Opened in 1816 and named after Arthur Wellesley, Duke of Wellington (1769–1852), created Duke after his command in the Iberian Peninsula brought about the abdication of Napoleon in 1814. Prime Minister (1828–30). Cast in iron in 1816 at Coalbrook in Shropshire, it was the only footbridge across the Liffey until the year 2000. On 25 March 1919, the turnstiles were removed and the bridge declared free to the public. On 8 May 2003, the restored bridge was awarded a European Union prize for Cultural Heritage at a ceremony in the Palais d'Egmont in Brussels. There were 282 entries to that year's awards and the bridge was one of 35 winning entries from 19 countries.

Wellington Bridge opened in 1816.

O'Connell Bridge
Between Westmoreland Street and O'Connell Street
Named after Daniel O'Connell (1775–1847), lawyer and politician who opposed the Union and championed Catholic emancipation. Built in 1794–98 by James Gandon and named Carlisle Bridge after the Viceroy, it replaced a ferry and was the lowest bridge on the river for many years. It was widened in 1880 and the hump levelled. In 1882, it was renamed when the statue of O'Connell was unveiled.
See **Statues.**

Butt Bridge
Between Tara Street and Beresford Place
Named after Isaac Butt (1813–79), barrister and politician, founder in 1873 of the Home Rule League. Given the freedom of the city on 4 September 1876. The present structure was built by the Dublin Port and Docks Board in 1932 and named Congress Bridge (1932 was the year of the Eucharistic Congress*). It replaced a centre-pivoted swing bridge, designed by Bindon Blood Stoney (1828–1909) and erected in 1879, which rarely opened to river traffic.

Talbot Memorial Bridge
Between Custom House Quay and George's Quay
Opened in 1978. Named after Matthew Talbot (1856–1925). Having taken the pledge about 1884, he became devout and imposed severe mortifications on himself. In 1976, the Roman Catholic Church gave him the title of 'Venerable'. He spent his last years at no. 18 Rutland Street.

Sean O'Casey Bridge
A new pedestrian bridge from Lombard Street East on City Quay to Custom House Quay at the Irish Financial Services Centre opened in July 2005. Designed to swing open by Moveable Bridges Ltd. Architects: Brian O'Halloran and Associates. Main Contractor: John Mowlem Construction Ltd for DDDA.

As yet unnamed bridge to be built
Linking the Grand Canal Harbour and the IFSC across the river from Macken Street to Guild Street
A new bridge designed by Santiago Calatrava, it is 26 metres wide with a span of 120 metres and accommodates two lanes of traffic, pedestrian walkways and a cycle lane. A cable-stayed bridge, pivoted to swing open to allow tall-mast ships to travel upriver as far as Talbot Memorial Bridge.

East Link Toll-Bridge
From York Road to East Wall Road
Opened in 1985. The combination of this and the Frank Sherwin Bridge eased former congestion at their crossings on the river. They afforded the facilities of reversing traffic flows on the North and South Quays with their beneficial effects of freer movement around and access to the city. On 20 October, the day before the bridge opened, the River Liffey ferry made its last trip, thus ending a tradition that dated back to the late fourteenth century. It crossed from the Ringsend slipway to near the Point Depot Theatre. The boat carried sixty passengers plus a crew of two and operated all day from 7.30 a.m. to 7.00 p.m. except on Sundays. The trip cost one penny each way.

Bridgefoot Street
From Thomas Street to Usher's Quay
Formerly Dirty Lane, from the foot of the old bridge that spanned the river. Bridgefoot was the name of the residence of Sir William Usher (1610–71), situated to the west of Bridge Street. Its gardens covered Usher's Quay and Usher's Island, vacant ground and tenements.

Broadstone
Phibsborough Road
Probably from a broad stone which crossed the river Bradogue. The now disused railway station designed by John Skipton Mulvany as the railway terminus for the Midland Great Western was commenced in 1841 and opened in 1847 but was not

completed until 1850, with an additional colonnade being added in 1861. The Royal Canal was carried over Phibsborough Road by the Foster Aqueduct* designed by Millar and Ruddery. This was removed in 1951. The station used to be reached by a floating drawbridge over the Royal Canal basin, but this was filled in 1879.

Broadstone Railway Station

In 1845, the Midland Great Western Railway Company was founded to run a line from Dublin to Mullingar, Longford, Athlone and Galway along the banks of the Royal Canal.* The canal had been purchased by the railway company in 1845 for £298,059.

The railway company architect was John Skipton Mulvany (1813–70) who held that post until 1850. He submitted designs for a new terminus in 1846 and work continued until completed in 1850. These included the normal station areas, the main work being carried out by the builders Gilbert Cockburn while the roof of the passenger terminal was erected by Richard Turner, the noted Victorian designer who had erected the curvilinear glass house in the Botanic Gardens.* In 1861, George Wilkinson, the architect of several railway stations including Harcourt Street,* carried out a major reconstruction including a new carriage shelter and waiting rooms accessed by a cast-iron colonnade.

The impressive frontage known as the Director's House is a large exotic-style, stepped, two-storey structure with a centre pediment over a large plaque which bears the legend 'Erected A.D. 1850'. The station operated until 1937 and is now used as a depot for Dublin Bus.

See **Broadstone, Constitution Hill.**

Brunswick and Shamrock Pneumatic Cycle Factory

Founded by Cornelius Mannin (1835–1913) who ran a profitable druggist business at no. 2 Great Brunswick Street (Pearse Street) and sold theatrical grease paint to the actors in the Queen's Theatre* opposite. In 1890, he decided to establish a bicycle

factory which opened on the west side of the street below the theatre and produced its first cycles in 1892. The title 'shamrock' was used to denote the first all-Irish manufactured machine. By 1896, there were eighty full-time workers producing eighty bicycles per week. In 1897, he sold the business to the newly formed Shamrock Cycle Syndicate Ltd who moved to a new factory in Marks Lane. He remained as managing director with Charles Loftus Townshend, Chairman, and George Furney, Secretary, the other directors being E. Chambré Harman and Christopher Somer Spear. The Marks Lane factory proved to be an over-ambitious enterprise and closed in 1909 with the bankruptcy of Mannin. He discharged himself before his death in 1913.

Brunswick Street, Great
See **Pearse Street.**

Brunswick Street, North
From Church Street Upper to Stoneybatter. Formerly Channel Row (1697)

Sarah, the wife of the Duke of Marlborough, died in 1730 at no. 63 North King Street. In 1707, she gave part of her property in Channel Row to six Dominican nuns from their disbanded Galway community. There was a disused convent and chapel there, which had been built by the direction of James II in 1689. Here the Dominican nuns opened a school for young ladies, which continued until 1808. It also housed parlour boarders, ladies of distinction who resided there from time to time, including the Duchess of Tyrconnell, Lady Dillon, Lady Mountcharles and the Countess of Fingal. The House of Industry,* opened in 1773, became the North Dublin Union Workhouse (*see* workhouse, James's Street) and the Richmond Lunatic Asylum. These would form part of the St Laurence's Hospital complex with the Richmond Hospital, founded in 1811, and, by 1813, two other hospitals, the Hardwick and Whitworth, had been added to the group. The first Irish operation under anaesthetic took place in the Richmond in 1847. In 1987, the hospital group closed and became part of the new Beaumont Hospital,* Beaumont Road. The Richmond buildings now house the Dublin Metropolitan district court with a proposed courts communication link with the Four Courts, Inns Quay and Dolphin House, Essex Street. Carmichael House at 83–88 was built for the Christian Brothers in 1864. The Hardwick at the side of the Richmond on Morning Star Avenue is now an apartment complex. Also in the area are the Richmond Business Campus, the Morning Star Men's Hostel, the Legion of Mary at de Montfort House and the Regina Coeli Hostel for Women.

Bull Alley

Encompassing Ross Road, Bride Street, Bull Alley Street

Part of the Parish of St Nicholas Within in 1680.

By the end of the nineteenth century, the area between St Patrick's Cathedral and Werburgh Street had become one of the worst slums in Dublin. Starting with Sir Arthur Edward Guinness and continued by Sir Benjamin Lee Guinness, then finished by his son, the 1st Earl of Iveagh, the entire area was cleared and a new park built beside the cathedral. The Iveagh Trust was founded in 1903. The Earl cleared seven acres of slums at a cost of £250,000, plus a further £50,000 towards the construction of housing for the poor. He endowed the Iveagh Hostel for working men, also the Iveagh Baths, recently closed and now housing a leisure centre and sports club. In St Patrick's Park are effigies of Dublin's Nobel Prize winners for Literature, together with a modern sculpture, 'Bell Sound' by Vivienne Roche, erected in 1988. The Iveagh Trust Act 1903 amalgamated the Guinness Trust (Dublin) Fund with the Dublin Improvement (Bull Alley Area) Scheme and gave the trustees enlarged and extended powers making one consolidated fund. At the time it provided 585 tenements for the artisan and labouring classes.

The flats on five storeys were designed by Joseph and Smithem with Parry and Ross. The impressive hall and recreation complex known to generations of children as the 'Bayno' was designed by McDonnell and Reid. The word 'Bayno' is a derivation of 'Beano' meaning a feast, as a bun and cocoa were given daily to the children.

Iveagh Trust public baths and laundry. Built 1905 after an architectural competition won by F. G. Hicks.

Bull Wall, North

From Clontarf to within 100 feet of the Poolbeg Lighthouse

Built in 1820, joins with the North Bull Island, a popular bird sanctuary, also home of the Royal Dublin Golf Club, founded in 1885 and, on the northern side, St Anne's Golf Club. A breakwater continues to the North Bull Lighthouse. Built by the Corporation for preserving and improving the port of Dublin.

See **Dublin Port and Docks Board.**

Bully's Acre
Within the grounds of the Royal Hospital, Kilmainham

One of the oldest burying grounds in Dublin was a repository for the dead since the time of St Maighneann. A great variety of people laid to rest here including Monk, Prince, Knight Templar, Knight Hospitaller, and there is a simple stone marking the grave of an English soldier who lost his life in the 1916 rebellion. The oldest stone still legible bears the inscription, 'Here lieth the body of Hive Hacket and Elizabeth Hacket who died in the year 1652'. Bully's Acre was closed to interments of the general public in 1832, the year of the great cholera epidemic. The body of Robert Emmet was interred here following his failed rebellion of 1803. It was later removed to a secret location which has never been found. Also Dan Donnelly (died 17 February 1820), pugilist. Son of a carpenter, he lived in Ringsend and was noted for his strength. He fought the English boxer, Hall, at the Curragh on 14 September 1814, beating him after seventeen rounds. He defeated the English champion, George Cooper, in eleven rounds in 1815. He opened a successful public house in Pill Lane. The elaborate altar-tomb has not survived, allegedly vandalised by soldiers stationed at Kilmainham.

Bushy Park

On the east side of Terenure House was a seventeenth-century house built by Arthur Bushe of Dangan, Co. Kilkenny, who was secretary to the Revenue Commissioners. The house had eleven acres and was sold in 1743 to a butcher, John Counly. In 1772, John Hobson changed the name from Bushe House to Bushy Park. It was sold in 1791 to Abraham Wilkinson, with eleven acres to which he added a further 100 acres as a dowry for his daughter Maria who married Robert Shaw Junior in 1796. There was an entrance to Rathfarnham Road at Rathdown Park and another exiting at Fortfield Road.

From 2002 and 2004, 200 apartments and seven penthouses designed by O'Mahony Pike Architects were built in the grounds of the house, off a tree-lined avenue around landscaped courtyards.

See **Terenure** *and* **Templeogue Road.**

Butter Lane, Great

From the Irish word *bóthar* meaning a road. Part of the *Slí Dála*, the great road from Cork, and the portion of what is now Kevin Street Upper and Bishop Street was so named. The road continued along part of the Coombe. It joined the *Slí Chualann*, the great Waterford Road, somewhere near Crosspoddle.*

Butter Lane, Little
See **Drury Street.**

Byrne's Hill
From John Street South to Ardee Street

Part of the grounds and lands of the Abbey of St Thomas in Thomas Court which were granted to William Brabazon's family on 31 March 1545 after the dissolution of the monasteries. In 1616, the Brabazons were created Barons of Ardee, and the Earldom of Meath was added on 16 April 1627. Mrs Margaret Boyle, founder of the Coombe Lying-in Hospital, opened a nurses' home here in 1826. Anne Devlin (1778–1851), the patriot and follower of Robert Emmet, died on Byrne's Hill. She is buried in Glasnevin Cemetery. Dr Richard Robert Madden (1798–1886), the historian, paid for her memorial.

See also **Booterstown.**

C

Cabbage Garden, Cathedral Lane
Off Kevin Street Lower
When Oliver Cromwell arrived in Dublin, a large house on the corner of Castle Street and Werburgh Street was selected as his residence. This was demolished in 1812 by the Wide Streets Commissioners. In order to supply green vegetables for his soldiers, he rented a garden from Philip Fernley who owned two houses in St Bride Street, and a garden in St Kevin Street on which he built five houses. Here, in 1649, Cromwell ordered cabbages to be planted and the name has survived to the present day. In 1685, French Protestant refugees were allotted a strip of the garden 150 feet long and 30 feet wide at one end and 38 feet wide at the other, by the archbishop of Dublin, as a burial ground which was used until 1858. Entrance is through a gateway, and many of the old gravestones are ranged around one side. It is now a public park with some trees and seats.

Cabbage Garden Lane
See **Cathedral Lane.**

Camden Row
From Camden Street Lower to New Bride Street
This entire area covering Camden Row, Camden Street and Wexford Street was originally known as St Kevin's Port, after the Abbot of Glendalough. The remains of the present church, built about 1780, and the adjoining graveyard are now a public park. On the corner of New Bride Street a large stone building originally housed St Peter's infant school and St Peter's female boarding and day school. Opposite is

Gascoigne Court, a modern apartment block opened in 2003 on the site of the former Gascoigne Home which had been built on ground purchased in 1902 by Colonel Trench Gascoigne for a home opened in 1904 to be known as the 'Rest for the Dying', until the name was changed in 1962. The building was demolished in 2002 and the home moved to the grounds of the Mageough Home in Cowper Road, founded in 1869 by the will of Miss Elizabeth Mageough, which has accommodation for women in 36 two-storey houses arranged in three terraces around a quadrangle.

Prior to the 1916 Rising, Eamon de Valera drilled his troops of volunteers in the garden behind the Gascoigne. A row of cottage-style residences (Belluvilla) was built in 1838. There is an entrance to the Kevin Street Dublin Institute of Technology, also assorted business premises and public houses.
See **St Kevin's (C of I)**

Camden Street
From Harrington Street to Wexford Street
An ancient highway leading from the city, known as the Highway to Ranelagh or the Highway to Cullens Wood.

In 1710, 'The Bleeding Horse Inn' was opened. James Clarence Mangan, the poet, was a frequent visitor. With the opening of the South Circular Road,* a turnpike was installed beside the inn, controlling access to the new road. It was renamed Camden Street after the Earl of Camden, Lord Lieutenant who sailed his yacht from Portobello to Sallins in 1779. When Portobello Harbour on the Grand Canal

opened in 1797, the street was aligned with Richmond Street, giving a straight run for traffic to Rathmines. Many of the nineteenth-century houses originally had front gardens and granite steps up to the front door. The gardens were later built over to accommodate shops, and the entrance to the houses lowered to street level. An example of this is no. 75 where Pleasants' Asylum was opened in 1818, Thomas Pleasants, the great philanthropist, having bequeathed £15,000 for establishing a female orphan house for the daughters of respectable householders in the parishes of St Peter and St Kevin. It amalgamated with Kirwan House in 1949. From 1892 to 1916 there was a Hebroth at no. 52; this was a small group formed by members of the Jewish immigrant community, for religious and charitable purposes, as a stage of transition for those with differences of language and temperament, which kept them apart from their Irish-born brethren. There were six of these in the Portobello area, one of the earliest being at no. 7 St Kevin's Parade, founded in 1883 for Lithuanian immigrants. The building also housed the headquarters (1912–1915) of the Inter-national Tailors', Pressers' and Machinists' Union, established by Jewish workers. At no. 34, in 1902, the National Dramatic Company owned by William and Frank Fay rehearsed its productions. It merged in 1904 with the Irish Literary Theatre Society to form the Irish National Theatre Company, which opened 27 December 1904 at the new Abbey Theatre in 27 Lower Abbey Street. Opposite the Bleeding Horse Inn is the Camden Hall Hotel, which was originally a convent of the Little Sisters of the Assumption, a nursing order for the sick and poor in their own homes. A fashionable residential street in the nineteenth century, today it is a busy shopping area with street traders selling fruit, flowers and vegetables. Fish is also sold on Fridays.
See **Abbey Theatre** *and* **St Kevin's Port.**

CANALS
Grand Canal
In 1715, an Act was passed proposing a link between Dublin and the Rivers Shannon and Barrow. In 1755, the interest was revived, and Thomas Omer, the surveyor, was appointed engineer. By 1763, 12 miles, commencing at Clondalkin, had been completed, including locks and bridges, at a cost of £57,000. In 1763, Dublin Corporation took over the construction as it was interested in an additional water supply for the city basin. By 1772, the Canal was again in private ownership under the Company of the Undertakers of the Grand Canal who held their first meeting on 18 July at no.105 Grafton Street. The Canal was opened to cargo boat traffic on 2 February 1779, and the first passenger boat commenced operating between Dublin and Sallins (Oberstown) in August 1780. Four years later, this was extended to Robertstown. In 1791, the canal had reached Ringsend and, on 23 April 1796, the Grand Canal Docks were opened when the Earl of Camden sailed his yacht, *Dorset*, through the locks at the River Liffey. This event was commemorated in an oil painting by William Ashford, 'The Grand Canal Docks opened on St George's Day 1796 by Earl Camden, Lieutenant'. It was sold in Sothebys on 2 June 1995. Huband Harbour (after Joseph Huband, a director) near Dolphin's Barn was opened in 1805 as a mooring area on the circular line, but has long since been filled in. The company had five hotels between Dublin and the Shannon, including the one at Portobello* which opened on 13 July 1807. The introduction of the railways brought about a decline in traffic and, in 1950, the company amalgamated with Córas Iompair Éireann, with the last boats being withdrawn in 1959–60. Company ownership has now been transferred to the Office of Public Works. On 13 May 2003, the Lord Mayor, Cllr Dermot Lacey, officially launched the Grand Canal Enhancement Project. The improvement works to date between Emmet Bridge,

Grand Canal at Upper Leeson Street, 1854.

Harold's Cross Bridge and Charlemont Street Bridge include upgrading of towpaths, new seating, lighting and litter bins, new planting, repaving of footpaths along Canal Road and Grove Road, and laying of granite setts around the lock areas at La Touche Bridge and Charlemont Street Bridge. Ongoing improvement works to the Grand and Royal Canals result from the City Canals' Plan prepared in 1998 by Dublin City Council on behalf of itself and Waterways Ireland.
See Dublin Docklands Development Authority.

Royal Canal
In 1789, The Royal Canal Company was formed by royal statute to build a canal between Dublin and Tarmonbarry on the Shannon. It was to have two lines, one commencing below the Custom House on the Liffey, and the other near Bolton Street, both to join at Prospect (in Co. Kildare). The latter was changed when the Broadstone Harbour was built, and the boats crossed Constitution Hill via the Foster Aqueduct.* Work on the construction was slow but it had reached Thomastown in 1805 and Coolnahay in 1809. The first packet boat travelled from Dublin to Mullingar in 1806. The canal was

completed in 1817 and a new company was formed under Act of Parliament in 1818 and named the New Royal Canal Company. The canal had never been able to compete with its rival, the Grand Canal, and, in 1845, it was sold to the Midland Great Western Railway Company Limited for £298,059. Because of competition from the railways, the canal went into a decline. It was taken over by Córas Iompair Éireann in 1944 and was closed in 1961. Recently work has commenced on restoring certain areas with a view to encouraging tourist traffic.
See also Portobello House, Dublin Trams.

Canon Street
From Bride Street to Patrick's Close
Name comes from the minor canons of St Patrick's Cathedral, hence its earlier name of Petty Canon Street. Shaw's directory of 1850 lists twelve houses but when the street was demolished in the 1960s only one house remained, that of Rutledge and Sons, the publicans, at no. 1. For years, the bird market was held in the street on Sunday mornings. One story told about the market recalls how the local children would catch sparrows (called spadgers) with a twig and bird lime and take them to a man who would paint them red and yellow and pass them off as goldfinches.

Capel Street
From Ormond Quay to Bolton Street
Named after Arthur Capel, Earl of Essex, Lord Lieutenant (1672–77).

Sir Humphrey Jervis, a wealthy merchant and later Lord Mayor, together with some associates bought some of the lands of St Mary's Abbey about 1674. He promised the Lord Lieutenant that he would lay out a new street and call it after his family name. It immediately became a fashionable residential area. It also housed, at no. 27, King James' Royal Mint house of brass money fame, in 1689. Today it is a busy commercial and shopping area.

Carman's Hall
Between Meath Street and Francis Street
Rocque's map of 1756 names it Cammon Hall after the tavern where the coaches left for Wexford. A street of small dwellings.

Carmelite Nuns
Established in Ireland between 1638, the year the Irish Province of Carmelite Friars was established, and 1641. Their first convent was probably somewhere in the centre of Dublin. During the Williamite Wars, the nuns took refuge in Loughrea where a Carmelite convent had been founded. They returned to Dublin in 1730 and re-founded the convent there, first in Fisher's Lane (St Michan's Street), then on Arran Quay until 1788, when they moved to Ranelagh, and then in 1975 to St Joseph's Carmelite Monastery, Sea Park, Malahide.

Casino at Marino
Created by James Caulfield, 1st Earl of Charlemont (1763), born in 1728, who at the age of 18 went on a grand tour of Europe and Asia Minor that was to last for nine years. In 1759, William Chambers, the Scottish architect, published drawings for the Casino (from the Italian casina, a small house) in the antique taste of a classical temple. Simon Vierpyl, the Italian sculptor, came to Ireland in 1756 and worked on various projects, including Chambers' Casino which is considered to be one of the finest garden temples in Europe and took

nearly twenty years to complete. He supervised the erection and the carving of this splendid building in the Franco-Roman style of neo-classicism. Lord Charlemont entertained regularly in the house for nearly twenty years before his death in 1799. A major conservation and restoration programme was carried out by the Office of Public Works, and the newly refurbished building was opened to the public on 6 July 1984, having been closed for the previous ten years.

Castle Avenue
Clontarf
Part of an old road which led from Artane through Killester to the sea. Named after Clontarf Castle, the residence of the Vernon family, the present castle was built in 1835. The original castle, erected by the Normans, was the residence of Adam de Phepoe (Feipo, Faypo) who later granted it to the Knights Templar, later to become the Knights Hospitaller. The castle eventually came into the possession of John Vernon, a quartermaster of Cromwell's army in Ireland. The estate then passed to the Oulton family who have since disposed of their interest in it. The castle is now a hotel. Red-brick houses in a residential area.

Castlesteps
See **Cole's Alley.**

Castle Street
From Werburgh Street to Cork Hill
Appears to have been in existence since the building of Dublin Castle from which it received its name. As early as 1260, the King's Exchange was situated in the street and, in 1338, an order was issued for the making of dies for coining pence, halfpence and farthings. Entry to the castle from the street was by a drawbridge with a portcullis at the entrance. In the seventeenth and eighteenth centuries, it was a busy commercial street with a great many printers and booksellers, tradesmen including silver and goldsmiths, several taverns and banks. The pleas office of the Court of Exchequer had its offices there

until 1770 and the Masonic Lodges met at the Hen and Chickens tavern about the same time. In 1773, the Irish Woollen Warehouse, established for the promotion of that manufacture and under the management of the Dublin Society, opened in the street, which also held the guildhall of the Corporation of Joiners and Coopers. Today, as well as an entrance to the Castle, there are houses belonging to St Werburgh's Church and a variety of buildings housing departments of Dublin City Council. The street originally extended into Cow Lane, which joined with Fishamble Street. In 2003, De Blacam and Meagher's building on the corner of Castle Street and Werburgh Street won the RIAI housing medal for the composition of the exterior and the beauty of the double-height penthouse apartment with its gallery library. At no. 4, a late eighteenth-century building occupied for many years by Barnewalls shoe repair shop and due for demolition after the owner died, has now been restored and is the headquarters of the Dublin Civic Trust.

Cathal Brugha Street (1931)

From Sean MacDermott Street to O'Connell Street

Named after Cathal Brugha (1874–1922), revolutionary, fought in O'Connell Street on the republican side at the beginning of the Civil War and died 7 July 1922. The parish Church of St Thomas (C of I),* built 1758–62, was extensively damaged in July 1922 when the area was occupied by the irregulars. The church faced onto green fields but with the building of Gloucester Street it appeared at the end of a long vista. Rather than restore the building, a new church was built on an island that extended Gloucester Street (now Sean MacDermott Street) with a new street, Cathal Brugha Street, which extended the thoroughfare through to O'Connell Street.

Cathedral Lane

*From Upper Kevin Street to the Cabbage Garden**

Part of a new housing scheme and public park provided by Dublin Corporation on the site and leading to the disused Capuchin and Huguenot cemeteries generally referred to as the Cabbage Garden,* which were in use from c. 1668. The scheme was officially opened on 30 April 1982.

Catholic University of Ireland

86 St Stephen's Green

The origins of the university date to 1845 when Sir Robert Peel's bill to establish the Queen's University of Ireland was passed, providing for the founding of an alternative university to Trinity College. The plan proved unacceptable to the Irish Catholic bishops.

Under the leadership of Archbishop Paul Cullen, the Catholic University Committee was formed in 1850, but little happened until February 1852 when Archbishop Murray of Dublin died. On 18 May 1854, the Irish bishops met in synod to agree the university's statutes and to appoint John Henry Newman as its first rector.

From the start, Cullen and Newman disagreed on policy, mainly because of Newman's wish to make the laity a substantive power in the university. The university lacked support and success mainly through not having the authority to grant degrees. An act of 1879 established the Royal University, a non-teaching body which was empowered to bestow degrees through examination, thus enabling Catholic students who had attained the required standards to have an academic qualification without being obliged to attend Trinity College Dublin. The Catholic University came under the control of the Society of Jesus from 1883 until the passing of the Irish Universities Act of 1908 which founded the National University of Ireland which incorporated the newly named University College Dublin as part of a grouping with Cork and Galway.

The Catholic University opened on 4 June 1854 in a house built in 1765 for Richard Chapel Whaley at no. 86 St Stephen's

Green, with very fine plasterwork attributed to Robert West. In 1865, no. 85 was purchased and the university extended. This house was begun in 1738 for Hugh Montgomery, MP for Co. Fermanagh, with plasterwork by Paul and Philip Lafranchini. In 1855, a premises at Cecilia Street was purchased for the establishment of a medical school. A further building, the Aula Maxima, was added to the east side of no. 85 in 1876.

Newman resigned in November 1858 and three years later Dr Bartholemew Woodlock was appointed as his successor. He envisaged a great university to be built at Drumcondra with James Joseph McCarthy as architect. The foundation stone was laid on 20 July 1862 but nothing more came of the project and the land was sold to the Irish Redemptorists.

See **Cecilia Street, Crow Street, Earlsfort Terrace *and* University College Dublin.**

Cavendish Row
From Parnell Street to Parnell Square East
From William Cavendish, 3rd Duke of Devonshire, Lord Lieutenant, 1737–45. Building leases date from 1753 when Luke Gardiner laid out a roadway 72 feet wide from Sackville Street through the gardens of the Bunch of Keys. Originally Cavendish Street and renamed Cavendish Row in 1766, it formed one of the sides of Rutland Square. Built as a shopping and residential street.

Cecilia Street
Like Cope Street it was named after one of the Fownes* family who developed the area. In 1756, it appears as the 'T' junction in Crow Street. On this site a monastery was erected about 1259 by the Talbot family for the friars of the Order of Augustinian Hermits. The medical school of the Catholic University of Ireland* was situated from 1855 to 1931 in the premises now known as Cecilia House.

See **Fownes Court *and* Catholic University of Ireland.**

Centenary Church (Methodist)
St Stephen's Green
Built in the neo-classical style to a design by Isaac Farrell, with four Ionic columns supporting a pediment. It was opened in 1843. In 1969, the interior was seriously damaged by fire, and the congregation moved to Christ Church Leeson Park to share the building with the C of I congregation there. The Centenary Church was sold in 1972 and converted into office accommodation for a private bank.

Chamber or Chambré Street
Newmarket, Coombe
So named after the Chambré family of Stormanstown, near Ardee. Mary Chambré married Edward, 2nd Earl of Meath.

The building lease is dated 1696 and the houses with plain triangular gables were occupied by master weavers. Returns were

Chambré Street photographed in March 1947 showing the triangular gabled houses.

added to the terraced houses about 1700. By 1798, the street had degenerated, being then inhabited mostly by small weavers and artisans. In 1955, a preservation group was set up to try to save what was left of the street, but nothing came of it and most of the houses had been demolished by 1964.

Champion's Avenue
From Summerhill to Sean MacDermott Street.
An attractive complex of red-brick Corporation houses opened in 1986 and named after the champion boxers who lived in the area 1930–40, including Paddy Hughes who held eleven titles and, together with Spike McCormack, a professional middle-weight champion of Ireland, Blackman Doyle and Peter Glennon, returned from America to a hero's welcome having defeated three American champion boxers. At the side facing Gardiner Street is an IDA Small Business Centre developed in association with the local community, beside which is a park facing onto Sean MacDermott Street.
See also **Rutland Street Upper.**

Chancery Lane
From Golden Lane to Werburgh Street
So named because of its proximity to Darby Square where there was the Examiner's office of the Court of Chancery and the office of the Master of Chancery (1738–43). Many important lawyers lived in the street during the eighteenth century. It is now a street of no merit.

Chancery Place (1825)
From Inns Quay to Chancery Street
From its proximity to the Court of Chancery. Also called Mass Lane after the Jesuit church which was there until 1697, later becoming the Huguenot Chapel* of the French Church of the Inns. The Presbyterians purchased the building in 1773 and demolished it in 1825. Also known as Lucy Lane* and Golblac Lane.

Chancery Street
See **Pill Lane.**

Channel Row
See **Brunswick Street North.**

Chapelizod (Séipéal Iosóide)
Four miles from Dublin on the northern bank of the River Liffey on the road to Lucan. The earliest documentary evidence would appear to be an appointment of a priest to the Chapel of Chapelizod in 1228. In the Pipe Roll of Henry III, 1229, Chapel Ysonde and Chapel Isoulde are mentioned. The Civil Survey of 1654 names Chapel Lizard. The lands of Chapelizod were bestowed on Hugh Tyrrell, Baron of Castleknock, by Hugh de Lacy. Tyrrell later transferred them to the Knights Templars at Kilmainham. Chapelizod also includes the townland of St Laurence on the south bank of the river near Palmerstown* where there was a leper hospital. Leprosy usually referred to incurable skin diseases. With the coming of the Normans, Chapelizod became a walled town.

In 1615, Sir Henry Power obtained lands consisting of ten messuages, 200 acres, a watermill and weir; he erected a brick house with fifteen chimneys. King William III was a guest there and the mansion became known as the King's House. It was used as a country residence for the Lord Lieutenants, including Capel, Ormonde, Grafton and Galway, Lord Dorset being the last one to live there. It became the officers' residence in 1760, the Irish Artillery Regiment being stationed in the village. Following a fire in 1832, the ruin and ten acres were sold. In 1864, the Sisters of St Joseph of Cluny bought Mount Sackville, a residence built for Lord George Sackville, youngest son of Lord Dorset. St Laurence's (C of I) is allegedly the site of the old church of Isolde's Chapel. The present church was built in 1832. The fourteenth-century tower was remodelled in 1859. One of the bells was donated in 1720 by a warden named Parker, with the name Chappellizard inscribed. There are several seventeenth-century memorial tablets on the walls of the church. The Church of the Nativity (RC) was built in 1845 as a chapel of ease to Blanchardstown. Because it was built on a slope close to the river, the foundations are as deep as the church is high.

Charitable Dispensary
71 Meath Street

Opened November 1794 and supported by annual subscription for administering medical and surgical aid to the sick poor and assisting them and their families with the necessaries of life during sickness, and preventing the spreading of contagious diseases. Externs were attended at their own houses if within the parishes of St James, St Catherine, St Luke, St Nicholas Within or St Audoen. (From a statistical survey prepared for the Dublin Society 1801.)

Charitable Infirmary
Jervis Street

The hospital was established in 1718 by six doctors, George and Francis Duany, Patrick Kelly, Nathaniel Handson, John Dowdall and Peter Brennan. It opened in Cook Street, moved to Inns Quay in 1728 and then to Jervis Street in 1796 on part of the site of Charlemont House, formerly the home of James 1st Earl of Charlemont. The Sisters of Mercy took over the hospital in 1854. It was rebuilt in 1877 and became one of the main casualty hospitals. It was again enlarged in 1886. An out-patients department erected at a cost of £4,000 was opened by the Lord Lieutenant on 17 October 1910. The hospital was closed in 1987 and its services were transferred to the new hospital at Beaumont.*

Charles Street West
From Ormond Quay Upper to Chancery Street

Named after Charles Coote, Earl of Mountrath 1660, one of the peers in the first parliament convened in Ireland on 8 May 1661, after the restoration of Chichester House. A family of military adventurers and premier baronets of Ireland. A small part of the Quay named Mountrath Street.
See also **Coote Lane** *and* **Kildare Street.**

Charlemont House
Palace Row, Parnell Square

Built in 1761–63 by Sir William Chambers for James Caulfield, Earl of Charlemont (*see also* Casino at Marino). As Commander-in-Chief of the Irish Volunteers, Charlemont was instrumental in securing the independence of the Dublin legislature. The house was considered one of the finest of all the Dublin houses. It was built on a double site in the centre of Palace Row—so called because of the palatial character of Charlemont House. Now the Dublin City Gallery, The Hugh Lane.
See **Rutland Square.**

Charlemont Street
Between Harcourt Road and the Grand Canal

Named after James Caulfield, 4th Viscount and 1st Earl of Charlemont (1728–99). He built the Casino* at Marino and Charlemont House,* Rutland Square.

Building commenced about 1780 and consisted of three-storey red-brick houses. Some of these were demolished in the 1950s and the Corporation levelled a large section in 1967 for urban renewal. A series of three Corporation flat buildings occupies a large section of the street: Tom Kelly Road flats, Ffrench Mullen House flats and Charlemont Gardens. Teac Ultain built for St Ultan's infant hospital opened in 1919, and became part of the new Charlemont Clinic in 1987 with an entrance at the Grand Canal.

In the 1950s, Michael Scott designed a four-storey block of thirteen flats for a philanthropic society, the Charlemont Public Utility Society.

The sculptor Augustus Saint-Gaudens (1848–1907) who designed the Parnell Monument was born at no. 35. His parents emigrated to the United States six months after his birth.

Charlotte Street
From Camden Street to Harcourt Road

Named after Queen Charlotte (1744–1818), wife of George III. Part of the ancient road to Cullenswood. Practically nothing

Chatham Street. The premises of Lambert Brien & Co. on the corner of Chatham Street and Grafton Street.

remains of what was once a fashionable and busy trading street. Europa House, a large office block extending to Harcourt Street, developed by Aranas Ab Sweden and built by Sisk, was opened in 1991. On Monday, 2 November 1992, the street was permanently closed to traffic.
See **Charlotte Way.**

Charlotte Way
From Camden Street to Harcourt Street
On Monday 2 November 1992, a new link road was opened to traffic, replacing Charlotte Street. In the 1980s, Clancourt Investments constructed the Harcourt Centre at the end of Harcourt Street and then built the new road between the Garda Headquarters* and Europa House. The Camden Court Hotel designed by Aranas Ab Sweden opened in 1981.
See **Police.**

Chatham Row
From Chatham Street to Clarendon Row

Chatham Street
From Grafton Street to Clarendon Row
Named after William Pitt (1759–1806), son of the 1st Earl of Chatham.

The nineteenth-century red-brick School of Music building, formerly the premises of Dublin Corporation Technical Printing School, occupies the site of the Clarendon Market, originally an open-air market laid out in 1684 by William Williams. In 1783, Sir John Allen Johnston built an enclosed market to a design of Samuel Sproule, who also built part of Merrion Square. With the formation of the Irish Volunteer Corps,* Sir John commanded the Rathdown Light Horse, all mounted on fine hunters. For generations, the premises occupied by the Allied Irish Bank, on the corner with Grafton Street, housed the firm of Lambert Brien and Company Ltd, established in 1798. Lambert Brien and Company were wax chandlers, lamp and oil merchants and they also had their factory in the street. AIB sold the premises in 2003 for a figure in the region of €18 million to a group of Cork businessmen. It is leased to a leading UK fashion multiple, Monsoon. The street also boasts a variety of shops, restaurants and public houses.

Chequer Street
See **Exchequer Street.**

Chester Beatty Library
See **Alfred Chester Beatty Library.**

Chichester House
College Green

At the end of the sixteenth century, Sir George Carew or Carye, President of Munster and Lord High Treasurer of Ireland, built a large house intended for a hospital but never used for this purpose. During 1605, the courts of law met at Carye's hospital. It passed through various hands until it was sold to Sir Arthur Chichester who had returned from exile in France to command the forces in Ulster. In 1604, he was appointed Lord Deputy. After his death, the house was purchased and completely restored by Sir Samuel Smith. The first parliament convened after the restoration of the monarchy met here from 8 May 1661 until 1666. William Robinson was appointed Keeper of the Parliament house in 1677 and, by 1709, the house was again in a bad state of repair, the banqueting hall having collapsed. It was demolished in December 1728 following a report that the edifice was beyond repair. The foundation stone of a new building was laid in 1729.

See **Parliament House.**

Christ Church Cathedral

In 1038, Donat, the first Bishop of Dublin, with financial help from Sitric, the Danish King of Dublin, built a cathedral on the site of the present one. Sitric also gave rich farmlands as a gift, the revenues from which financed the cathedral until the Church of Ireland was disestablished and disendowed in 1871. Little is known of the original building apart from the fact that it had a nave and wings.

In 1170, Dublin was captured from the Danes by the Normans and Richard De Clare, Earl of Pembroke, better known as Strongbow. Shortly after, King Henry II visited Dublin and received Holy Communion at the cathedral on Christmas Day 1171.

After the conquest, Strongbow and Archbishop Laurence O'Toole (who was uncle to Strongbow's wife, Eva) and the Prior of Christ Church joined in a scheme for the rebuilding of the cathedral. This included the digging out of the crypt which is extant, with a chapel on either side, and on the ground level they built the east end of the cathedral. To the north and south, the magnificent transepts in Romanesque style date from the Anglo-Norman period. The west end of the cathedral is built in early English or lancet style of Gothic architecture. The wall on the north side is the original thirteenth-century wall. The south wall and roof collapsed in 1562, wrecking Strongbow's monument of 1176. The present south wall was built over a hundred years ago. St Laurence O'Toole's heart is enclosed in a casket in the cathedral.

During the Archbishopric of John de St Paul (1349–63), the choir was extended by a further 40 feet and was used from 1358 to 1871. The remains of the eastern wall may be seen in the grounds outside the door of the Chapter House. It was from this long choir that the prayer book was first read in English in 1551 and the bible was read in English from 1560 onwards.

In 1541, King Henry VIII dissolved the priory and established a new order, which has continued with modifications to the present day. On 22 December 1541, Robert Painswick, the thirty-sixth prior since the time of St Laurence O'Toole, became the first Dean of Christ Church.

By 1870, the building was almost in a state of collapse and a Dublin citizen, Henry Roe, agreed to underwrite the entire cost of reconstruction. George Street was employed as architect and the long choir was taken down and not replaced. The cathedral was reopened for public worship on 1 May 1878. As well as restoring the cathedral, he also paid for the building of the Synod Hall. Upon the cathedral and the synod hall, Henry Roe junior, who was from the brewing family in Thomas Street,* expended some £250,000. The hall now houses 'Dublinia', a striking recreation of the streets of Dublin as they were many centuries ago.

The organ was built by Telford and Telford in 1857 and moved to its present position in 1878. It was rebuilt and enlarged in 1923 and, in 1961, a new console was fitted. A complete reconstruction of the organ was undertaken by Jones in 1982.

In 2001, the Treasures of Christchurch was opened in the medieval crypt, displaying information on how the Vikings built the cathedral. It also contains the Tabernacle used when James II worshipped there, the magnificent altar plate given by William of Orange in 1697 to celebrate his victory at the Battle of the Boyne in 1690, and many other items including ancient documents and books.

Christchurch Place
From Lord Edward Street to High Street
After Christ Church Cathedral* the mother church of the Protestant archdiocese of Dublin and Glendalough. A cathedral has stood on this site since 1038. Formerly known as Skinners' Row or the street of the curriers, an area where the citizens traded in hides and leather that were a valuable export to the continent of Europe for many centuries. The Tholsel* or city hall which stood at the High Street was demolished in 1676 and a new Tholsel was completed, having been extended into Skinners' Row by the purchase of additional adjoining sites. It survived until 1791. Near the Tholsel stood Carbrie House which was occupied in the early part of the sixteenth century by the 9th Earl of Kildare. Part of this was converted into a coffee house in the 1640s by Richard Pue, a printer. It was known as Dick's Coffee House and became one of the most popular establishments of its kind in the city. Until 1821 it was a fashionable street with booksellers, jewellers and goldsmiths' shops but in that year this thoroughfare, which was only about 12 feet in width, had its entire north side demolished and the newly laid-out area was renamed Christchurch Place. An attractive 'peace garden'* opened in 1988 faces onto the corner with Nicholas Street.
See **Peace Garden.**

Church Lane
From College Green to St Andrew Street
Facing the Church of St Andrew.* Jammet's Restaurant* was at no. 6 until the lease reverted to the Hibernian Bank in 1926. The bank premises were then extended the length of the street and were again rebuilt in 1980. Now the National Irish Bank with the entrance at 27 College Green. On the opposite side, the North British and Mercantile Insurance Company built an office block in Glasgow freestone in 1855 on the corner of College Green. This was sold to the Post Office in 1909 and used by them until the St Andrew Street post office was opened in the 1950s. The 1885 building was demolished in 1975 and a modern office block now forms part of the Ulster Bank.

Church Street
From Arran Quay to Constitution Hill
Name comes from the church dedicated to St Michan the martyr* on 14 May 1095. The church was rebuilt 1685–86 and reroofed in 1828. The vaults constructed from magnesium limestone absorb moisture, resulting in mummified corpses, making them a popular tourist attraction. At nos. 131–137 is the Father Mathew Centenary Temperance Hall built in 1890 and in nos. 138–142 the Franciscan Capuchin Friary, built in 1881. Both buildings were purchased in 2001 by Ossory Park Management and in 2004 planning permission was granted to convert the Temperance Hall into three office units. St Mary and All Angels (RC) Church was opened in 1881 with J. J. McCarthy as architect. It has a rose window and two pinnacles beneath which are three carved figures under canopies.

Circular Road, North
From Phoenix Park to Portland Row
Laid down in 1763 as one of the boundary roads of the city under an act of 1763 (3 Geo III 36). When it was first laid out it was a fashionable thoroughfare to drive along to the Phoenix Park. The total length from the Park to the North Wall is about 3 miles.

Nicholas Lawless, the 1st Lord Cloncurry, who lived in Upper Merrion Street, wrote: 'Upon that magnificent drive I have frequently seen three or four coaches and six, and eight or ten coaches and four, passing slowly to and fro in a long procession of other carriages and between a double column of well mounted horsemen.' There are many accounts of it being both a scene of pleasure and gallantry. At the junction of Cabra Road is St Peter's (RC) Church of the Vincentian order of St Vincent de Paul, a large Gothic revival building designed by George Goldie of London in 1869. This was a final extension to a church built in 1831. The spire which is over 200 feet high and probably the highest in Dublin dates from 1907. It is in the parish of Phibsborough named after the (Phipps) Phibbs family, large property owners and landlords of the area. Some fine windows by Harry Clarke. From nos. 7 to 62 were the sheds and offices of the Dublin United Tramways Company and at no. 72 the entrance to Bohemian Football Club, Dalymount Park. On the south side, in 1911, there were forty-four houses occupied by the employees of the Midland Great Western Railway. The old cattle market stood until recently at the corner of Aughrim Street. Just past Abercorn Terrace stood the female orphan house or Kirwan House which opened initially at no. 42 Prussia Street in 1790. A new building designed by Whitmore Davis on the NCR was completed in 1793. A further addition was made in 1796 following a charity sermon by the Rev. W. B. Kirwan. The chapel and east wing were added in 1818. It was demolished in 1966 and an office block stands on the site. Under the same act of 1763 the South Circular Road was commenced, giving an elliptical boundary to the city.

Circular Road, South

From Phoenix Park to Harrington Street
This road, together with the North Circular Road, was commenced in 1763 under an act of 1763 (3 Geo III 36) which set up Commissioners for making a circular road. Further acts of 1775–76 and 1777–78 (15 & 16 Geo III 28) decided that the lengths of both roads should be extended and the south road should take in an old circular road of Adelaide Road, Mespil Road and Haddington Road. The south road extends 4¼ miles. It took years to complete the two roads and the work was kept going for years as a relief scheme to provide employment. The shapes of the two roads divided the inner city into an ellipse. At no. 27 SCR stands St Kevin's* (C of I) built in 1888–89 and sold in 1987. It was resold in November 1990 and converted into apartments on a three-floor level. The Griffith (Wellington) military barracks was vacated in 1987 and is now an educational college. Donore Presbyterian Church and manse were sold recently and have been replaced by a Moslem Mosque. At nos. 45–70 a large stone building erected for the Little Sisters of the Poor, St Patrick's House, was sold by the order because of the advanced age of the sisters, and converted into apartments. Also there is a large nineteenth-century church (RC), Our Lady of Dolours, at Dolphin's Barn. A Jewish Synagogue in the classical style has recently been sold for commercial purposes. The portion SCR from Kilmainham Court House to Sarah (Island) Bridge was St John's Road West* until a few years ago. There was an entrance to the Memorial Park. The Island Bridge Cavalry (Clancy) Barracks is also situated near Sarah Bridge.

City Assembly House

58 South William Street
The painters, sculptors and architects resident in Dublin in the 1760s were discouraged by the frequent importation of inferior foreign pictures and mediocre copies of old masters palmed off as originals. Observing the advantages derived in England from annual exhibitions of paintings, they formed themselves into an association under the name of the Society of Artists and, in February 1765, held an exhibition at Napper's Great Room in George's Lane. Its

success exceeded the expectations of its promoters who decided to apply the proceeds to the erection of an exhibition room and school.

A subscription was opened in 1765 and about 100 persons each contributed three guineas, receiving in return a silver ticket to admit him and his heirs to the future exhibitions. With these funds and the promoters' own contributions, an octagonal exhibition room costing £1,307-5-11 was opened in South William Street, the entrance being from Coppinger Row, leaving a debt of £380. The first exhibition in the new premises was opened on 10 March 1766. The Society applied to parliament for aid and, on a second application, in 1767, was granted £500. With this and £200 presented by the trustees of the Royal Exchange building, together with receipts from exhibitions, they erected the new building at no. 58. As parliament did not make any further grants the premises were completed at a cost of £1,730-11-4 with funds advanced by some of the members of the Society. Unfortunately the Society of Artists had a short life and broke up after its last exhibition held in May 1780.

A Richard Cranfield took up the lease and hired out the building for meetings and concerts. By 1791, the Tholsel* was in such a dangerous state of dilapidation that the Assembly hired the exhibition rooms at 30 guineas per year. The premises became the City Assembly House by which name it is known today. In 1809, Mr Cranfield sold his interest in the building to the Assembly who then refurbished the octagonal room for meetings of the Commons and drawing rooms for the Lord Mayor and Aldermen. In October 1851,the Lord Mayor took over the Royal Exchange building* and moved there in 1852. The Court of Conscience, a mayoral court for the settlement of trade disputes and small debts, then moved to the octagonal room from the chamber below.

During the years 1920–22, the outlawed Supreme Court of the Irish Republic met there. Today the building which housed the Dublin Civic Museum, formed from a joint committee of Dublin Corporation and the Old Dublin Society, is closed for refurbishment. The architect is unknown.

City Charters

The corporation possesses 102 charters. These charters were granted to the city by various kings and queens between 1172 and 1727; also 124 deeds, grants, rolls and other documents dating from 1225 to 1828. The charters were granted as a means of securing loyalty from the citizens by conveying various rights and privileges on them. They form the basis of municipal legislation and government. The earliest, issued by Henry III in 1171–72, grants to his men of Bristol his city of Dublin with all liberties and free usages which they have at Bristol and throughout the land. They were to assert their authority over the Norman adventurers who had captured the city.

See **Armorials of the City, Civic Regalia** *and* **Civic Plate.**

City Hall

On 8 October 1851, an Indenture transferred the Royal Exchange* from the Corporation of Merchants or the Guild of the Holy Trinity and vested it in the Right Honourable, the Lord Mayor, Aldermen and Burgesses of Dublin. The trustees also vested in the Lord Mayor, the Rt Hon. Benjamin Lee Guinness, £1,721-14-10 from the sale of government funds, less liabilities of £207, the surplus to be used to refit the building for use and occupation of the Corporation (see Dublin Corporation). Alterations were carried out by Samuel Roberts of Upper Leeson Street, care being taken to preserve the architectural beauty of the edifice. The first meeting of the Corporation in the refitted building took place on Thursday 30 September 1852 when a motion was proposed and agreed 'that this building for the future be denominated the City Hall'.

Following the refurbishment of the City Hall in 2000, a permanent multimedia exhibition centre called 'The Story of the Capital' is housed in the basement, tracing the evolution of the city from before the Anglo-Norman invasion of 1170 to the present day. Also on display are the Civic Regalia.*

See also Assembly Rooms, Royal Exchange and Tholsel.

City Seal

Since the early thirteenth century the city had a common seal: a stamp placed on Corporation documents to make them official. By a charter dated 23 July 1215, civic independence (which the citizens had long been striving for) was assured and this was completed by a charter of Henry III in 1229 which authorised the citizens to elect from among themselves a loyal and discreet Mayor proper for the government of the city. The ancient two-disc seal is made of copper with small additional percentages of silver, zinc and tin, being 3⅜ inches in diameter and having four pierced tags at the side for the insertion of pins to keep the discs in place so that they fitted accurately over each other during sealing. On the obverse is a triple-towered castle, and on the top of each side tower is an archer with a cross bow; from the battlements lower down a figure blowing a trumpet. On the top centre tower, two men blow horns. In the open doorway is an armoured figure bearing a shield and sword. Over the door are three circular niches containing human heads. Around the circular collar is the inscription *SIGILLUM COMMUNE CIVIUM DUBLINIE*. On the reverse is a galley in full sail. At the bow and stern are figures blowing horns. In the galley is the bust of a man wearing a crown while a woman faces him. A man is offering them a cup while a sailor at the stern is hauling on a rope. As on the obverse the motto *SIGILLUM COMMUNE CIVIUM DUBLINIE* is repeated. The old seal is no longer in use and double wafer seals were replaced in 1923 with an embossing seal.

Civic Plate

In the sixteenth and seventeenth centuries, the city possessed a collection of some importance. Nothing now remains except two splendid standing cups, the Williamson and the Fownes, together with a cup presented by Queen Victoria.

Williamson Cup and Cover 1695 Dublin silver goblet-shaped cup made by Thomas Bolton with the arms of Sir Joseph Williamson impaling those of his wife. The cover is surmounted by Sir Joseph's falcon crest issuing from a coronet. 28½ inches high, it is the longest extant Irish cup made. The cup was presented in 1696 by Sir Joseph who was sometime Secretary of State for England, in recognition of the action of the Corporation who presented him with the freedom of the city for his great interest in its affairs.

Fownes Cup and Cover 1700 Dublin silver goblet-shaped cup made by Thomas Bolton with the arms of the City of Dublin. The cover is surmounted with a demi-falcon issuing from a coronet and is 25½ inches high. Sir William Fownes was one of the wealthiest merchants in Dublin and was Sheriff in 1708. In the assembly rolls of the fourth Friday after 25 December 1699–1700 there is an entry: 'It is ordered by the authority of the said assembly on the petition of Alderman William Fownes that the petitioner surrendering the present lease, formerly made to Alderman George Jones, and giving the citty a piece of plate like to and equall value with that given to the citty by Sir Joseph Williamson, Knight, shall have a lease of part of Hoggen Green, alias College Green.'

Queen Victoria Cup and Lid 1899 London silver gilt cup and cover made by R. and S. Garrard and Co. The cup is 17½ inches high and is supported on a squat spreading base. It has harp handles and on one side are engraved the royal arms, while on the reverse are the arms and motto of the city of Dublin and an inscription: 'Presented by Queen Victoria to the citizens of Dublin as a memento of her Majesty's visit to the viceregal lodge April 1900.'

See Fownes Court.

Civic Regalia

The Great Mace 1717–18 Dublin silver gilt probably incorporating parts of an earlier mace supplied in 1665 by Daniel Bellingham, goldsmith, the first Lord Mayor* of Dublin. The present mace was fashioned by Thomas Bolton, goldsmith, who was Lord Mayor in 1716. It measures 60¾ inches in length and 24 inches around the head, the arches of which are topped with an orb and cross plate under which are the arms of George I.

Minor Mace 1762 Dublin silver is 12 inches in length. The head has applied harp, rose and thistle, also a fleur de lys, all surmounted by crowns. Maker Thomas Johnston.

Two *minor maces* One dated 1717 Dublin the maker not known, and the other 1760 maker William Townsend. The heads of each are 8 inches in length and are fitted into turned shanks of mahogany. They have applied harps, roses and thistles, also fleurs de lys. All three minor maces also bear the royal coat of arms.

The Great Sword Cruciform with a pommel and cross of iron encased in thick silver gilt sheet decorated with engraved designs and inscriptions; enclosed in a scabbard of wood covered with red velvet and mounted in silver gilt. The sword measures 54⅝ inches and the scabbard 43⅝ inches. It was made for Henry IV's use in the 1390s and delivered to the city of Dublin in 1409 or 1410.

The King's or City Sword Cruciform in shape with a hilt of engraved silver gilt including the grip. It measures 44¹¹⁄₁₆ inches. This possibly dates to the late fifteenth century but before 1609. According to the Friday book, in 1609, a new pommel and cross was set on the king's sword, weighing 23 ozs of pure silver.

The Great Chain Made of 22 carat gold and worn up to 1988 by the Lord Mayor, it was given to the city by King William III in 1698. It is composed of links representing the Tudor Rose, followed by a trefoil-shaped knot and another in the shape of the letters SS. The design is repeated throughout the length of the collar. On each side is a harp and at the lowest point a link in the shape of a portcullis which is repeated in the centre. A 3¼ inch gold

medal with the bust of William III in relief is suspended from the chain, it being the work of James Rottier. Because of its antiquity and danger of wear through constant usage, a gilt replica was donated to the Corporation in 1988 and this is now worn by the Lord Mayor.

Deputy Lord Mayor's Chain Made in 22 carat gold, it consists of 167 folded links and is approximately 10 feet in length, connected by a small ornament now much worn, probably a castle with two swords behind. It was made in Dublin in 1796 by Jeremiah D'Olier, one of the founders of the Bank of Ireland* and a member of the Wide Streets Commissioners.* His name is honoured in D'Olier Street. This chain replaced one made by Thomas Bolton in 1701. It cost fifty guineas and the value of the old chain.

Lady Mayoress Chain Made in 18 carat gold, it is a triple close-link chain with a medallion in the centre having three castles imposed on a background of blue enamel. The safety chain is in the form of an 18 carat gold Tara brooch with a short chain. It was made in Dublin in 1961 by J. J. McDowell who presented it to the then Lady Mayoress Isobel Dockrell.

Sheriff's Chain Made in 22 carat gold, it consists of 141 links with a small ornament in the form of a tower. Attached to this is a circular gold medal with an inscription stating that it was presented by the Gray Indemnity Committee, December 1882. The chain was made in Dublin 1792 and the medal in Dublin 1882 by John Wodehouse. Edmund Dwyer Gray, while High Sheriff, was committed to Richmond prison on 16 August 1882 for three months for contempt of court. He was a journalist and politician, his father being the owner of *The Freeman's Journal*, a supporter of Parnell and the Land League. Each Sheriff was supposed to add a link with his name. The earliest name appears to be James Moore for 1826. James Moore was a goldsmith and was a Sheriff's peer until 1842. He died in 1849.

Court of Conscience Chain Made of 22 carat gold it consists of 179 fold-over links, is 108 inches in length and was originally worn by the President of the Court of Conscience. The Court of Conscience was a mayoral court for the settlement of trade disputes and small debts.

John Clancy Chain Made in 18 carat gold, it has two types of links—square with book of Kells motifs and elongated with celtic ribbons. It is 26 inches in length. At the base is a circular centrepiece with a copy of the Tara brooch suspended from which are the arms and motto of the city in blue and red enamel. It was made in Dublin in 1914. This chain was presented to Alderman John Clancy, Sub-Sheriff, in 1914, after his election as Alderman for the east ward of Clontarf.

The Corporation purchased the chain in 1951. Alderman Clancy was elected on 23 January 1915 to be Lord Mayor but died on 29 January.

See **Armorials of the City, City Charters** *and* **City Seal.**

Clanbrassil Street Lower

From South Circular Road to New Street
Named after James Hamilton, 2nd Earl of Clanbrassil KP (1729–98), one of the founder members of the Royal Irish Academy.*

In the early 1990s, a dual carriageway, 88 feet wide, replaced most of the small dairies, public houses and butcher's shops that had been operating for generations. A bitter conflict, with widespread opposition from local residents and fifteen organisations, failed to stop the new roadway that continues along New Street and Patrick Street.

Clanbrassil Street Upper

From South Circular Road to Harold's Cross Road
At no. 52 a blue plaque on the house states, 'In James Joyce's imagination was born in May 1866 Leopold Bloom, citizen, reincarnation of Ulysses'. This unfortunately is not correct, the plaque should have been attached to no. 52 Lower Clanbrassil Street. A new corporation development, Clanbrassil Close, is situated near Robert Emmet Bridge. The bridge over the Grand Canal was rebuilt and renamed Robert Emmet Bridge on 31 January 1937.

See **Leopold Bloom Sculpture Trail.**

Clanbrassil Street Lower. Some of the last remaining houses on the west side of the street.

Clare Street

From Leinster Street to Merrion Street Lower

Named after Denzille Holles, Earl of Clare. A street of mid-Georgian houses. Among the present occupants are the Chamber of Commerce, founded in 1783 superseding the Galley Society, and the Mont Clare Hotel.

The modern office block designed by Desmond Fitzgerald and built in 1980 replaced four Georgian houses. At no. 3 lived Dr George Sigerson, eminent doctor and president of the National Literary Society from 1893 until his death in 1925. In May 1909, he unveiled the James Clarence Mangan memorial in St Stephen's Green (see page 237). In the 1930s, Samuel Beckett (1906–90), writer and playwright, who in 1969 was awarded the Nobel Prize for Literature, lived on the top floor of no. 6 above his father's offices, Beckett and Metcalf.

Clarence Mangan Road

From Blackpitts to Mill Street

Pre-war housing estate. James Clarence Mangan, poet, born 1 May 1803 at no. 3 Fishamble Street, died of malnutrition in the Meath Hospital on 20 June 1849. There is a bronze bust of him by Oliver Sheppard RHA, RBS (1865–1941) in St Stephen's Green, unveiled in 1909. Inserted beneath the bronze is a carved stone female head, representing Mangan's poem 'My Dark Rosaleen', by James H. Pearse (1881–1900). *See* **Pearse Street.**

Clarendon Market

See **Chatham Row.**

Clarendon Street

From Wicklow Street to Chatham Street

Named after Henry Hyde, 2nd Earl of Clarendon (1638–1709), Lord Lieutenant 1685.

In 1671, Dublin Corporation leased a plot of land to William Williams for a period of 99 years. This included what is now William Street South* and Clarendon Street which was developed by Williams in 1685. In Mediaeval times, the area was bisected by the River Steyne, a tributary of the Liffey and was part of the lands of the Monastery of All Hallows. In 1684, Williams applied to the Corporation for the liberty to open a market called Clarendon Market on the site where the School of Music now stands in Chatham Row. In 1793, St Teresa's Church was built for the discalced Carmelites, but not consecrated until 1810. It became a fashionable residential street and some members of the Irish parliament resided there, but after the Act of Union many of the houses became gaming halls and dancing rooms. In 1873, the Sisters of the Holy Faith moved from Crow Street and opened a convent and school, where the Westbury Hotel now stands, at a time when there were brothels and illicit drinking houses especially at the Wicklow Street end (*see* Exchequer Street). Brown Thomas, formerly Switzer's, department store forms part of the corner of Wicklow Street.

Some shops trading in antiques and general trading.

Clonliffe Road

Originally Fortick Road after Tristran Fortick who built the Redd House (now known as the Red House) occupied by Frederick E. Jones (*see* Jones's Road). After Jones's death in 1834, the house became part of the Feinaglian Institution.* In 1859, Archbishop Cullen (1803–78) founded Holy Cross College Clonliffe on the site.

Clonmel Street

Cul-de-sac off Harcourt Street

From John Scott (1739–98), Earl of Clonmell, Solicitor General 1774, Attorney General 1777, Chief Justice 1784, created Viscount 1789. Lived at Clonmell House, Harcourt Street opposite Clonmel Street and owned extensive pleasure grounds from Harcourt Street behind St Stephen's Green to Earlsfort Terrace. The street originally joined with Earlsfort Terrace. *See also* **Earlsfort Terrace** *and* **Coburg Gardens.**

Clonskeagh

It would appear that this area was always under the jurisdiction of the Mayor of Dublin as there are several sixteenth-century references 'to the riding of the franchises' passing through Clonskeagh on their way back to Dublin. Horse omnibuses commenced in Dublin about 1836 and soon extended to this fast-growing suburb. (*See* Dublin Trams.) Vergemount Fever Hospital was opened in 1938 and became a psychiatric hospital in 1969, but by 1979 was being used mostly for geriatrics. In the late eighteenth and early nineteenth centuries, Dubliners would ride out this far for a day's rough shooting.

The Church of the Miraculous Medal on Bird Avenue is a large brick building with an extensive front porch having open archways. Designed by Felix Jones, it was opened in 1955.

Clontarf and Dollymount

Cluain Tarbh, Meadow of the Bulls.

Amalgamated with the City of Dublin by Act of Parliament 1900. Formerly a maritime parish in Coolock barony, 3 miles E.N.E. from the General Post Office. On Good Friday, 23 April 1014, the Battle of Clontarf took place when Maol Mórdha, the King of Leinster, rose against Brian Borumha, the High King. It was a long and bloody battle, which appears to have stretched from Summerhill towards Fairview and part of Clontarf, resulting in a win for the forces of Brian Borumha. The battle put a curb on Viking expansion in Ireland. Brian, his son and grandson were killed in the fight. Maol Mórdha did not personally take part in the battle.

A castle (*see* Castle Avenue) was erected here by the Normans and, in 1179, when Clontarf was given to the Knights Templar, Adam de Phepoe (Feipo, Faypo), the owner of the castle, gave it to the order. Rebuilt in 1835 and designed by William Morrison, it is now a hotel. Near Vernon Avenue, on 38 acres, stood the sheds erected in the late seventeenth century for the curing, smoking and salting of fish. The sheds area remained into the nineteenth century and

became a popular seaside resort. Howth Road between Castle Avenue and Killester Lane was widened in 1923. Houses already existed on Vernon Avenue at this time and, in 1925, thirty new semi-detached houses were built. The Vernon estate owned extensive lands in the Clontarf area and, in 1928, entered into an agreement with Dublin Corporation that it would lay out a road network on the estate. Houses were also being built at the newly developed Vernon Grove and Vernon Avenue with a new road linking them to Castle Avenue, while Mount Prospect Avenue was extended to join Howth Road. The area was rapidly expanding with an assortment of houses being built on Belgrove and Kincora roads. Development continued into the 1930s with the opening of shops and thoroughfares including the link road, Copeland Avenue, between Howth Road and Malahide Road.

To coincide with the expansion of population, St John the Baptist (RC) Church was opened in 1835 on Clontarf Road and was redesigned and greatly enlarged in 1895. This was followed by the (C of I) church of the same name on Seafield Road in 1866. The foundation stone of the Presbyterian Church was laid by Mrs John Findlater on 26 July 1889. The fine town hall erected in 1894 and enlarged in 1898 was no longer used when Clontarf was amalgamated with the City of Dublin, and was converted to serve as St Anthony's (RC) Church. It was replaced in 1975 with a new church.

The attractive St Anne's Park, on the James Larkin Road at Dollymount, was part of a 52-acre site purchased by the Guinness family in 1835 from the Vernons of Clontarf Castle. Thornhill, the eighteenth-century house on the estate, was redesigned and enlarged and, renamed St Anne's, it became the home of Benjamin and Elizabeth Guinness. Various additions were added to the house over the next fifty years. By 1939 the estate had expanded to take in 484 acres when Dublin Corporation took it over under a Compulsory Acquisition Order. The house was badly damaged by fire in

1943 and eventually demolished in 1968. A golf course is situated between the Howth and Malahide roads.

See **Castle Avenue, Bull Wall, Drumcondra, Marino** *and* **North Bull Island.**

Clontarf Sea Wall

The Dublin Corporation on 23 September 1938 adopted a report approving of the raising of a loan of £90,000 for the purpose of constructing a sea wall from the Great Northern Railway bridge to Dollymount. 'A sum of approximately £104,000 has been expended to date and the City Engineer estimates that a further expenditure necessary to complete the work will involve a total cost of approximately £110,000. The City Engineer is of the opinion that permanent road works cannot be taken on the land before the summer of 1940.'

See **Castle Avenue.**

Coat of Arms

See **Armorials of the City.**

Coburg Gardens

From Harcourt Street to Earlsfort Terrace

John Scott (1739–98), Earl of Clonmell, lived at Clonmell House, Harcourt Street, and owned extensive pleasure grounds opposite, bordering St Stephen's Green and Hatch Street. These were opened to the public from 1817 until Benjamin Guinness bought them on the completion of Iveagh House at St Stephen's Green. Guinness leased part of the grounds for the 1865 and 1872 exhibitions at Earlsfort Terrace where the National Concert Hall now stands.

See **Earlsfort Terrace** *and* **Clonmel Street.**

Cock Hill

From St John's Lane across Winetavern Street to St Michael's Lane

A sixteenth-century thoroughfare where the fish market was held. In 1537, new houses were built and, in 1695, the offices of the various law Courts moved there while the Four Courts in Christchurch Lane were being rebuilt. Thomas Maule, the Queen's Remembrancer, stated that the

offices were in great danger of fire by reason of the adjacent houses being of timber-work and the cellar under the offices being an ale house. The office was removed to Kennedy's Court in 1716. The area was demolished by the Wide Streets Commissioners.*

Cole's Alley

From Little Ship Street (Hoey's Court) to Castle Street

In the eighteenth century, it contained private residences and the Royal Chop House, a tavern much frequented for billiards. The houses at either side were moved and a steep flight of steps, known as the Castle Steps, was erected, and the passageway extended to Ship Street to give access to the Lower Castle Yard.

College Green

From Dame Street to College Street

From its proximity to Trinity College, originally Hoggen Green from the nunnery of the Blessed Virgin Mary del Hogges built in 1156 by Dermot McMurrogh, King of Leinster. The Green lay outside the east wall of the medieval town.

On the east side is Trinity College,* founded in 1592. The Palladian façade on the west front was designed by Theodore Jacobsen in 1751. Within the College railings are the statues of Edmund Burke and Oliver Goldsmith which, together with the statue of Henry Grattan at the centre of the Green, are by John Henry Foley (1818–74).

On the north side is the Bank of Ireland,* built originally as the Parliament House by Sir Edward Lovett Pearce, and later enlarged by James Gandon and Robert Parke. This was built on the site of an old parliament house that was built as a hospital and later became Chichester House,* the residence of Sir Arthur Chichester. In 1677, William Robinson, architect, became keeper of the Parliament House, under a lease in which he agreed to keep it in good repair.

In 1769, Patrick Daly opened new premises designed by Richard Johnston for his gambling house and club between Foster Place and Anglesea Street. Founded in 1750, it closed in 1823. Part of the centre portion is incorporated in commercial premises. Jury's Hotel commenced life at no. 7 in 1839 as commercial lodgings. It was rebuilt in 1859 and again in 1882. In 1973, the hotel moved to Ballsbridge and the building was demolished in 1980. The new Blooms Hotel stands on the site.

A great part of the south side from Grafton Street to Church Lane is occupied by the Ulster Bank headquarters. In 1962, the Ulster Bank demolished the Irish poplin shop of Richard Atkinson and Co., which had been occupied since 1835 by the firm. Richard Atkinson was Lord Mayor in 1857 and 1861. The bank then demolished the post office building in 1975, after the post office had been moved to Andrew Street. This building on the corner of Church Lane was built for the North British and Mercantile Insurance Company in 1855, and sold to the Post Office in 1909. In 1966, as part of the celebrations to mark the fiftieth anniversary of the Easter Rising, a memorial was erected in the form of a statue of Thomas Davis, together with a fountain designed by Edward Delaney. Thomas Davis (1814–45), the poet and nationalist, founded *The Nation* newspaper in 1842 and wrote 'A Nation Once Again' and 'The West's Awake'.

Numbers 16–17 housed the merchant bank founded in 1836 by Robert Guinness and John Ross Mahon in South Frederick Street. They moved to College Green in 1854. The present building was constructed in 1931.

College Street
Follows the curve of Trinity College railings from College Green to Pearse Street
The Royal Irish Institution for the encouragement and promotion of the fine arts in Ireland, founded in 1813, moved in 1829 to its new premises at no. 5, designed by Frederick Darley. This building was replaced in 1866 by the Provincial Bank, designed by William George Murray. This is now part of the 164-bedroom Westin

Hotel which extends into Westmoreland Street, designed by Henry J. Lyons and Partners and opened in 1998. This necessitated the demolition of four buildings apart from their façades, including the one on the corner with Westmoreland Street that was designed by the Deane Partnership for the Scottish Widows Insurance Company. In 1966, the Provincial Bank came under the new grouping of Allied Irish Banks who owned the site, and is now situated in the complex at nos. 40/41 Westmoreland Street. The Crampton Memorial,* erected in 1862 and removed in 1959 after it had partially collapsed, stood in the centre of the street at the Pearse Street end.

On the traffic island at Pearse Street, a stone sculpture, 'Steyne' by Cliodna Cussen, was erected in 1986. Steyne is the Viking word for stone. In the ninth century, the Vikings erected a long stone at the edge of the River Liffey to prevent their ships from running aground. It remained standing until about 1720 and is shown on a map in Dublin City Council Archives.* The present 'Steyne' is a copy of the original and stands in the same location. Outside the Screen Cinema is a bronze statue, 'Mister Screen' by Vincent Browne. It is in the form of a uniformed usher directing people to the cinema with his torch. Erected in 1988, it was sponsored by the Dublin Cinema group.

Collins Barracks (Royal Barracks)
See **Barracks** *and* **Benburb Street.**

Commercial Buildings
See **Fownes Court.**

Conciliation Hall
Burgh Quay
Built in 1841 to house the campaign head-quarters of the Repeal Association founded by Daniel O'Connell on 15 April 1840, an organisation working for the repeal of the Union between Great Britain and Ireland. Forty-eight clerks were employed there in 1843. The organisation was dissolved shortly after O'Connell's death in 1847.

Conciliation Hall was a large plain building with a plaster ceiling having three rosettes painted green with shamrock decoration, the centre one having the Brian Borumha harp in relief. The building was later used as a grain warehouse. In 1896, it was converted into the Grand Lyric Hall to a design of William Henry Byrne, when a new front was erected with Corinthian pilasters, a pediment and a scroll-topped rail surmounted with the figure of the Goddess of Music. The auditorium had elaborate rococo plasterwork. The name was later changed to the Tivoli Theatre. The newly formed Irish Press newspaper bought the building in 1930 when it was converted into a printing works and office accommodation.

Constitution Hill
From Church Street to Dominick Street
On the east side are the gardens and a fine view of the King's Inns (*see* Henrietta Street). To the left is the old Broadstone station, built 1841–50 in the typical exotic style of railway termini designed by John Skipton Mulvany. Now a bus station. The gardens cover the filled-in Broadstone harbour built for the Royal Canal.* The boats crossed over the road via the Foster Aqueduct.*
See **Foster Aqueduct.**

Contemporary Music Centre
Fishamble Street
Ireland's national archive and resource centre for new music, supporting the work of composers throughout the Republic and Northern Ireland. The centre is used both nationally and internationally, by performers, composers, promoters and members of the public interested in finding out more about music in Ireland. Its library and sound archive, open to the public free of charge, contain the only comprehensive collection in existence of music by Irish composers.

Conyngham Road
From Parkgate to Chapelizod Road
William Burton Conyngham was appointed in 1767 to the Wide Streets Commissioners as a trustee for the building of an academy of painting, sculpture and architecture. Work on a narrow laneway to Island Bridge was commenced in 1786 and partly paid for by Mr Conyngham.

Cook Street
From Bridge Street to Winetavern Street
Le Coke Street or Vicus Cocoram, the street of the cooks, incorporated under the Guild of Cooks or Fraternity of St James the Apostle. Here may be seen the reconstructed arch, dating from AD 1240 and wall of medieval Dublin.

Originally there were numerous gates in the old wall along this area and in the sixteenth century the area had oak-beamed cagework houses, one of which was built in 1580 by John Luttrell, Sheriff in 1567–68. During the reign of Charles I, the discalced Carmelites opened a chapel, as did the Franciscans or Grey Friars whose large church and friary of 'Adam and Eve's' (the church of the Immaculate Conception) back onto the street. Robert Burnell, Baron of Exchequer in Ireland in 1402, had a house here and, in 1613, James I granted Philip Hoare 'a ruinous stone house and an orchard or garden; called the garden of Burnell's Inns'. The Dublin Charitable Infirmary opened in Cook Street in 1718 before transferring to Inns Quay and then to Jervis Street.

There were also several Catholic stationers and printers in the area in the eighteenth century, printing mostly devotional literature. During the nineteenth century, from about 1850 onwards, many coffin makers worked here, opening shroud warehouses and displaying their wares in large open sheds that also housed the hearses. In 1851, Nugent started *Moore's Almanack* or as a rival concern termed it, 'The Rushlight of Coffin Colony'. Opposite the city wall there is Audoen's House, a block of Corporation flats, and a national school for boys and girls. A row of artisan dwellings stands between Schoolhouse Lane West and Winetavern Street.

Coombe
From Bride Street to Dean Street
A valley or hollow place from where the River Poddle ran eventually to the sea. In about 1670, a housing development began in the area, with houses known as Dutch Billies with their gables facing the street. The area became overcrowded with the weavers, making it an industrial zone. The Dutch Billies were replaced in the nineqteenth century by houses that cost £90 each. The River Poddle had for many years been covered in. One of the most important buildings was Weavers Hall, a red-brick building that housed the weavers, built in 1745–47. The head of Benjamin Rickshaw's lead image of George II disintegrated and was removed in 1937. The head reposes in the City Archive.* The building was demolished in 1965, including the alms houses on either side.
See **The Liberties** *and* **Stove Tenter House.**

Coombe Lying-In Hospital
On 10 October 1770, Lord Brabazon laid the foundation stone of the new Meath Hospital in the Coombe. In 1774, it became the County Dublin Infirmary. When the new Meath Hospital* was built at Long Lane, the patients were transferred on 24 December 1822 from the Coombe to the new premises.
In 1826, Mrs Margaret Boyle, a wealthy widow, was deeply affected by the case of a woman who, failing to get to the Rotunda, then the only lying-in hospital in the city, had her baby on the corner of Thomas Street and died there. Mrs Boyle founded the Coombe Lying-in Hospital in the building vacated by the Meath Hospital. The Guinness family became benefactors and built a dispensary block. On 8 May 1879, the Viceroy, the Duke of Marlborough, opened a new Georgian front wing designed by J. F. Fuller (1835–1924), which increased the number of beds from thirty-one to seventy. In 1967, a large modern 265-bed hospital complex was built in Cork Street. When the old building became vacant, the back courtyard area housed the St Laurence O'Toole Old People's Day Centre, run by the Red Cross. The building was eventually demolished to make way for a Dublin Corporation housing development. The large portico was preserved and is incorporated in the estate.
See **Meath Hospital.**

Coote Lane or Coote Street
From Leinster Street South, to St Stephen's Green North
Part of the Molesworth fields and now Kildare Street since 1753. According to Gilbert, John Ensor erected several houses in the locality and, in 1753, set the dwelling house on the north-western corner of 'Coote Street otherwise Kildare Street to Mary Countess Dowager of Kildare for 999 years at the annual rent of £36'.

Cope Street
From Fownes Street to Anglesea Street
From Robert Cope of Loughgall who married Elizabeth, the daughter of Sir William Fownes.
See **Fownes Court.**

Copper Alley (1608)
From Fishamble Street to Blind Quay
Erected on portion of the ground known as Preston's Inns. Received its name from the copper money coined and distributed by the charitable Lady Alice Fenton, widow of Sir Geoffrey Fenton, Secretary of State in Ireland 1581–1608. Lady Fenton had the tenure of Preston's Inn, an old house with barns and 'backsides' on which were built tenements, together with an orchard on the south side of the house. Barnaby Rych, writing about this time, describes it as a flourishing street. Next to the church of St John the Evangelist stood the courtyard and deanery of Christ Church Cathedral. It was the last building on the western side of Fishamble Street. It was an early eighteenth-century building but replaced an earlier seventeenth-century building that had stood nearby. It was used as a deanery until 1770. From 1842, it was used for St John's United National Schools until it was demolished with St John's Church as

part of a road-widening scheme and the opening of Lord Edward Street.

Coppinger (Lane) Row
From William Street South to Clarendon Street
Maurice Coppinger, Serjeant at Arms.
In March 1765, Vierpyl, the extensive house builder and developer, leased land on William Street South to build an octagonal exhibition room with an entrance in Coppinger Lane. These were to become the City Assembly House.* A fire station was built in the Row in 1862 with telegraphy in order to liaise with its sister station in White Horse Yard.* Powerscourt House sides onto the Row which is now pedestrianised.
See White Horse Yard, City Assembly House, Powerscourt House.

Cork Hill
From Lord Edward Street to Dame Street
Named after Richard Boyle, 1st Earl of Cork. About 1600, he erected a mansion house known as Cork House* on the site of the demolished Church of Sainte Marie del Dam* which, apart from Dublin Castle,* was the earliest building of any significance in the area.
Opposite Cork House stood another house erected by John Bysse, Recorder of Dublin and Chief Baron of the Irish Exchequer (1666–79). His daughter Judith married in 1654 Robert Molesworth, father of the political writer. This property then passed to the Molesworths and together with the adjacent buildings was demolished in 1762 to make an opening for the new Parliament Street.
In *Faulkner's Journal,** dated 12 July 1768, an entry states, 'Yesterday the workmen began to throw down the old Buildings of Cork Hill, in order to widen the Avenue, and prepare the ground for erecting the New Exchange.' (*See* Royal Exchange.)

Cork House
A mansion house built by Richard Boyle, 1st Earl of Cork, on Cork Hill about 1600. After his death, it was used for various government offices. During the rising of

1641, it was used by the Council which had moved out of Dublin Castle and subsequently became the headquarters of Cromwell's government in Ireland. It was also used as an exchange and later housed Lucas's Coffee House.*

Cork Street
From Dolphin's Barn Street to Ardee Street
The old Fever Hospital* was opened here in 1804 and remained until it was replaced by the Cherry Orchard Hospital in Blanchardstown. Like so many streets in the Coombe area, the houses were built in the 'Dutch Billy' style. Charles and John Wesley, the founders of Methodism, rented a weavers' store at 46–48, about 1745, and then moved to a larger weavers' store at 104 around 1750. A further move took place in the 1770s to 148 and this was rebuilt as a Methodist Chapel in 1812 and closed in 1902. In 1829, Donnelly established a bacon factory and, in 1891, amalgamated with two other bacon factories, James Pakenham of Brickfield Lane and Matthew Keogh, Francis Street and 13–15 Spitalfields. In 1906, O'Mara's Bacon Company bought Donnelly's who eventually went bankrupt in March 1967 when they were taken over by Clover Meats of Waterford. They closed on 13 July 1979. The Primitive Wesleyans formed a new group in 1834 near the present Donnelly Centre. It later became a widows' home. The James Weir home for nurses was built in 1903 on the site of a former Quaker burial ground. In 1873, the Sisters of Mercy opened the present convent (*see* Stove Tenter House for details). In 1967, a new 265-bed hospital, designed by T. P. Kenny and Partners, replaced the Coombe Lying-in Hospital. In 2003, the Cork Street/Coombe Relief Route was completed with a two-lane highway and bus corridor. Mitchell and Associates, consultant architects, were appointed to prepare a road enhancement scheme, which included the planting of trees. A multi-disciplinary team was established to regenerate the area, which covered the physical, soft environmental improvements, development potential and community issues. In 2003, work

commenced on 46 apartments designed by architects Horan Keogan Ryan, consisting of two blocks, one fronting onto Marrowbone Lane and the other with frontage onto Cork Street. A further development at nos. 46/47, of 18 one- and two-bedroom apartments, was built in 2004.

Cornmarket
High Street

Because of its situation at the west end of the street it was one of the most important trading positions in the ancient city. The charter of King John enacted that no foreign merchants should buy corn, hides or wool from any but the citizens.

From the thirteenth century onwards, large quantities of corn were traded and exported. The chief magistrate was responsible for checking the weights and measures and for keeping law and order. Nothing remains of the cornmarket except the name given to a portion near St Audoen's Church.* With the widening of the High Street and Bridge Street, many of the eighteenth- and nineteenth-century houses were demolished, including the Winstanley Memorial Hall at nos. 1–2, built by the shoe firm in Back Lane for St Audoen's in 1894. A park laid out by Dublin Corporation stands on the site which is now part of Bridge Street.

Corry's Lane
Now Botanic Avenue

Named after James Corry, a linen merchant who had a house here.
See Glasnevin.

Cow Lane
Originally from Castle Street to Fishamble Street. With the opening of Lord Edward Street in 1886 it now extends from there to Essex Street West.*

Mentioned as early as 1397. In 1598, it was set by the City to John Weston, and many fashionable houses were built on it, including one erected by Sir Daniel Bellingham, first Lord Mayor of Dublin in 1665, which was described as 'a large

elegant structure across the ancient entrance to Cow lane at the corner of Fishamble Street and Castle Street'. In 2000, the street was realigned when five architectural practices working to a social, cultural and environmental brief designed 191 apartments and 24 retail units in a pedestrian street renamed Cow's Lane. In 2003, the area was awarded the London, Royal Town Planning Institute's 'Planning and City Renaturation' award.

Cow Pock Institution

Opened in North King Street on 14 January 1804 when vaccinations against smallpox were administered in Dublin for the first time. The institution later moved to larger premises in no. 62 Sackville Street. From its institution to 1 November 1826, 99,128 patients were inoculated and 73,910 packets of infection distributed.

Crampton Court
Off Dame Street

Opposite to Castle Lane was the station of the Horse Guard of Dublin. On the removal of the military in the early part of the eighteenth century, this locality became the property of Philip Crampton (1696–1792), a wealthy bookseller who continued to reside in it for many years after he had retired from business. The court was built in 1745. In 1755, his brethren of the Corporation of Stationers presented him with a large silver cup in acknowledgment of his work as Sheriff. Crampton was elected Lord Mayor in 1758 and died in Grafton Street in 1792, at 96 years of age. In the eighteenth century, the court was frequented by merchants and insurance companies. The Little Dublin Coffee House was located at no. 20. After 1799, the merchants moved to Commercial Buildings and the area became tenanted by jewellers and watchmakers. By the 1960s, most of the houses had been reduced to one storey. All of the original houses have now been demolished.

Crampton Memorial

Sir Philip Crampton MD (1777–1858) was

surgeon general to the forces in Ireland and surgeon in ordinary to Queen Victoria. He was a founder member of the Royal Zoological Society and obtained the present garden site for the zoo in the Phoenix Park. The monument by Joseph Kirk (1821–94) was in the form of a high foliate decoration with the bust of Crampton amid three swans supported on a trifid plinth with lion masks emitting water to shell basins. Three lamp-posts at the edge of a circle completed the memorial which stood at the corner of College Street and Hawkins Street. It collapsed in 1959 and was removed. In 1960, plans were drawn up for another fountain but these plans were never put into operation.

An amusing anecdote recalls that in 1836 on the day when the equestrian statue of William III* was blown up, a message was sent to the surgeon that an important person had fallen from his horse in front of the Bank of Ireland.

Crane Lane
From Dame Street to Essex Street

A lease dated 1620 granted to King James I from Jacob Newman for ninety years 'a certain parcel of ground lying in or near Dame Street, in the suburbs of Dublin . . . for the purpose of erecting cranes and making wharves, whereby the merchants might land their goods at a convenient place . . . with free ingress and egress through a lane leading from the said street to the Liffey containing in breadth 18 feet'. The first Jewish synagogue was in the lane possibly as early as 1663, in the house of a merchant named Phillips.

Crann sa Chathair

A Dublin millennium project, initiated by Crann (founded in 1986 with the aim of releafing Ireland with broad-leaf trees), funded by AIB and assisted by the co-operation of Dublin Corporation Parks Department. Its aim was to assist Dublin people in ten districts of the city with the job of planting 10,000 broad-leaf trees during 1988. The organisation supplied the trees, expertise and advice. Initial plantings took place in February/March in five of the areas and recommenced in September.

Crockers' Street
North of Thomas Street

A twelfth-century street, Vicus Figulorum, or the potters' quarters, it was the approach to Gormond's Gate from the west. It was eventually reduced to Crockers' Lane and Rocque's map of 1756 shows the lane as Mullinahack.* Most of the lane disappeared with the building of John's Lane Distillery, now the National College of Art and Design.

Croke Park
Jones's Road

Named after Thomas William Croke (1824–1902), Archbishop of Cashel, first patron of the Gaelic Athletic Association (Cumann Luthcleas Gael), founded 27 October 1884. Jones's Road was first rented by the GAA for an athletics meeting on 10 September 1892 and the first All-Ireland finals played there were on 21 March 1896. Prior to this, matches had been played on different grounds, including a muddy field at Inchicore, where Tyrconnell Park housing estate now stands. In 1907, Frank Dineen bought the field at Jones's Road for £3,250 and, on 22 December 1913, sold it to the GAA for £3,500 plus fees. The memory of the event of Bloody Sunday 21 November 1920, when thirty people died including the Gaelic footballer Michael Hogan, would be perpetuated with the opening of the Hogan Stand in 1926, the same year the first outdoor radio broadcast of a match, anywhere in Europe, took place there. This stand was replaced 7 June 1959 with the new Hogan Stand. On 21 August 1938, the Cusack Stand was opened, named after Michael Cusack (1847–1906) the founder of the GAA.

In the 1980s, a decision was made to rebuild the Park completely and in 1993, planning permission was granted and demolition work commenced. Construction took place between then and 2004. Today it is a stadium built to world-class

Croke Park, Jones's Road, opened in 1892. Today it is a stadium built to world-class standards with accommodation for 80,000 at any one event.

standards with 1.5 million people attending matches in the season, with accommodation for 80,000 at any one event. It also houses the GAA museum with visitor numbers increasing each year to over 45,000.

Croppies' Acre Memorial Park
South of Benburb Street, near Wolfe Tone Quay
The United Irishmen had, in imitation of the French Republicans, adopted the fashion of wearing the hair cut short, from which they obtained the name of Croppies, and any person with closely cut hair was at once denounced as a rebel and forced to undergo the torture of the pitched cap. This was made of coarse linen or strong brown paper and the inside smeared with pitch, which when well heated was pressed down on the head. When cooled, it was extremely painful to remove.
While no fighting took place in Dublin during the 1798 rebellion, cartloads of bodies of revolutionaries were brought into the city and dumped at Barrack Street

(Benburb Street) and, together with the bodies of those who were executed in the Prevost prison at Arbour Hill, are interred in a park in front of what was once the grounds of the Royal Barracks (Collins Barracks). Large, flat, granite slabs represent the unmarked graves. There is an attractive water feature while double rows of yew trees lead to a wall carved with a cross and Seamus Heaney's poem, 'Requiem for the Croppies'.

Crosspoddle
See **Dean Street.**

Crow Street
From Dame Street to Cecilia Street
About 1259, a monastery was built for friars of the order of Augustinian Hermits. This stood on what is now Cecilia Street and part of Crow Street. The site was granted by Henry VIII to Walter Tyrrel whose heirs assigned the site to William Crow who in 1597 had been granted the offices of Chirographer and Chief Prothonotary to the Court of Common Pleas in Ireland;

also in 1605, at the same court, Clerkship of the King's silver. Gilbert records in a document of 20 January 1627: 'one large garden with one capital messuage thereupon lately built by William Crow esq., . . . adjoining unto the King's pavement called Dame's Street on the south and upon the lane going to the river of the Liffey on the west'. The building, named The Crow's Nest, housed various government offices including the Survey of the Forfeited Irish Lands when forty clerks were directed under Dr Petty. On 14 April 1684, the Dublin Society moved from Cork Hill and took rooms in the building, establishing a botanic garden together with a museum and a laboratory. The house remained standing until the death of its owner, Colonel Weatheral, in 1730. The street also housed a famous theatre.
See **Crow Street Theatre and Music Hall.**

Crow Street Theatre and Music Hall

On a slab in St Werburgh's churchyard is inscribed an epitaph to John Edwin, an actor of Crow Street Theatre who died in 1805 from chagrin at the criticism of the author of the *Family epistles on the present state of the Irish Stage.* Spranger Barry opened the Crow Street Theatre in opposition to the Smock Alley Theatre known as the Theatre Royal. Thomas Sheridan, manager of the Theatre Royal wrote: 'Let all farther progress in the Theatre of Crow Street be stopped'. Finding his propositions disregarded, Sheridan soon withdrew from Ireland after the opening of the new theatre in Crow Street.

Dublin owed the establishment of a hospital for incurables to the charitable musical society of Crow Street which agreed in 1743 to appropriate funds to that purpose, and fitted up a house which opened in 1744. Spranger Barry took a lease of the building in 1757, paying a fine of £500 and an annual rent of £50. He knocked down this house and erected a new theatre costing £22,000. Spranger Barry died in 1777. His background is interesting as he took over the family firm

of silversmiths in Skinners' Row, but through his mismanagement, the firm went into bankruptcy. He had a brilliant career in the theatre.

In 1836, a portion of the site of the theatre was purchased by the Company of the Apothecaries Hall* of Dublin who erected on it a building with spacious lecture rooms and a laboratory for their medical school. These premises were sold in 1855 to the Catholic University of Ireland.

'Crown Jewels' of the Order of St Patrick

The Most Illustrious Order of St Patrick was founded for Irish Peers in 1783 on the order of King George III. The banners of the knights, together with their symbolic swords and crested helmets, are placed over their stalls in St Patrick's Cathedral. The jewels and insignia of the order, together with the collars of five knights and another badge, were kept in the safe in the Office of Arms in the Bermingham Tower, Dublin Castle. The two principal pieces that were worn only by the Lord Lieutenant or a visiting member of the royal family consisted of an eight-pointed diamond star, mounted on a blue enamel and gold background with an emerald-set shamrock in the centre, and a badge having an emerald-set shamrock mounted on a cross set with rubies. Attached was a blue enamel border with old cut diamonds, having a motto and date, the entire having a border of large diamonds. This was suspended from a diamond-set harp. These were made in London in 1830, by Rundell and Bridge. King Edward VII visited Ireland on 10 July 1907 and, among his many engagements, including a visit to the Irish International Exhibition* in Herbert Park, was the Investiture of Lord Castletown as a Knight of the Order. On 6 July, the safe was discovered unlocked and the jewels missing. In spite of a police reward of £1,000, a vice-regal commission and many accusations, the perpetrators of the crime were never caught or the jewels recovered. The King made it known that he was very annoyed with the results of the enquiry, and Lord

Castletown's investiture did not take place.

Crumlin
Off Parnell Road and Dolphin Road
A settlement dating from the Stone Age, eventually becoming a crown manor on the instructions of King John. It was an area of open fields with dairies and farmland centred round a small village. Local horse races were held on the common until the beginning of the nineteenth century. In the 1920s, 702 houses were built by Dublin Corporation and, commencing in 1935, 2,915 houses were built as a result of new legislation giving the Corporation wide powers of compulsory acquisition. In 1926, the Iveagh Trust had erected 136 houses on a 30-acre site off Crumlin Road, designed by O'Callaghan and Webb. From 1938 to 1945, the Corporation built a further 2,416 houses in an area north of Kildare Road, now called Crumlin North. Two schools, St Agnes's Convent and the Christian Brothers opposite, catered for almost 7,000 children between the ages of six and fourteen. For many years during the nineteenth century, Brickfields Park produced the yellow clay used for making bricks, commonly used in the expanding urban development. Our Lady's Hospital for Sick Children was opened in 1956. The old church of St Mary the Virgin (C of I) stands on the site of a twelfth-century building. Because of the great housing expansion a new yellow-brick church was opened in 1942, designed by McDonnell and Dixon. St Agnes's (RC) Church, built in granite, was opened in 1935.

Cuala Press
Following a split with the Dun Emer Guild,* Lolly Yeats (Elizabeth Corbet) and Lily Yeats removed their printing business which they had started in 1903 to Churchtown. W. B. Yeats was their editor and the first book to be published in 1903 was his *In the Seven Woods*. The sisters produced broadsides by their brother, Jack B. Yeats, together with Christmas cards. Other broadsheets were then produced, being hand-coloured and having poems by Yeats and others. The business was continued in the home of Anne Yeats (1919–2001), painter and daughter of W. B. Yeats, until it ceased to operate in 1986.

Cuffe Street
From St Stephen's Green to Kevin Street Lower
Name comes from Sir James Cuffe MP who married in 1656–57 Alice, daughter of Sir Francis Aungier whose descendant, the 1st Earl of Longford, laid out Aungier Street, Longford Street and Cuffe Street c. 1677.
The street was redeveloped in the late eighteenth century when four-storey red-brick terraced houses lined the street. These have now disappeared and Corporation flats stand in their place. On the corner of no. 24 Cuffe Street and no. 106 St Stephen's Green stood the Winter Garden public house. It was acquired together with other properties in the area by a Compulsory Purchase Order in 1968 and demolished in 1975 to make way for a six-lane dual carriageway, part of the inner loop tangent.

Cumberland Street North
From Sean MacDermott Street to Waterford Street
Named after William Augustus, Duke of Cumberland (1721–65).
A fashionable street laid out in the second half of the eighteenth century. One famous resident was Richard Crosbie who, on 19 July 1785, became the first Irish aeronaut by ascending from Leinster Lawn in a balloon which landed in the sea at Dún Laoghaire where a barge towed it to safety. By 1850, many of the 42 houses were occupied by solicitors and barristers. Nothing has survived from this era and the street now contains a block of Corporation flats, Avondale House, a Department of Social Welfare Employment Exchange and a small office block.

Custom House (New)
Custom House Quay
James Gandon arrived in Dublin on 26 April 1781, having been guaranteed financial security by Lord Carlow and Lord Beresford. The foundation stone for his

Head of a river god by Edward Smyth (1749–1812). Custom House.

great masterpiece, the new Custom House, was laid by Lord Beresford on 8 August 1781. There was an amount of opposition to the building and several riots took place, some led by Napper Tandy, as merchants had their warehouses further up river at the old Custom House, and the dockers also would have much further to travel. There was opposition too from the owners of fashionable town houses in Lower Gardiner Street and surrounding areas who feared that their property would be reduced in value by the proximity of commerce. Many difficulties arose regarding the construction as it was built on reclaimed slob lands.

The building was completed in 1791 at a cost of £400,000. It was gutted by fire in 1921 when the IRA burned it. The Office of Public Works rebuilt the interior to a new design. A further major restoration and reconstruction took place in 1986–88. The large sculpture of Commerce on the dome is by Edward Smyth. Prior to the burning in 1921, there stood above the pediment statues of Neptune, Mercury, Plenty and Industry. These were replaced in 1991. Smyth also did the keystones representing the Atlantic Ocean and the thirteen

principal rivers of Ireland; and, to a design of Carlini, he carved the marine chariot drawn by sea horses, with Neptune banishing famine and despair placed in the tympanum.

At the west front is a memorial to the Dublin Brigade, IRA, by Yann Renard Goulet.

Custom House (Old)
Wellington Quay

In 1620, the government erected a Custom House, crane and wharf for the 'convenient loading, landing, putting aboard and on shore merchandize as should at any time thereafter be exported or imported'. Prior to this an edifice known as The Crane on Merchant's Quay at Winetavern Street was used as a Custom House. In 1596–97, a quantity of gun powder exploded accidentally beside The Crane, causing destruction of life and property. It was rebuilt several times and used as a store until about 1800. In 1707, another Custom House was built where the Clarence Hotel now stands, with principal entrances in Temple Bar and Essex Street. The upper two storeys built in brick each had fifteen windows. The lower storey was an arcade of cut stone with fifteen arched entrances. Custom House Quay formed the width of the building and could berth only four small ships at any one time. Larger ships had to unload their cargoes into barges and lighters and transport them from the harbour. The upper part of the building was declared unsafe in 1773. In March 1774, the House of Commons after a long investigation decided that the situation of the existing Custom House was inconvenient to trade and, after much public objection, the foundation stone of the new Custom House* was laid down-river in 1781 and the old building was converted into a barracks in which the Dumbarton Fencibles were housed in 1798.

Custom House Docks Development Company
See **International Financial Services Centre** *and* **Dublin Docklands Development Authority.**

Custom House (New) completed in 1791. The photograph shows a view of the river before the Custom House was shadowed by the City of Dublin Junction Railway Bridge—familiarly known as the Loop Line—which opened in 1891, an unsightly metal box affair covered to this day by advertising slogans.

D

Dalkey

Eight miles S.E. from the General Post Office, it is picturesquely situated on the southern shore of Dublin Bay. It was a thriving port from Norman times and the town has a Charter of Incorporation of 33 Edward III, dated 8 February 1358. Until the seventeenth century, it maintained the character of a port and was protected by seven castles; the remains of two are still to be seen on the main street. One, the Goat castle, dating from 1498, was restored for the Town Hall and is now the rates office. The other, Archbold's castle, is on the other side of the street. There is a third fortified building, Bullock castle, at Bullock Harbour, built probably by the Cistercian monks of St Mary's Abbey in Dublin who owned land here. In the main street there are the ruins of a medieval church dedicated to St Begnet, a local virgin saint. (See Dalkey Island.) The district became popular after the building of Dún Laoghaire harbour and the extension of the railway to Dalkey. In 1838, a Loreto school was set up in Bullock Castle and the buildings greatly extended with the purchase of several private dwellings. St Patrick's (C of I) Church, which opened in 1843, was built of stone from the local quarry. The Church of the Assumption (RC) was opened in 1840 but added to over the years. The square tower is a later construction.

Dalkey Island

Comprising an area of 22 acres, lies 300 yards offshore from Dalkey. The old name was *Deilginis*, meaning Thorn Island. There is evidence that it was inhabited in the fourth millennium BC and was also used as a Viking base. There are the ruins of St Begnet's Church, dedicated to a local virgin saint. It was used as a dwelling for the builders of the nearby Martello tower.* A large herd of goats was removed because of disease and malnutrition. In the end of the eighteenth and beginning of the nineteenth century, a convivial Dublin club used to assemble on the island in June to go through a mock coronation of the King of Dalkey, with officers of State, etc. and proclamations from the 'Kingdom' issued from 'The Palace, Fownes Street'. This custom was re-introduced about twenty-five years ago when Norman Judd was crowned King of Dalkey and invested with the Order of the Lobster and Periwinkle.

Dame Street

From College Green to Cork Hill

Dame's Gate in the city wall* opposite Palace Street was demolished in 1698. It adjoined the Church of the Blessed Virgin Mary del Dame, built 1385. Charles Haliday in the 'Scandinavian Kingdom of Dublin' derives the name from the dam or millpond close to where the gate and church stood. The street was widened in 1769 by the Wide Street Commissioners. The Central Bank, commenced in 1973 to a design of Sam Stephenson, dominates the street. When completed, it was found to be almost 30 feet higher than shown in the original plans. Following an inquiry, the height was reduced by omitting the copper roof. The building was completed in 1978 at a cost of £10 million. In 1991, a large sculpture, 'Crann An Oir' by Eamonn O'Doherty, commissioned by the bank for the forecourt, was unveiled by Charles J. Haughey. Much of the ground on which the bank now stands housed a fine classical grouping of buildings commenced in 1796 and opened under the name of Commercial Buildings in 1799. (*See* Fownes Court). The architect was Edward Parke. The courtyard of the building was used as a short cut to Merchant's Arch and the metal footbridge. Also demolished to make way for the bank was the Royal Insurance office at nos. 44 and 45, designed by W. G. Murray and opened in 1869 having exceptionally fine plasterwork ceilings. At no. 75, the Olympia Theatre, designed by John J. Callaghan, opened in 1879 as the Star of Erin Music Hall, owned by Dan Lowry. Closed in 1897 and reopened as the Empire Palace under the proprietorship of Star Theatre Varieties Ltd, a company in which John Findlater, of the grocer family, had a financial interest, and eventually renamed the Olympia Theatre. There was a fashion in the first half of the nineteenth century to face red-brick eighteenth-century houses with stucco work. Up to recently, the horse's head mounted over the door of T. J. Callaghan, the outfitters, saddlers and harness makers at nos. 13–16, was a familiar landmark. The building was designed by J. J. O'Callaghan. Another familiar sign, until it was removed recently, was the clock erected over Waterhouse the jewellers at no. 24. Waterhouse made the first two copies of the Tara brooch. Dame Street is a busy commercial street with offices, restaurants, banks and insurance companies.

Dame's Mills

A series of mills along the River Poddle east of Dame's Gate. The Assembly rolls record the commencement of a wall from the gate to the mills. Jacob Newman leased them from Buyshopp in 1607 and they then passed through various ownerships until they were leased by Keane O'Hara in 1704.

Darby Square
Werburgh Street

Possibly named after John Darby, a pewterer who lived there and was church-warden in St Werburgh's in 1694. Gilbert notes a death in 1729 of Mr Thomas Connor who married the widow Darby, owner of Darby Square. It was originally surrounded by twelve houses, which were occupied mostly by the legal profession. It also contained the examiner's office of the Court of Chancery and the office of the Master of Chancery 1738–43. It was lighted by five large globe lamps, which, with the iron gates to the square, were taken down about 1820. The original granite entrance with the name of the square was removed to make way for the entrance to a large multi-storey car park. It is at present stored with Dublin City Council. At the rere of the square was a large plot of ground that was used for various forms of entertainment and, in 1798, the Liberty Rangers and Yeomanry Corps of about 200 men trained there. It was here at Mr Courtney's Academy that James Clarence Mangan (1803–49), poet, would receive his education until the age of 15 years.

Darby Square showing the original entrance from Werburgh Street.

Davy Byrne's
21 Duke Street

By the end of the eighteenth century, there was still a lot of grassland as well as small farms and dairies bordering South Anne Street, Duke Street and Grafton Street. Number 21 became a licensed premises in 1798 when a tenement was leased to Michael Deering. It passed through several ownerships until Davy Byrne bought the premises in 1889 and ran a most successful and popular establishment until he retired in 1939. Like the Bailey Tavern opposite, it was patronised by a literary clientele, including James Joyce who mentions it both in *Dubliners* and in *Ulysses* when Leopold Bloom* has his gorgonzola sandwich and glass of burgundy. James Stephens, Patrick Kavanagh and Brendan Behan were frequent visitors. Since 1942, the Doran family, owners of The Old Stand in Exchequer Street, have kept the traditional pub alive. The murals in the front are by Cecil Ffrench Salkeld (1904–69).

Dawson Street
From St Stephen's Green to Nassau Street

Joshua Dawson purchased the site in 1705 from Henry Temple of East Sheen, Surrey, and the representatives of Hugh Price of Dublin, and by 1707 had formed a wide roadway considered at the time to be the finest in Dublin. In 1714, a committee was set up to consider the building of a house for the Lord Mayor. It recommended that a house built by Mr Joshua Dawson for his own use but as yet unoccupied and unfinished should be purchased. On 25 April 1715, the Corporation agreed to purchase the house for £3,500 and also pay a yearly rent of 40 shillings and a loaf of double refined sugar weighing 6 lbs at Christmas. The house as purchased had brick walls and a different parapet at the top of the front wall. It has since been changed in appearance by external plastering and the addition of a nineteenth-century portico at the entrance. The round room beside the Mansion House was built in 1821 for a visit of George IV. It was built in a period of six weeks. This is now used for functions and exhibitions and also houses a large restaurant. To the right of the Mansion House a large office block was opened in 2002. Number 19, formerly Northland House, was built in 1770 for the Knox family. In 1852, it was acquired by the Royal Irish Academy.* St Ann's Church* also graces the street which today is a busy commercial and shopping area with several fine bookshops. In 1982, Trust House Forte sold the popular Hibernian Hotel to a property developer and, in 1984, planning permission was granted for the Hibernian Way, a large office and shopping complex opened in 1988, leading from Dawson Street to Duke Lane.

Dean Street
From the Coombe to Patrick Street

Name comes from its close proximity to the deanery of St Patrick's Cathedral, originally named Crosspoddle Street, where, at the junction of Patrick Street, women washed their clothes in the River Poddle. After a bad flood in 1860 when the Cathedral was awash, the river was piped. The Poddle like the Liffey was tidal as far as a small island at Crosspoddle where the river divided; the smaller channel was bridged here right up to the beginning of the seventeenth century, the lower stretches of the river being marshy and subject to flooding.

Dean's Grange Cemetery
Dean's Grange Road

Established by the Board of Guardians of the Rathdown Union acting as a burial board, in 1865, and put under the management of a joint burial board known as the Dean's Grange Joint Burial Board by a provisional order of the Local Government Board confirmed by Act of Parliament 1899. The first burial took place on 28 January 1865. The cemetery contains two churches and is open to all religious denominations. Originally Roman Catholics were buried in the North section and Protestants in the South section. The cemetery covers over 60 acres and is the largest in South Co. Dublin. The old part contains many headstones to eminent people including Augustine Henry (1857–1930), physician and botanist who in 1881 joined the customs service in China. While there he studied the flora of the country and collected a thousand plants, which he sent to Kew Gardens, London. He was appointed Professor of Forestry at the College of Science, Dublin, 1913. His wife, Elsie (1882–1956), who continued his interest in collecting plants for the National Botanic Gardens, is interred with him.

Delville
Glasnevin
Originally named Heldeville. Home of Patrick Delany, a clergyman of Swift's circle, and his second wife, the former Mrs Mary Pendarves, whom he married on 9 June 1743. Through her influence he was appointed Dean of Down. The house, built on an eleven-acre site, was commenced in 1722. It was here that Mrs Delany entertained the intellectual society of Dublin, wrote her diaries, painted and made her famous flower decorations. The house survived until 1951. The Bon Secours Hospital now stands on the site.

Denzille Lane
Off Holles Street
Named after Denzille Holles (1597–1681), Earl of Clare.

Derby Square
See **Darby Square.**

Designated Areas Scheme
Under the 1986 Finance Act, certain designated inner-city areas have the advantage of tax incentives. Commercial property developers receive a 50 per cent allowance against tax, and tenants are entitled to an allowance of twice their rent for ten years. This scheme, which got off to a slow start, is now progressing with developments on derelict sites at High Street, Christchurch Place, Church Street, parts of the Quays and stretching northwards to Gardiner Street and Mountjoy Square.

Digital Hub (The)
The digital hub is an initiative of the Irish Government to create an international digital enterprise area in Dublin city. The Department of Communications, Marine and Natural Resources, Dublin City Council, Enterprise Ireland and IDA Ireland are the sponsoring partners. The core development of approximately nine acres is located within the Liberties Area.* It includes a public-sector investment of €130 million from the Irish Government to encourage established and high-potential start-up companies working in the digital media sector. Included in the area is Media Lab Europe, opened in July 2000 on the top floor of the Hop Store, formerly part of Guinness Brewery. It is a new university-level research and education centre in conjunction with the Massachusetts Institute of Technology. Media Lab Europe is made up of a team of scientists, engineers, technologists and artists from a variety of backgrounds and skill sets, from Ireland, Europe and around the world. Their research focuses on the ways in which new technologies can impact on people's lives and environments in order to enhance the quality of life through research and education. Media Lab Europe went into voluntary liquidation in January 2005 as the Massachusetts Institute of Technology and the Irish government were unable to reach agreement on future funding, €35 million already having been invested in the project. The project office of Digital Media Development Ltd is at 10–13 Thomas Street. In 2003, Digital Hub attracted its first five companies to locate at the site, Educational Multimedia Group, Unlimited, Journeyman Productions, Zenark and Pixel Soup. Educational Multimedia and Unlimited have since ceased trading but Digital Hub is in the process of attracting other digital media and technology firms, and over forty have relocated to the Liberties.
See **Thomas Street.**

Dirty Lane
See **Bridgefoot Street.**

Dispensary for the Parishes of St Mary, St Thomas and St George
Denmark Street

'This charitable institution was the first of the kind established in Dublin. Medicures and advice are given thrice weekly at the dispensary or at their own dwellings, every day, if necessary, to such of the resident parishioners as are able to procure the common necessities of life but whose age, complaints, or situation render them improper objects for public hospitals' (from a statistical survey prepared for the Dublin Society 1801).

Dr Steevens' Hospital
Steevens' Lane

Richard Steevens (1653–1710), the son of an Anglican clergyman, studied theology at Trinity College* before taking an MD degree in 1687. He amassed a large fortune and died while holding the office of President of the Royal College of Physicians.* He bequeathed his estate to his twin sister Madam Grizel for her lifetime and, on her death, to be used for the building of a hospital. His sister decided to build the hospital in her own lifetime, retaining £100 a year for herself. Thomas Burgh drew up a set of plans in 1713 but it was not until four years later that the present site was purchased and work commenced in 1721. This took twelve years to complete and the hospital opened in 1733. As part of the agreement, Grizel Steevens lived in the hospital until her death in 1747 in her ninety-third year. The design included a clock tower and an internal arched courtyard for patients to walk in.

The hospital closed in 1987. It contained a splendid library bequeathed by Edward Worth, one of the trustees, having early printed works and beautiful bindings. This collection of 4,000 volumes is now contained in its original setting. Thomas Burgh (1670–1730) died before the hospital was completed and the work was then supervised by Edward Lovett Pearce (1699–1733), who designed the attractive boardroom that houses Worth's books. The hospital was sold in Spring 1988 for £800,000 and reopened in 1992 as the headquarters of the Eastern Health Board. A new entrance was created on the north front, facing Heuston Station,* with a flight of nine granite steps leading to a new limestone door case. The architects were Arthur Gibney and Partners and the restoration and conversion cost £4.4 million.

Dogs' and Cats' Home
Mount Venus, Rathfarnham

A Galway MP, Richard Martin, nicknamed 'Humanity Dick', had a law passed in 1822 concerning the welfare of animals. As a result of this, the Society for the Prevention of Cruelty to Animals was founded in 1824 and, in 1840, the Dublin Auxiliary to the Royal Society for the Prevention of Cruelty to Animals was founded under the patronage of Queen Victoria and the Earl of Bessborough, with an address at 2 Lower Ormond Quay. In 1883, Richard Barlow Kennett, an Englishman, offered £500 for general purposes on condition that it was matched by a similar amount, and a further £500 for a house for lost and starving dogs and cats.

In 1884, half an acre was leased from the Dublin Sugar Refinery at Grand Canal Quay, with 306 feet along the railway, 161 feet onto the Quay and 267 feet along the Sugar Company's premises. The building was opened in 1885 behind boundary walls 8 feet high. There was a caretaker's residence, a boardroom and a separate building for 200 dogs and a section to house the cats. In 1906, an Act of parliament made it the official pound for stray dogs. They were to be kept for seven days, then sold or destroyed. In 1950, infra-red lamps were installed to keep the animals warm and the bedding dry. By 1960, the buildings were in a dangerous condition and, after a successful fund-raising project, a new block was opened in 1967 and new kennels for badly injured dogs were built in 1969. Whitney, Moore and Keller, the solicitors, gave £1,750 to pay off the loan, together with £3,000 towards rebuilding costs, and a further £15,000 was received through their office in 1972. A further £26,250 was given in 1975 by an anonymous donor. In 1992, the home moved to Stocking Lane, Rathfarnham, and in October 2003 was housed in a new 30-acre complex at Mount Venus, Rathfarnham.

Dodder Valley Drainage (1975)
See **Main Drainage System.**

D'Olier Street
From College Green to O'Connell Street
Named after Jeremiah D'Olier (1745–1817), Sheriff 1790, one of the founders of the Bank of Ireland. Prominent goldsmith and member of Wide Streets Commissioners. D'Olier Street and Westmoreland Street were the last two major schemes to be carried out by the Wide Streets Commissioners.* The new street (D'Olier

Sea horses from the base of a 19th-century lamp standard in College Green. It was originally a gas lamp.

Street) was constructed at the beginning of the nineteenth century and consisted of brick buildings with shops at street level over basements. Brocas's engraving of 1820 shows the street with the impressive stone-built Carlisle Building no. 28 that cornered onto Burgh Quay. This was demolished and the new towering O'Connell Bridge House opened in 1965, and was extended in 1968 by demolishing two more of the original houses. Numbers 21–24 were remodelled in 1883 to house the Junior Army and Navy stores. They were altered again in 1926 when T. and C. Martin, the builders' providers, moved in. This firm went into liquidation and in 1968 an office block called D'Olier House was erected. Between the two office blocks (D'Olier House and Carlisle Building) designed by Desmond Fitzgerald stand the 1920s former offices and showrooms of the Dublin Gas Company. The Gothic building in the angle of D'Olier Street and Westmoreland Street was built in 1894–95 and for many years housed Purcells, the tobacconists.

On the traffic island at Westmoreland Street, set into the concrete paving slabs, is a series of metal footprints entitled *Oileán na nDaoine* (People's Island), by Rachel Joynt, sponsored by Allied Irish Banks in 1988 for the Sculptors' Society of Ireland.

Dolmen Press
Printing press founded in 1951 by Liam Miller (1924–87) who studied architecture in UCD and worked in London on various projects after the Second World War. He returned to Dublin and founded the Dolmen Press, working at home and experimenting with type layout and design. His first publications were mostly small volumes of poetry. He moved to 23 Upper Mount Street in the 1960s and expanded the business to include an assortment of publications including *The Importance of being Oscar* by Micheál MacLiammóir. He also commissioned artists to illustrate his works, including Louis le Brocquy's designs for Thomas Kinsella's translation of the mythological *Táin Bó Cuailgne* in 1969,

THE DOLMEN PRESS

The Dolmen Press logo.

which after more than thirty years is still considered to be one of the finest examples of Irish printing. He expanded his readership by printing a number of his publications in conjunction with Oxford University Press. His book layout and design won many awards and established him as an international typographer. He also designed sets for the Abbey Theatre and was the first president of Clé, the publishers' association. He died on 17 May 1987 and with his death came closure of the Press and the end of one of the finest periods in book design.

Dolphin's Barn
From Cork Street to Dolphin's Barn Street
Known in medieval times as Dolfynes Berne or *Carnan Cloch* (Mound of Stones). In the thirteenth century, there are several mentions of the Sign of the Dolfyn, possibly an inn or dwelling belonging to a family of that name as Dolfyn (David) is recorded as owning lands in the area. There is a mention in the Liber Albus (White book of Dublin Corporation 1396) of O'Donacha's Carn (O'Donacha's burial place) from which the name Dolphin's Barn could have originated. At the riding of the franchises* the city boundary was beyond Dolfynes Berne. Thomas Amory (c. 1691–1788), the eccentric author of *The Life of John Buncle* and *Memoirs of Several Ladies of Great Britain*, refers to the hurling matches we have played at Dolphin's Barn. There were extensive limestone quarries and yellow-brick works in the area, which operated until the late 1940s. A Roman Catholic Church was built in 1798 and served until 1893. The foundation stone for

the present church, Our Lady of Dolours, designed by the architect William Hague, was laid in 1890 and the church was consecrated in 1893. In 1902, it became a separate parish of Dolphin's Barn from St James.
See **Cork Street.**

Dominick Street
Lower, from Parnell Street to Bolton Street
Upper, from Bolton Street to Western Way
Part of a parcel of land in the possession of Sir Christopher Dominick who started to build in 1720. In 1727, a lease was given to Lady Alice Hine on land which was bordered on the north by Sir Christopher's house. He was a member of the established church and when he died in 1743, his will stipulated that any bequest to his wife or family be revoked if she allowed any of their children to be carried to any Presbyterian church, meeting or assembly. Robert West, the stuccodore, lived at no. 20 and designed it to his own specification with outstanding plasterwork. The house passed through various hands including those of the Rt Hon. John Beresford until it was opened in 1856 as a Protestant school. Seán O'Casey's sister Isabella taught there and Seán resided there with his mother after 1887. In 1927, the house was taken by the Dominicans as an orphanage for boys.
Number 41 was the town residence of the Earl of Howth who gave it to the Carmelite friars, and, in 1902, it was transferred to the Sisters of the Holy Faith. Sir Rowan Hamilton, the mathematical genius, was born at no. 38 in 1805. The street, which was one of the most fashionable when it was built, rapidly declined after the Act of Union. Most of the houses which eventually became slums have been replaced with flats belonging to Dublin Corporation. The upper part of the street was commenced after 1810 and Arthur Griffith was born in no. 4 in 1871.
In 2004, Dublin City Architects, as part of the Dublin Development Plan, designed, at nos. 65–79, a five-storey council house scheme, incorporating 46 apartments into

a 0.42 acre site, as well as a canteen and a changing area for the employees of Dublin City Council Cleansing Department. The complex has a raised pavement and private walkway. This is part of an ongoing scheme for the upgrading of the street, and some of the residents from lower Dominick Street have moved into these apartments.
See also St Saviour's and Dublin Artisans' Dwellings Company.

Donnybrook
Domhnach Broc, The Church of Broc
The site of an ancient settlement on the banks of the River Dodder founded about AD 750 by a lady named Broc who built a church here dedicated to the Blessed Mother of God. In 1524, on the marriage of Alison Fitzwilliam to Christopher Ussher, she received the lands of Donnybrook. Her husband built Donnybrook Castle. A smaller house was built on its ruined site in 1798 and was purchased by Mother Mary Aikenhead in 1837. This became the St Mary Magdalen Home of Refuge.
The village was the scene of a famous fair founded in 1204. It lasted for eight days; originally held in May, it was extended to fifteen days commencing on 26 August. It was suppressed in 1855. The rugby pitches and on the other side the CIE depot cover part of the green. The Sacred Heart Church, designed by Michael Healy (1914–15), has a fine window by Harry Clarke. Further along is University College Dublin* and, in the grounds of Montrose, Radio Telefís Éireann.* St Thomas's Church on the corner of Foster Avenue has a window by Evie Hone. The Irish Christian Brothers occupied St Helen's from 1926 to 1988. Built in 1750, it was one of the country houses built for the Fitzwilliam Estate. The area is divided by the Stillorgan Road dual carriageway.
Eight attractive cottages in the village were demolished between 1965 and 1970 and replaced with two-storey shops and a new fire station.
The Westmoreland or Lock Hospital for Incurables moved from Townsend Street to Donnybrook in 1792. It was rebuilt at the end of the nineteenth century to J. Rawson Carroll's plans and, in June 1887, it was renamed the Royal Hospital for Incurables, Dublin. The name was changed again in July 1974 and it has been known since then as the Royal Hospital, Donnybrook.

Donnybrook Fair
Founded in 1204 by Royal Charter. As the centuries progressed, it became an occasion for debauchery, drunkenness and prostitution. The area was covered with ragged tents, having signs advertising the various wares for sale. The fair lasted for fifteen days from 26 August and was primarily a horse fair but traders travelled from abroad to buy and sell their wares. The traders included an assortment of craftsmen and money dealers. By the middle of the nineteenth century, Donnybrook was developing into a residential area and the residents had the fair suppressed in 1855 with the buying out of the original Charter.

Dorset Street
From Bolton Street to Drumcondra Road
Named after Lionel Cranfield Sackville, Duke of Dorset, Lord Lieutenant 1731–37, 1751–55. Originally Drumcondra Lane following the old highway to the north. Richard Brinsley Sheridan was born at no. 12. In his autobiography, John O'Keefe recalls playing marbles in the back yard of Dr Sheridan's school. Number 80, which was demolished at the end of the nineteenth century, was built by Richard Synnott, whose father became Lord Mayor. The Bethesda Chapel was taken over by W. M. Shanley who opened it as the Plaza Cinema in 1913. The Bank of Ireland building now at no. 85 occupies the house where Seán O'Casey (1880–1964) was born. He also lived at 20 Dominick Street after 1887. He left for London in 1926.

Drimnagh Castle
Situated within the grounds of the Christian Brothers School off the Long Mile Road, it was built by the Barnewell family in the thirteenth century and is the

only surviving Irish castle to be surrounded by a flooded moat. It consists of a great hall over a vaulted undercroft with a sixteenth-century gate tower. The original drawbridge was replaced in 1780 by a fixed bridge which gives access to the yard. There are also some nineteenth-century buildings.

The building was restored through the Drimnagh Castle Restoration project which commenced work in 1986 with a grant of £3,000 from Dublin Corporation and a further £16,000 from its Conservation Fund. The work was supervised by a local committee under the auspices of An Taisce and an AnCO training scheme. Two stone masons and a carpenter came from France on an exchange programme and, together with Irish trainees, made the roof.

Drogheda Street
From Great Britain Street (Parnell Street) to Abbey Street

Part of the lands of St Mary's Abbey that were divided up at the dissolution of the monasteries in the sixteenth century. This parcel, called the Drogheda Estate from Viscount Moore then Earl of Drogheda, was purchased in 1714 by Luke Gardiner. In the 1750s, Gardiner widened it by 150 feet by demolishing the houses between Great Britain Street and Henry Street. It had a central mall named Gardiner's Mall. The stretch between Henry Street and Abbey Street remained as Drogheda Street and the new development was named Sackville Street.
See **Sackville Street.**

Drumcondra
A suburb on the main N1, Belfast Road, 2 miles north of Dublin. The road originally being known as the Royal Way. In 1878, the Local Township Act 41/42 Vict. CH. CLVII was passed, forming the districts of Drumcondra, Clonliffe and Glasnevin into a township. Donnycarney and Goosegreen were not in the township but the entire area was added to the City of Dublin by the Boundaries Bill of 1900.

Drumcondra. Folly in the grounds of Drumcondra House. It was designed by the Florentine architect Alessandro Galilei c. 1718–20 and closely resembles the front of Castletown house, Celbridge.

James Bathe built a castle here in 1560. The site is now occupied by what was known as St Joseph's Asylum for the Male Blind, opened by a group of Carmelites in 1882, now known as St Joseph's School for Visually Impaired Boys and run by the Rosminian Fathers since around 1958. St John the Baptist (C of I) Church built in 1743 on the instructions of Mary Coghill whose brother Marmaduke Coghill (1673–1738) is portrayed in an impressive monument in the church, by Scheemakers. James Gandon (1742–1824), the architect, and Francis Grose (1731–91), the antiquarian, are buried in the one grave. St Aidan (C of I), designed by Caulfield Orpen, opened in 1902 on Drumcondra Road. A new Roman Catholic parish was created in 1902 from Berkeley Road and, in 1905, St Columba's Church, designed by George Ashlin, was completed. Land was purchased from the Lindsay estate to build the new Iona Road to give access to the front of the building. Sir Marmaduke Coghill lived in Belvedere House built for Sir Robert Booth in 1785, which was purchased by the Archbishop of Dublin in 1883 and is now incorporated in St Patrick's

Training College. The Missionary College of All Hallows, designed by J. J. McCarthy, incorporates Drumcondra House, designed by Sir Edward Lovett Pearce in 1725 for Sir Marmaduke Coghill. The College chapel has a window by Evie Hone. In April 1927, a road running from Howth Road to Ballymun Road, known as the 100 Foot Road, was renamed Griffith Avenue. Dublin Corporation had previously acquired 32 acres of the Butterly estate and, by the end of 1927, approximately 534 houses had been built. Further land was then purchased and Home Farm Road, built in 1911, was then extended and many of the local farms and fields were built on. With the completion of Griffith Avenue, Collins Avenue was extended by 73 yards in 1936 and extensive building in the surrounding area took place, including shops on Collins Avenue and a cinema.

Beyond Drumcondra was the small village of Goosegreen. Goosegreen Road is now Grace Park Road. The RC Archbishop's residence is situated on Drumcondra Road Lower. Binns Bridge on the same road is named after John Binns, a founder member of the Royal Canal Company* and a director of the Grand Canal Company.* He also had a bridge on the Grand Canal at Robertstown perpetuating his name. He represented the weavers on the Common Council and later became a representative of the merchants.

See **Clontarf and Dollymount, Castle Avenue, Marino** *and* **North Bull Island.**

Drury Street

From Exchequer Street to Stephen Street

Originally Little Butter Lane according to Brooking's map of 1728. Renamed Drury Lane about 1766. In 1876, a group of businessmen acquired properties in the lane, mostly tenements, in order to build the south-city markets.* The lane was widened and renamed Drury Street 1880–81.

Dubhlinn

The origins of the name of the city are unknown and tend to enter the realm of legend. Along the old town wall at Wood Quay there would appear to have been an area that flooded at high tide and this possibly was *An Linn Dubh,* the black pool where the Liffey and Poddle met. The name possibly predates the coming of the Vikings. Françoise Henry and Howard Clarke both suggest that the name may have referred to a monastic settlement south of the blackpool, and Clarke considers that the reason for the two names is that Dubhlinn referred to the monastic settlement near the pool and Áth Cliath was further upstream where there was a community at the ford of the hurdles.

See **Baile Átha Cliath.**

Dublin and Blessington Steam Tramway

About 1880, it was proposed that a light railway with a 3-foot gauge should be built from Dublin to Blessington with a terminus near St Patrick's Cathedral. Dublin Corporation turned down the proposal as steam was not acceptable within the city limits. In 1887, an act was passed to run a 15½-mile tramway from Terenure to Blessington and a connection made with the Dublin Tramway Company to the city centre. The railway opened on 1 August 1888. The line was extended to Poulaphouca on 1 May 1895 with a separate company formed in 1889 called the Blessington and Poulaphouca Steam Tramway. This section was closed on 30 September 1927.

In 1887, the Company had six four-wheeled coupled tank locomotives costing £900 each, ten passenger vehicles, ten goods vehicles, four cattle wagons, two closed vans and two brake vans. This rolling stock was increased over the years. In 1897, it was proposed to extend the line over the Wicklow Gap to Glendalough but this never materialised. The Paragon Bus Company in 1929 commenced a service from the city centre to Poulaphouca and Ballymore Eustace, which eliminated the problem of having to change cars at Terenure. The steam tram went into decline from then on and eventually closed on 31 December 1932. Since the tram ran at the side of the road, many people were killed over the years and many others seriously injured. The route was known as the longest graveyard in Ireland, as crosses were erected along the route to mark the spots where fatal injury had occurred.

Dublin and Lucan Steam Tramway Company

On 1 June 1881 a 3-foot gauge tramway opened and ran from Conyngham Road to Chapelizod. It was extended to Palmerstown in November and finally to the Spa Hotel at Lucan on 20 February 1883. An extended service to Leixlip opened in June 1890 and closed in 1897 when the terminus reverted back to the Spa Hotel. The line was electrified in 1900 and the gauge changed to 3-foot-6-inch tracks. The company changed its name to the Dublin and Lucan Electric Railway. After the First World War, competition from motor buses affected the company which eventually became bankrupt on 29 January 1925. The Dublin United Tramways Company* took over the assets of the company and laid new lines to the east end of Lucan village and commenced a service in May 1928. It ran at a loss until it closed in April 1941.

Dublin Artisans' Dwellings Company

Started in 1876 by some members of the Dublin Sanitary Association including Lady Brabazon. Sites that were already cleared by Dublin Corporation under Public Health Acts and the Artisans and Labourers Act of 1875 were then leased to the company and red-brick one-storey cottages and two-storey houses were built. The Coombe area, bordering Pimlico and Meath Street, was covered with 216 of these. Two references were required before a tenant could occupy a building; the tenant also had to be in steady employment. Rents ranged from three shillings and sixpence to seven shillings and sixpence, and the company's first report states that it was working on thoroughly sound commercial principles and not as a charitable undertaking. By 1907, there were 2,961 dwellings, housing 2,884 families (the number of individuals housed being 13,330), with a rent for the year of £40,450. Each house had a water supply, a yard and water closet. Lord Ardilaun and Lady Brabazon invested heavily in the company. Lady Ardilaun was also involved in the London Artisans' Company. The Corporation also erected artisans' dwellings for the amelioration of the living conditions of the working classes, as did the Iveagh Trust.* In 1885, the Prince of Wales and his son, the Duke of Clarence, visited some of the houses in the Coombe area. In 1897, the company tried to raise the rents by three pence per week, but following mass demonstrations it was agreed to postpone the increase until 1 January 1899.

The Dublin Artisans' Dwellings Company started by building tenements in Buckingham Street and Dominick Street Upper. They also built houses at Harold's Cross, Infirmary Road, Manor Street, Plunkett Street, Portobello, Seville Place and at Dún Laoghaire.

See **Golden Lane.**

Dublin Boundaries Act

The act which received royal assent on 6 August 1900 included the districts of Clontarf, Drumcondra, Glasnevin, New Kilmainham and portions of the county of Dublin within the city boundary.

Dublin Burns Club

Instituted 1905, having for its object the perpetuity of the memory of Robert Burns (1759–96), the Scots poet and songwriter, by the celebration of his birthday and otherwise, and for intellectual improvement as well as the social intercourse and enjoyment of its members.

Dublin Castle

Entrance from Castle Street or Palace Street

The Castle was constructed on the instructions of King John and was completed about 1215. The Record Tower and the Bermingham Tower are the

Dublin Castle. The former Genealogical Office now restored to its original state with the third storey removed.

principal remains of this structure. Frequent repairs were carried out in the fifteenth century and a major rebuild was carried out 1565–78 by Sir Henry Sidney. A major reconstruction took place during the eighteenth century, leaving the format similar to the present layout. The old Chapel Royal was replaced in 1814 to a design of Francis Johnston. George's Hall was built in 1911 as a supper room for the visit of George V and, for the same occasion, the State Apartments were modernised. A serious fire destroyed the greater part of the State Apartments in 1941, after which the external walls and first floor were restored in the character of the original building. A new cross block, separating the upper and lower yards, was built 1961–64, and replaced late eighteenth-century buildings. For 700 years the Castle was the seat of English rule in Ireland until it was taken over by the provisional government in 1922.

From 1985 to 1989, a major reconstruction programme took place that cost over £20 million, and a major conference centre was built for Ireland's presidency of the European Community in 1990. During the excavations for the new building, a section of the Viking town defences was exposed in the form of a stone-faced earthen embankment dating from the ninth or tenth centuries. This has now been preserved and is on view to the public. During reconstruction, the eighteenth-century building that housed the Genealogical Office was extended and the third storey removed to reveal the cupola topped Bedford Tower. A new hump-back bridge leading from the Gate of Fortitude crosses an ornamental pool to Castle Street. The Castle is used principally as government offices. The Presidents of the Republic of Ireland are inaugurated in St Patrick's Hall.

The architects appointed for the restoration and new conference centre were Klaus Unger, David L. Byers, Angela Rolfe and Michael Carroll.

Dublin Cemeteries Committee

A body responsible for the cemeteries at Glasnevin, Goldenbridge and, after July 1978, Palmerstown.

Established by the Dublin Cemeteries Committee Act 1970 (No. 1 (Private) of 1970): 'An Act to establish a body corporate to undertake and carry out the functions at present carried out by the 'Dublin Cemeteries Committee' and to enlarge and extend such functions.' Originally established in 1846 under 'An Act for the maintenance of the cemeteries at Golden Bridge and Prospect in the County of Dublin, and to create a perpetual Succession in the governing Body or Committee for managing the same.' (The Act of 1846 was repealed by the Act of 1970.)

The Dublin Cemeteries Committee is a body corporate with perpetual succession and an official seal, and power to sue or to be sued, and to purchase, take hold and dispose of land and other property.

The objects for which the Committee is established are:

(a) to maintain, improve and extend the existing cemeteries and to preserve the bodies interred in them from disturbance and desecration;

(b) to acquire, provide, maintain, improve, lay out, construct and operate in the County and County Borough of Dublin, cemeteries, burial grounds, and other places and means for the burial, interment, preservation or disposal of human remains.

The logo of Dublin City Council, ratified in March 2002.

Dublin City Council

Under a new Local Government Act, Dublin Corporation changed its name to Dublin City Council, which was ratified by the Council in March 2002. A new logo was adopted using a version of the three castles, which have been used since 1229 when they first appeared on the common seal of the citizens of Dublin. The castles have been used as a logo since 1324 and were entered as the official arms of the city in 1607. On the new logo the figures of Law and Justice have been omitted together with the floral emblems. There are three important additions—the City Sword, the City Mace and the Cap of Maintenance.

See **Armorials of the City**
See also **Introduction.**

Dublin City Council Economic Development Unit

Dublin City Council's Economic Development Unit has been established to plan for the continued economic development of the City. Working in partnership with the relevant private and public-sector bodies and other support agencies, Dublin City Council's Development Unit provides a dedicated service to encourage business start-ups, inward investment and tourism in the area. A Development Advisory Team has been set up to assist property owners and developers in progressing development proposals to planning application stage and to advise on the range of tax incentives available for development.

Attracting inward investment is a major challenge for Dublin City Council. To this end the Economic Development Unit aims to:

Secure maximum economic development through a co-ordinated approach with all participating agencies.

Promote a positive image of the City.

Market the City as a place for inward investment.

Undertake specific developments, which add to the attraction of the City.

Form partnerships with others to deliver key projects for the City.

Be a catalyst for change and lobbyist on issues impacting on regeneration of the City.

Dublin has the lowest corporate tax rate in Europe at 12.5 per cent until 2025 and offers investors: a stable, profitable, English-speaking base to service the European market and beyond, a young highly skilled workforce—almost half of Dublin's population is under the age of 25, highly developed infrastructure and telecommunications network, quality of life—strong cultural structure and wide range of leisure facilities, opportunities for public and private partnerships through a €7.6 billion infrastructure programme over six years. Dublin plays an important role in the national economy. Its ports and airport make it an important entry point to the

Tower cranes over Dublin seemed to increase daily caused by an unprecedented activity of building during the 1990s.

country and a gateway to the EU and the rest of the world. While Ireland's GNP growth levels have averaged 7.5 per cent each year since 1998, Dublin has outperformed the national average. Dublin accounts for 38 per cent of GNP.

1998 saw: The establishment of two new city quarters, the International Financial services Centre and Temple Bar.

13,000 new residential units

25,000 people returning to the Inner City

Capital Investment in excess of £3.5 billion

A living and vibrant city with an improved city image

Plans for a third cluster in the city — the Digital Media District.

The 1999 Urban Renewal Scheme differs substantially from its predecessors. While previous schemes concentrated on physical development, the new scheme looks at physical, environmental, social and economic development, and tax incentives are available only where all four elements are addressed. Under the Integrated Area Plans approach, the local authority targets a number of sites in each area to be developed in particular ways and make tax incentives available to developers who agree to carry out such developments.

In Dublin, six Integrated Area Plans (IAPs)

were designated under the Urban Renewal Act 1998, five of which are in the inner city. The six areas covered by these plans are: Ballymun, Kilmainham/Inchicore, O'Connell Street, North East Inner City, Liberties/The Coombe and Historic Area Rejuvenation Project (HARP).

Tax incentives apply to specific sites and will be granted only if the development contributes some element of 'community gain' to the area. Unlike Urban Renewal initiatives, these plans take into account the cultural, employment and educational needs of the existing community. Designated project teams and a development advisory team have been set up by the City Council to work in partnership with private investors and developers in an effort to regenerate the six areas. In the residential sector, the concept of community gain can be achieved by including a percentage of development for social or affordable housing, to be purchased by the Local Authority. Alternatively, a financial contribution based on a percentage of the current site value can be invested in community and leisure facilities in the area.

Development opportunities across the full spectrum of uses are identified and project teams are in place to work in partnership with the private sector to realise the enormous regeneration potential that exists in these areas. One of the most important aspects of Dublin City Council's approach to the Integrated Area Plans is its development advisory team. This multi-disciplinary team has been set up to assist developers in bringing their projects to the planning application stage. This ensures that promoters are not left in a position of effectively having to guess what form of development will qualify for tax relief.

Tax Incentives for Development:

There is a range of tax incentives available nationwide to encourage the supply of different categories of development. These tax incentives are all property related and apply to the construction of new buildings or refurbishment of existing buildings and the incentives available depend on the use to which the property is put. In Dublin, additional tax incentives apply to desig-nated areas in Integrated Area Plans.

Dublin's Integrated Area Plans:

The following are categories of tax incentives available for targeted sites in IAP areas:

Commercial—Car Park
Commercial—Office
Commercial—Retail/Other
Industrial
Residential Owner Occupier—New Building
Residential Owner Occupier—Refurbishment
Residential Investor—New Building
Residential Investor—Refurbishment
Hotel.

Dublin City Council Freedom of Information Unit

2nd Floor, 16/19 Wellington Quay

The Freedom of Information Act, 1997, provides that every person has the following new legal rights:

The right to access official records held by public bodies listed in the Act;

The right to have personal information held on them corrected or updated where such information is incomplete,

incorrect or misleading; and

The right to be given reasons for decisions taken by public bodies that affect them.

These rights mean that, from 21 October 1998, people can seek access to personal information held on them no matter when the information was created by Dublin City Council, and to other records created after 21 October 1998. The Act requires Dublin City Council to respond to requests from the public for information held by them.

Dublin City Council is obliged to:

Acknowledge receipt of the request within two weeks.

Make a decision on the request within four weeks, or eight weeks in certain cases.

If Dublin City Council does not respond within four weeks, the decision is deemed to have been refused and the requester can proceed to the review stage. Dublin City Council has two publications available to help in understanding the structure of the organisation and the types of information held.

Section 15 Reference Book—Guide to the Structure, Functions, Powers, Duties, Services and Records of Dublin City Council.

Section 16 Information—Rules, Procedures, Practices, Guidelines, Interpretations and Precedents used by Dublin City Council for the purposes of Decisions, Determinations or Recommendations.

These publications are available for reference or purchase in every public office and public library. The Act provides for greater public access to official informa-tion. The experience of other countries with FOI legislation is that, because the papers produced by public servants are more likely to be seen by the public, the process of making decisions and giving reasons for them has improved greatly.

Dublin City Enterprise Board

17 Eustace Street

A body supported by the Department of

Enterprise, Trade and Employment. It exists to encourage and support smaller companies employing ten people or fewer in the city area. The services include: Financial assistance, Grants, Refundable aid, Equity together with business information, advice and mentoring. Since its foundation in 1993, almost 1,000 business projects have been supported by DCEB, creating thousands of jobs.

Dublin City Library and Archive
138–144 Pearse Street
The library contains manuscripts and books accumulated by Sir John T. Gilbert in more than 50 years of assiduous searching. Dublin Corporation of 1900 voted to buy the collection from his widow for £2,500. It also includes transcripts of the municipal records of the City of Dublin and records of the Dublin Guilds. The Dix collection, donated by the Irish bibliographer E. R. McClintock Dix, contains some 300 books and pamphlets of mainly seventeenth- and eighteenth-century Dublin. The Yeats collection has material relating to the poet William Butler Yeats and items printed at the Dun Emer Press by the Yeats sisters. The library continues to collect and acquire material relevant to the city, including books, newspapers, photographs, maps, prints and drawings. It includes a wide variety of material dating from the eighteenth century. Following the re-opening of the library, after complete refurbishment, on 2 July 2003, the Dublin Corporation Archive* collection moved from City Hall. The library has a 100-seat public reading room with a reader's café adjacent. The collections are housed on purpose-built storage floors equipped to the highest international standards for conservation and document retrieval.
See **Pearse Street.**

Dublin City University
Glasnevin
A Commission on Higher Education set up to investigate higher education in Ireland issued its report in 1967. Among

the various recommendations was the establishment of the National Institute for Higher Education at Limerick in 1972, and at Dublin in 1980, using the old UCD Albert Agricultural College buildings at Ballymun. The first new buildings were designed by Robinson Keefe and Devane in 1984, with various additions by Arthur Gibney, which include an internal glazed street. By 1989, there were approximately 3,000 students at the Dublin Institute which was raised to university status in 1990 to respond to the challenges which a diversifying industrial sector and changing community needs were setting for higher education. The new university is located on a 50-acre campus bordering Ballymun Road with the main entrance at Collins Avenue extension. The development plan envisages a campus population of 5,000 after the completion of a large science and engineering complex. Limerick NIHE was given university status in 1989.

Dublin Corporation and Dublin City Council Archives
138–144 Pearse Street
The Archives are the historical records of the municipal government of Dublin, from the twelfth century to the present. Included are a number of medieval documents, including two important bound manuscripts written on vellum: 'The White Book of Dublin' (also known as Liber Albus) and 'The Chain Book of Dublin'. The archives also include a series of Assembly rolls, which record the minutes of Dublin City Assembly from 1447 to 1841. There is the magnificent series of 102 Charters, the earliest of which was issued by King Henry II in 1171–72, giving the men of Bristol the right to live in the city of Dublin. In addition, the archives contain a wealth of records, which have not been published.
See **Dublin City Library and Archive.**

Dublin Crisis Conference
At the end of a three-day Dublin Crisis Conference held in the Synod Hall, Christchurch Place, in February 1986, the

participants called upon the government and Dublin local authorities to recognise and accept that the city was in crisis, and called for radical changes in public policy. The document then laid down eleven points that were needed to revive the inner city. In 1989, a large group representing residents' associations and bodies interested in the welfare of the city drew up a 16-point Citizens' Alternative Programme for Dublin, demanding a strategic plan for the city region, which included preserving the city's architectural and archaeological heritage.

Dublin Docklands Development Authority

The Dublin Docklands Development Act, 1997, produced a master plan to guide the durable economic and physical development of the area and to capture the vision of an attractive and sustainable environment. It proposed a development framework for people wishing to avail of the benefits of urban living in an attractive setting. This in turn would translate the aspirations of the communities and other interests in the docklands into gain to be shared by those working and living in the area and provide a renewal strategy for progressively rehabilitated areas, which are underutilised, contaminated or aesthetically deficient. The plan would capitalise on the appeal of significant water bodies for living and leisure, and develop a framework for promoting architecture of world standard and urban design.

This far-sighted development, which is the largest ever undertaken in Ireland, is currently underway. It involves strategic partnerships between the public and private sectors working together in the regeneration of 520 hectares (1,300 acres) of riverside land. New offices, retail outlets, hotels and homes are being built beside high-quality public realm and leisure facilities in a waterfront environment.

The 15-year-long project, started in 1997, will result in the population of the Dockland increasing by 25,000 to 42,500 by the year 2012, and the construction of

Mayor Street, between Commons Street and Guild Street. Part of the Dublin Dockland Development Act and the International Financial Services Centre near Spencer Dock on the Royal Canal where 600 apartments were built. Including a social housing block at Mayor Street providing a total of 184 new apartments.

more than 11,000 new homes, including 2,200 social and affordable homes.

At the west end there is the International Financial Services Centre.* The development of the Grand Canal docks area encompassing 38.2 hectares to the south of the River Liffey, creating a double frontage to the river and the Grand Canal basin, is ongoing. This includes the area from Pearse Street along Macken Street to the Quays and, when completed, will provide approximately 3,500 apartments and 400,000 square metres of offices, together with hotels, retail and other facilities. The DDDA built a public Piazza at Gallery Quay, Grand Canal Square, with fountains, under which is a car park with 150 spaces. This complex includes 300 apartments and 100,000 square metres of offices, restaurants, bars and shops. The Grand Canal Harbour is mainly a residential quarter, located on 10 hectares, and includes 1,200 apartments and two office buildings with frontage onto the river. Riverside 1, comprising 10,000 square metres, and Riverside 2, comprising 23,500 square metres, form the Northern Gateway to the Grand Canal Harbour. At no. 1 Grand Canal Quay, between the railway and the quay, a glass-fronted triangular building designed by DeBlacam and Meagher for Esat Headquarters, opened in 2001. They are linked with the IFSC* across the river by a new bridge, designed by Santiago Calatrava, opened 16 June 2003, which is 26 metres wide and accommodates two lanes of traffic, pedestrian walkways and a cycle lane.

Barrow Street from Grand Canal Street to Ringsend Road
The name comes from the River Barrow which enters the Grand Canal. There are mentions of this river in the sixteenth century but it was laid out as a street in the late eighteenth century. Small c. 1830 two-storey red-brick originally railway cottages. It borders on the former Bord Gáis Eireann site and is scheduled for redevelopment. In 2003, work commenced on the 'Gas Works', a complex of 70 apartments around a courtyard. A sculptural effect is created by the cast-iron framework of the old gasometer, designed by Clayton and Sons, Leeds, in 1871, which has been newly painted and beneath which is a multi-storey car park.

Spencer Dock between Mayor Street and Sheriff Street on the Royal Canal
A new development designed by Architects Scott Tallon Walker and built by John Sisk and Son Ltd. Has 600 apartments in a square with ample underground parking and tree-lined pathways and landscaped gardens. When completed, this 51-acre development will have 3,000 apartments with a capital value of €2 billion, designed by a multi-disciplined team of architects, planners and designers. The dock is of strategic importance for future navigation linking it to inland waterways. On Friday 28 May 2004, the Authority announced plans for a €475 million 2,000-seat performing arts centre, designed by Daniel Libeskind, plus a hotel designed by Manuel Aires Mateus. An office building designed by Duffy Mitchell O'Donoghue will border on the proposed arts centre on Grand Canal Square.

The Scherzer Bridge is a protected structure.

Waterways Ireland has a visitor's centre, housed in a modern building, situated on the Grand Canal Basin in Ringsend. The centre houses an exhibition showing art and literature connected with the waterways. It also inc udes working models of important engineering features associated with the canal. Navigation charts and guides are available for purchase.

The lighting contractors Wink were employed in 2004 to install a lighting project that illuminated the North Quays from Butt Bridge to the Point Depot.

See Ballast Board, Dublin Port, International Financial Services Centre, North Wall Quay, Custom House Quay, Ringsend.

Dublin Electric Light Company

The first electric light in Ireland was an arc lamp outside the office of the *Freeman's Journal** in Prince's Street in 1880.

In the same year, William Martin Murphy and John Findlater set up the Dublin Electric Light Company with paid-up capital of £15,000. There was a small experimental station in Schoolhouse Lane, from which Kildare Street, Dawson Street and part of St Stephen's Green were lighted with arc lamps on wooden posts.

See Public Lighting.

Dublin Evening Post

First made its appearance in 1732 and continued until 1736. It reappeared in May 1757 but ceased in July of that year. The paper appeared again in 1778 with John Magee as proprietor at no. 11 Trinity Street and continued publication up to August 1875. It was an influential paper and, by 1826, was appearing three times weekly, priced 5d. Robert Peel, Chief Secretary to Ireland 1812–13, writing in 1813, states: 'Most of the faction in this country arises from the immense circulation of that nefarious paper the *Dublin Evening Post*. It is sent gratuitously into many parts of the country and read by those who can read to those who cannot; and as it is written with a certain degree of ability, and a style which suits those upon whom it is intended to work, it does, no doubt, great mischief.'

Dublin Fishery Company, 1818–30

On 2 November 1818, a meeting was held at the Leinster Tavern, also known as Morrison's Hotel in Dawson Street, with a view to forming a company that would supply the Dublin market with a better supply of fresh fish. The proposals were submitted by Captain James Steward, an official in the Civil Branch of the Ordnance Board, employed as Superintendent of the Pigeon House Docks. Following a deputation to the Lord Mayor, a further meeting was held at which a prospectus was drawn up asking for £2,000 divided into £50 shares to purchase five boats of about 30 tons each to trawl off the coast. Allowing for bad weather, it was estimated that 335 days at sea would produce £10 worth of fish per day, with an annual income of £3,350, allowing for the fact that each boat would be four to five days at sea. One boat would land each day at Pigeon House Dock, and the catch would be taken by horse and cart to the market.

The company was formed on 17 December 1818, and Captain Steward spent five weeks in England looking for suitable boats; four came from Brixham and one from Plymouth. These were: the *Armada*, 41 tons, cost £371; *Rosebank*, 36 tons, £461; *Maria*, 37 tons, £410; *Pheasant*, 32 tons, £325; and the *Frederick*, 39 tons, £490. An order for another vessel was given to Mr Morton, a Dublin shipbuilder, to cost £675, and two more boats were ordered from England in April 1819, the *Mary*, 39 tons, £430, and the *Mariner*, 39 tons, £480. In the same month, the capital was

increased to £5,000. The captains and seamen were brought from England as trawling was unknown or practically non-existent before this time. As a result of severe competition in 1820 from English trawlers and eight trawlers from Ringsend, the average price of fish dropped to about one penny a pound. The company, which was wound up in 1830, had achieved much in its time that was of benefit to the city, including the discovery of new fishing grounds in the Irish Sea.

Dublin Free School
See **Dublin Weekly Schools.**

Dublin Gate Theatre
See **Gate Theatre.**

Dublin Gazette or Weekly Courant
A government publication launched by James II. It was suppressed by William of Orange but was relaunched in 1705. In 1727, it was at the Custom House printing house in Essex Street. It has survived to the present day and is published twice weekly under the banner *Iris Oifigiúil*.

Dublin Grand Opera Society
Founded in 1941 by Professor John F. Larchet and Colonel William T. O'Kelly, it staged a great variety of operas from many countries and, until recently, a three-week spring Italian season in the Gaiety Theatre.* From 1953 to 1965, a grant from the Italian government enabled the society to attract many famous singers, including Luciano Pavarotti and Guiseppe Di Stefano. The members of the chorus are employed on a voluntary basis. It is now known as Opera Ireland.

Dublin International Exhibition 1865
The Dublin Exhibition and Winter Garden Company Ltd with a guaranteed capital of £50,000 and with three trustees, Duke of Leinster, Lord Talbot de Malahide and Benjamin Lee Guinness, opened an exhibition on a 15-acre site at the Coburg Gardens* on 9 May 1865 at which the Prince of Wales attended. At a time of the

Celtic Revival there was an emphasis on Irish motifs and symbolism, which were used in exuberant fashion by the makers of all the applied arts, including furniture, bog oak, jewellery and weaving.
See also **Great Industrial Exhibition 1853** *and* **Irish International Exhibition 1907.**

Dublin Journal

Founded in 1725 by George Faulkner (1699–1775) who had a printing works and bookshop at the corner of Essex Street.* He also printed many pirate editions of books. Became Alderman in 1770 and declined a knighthood. He was Swift's publisher and enjoyed a great social position both in Dublin and London where he lost a leg. He entertained lavishly in his house in Essex Street, and Philip Stanhope, Earl of Chesterfield, was a regular visitor when Viceroy.

Dublin Magazine (The)

Founded in 1923 by the poet and bibliophile Séamus O'Sullivan, penname of James Sullivan Starkey (1879–1958), it was edited by him until his death. All the leading writers of the time were contributors. Together with *The Bell*,* it was the longest-running literary magazine of its day. O'Sullivan, a Methodist, was a friend and partner of the Jewish painter, Estelle Solomons, who worked with him on the magazine and whom he married after her parents had died. After O'Sullivan's death, it was found impossible to get an editor with his talent and commitment and the magazine closed.

Dublin Metropolitan Police
See **Police.**

Dublin Newsletter

A newspaper printed in 1685 by Joseph Ray in College Green for the publisher and bookseller, Robert Thornton, of Skinners' Row. It consisted of a single sheet printed on both sides. It was from the offices of the *Dublin Newsletter* at Molesworth Court that John Harding printed Swift's *Drapier's Letters* in 1724.

Dublin Opinion

An illustrated humorous paper first published on 1 March 1922 with a staff of three, Arthur Booth, its editor, was a clerk in the traffic department of the Tramways Company, Charles E. Kelly, who also did many of the illustrations, and Tom Collins were both junior clerks in the office of National Education. It ceased publication in 1972 and was purchased by Louis O'Sullivan who published a volume entitled *Forty Years of Dublin Opinion.* From 1923, it was printed by Messrs Cahill and Co.

Dublin Penny Post 1773–1840

On 11 October 1773, a postal system was set up, designed to provide an efficient distribution of letters within the city limits. A special act of that year gave the necessary powers to the Post Master General. According to Faulkner's *Dublin Journal:** 'all letters and packets not exceeding the weight of four ounces will be forwarded from the penny post office in the General Post Office Yard twice every day (Sundays excepted) at nine o'clock in the morning and four o'clock in the afternoon to any part of the city. A penny is to be paid with every letter put into the penny post office or into any of the receiving houses for which penny every such letter will be delivered to the person to whom it is addressed.' Eighteen further receiving houses were also established throughout the city. In 1810, 54 city and 29 country receiving offices were opened. A notice of that time quotes: 'So expeditious and regular is the dispatch and delivery of letters by this office that two persons residing in the most distant parts of the city from each other may write four letters and receive three answers in the day for the trifling expense of one penny on each.' From 1822, there were six deliveries daily. In 1841, the Irish office ceased to be a separate operation and was put under the control of London, and Rowland Hill's uniform penny post took over.

Dublin Port and Docks Board

Alexandra Road, Dublin 1

The first authority to oversee the port of Dublin was the Ballast Board* set up in 1708 with responsibility for improvements to the port in general. Under its guidance, the South Wall was constructed, also the Poolbeg lighthouse. The entrance channel was straightened and parcels of land divided into the North and South Lotts were sold for reclamation. In 1786, the Corporation, for preserving and improving the port of Dublin, took over the duties of the Ballast Board and, during its term, the North Bull Wall was built and the quays extended on either side of the river. The Dublin Port and Docks Board replaced this body in 1868. George Halpin who was inspector of works to the Ballast Board was concerned with the building of the North Wall, various lighthouses, also the Whitworth and Richmond bridges and possibly the Corn Exchange on Burgh Quay.

See **Westmoreland Street, Halpin's Row** *and* **Halpin's Pool.**

DUBLIN PORT

Dublin Port Company

Alexandra Road

Dublin Port Company is responsible, under statute, for the management, control, operation and development of its harbour and for the provision of such facilities, services and accommodation and hands in the harbour for ships, goods and passengers, as it considers necessary.

The company is also responsible for pilotage in the Dublin pilotage district. Pilotage is compulsory between Butt Bridge and the line of the sixth meridian between the parallels of latitude passing through the Bailey lighthouse and Sorrento point.

Dublin Port is the premier port in Ireland in terms of cargo handled, economic impact, freight and passenger services. In 2004, the throughput was over 21 million tonnes, the highest ever recorded for any port on the Island. Roll-on-Roll-off services account for more than 50 per cent of the total throughput. The five ferry

companies operating from Dublin provide, between them, 16 daily sailings to the UK, connecting with Liverpool, Holyhead and Heysham. Load-on-Load-off services represented about 20 per cent of the throughput.

Port Facilities

Entrance and depths: the approach to the port is well lighted and of easy access. There is a channel across the bar at M.L.W.S. of 7.8 metres.

Total Land Area: 270 hectares.

Berthage: Seven kilometres ranging in depth from 6 m to 11 m at L.A.T. Vessels drawing up to 10.2 can enter port on high waters of normal tides. Vessels drawing up to 7 m can enter at any state of tide. A.V.T.S. system is operated from the port radio station.

Transit Sheds: 14,000 sq. metres of covered accommodation.

Pilotage: Compulsory for vessels over 450 gross tonnage and for all vessels carrying petroleum or explosive cargo. Dublin Port Company is the pilotage authority for the Dublin Pilotage District. The pilotage service is based in a pilot shore station situated on the eastern breakwater and is operated by direct-boarding fast cutters, each capable of speeds up to 20 knots. The Harbour Office, Pilot Shore Station and Pilot Cutters are equipped with VHF radio, Hague channels 16, 12 and 6.

Towage: To cater for large ocean-going vessels using the port, the company has provided three modern diesel tugs fitted with twin Voith propellers. Two are of 35-tonne bollard pull, one of 16-tonne bollard pull. They are equipped with VHF radio, Hague channels 16, 12, 13, 9 and with modern fire pumps.

Graving Docks:

Number 1 — length 117 metres, width 11.5 metres.

Number 2 — length 202 metres, width 24.4 metres.

Warehousing: The port company operates a major warehousing complex providing storage in ordinary and bonded warehouses. Cold storage is also available in the port area.

Dublin Port is the premier port in Ireland in terms of cargo handled, freight and passenger services. Five ferry companies provide sixteen daily sailings to the UK.

Cruise Liners: Dublin Port was the most frequent port of call in Ireland during 2004 with approximately 40 calls. It is Ireland's foremost cruise-liner port.

Passengers: Up to 16 ferries daily to the UK (Liverpool, Holyhead, Heysham).

See **Ballast Board, Dublin Docklands Development Authority, International Financial Services Centre.**

Dublin Port Tunnel

In July 1998, the Environmental Impact Statement and the Motorway Scheme for the tunnel were published. Following a public inquiry, the Minister for the Environment and Local Government approved the project. Hailed as a transport milestone, it links the Dublin Port to the M50 at Fairview and is designed to remove the bulk of Dublin's HGV traffic from the city. It consists of two tunnel tubes, each approximately 11 metres in diameter. One carries northbound traffic and the other southbound vehicles, both tubes having two lanes. The overall scheme length is 5.6 km, of which the tunnel section is 4.5 km and 1.1 km surface road. It passes beneath Griffith Avenue under the mainly residential area of Marino. It then passes beneath the Dublin–Belfast and DART railway lines and Alfie Byrne Road. Crossing the Tolka River at ground level on a bridge, the route ends at the North Port Interchange, north of East Wall Road. The traffic flow for lorries is approximately 20,000 vehicles per day, rising to a projected figure of 31,000 in 2018. The travel time from the M50 (at M1) to Dublin Port is 6–7 minutes. There are 315 private residential properties and 13 institutional properties situated above the tunnel. The boring of the tunnel was completed on 18 August 2004 and the Minister for Transport, Séamus Brennan, attended the breakthrough. The overall cost was €715 million with the tunnel scheduled for

The Dublin Port Tunnel consists of two tubes. One carries northbound traffic and the other southbound vehicles. Illustration shows the boring machine breaking through on 18 August 2004.

completion in 2006. The main contractor was Nishimatsu Mowlem Irishenco Consortium.

Dublin Ring Road
A ring road to motorway standard encompassing the city area
Traffic entering the Dublin city area on a radial national primary road is able to bypass the central area by using the orbital route. The M50 Northern Cross route commences at the Woodlands roundabout crossing the M1 Belfast Road, Swords Road and Ballymun Road where it joins the Western Parkway motorway at the N3 Navan Road. It continues until it meets the N4 Dublin–Galway Road at Palmerstown. The section from the Galway Road to the Naas Road was opened to traffic on 2 May 1990. The Western Parkway Galway Road–Navan Road was constructed by a private investor, West-Link Toll Bridge Ltd, and was opened to traffic on 12 March

1990. The toll road covers a distance of approximately 3.2 km with a high-level bridge, approximately 385 m long, over the River Liffey. It then crosses the Lucan Road, Naas Road and Tallaght Road. The final section runs from Balrothery to Sandyford Road and on to the Bray Road.

Dublin Society for the Prevention of Cruelty to Animals
See **Dogs' and Cats' Home.**

(Royal) Dublin Society Schools
George Berkeley, Bishop of Cloyne, writing in the *Querist* in 1735, deplored the state of painting in Ireland and urged the necessity for starting an academy. The (Royal) Dublin Society, founded in 1731, started paying Robert West in 1746 to take students at his drawing academy in George's Lane. Berkeley appears to have been instrumental in influencing his friends, Samuel Madden and Thomas

Prior, to take this decision. By 1750, this had become the Dublin Society School at Shaw's Court. Under the direction of Robert West and James Manning, the decorative arts and the art of pastel drawing began to flourish.

See **National College of Art and Design** *also* **Royal Dublin Society.**

Dublin Trams

The earliest public transport in the city was operated with horse omnibuses which ran from about 1836. A serious accident occurred on 6 April 1861 when an omnibus from Terenure fell into the Grand Canal at Portobello Bridge and five passengers, including a baby, were drowned. (*See* Gaiety Theatre.) The idea of running on fixed rails was introduced in May 1867 when the City of Dublin Tramways Company was empowered to construct lines linking the railway termini. These would have run from Kingsbridge via the South Quays and Westland Row to Earlsfort Terrace. After work had begun on laying tracks at Aston Quay, the project was abandoned because of objections to the depression in the roadway between the rails. An act of 1871 authorised the Dublin Tramways Company, which had taken the rights of both the Rathmines omnibus service and the City of Dublin Tramways Company, to build tramways. On 1 February 1872, the first horse tram plied from College Green, via St Stephen's Green and Rathmines, to Terenure. On 3 June, the originally proposed line from Kingsbridge to Earlsfort Terrace was opened, and, on 1 October, another line to Sandymount via Haddington Road and Bath Avenue. In 1873, two further lines to Donnybrook and Dollymount were put into operation. The North Dublin Street Tramways Company commenced operation in 1875 with lines to Glasnevin, North Circular Road and Drumcondra via Capel Street. The line at Earlsfort Terrace was extended in 1878 along Hatch Street to Harcourt Street Station.

In that year, two new companies commenced operations. The Dublin Central Tramways Company ran from College Green to Rathfarnham via Harold's Cross to Palmerston Park, with a branch line from Ranelagh to Clonskeagh in 1879, and to James's Street via Castle Street and then to Inchicore. The Dublin Southern Districts Tramway Company operated from Haddington Road to Blackrock in April 1879 and was extended to Kingstown in 1883 by the Blackrock and Kingstown Railway Company. These two companies were taken over in 1893 by Imperial Tramways of Bristol. The line which was then electrified was opened to the public on 16 May 1896 and ran from Haddington Road to Dalkey.

In 1881, the Dublin Tramways Company, the North Dublin Street Tramways Company and the Dublin Central Tramways Company merged to form the Dublin United Tramways Company, and, in June 1896, they took over the Dublin Southern District Tramway Company and commenced electrifying their complete network by building a power station at Clontarf. New routes were also inaugurated in the city.

Another company, the Clontarf and Hill of Howth Tramroad Company, was founded in 1894 and commenced operating from Nelson Pillar to Howth on 26 July 1900. This was taken over by the Dublin United Tramway Company but the original company remained in operation until the line closed in 1941.

On 9 May 1901, the Great Northern Railway extended a line from Sutton Station to Howth Summit and to Howth Station on 1 August. The line was closed on 31 May 1959. The trams were finally withdrawn in Dublin when the last car left from the Ballast Office at 12.45 a.m. on 11 July 1949.

Dublin to Kingstown Railway

This was the first railway to be built in Ireland and was opened for passenger traffic on 17 December 1834. It was built by William Dargan who organised the International Exhibition* and it ran from Westland Row to the West Pier at

Kingstown (Dún Laoghaire) to serve the Dublin–Holyhead mail boat which had previously docked at Howth. The railway was 6 miles in length and was constructed at a cost of £418,000. A branch line to Dalkey was opened in 1844 as an atmospheric railway but was converted to a steam railway ten years later. The engine for the atmospheric railway was at the top of Dalkey Hill and, by a suction method, hauled the train to Dalkey. In 1856, the Dublin and Kingstown Railway Company ceased to be an independent company and was leased to the Dublin and Wicklow Railway Company. According to the *Dublin Evening Post* of 18 December: 'The average rate at which the trip was performed yesterday was nineteen minutes and a half, including a delay of about two minutes at the (Black) rock where passengers were taken up.'

Dublin Weekly Schools

First established in 1786, under the name of St Catherine's Sunday Schools, for the education of both sexes of all religious persuasions. At first, all who applied were admitted; the numbers increased and they were required to bring a note from a householder; the numbers still increased and it was judged necessary that they should bring a recommendation. The scholars were taught spelling, reading, writing and ciphering and were provided with books, slates, paper, etc. The Scriptures were read but no catechism or books of religious controversy were admitted. The Dublin Free School house was erected in 1800 and was capable of containing 1,500 scholars. The masters were paid two shillings and sixpence and the mistresses two shillings each week.

Dublin Women's Suffrage Association

Founded in 1876 by Mrs Anna M. Haslam, a member of the Society of Friends. From the beginning, the group was active through peaceful methods, keeping the cause of votes for women in the forefront of the news. Anna Maria Fisher married Thomas Haslam, a schoolteacher who later became a bookkeeper in Dublin. Her father was a miller from Youghal, Co. Cork, who was involved with the anti-slavery movement. The suffrage movement which started in Manchester in 1867 spread to London, and Dublin became the third active city in the cause. The title was broadened to the Dublin Women's Suffrage and Poor Law Guardians Association and then changed to the Dublin Women's Suffrage and Local Government Association. The Women Poor Law Guardians Act was passed in 1896 and, as a result, twelve women were elected. The Local Government Act of 1898 allowed women who had property of a certain value to vote for and be elected as district councillors.

In 1918, the Representation of the People Act extended the vote to women over the age of 30 and a separate act permitted women to be members of parliament. In 1922, in the Irish Free State, women over 21 had the vote. There is a seat made of Kilkenny limestone in St Stephen's Green which is inscribed: 'In remembrance of Anna Maria (1829–1922) and Thomas (1825–1917) Haslam, this seat is erected in honour of their long years of public service chiefly devoted to the enfranchisement of women.'

Dublin Writers' Museum

18 Parnell Square

The museum together with the Irish Writers' Centre at no. 19 is housed in restored eighteenth-century buildings, which had stood empty for some years. With grants from Bord Fáilte, the National Lottery and the European Regional Development Fund, refurbishing commenced in 1989 and the museum was officially opened on 18 November 1991 by An Taoiseach Charles J. Haughey. Number 18, originally built for Lord Farnham, has permanent displays illustrating the history of Irish literature from its earliest times to the present day. It also houses a large collection of letters, first editions, photographs and memorabilia.
See Rutland Square.

Dublinia
See **Synod Hall, Christ Church.**

Duke Street
From Grafton Street to Dawson Street
From second Duke of Grafton (Viceroy).
A map of 1685 describes the area which included this street as 'a piece of marshy land without even a lane crossing it'. In 1705, Joshua Dawson purchased a strip of ground which was to include Duke Street and Dawson Street. Shopping area with two popular taverns, the Bailey and Davy Byrne's.
See also **Bailey Tavern** *and* **Davy Byrne's.**

Dundrum
On the main Enniskerry Road in the civil parish of Taney. In 1853, Queen Victoria visited the International Exhibition on Leinster Lawn organised by William Dargan and was invited to his home at Mountanville, which he had bought in 1851, where she planted a Sequoia tree, *Wellingtonia gigantea*, shortly after the species was introduced into this country. Mountanville is now Mount Anville Convent. When William Dargan died on Thursday, 7 February 1867, aged 68 years, at 2 Fitzwilliam Square East, his was one of the largest funerals seen in Dublin for many years. The cortege, which was led by 700 railwaymen, the hearse with four horses, three mourning coaches, the Lord Mayor Sir John Gray's coach, then over 200 carriages, proceeded to Glasnevin cemetery. Dundrum Castle, now a ruin but in private ownership, was built in the thirteenth century. It was badly damaged in 1641 but renovated in 1653 by one of the Dobson family. Dundrum remained a village until the opening of the Harcourt Street–Bray line when a station was erected here and the area rapidly expanded. It became a popular health resort especially around the area of Windy Arbour where the Central Mental Hospital now stands, which was opened in 1845 as the Central Criminal Lunatic Asylum.
Taney (C of I) Church was built in 1818 to serve a small community, and the church as

Dundrum. A major landmark is the 185-metre-long cable-stayed Taney Bridge for the Luas.

it stands today with a central square tower was completed in 1872, being the last of a series of renovations since its foundation. An older church, St Nathi's, is used on special occasions. The name Taney comes from *Teach Nathi*, the house of St Nathi, an early Christian bishop. Holy Cross (RC) Church opened in 1878, built of granite with an open bell tower and greatly enlarged in 1953.
Some of the convent buildings at Mount Anville Road were designed for the Society of the Sacred Heart by Pugin and Ashlin in 1866, following the purchase of the original house from William Dargan in 1865.
In August 2002, a new bypass was opened to relieve the congestion caused by the expansion of development in the area. A major landmark is the 185-metre-long cable-stayed bridge for the Luas.* Named after William Dargan the railway engineer. There is a tram station near the former Dundrum railway station.

On 3 March 2005, the first phase of a new €650 million town centre opened. It is built on a 17-acre site and, when completed in 2008, will include the largest retail shopping centre in the state, with parking for 3,500 cars. The architects are Burke Kennedy Doyle, and it is being developed by Grossridge Investments, while the main building contractors are John Sisk and Sons Ltd.

Dun Emer Guild

Founded about 1902 out of the arts and crafts movement when the Roman Catholic Church was persuaded to employ Irish rather than foreign craftspeople. They worked a set of 24 embroidered banners for Loughrea Cathedral, with scenes of Irish saints made in silk and wool, to designs by Jack Yeats and his wife, Mary. These were worked by Lily Yeats and her workers. They also worked fine vestments and beautiful cloths. Their aim was to find work for Irish hands in the making of beautiful things. In 1903, under Elizabeth Yeats, they started printing on paper. The partnership split in 1908. Evelyn Gleeson retained the name Dun Emer and the Yeats sisters called themselves the Cuala Industries.

See **Cuala Press.**

Dún Laoghaire

A populous and wealthy township six miles E.S.E. from the General Post Office. Under the Towns Improvement Act of 1854, the district comprised Monkstown, Dún Laoghaire (Kingstown) and Glasthule. It had its own Town Commission since 1834 and, in 1930, Dalkey, Blackrock and Ballybrack were incorporated in the borough. The borough is named after Laoghaire a fifth-century king of Tara who built a fort here. Up to about the middle of the eighteenth-century it was a fishing village until a pier was completed in 1767, which, because of moving tides, caused the harbour to silt up. In the nineteenth century, work had commenced on the unsuccessful harbour at Howth* and a new harbour as we know it today was commenced in Dún Laoghaire

in 1817 and directed by John Rennie. By 1821, the east and west piers were completed but the work of reinforcing the east pier continued for at least another thirty years. On the East Pier, an Egyptian-style granite building erected in 1852 houses an anemometer, placed on the pier in 1845, a device for measuring the strength of wind, invented by Rev. Thomas Romney Robinson of Trinity College. A modern weather station replaced it in 1999. There is also a bronze plaque commemorating Samuel Beckett (1906–90), playwright and Nobel prize winner. The Holyhead–Dublin shipping fleet berths here, having moved from Howth in 1826, and the car-ferry service was introduced in 1965. George IV embarked here on 3 September 1821 but was detained by contrary winds until 7 September when the name of the town was changed to Kingstown and the harbour was called the Royal Harbour of George IV, as is inscribed on a granite obelisk surmounted by a crown, near the wharf erected by the Harbour Commissioners to commemorate the occasion. He should have arrived in Dún Laoghaire on 12 August 1821 where the Lord Lieutenant and a crowd estimated at 20,000 waited in vain. Instead, his ship, the *Lightning*, berthed at the West Pier in Howth due to storm conditions at sea. The town reverted to its original name in 1920. On the quay along the breast of the harbour is a wharf 500 feet in length known as Victoria Wharf, where Queen Victoria landed on her visits to Ireland in 1849, 1861 and 1900.

The railway to Dublin was opened in 1834 and cost £63,000 per mile to build. The station, completed in 1836, is to a design of J. S. Mulvany. The stone-fronted Town Hall was completed in 1880 with J. L. Robinson as architect. The former Mariners' Church, built in 1837 and extended in 1867, now houses the National Maritime Museum. At the end of Haigh Terrace is Andrew O'Connor's (1874–1941) sculpture of 'Christ the King', erected in 1978. At Sandycove, there is the 'Forty Foot', a famous bathing place originally for men only, but in 1976 women occupied what had been for generations that great bastion of men only. The Martello Tower is mentioned in James Joyce's *Ulysses* and is now a Joyce Museum. St Michael's (RC) Church, built in 1894 and designed by C. J. McCarthy, was completely destroyed by fire in 1968. Only the tall tower and spire remained. A new building, designed by Pearse McKenna, Naois O'Dowd and Sean Rothery, is attached to the old tower and was opened for worship in 1973. The Presbyterian Church on York Road was built in 1865 to a design of Andrew Heiton, with a church hall under the building. The three two-light windows are by Ethel M. Rhind.

Dún Laoghaire is a major yachting centre, having the Royal Irish Yacht Club, the National Yacht Club and the Royal St George Yacht Club. It is also the home of the Irish Lights Service which maintains the lighthouses and ships around the coast. St John the Evangelist Church was used by the C of I until 1975, when it was taken over by the Society of St Pius X. The Tridentine mass is celebrated there. The altar in the church was removed from the Dominican Convent in Eccles Street.

The borough also has an eighteen-hole golf course, two large shopping centres, new apartment blocks and a large ferry terminal. It is now the Dún Laoghaire/Rathdown County Council.

E

Earl Street North
From O'Connell Street to Marlborough Street
Originally part of the lands of St Mary's Abbey. Named after Viscount Henry Moore, Earl of Drogheda, who acquired the estate in 1614. The Drogheda Estate was purchased in 1714 by Luke Gardiner. On Saturday, 16 June 1990, Marjorie Fitzgibbon's statue of James Joyce sponsored by the North Earl Street Business Association was unveiled beside the Kylemore Café. Mostly retail shops.
See **also Henry Street, Moore Street, Drogheda Street.**

Earl Street South
From Meath Street to Thomas Court
Named after the Earl of Meath. An early eighteenth-century street which, after the Act of Union, rapidly went into a decline, most of the tall buildings becoming tenements. Part of the street was replaced with new tenement buildings in 1866. These have since been demolished. The street has remained derelict for some time. A scheme is being considered for a high-density street of four-level buildings of quality design.
See **Liberties** *and* **Pimlico.**

Earlsfort Terrace
From Leeson Street to Adelaide Road
Named after John Scott (1739–98), Baron Earlsfort and Viscount Clonmell in 1789 and Earl 1793. Solicitor General 1774, Attorney General 1777, Chief Justice 1784. He had extensive grounds from Harcourt Street to Earlsfort Terrace. In 1839, a row of gabled houses in Leeson Street was demolished and the terrace opened to join the street at St Stephen's Green. Developed late in the nineteenth century. In 1865, the Dublin International Exhibition* opened and again, in 1872, the Dublin Exhibition of Arts, Industries and Manufacturers was held on the same site. The statues representing the crafts of wood, metal and stone from this exhibition may now be seen in the Millennium Garden,* Dame Street. The exhibition buildings were converted by the architect Edward Kavanagh in 1886 to house the examination halls of the Royal University of Ireland (1882–1909). University College Dublin was built on the site 1914–19 to a design of R. M. Butler. Some of the exhibition buildings remain, as do the boundary wall and gates. In 1981, the Great Hall of the college was adapted to house the National Concert Hall. In the 1970s and 1980s, modern office blocks and a hotel were built on the opposite side, where Alexandra College had stood from 1866 until it moved to Milltown in 1972. In the sunken courtyard of the Conrad Hotel, an attractive bronze group of flying birds over a fountain bears a plate quoting from W. B. Yeats, 'For peace comes dropping slow'. This group was completed in 1989 by Colm Brennan and Noel Kidney. Another fine bronze, 'The Kiss' by Rowan Gillespie, cast in 1989, stands in front of the Earlsfort Centre at the corner with Hatch Street.
At no. 16, on 28 August 1892, W. H. S. Monck (1839–1915) and colleagues made the first electrical measurements of light.
See also **Coburg Gardens, Clonmel Street, Catholic University of Ireland** *and* **University College Dublin.**

Earlsfort Terrace. Alexandra College. Photograph from 1936 prospectus.

Eccles Street

From Dorset Street to Berkeley Road

This was considered to be one of the finest Georgian streets on the north side of Dublin. Built between 1750 and 1820, it was originally to have an elliptical circus at the west end. It complemented the view of St George's Church* in Hardwicke Place. Some of the houses were in ruins including no. 7, the home of Leopold and Molly Bloom, James Joyce's *Ulysses* characters. The front door of no. 7 is preserved in the Bailey* restaurant in Duke Street.

The Mater Hospital got planning permission to demolish the entire north side of the street, which included the former Dominican Convent schools, in order to build a large extension to the hospital. It was assumed that the south side would remain intact but in the High Court it was proved that the hospital owned 28 of the 42 houses. The Dangerous Buildings Committee of Dublin Corporation declared nos. 43, 44 and 45 unsafe and these were partly demolished. In spite of arguments that it was against the public interest to demolish the street as it was part of the architectural heritage of the city, and An Taisce stating that since 1979 it had been concerned with the preservation of the street, the houses were eventually demolished. Under the 1980 development plan, 60 per cent of the houses had been listed for preservation.

The Mater Misericordiae Hospital* run by the Sisters of Mercy had its foundation stone laid in 1852, and opened to the public in 1861. Francis Johnston (1760–1829), who designed the Chapel Royal, St George's Church, and the General Post Office, lived at no. 64. In 1923, the house was taken over by the Albert Retreat for

Eccles Street. Rear of no. 64, the home of Francis Johnston (1760–1829).

Women of the Domestic Class 'who have outlived their powers of work and have no relatives to give them a home or care'. The premises were sold in 1961 and in 1964 a new 12-roomed Albert House was opened in Gilford Road, Sandymount. Number 64 was recently converted into a hostel for homeless boys, by the Catholic Social Service Conference.

Ely Place
From Merrion Row to Hume Street
Laid out in 1770 by Sir Gustavus Hume MP, who was responsible for bringing the architect Richard Cassels to Ireland. Cassels also designed Castle Hume in Co. Fermanagh. Ely House, no. 8 Ely Place, was built by the Earl of Ely who lived in Rathfarnham Castle. In 1736, he married Mary, the daughter of Sir Gustavus Hume. The upper end of Ely Place was named Smith's Buildings after the builder Thomas Dodd Smith, who lived at no. 1 from 1836 to 1849. The name was then changed to Upper Ely Place as the residents did not think the name Smith's Buildings good enough.

Ely House, designed by Michael Stapleton for the Earl of Ely, is now the headquarters of the Knights of Columbanus. It has some very fine ceilings and an impressive staircase. Number 6 also has a Stapleton interior and was the home of John Fitzgibbon, Earl of Clare (1749–1802). He resisted any reforms connected with the emancipation of Roman Catholics and supported the Act of Union. There were violent demonstrations at his funeral. Number 4 was the town house of John Philpot Curran (1750–1817), popular orator and politician whose daughter, Sarah, was secretly engaged to Robert Emmet* (*see* Rathfarnham). George Moore (1852–1933), the poet, also lived there.

A street of commercial lettings and some government offices. In 1972, a house at the upper end that had once been the home of Oliver St John Gogarty was demolished and work started on a new building for the Royal Hibernian Academy.* The new building was to be the gift of the late Matt Gallagher. Unfortunately no provision was made in his will for funds for the completion of the building and the concrete shell stood unfinished until it was completed in 1987.

Emmet, Robert and the 1803 Rising

Robert Emmet was the grandson of Rebecca Temple, who came from an influential political dynasty at Stowe in Buckinghamshire, and Christopher Emmett. Their youngest son, Dr Robert Emmet, became state physician for Ireland from 1770 until his death in 1802. The family originally lived in a house on the corner of Molesworth Street and Kildare Street (demolished 1975). Dr Emmet was married to Elizabeth Mason and, as he prospered, moved to a large house, 109/110 St Stephen's Green (also demolished late 1950s). Robert, their seventeenth child, was born there on 4 March 1778. He was brought up in a home where his father was obsessed with politics and the winning of Irish Freedom, also the conflict between the American Colonists and Britain was continually being discussed. At home he developed a lifelong interest in military manoeuvres and history. He was educated first at Oswald's Academy near Golden Lane and then at Samuel Whyte's English Grammar School at 75 Grafton Street, which gave a good basic education (see Grafton Street). It was here that he learnt the art of public speaking and the ability to throw his voice, during speech giving and debating. Before entering Trinity College at the age of 15, on 7 October 1793, he was tutored by Rev. Mr Lewis of Camden Street. While at college, he also entered the King's Inns in 1795 to study for the Bar. The College, by 1798, was becoming concerned over students who admitted membership of the United Irishmen. Three students were expelled that year and, on 12 March, Emmet's elder brother, Thomas Addis, a leading radical, was arrested and would spend four years in prison. It would appear that Robert left college shortly after this time, never to return. He regularly visited his brother in Newgate Prison and these visits were noted by Dublin Castle. In March 1799, the authorities moved Thomas to Fort George

in Scotland where his wife Jane was allowed to live in the same cell. A daughter, Jane Erin, was born there. They emigrated to New York in 1802, having spent some months in Paris. Robert Emmet and Malachy Delaney, another member of the United Irishmen, visited Paris via Hamburg in 1801 and had several meetings with Napoleon Bonaparte. Emmet remained in Paris and became disillusioned with the General, considering that he was not interested in the Irish cause or in supporting a rebellion. In March 1802, Britain and France signed a peace treaty making the visit of the United Irishmen to Paris a disappointment, as they did not succeed in attaining their goals. While there, Emmet purchased and read Templehoff's *History of the Seven Years War*. These two volumes were to have an influence on the 24-year-old Emmet. At this time, the United Irishmen in Paris, consisting of people who had fled or emigrated to France, were deeply divided about the liberation of Ireland and the possible success of a rising. At the end of 1802, Emmet returned to Ireland and went to live with his ageing parents who had moved to Casino, a house at Milltown. His father, who had supported him financially while he had been abroad, died in December 1802 and Emmet now needed to get a job as the professions were closed to him. He entered into business with a tanner, William Norris, in Dolphin's Barn, while continuing to meet with members of the United Irishmen, including a wealthy merchant, Philip Long, who would eventually donate £1,400 towards the cost of the rising. However, under the terms of his late father's will, he received £2,000 in March 1803, which gave him independence and security, and he immediately started planning a rebellion for later in the year that he believed would succeed. One evening, at a dinner party given by John Keogh, who was responsible for the Act that allowed Roman Catholics to vote in the election of MPs, he met John Philpot Curran, the lawyer who defended many of the United Irishmen. Emmet was from then on a regular visitor to the Currans' home, The Priory, Grange Road, Rathfarnham, where he met and fell in love with their daughter, Sarah, and secretly became engaged to her. When Curran discovered this, he forced her to leave home and live with friends, the Penrose family in Cork. During this time, Emmet had obtained a depot at Marshalsea Lane off Thomas Street for the store of rockets, firearms and hinged pikes that could be concealed under a coat. A house at 26 Patrick Street was also leased and six months' rent was paid in advance. While this was being arranged, a recruitment drive was taking place and pistols and blunderbusses were being manufactured to order.

Emmet considered it prudent to go into hiding in case the authorities should arrest him. He rented a house in Rathfarnham near the Currans and adopted the alias, Robert Ellis. A frequent visitor was 22-year-old Anne Devlin who acted as his servant and carried messages between him and his colleagues. This would continue after the rebellion when he was in hiding. She was eventually arrested, tortured and suspended at the end of a rope from the shafts of an upturned cart. She spent two years in Kilmainham Gaol, refusing to give information about her employer. After her release, she lived in abject poverty and was found in St John's Lane East* by Dr Robert Madden MD (1798–1886), the historian and author of a seven-volume work, *The United Irishmen, Their Lives and Times*. While visiting America, he raised funds to help her but on his return discovered that she had died on 18 September 1851, aged 70 years, and was buried in the paupers' section at Glasnevin. He had the remains transferred to a different plot and erected a monument over her grave. Emmet was working on a plan to capture Dublin; this would include capturing the Pigeon House, the barracks at Islandbridge and Cork Street which would be set on fire, and he would lead the attack on Dublin Castle. Barriers would also be set at various parts of the city. On 16 July, an explosion almost demolished the house at 26 Patrick Street, caused by an

accident when some volunteers were working with gunpowder; it resulted in two men being taken to Dr Steevens' hospital. The remaining weapons were removed to Joseph Palmer's premises on the Coombe. Following the explosion, problems arose. People who had promised money did not honour their verbal agreements, resulting in a shortage of arms, also various rockets and explosives were not ready and Emmet's elaborate plan began to disintegrate and crumble. In spite of this, he believed that victory could be achieved, but at a meeting of the Command on the morning of 23 July, very few were convinced and thought that the rebellion should be aborted. Dublin Castle at this stage had become aware that there was a dangerous threat to the city and the authorities were also aware of the explosion at Patrick Street. Reports were arriving from various parts of the country suggesting that a rising was inevitable but no action was taken.

More difficulties arose on an hourly basis, there were not enough blunderbusses, rockets and explosives were not ready and the men were poorly trained, lacked discipline or were not in any way prepared for action. On the evening of 23 July, Emmet ordered his men to appear at the Marshalsea Lane depot in preparation for an attack on the Castle but only about eighty turned up. He then commenced his march but by the time he reached Thomas Street he had only about a dozen followers and cancelled the attack. A mob in Thomas Street attacked the carriage of Lord Kilwarden, a privy counsellor, and killed him and his nephew, Rev. R. S. Wolfe, the rector of Kilbeggan. At midnight, two companies of the army were called out and the rebellion was defeated. Emmet fled to the Dublin Mountains but returned to Mrs Palmer's house, in Hen and Chicken Lane, now Mount Drummond Avenue and renamed Emmet House, demolished in 1980, to visit Sarah Curran, where he was arrested by Major Henry Sirr.

Emmet's trial opened on Monday morning, 19 September 1803. He was led in chains to stand in the dock and nineteen witnesses gave evidence against him of his complicity in the rising. The case lasted the whole day and the jury after a few minutes delivered a verdict of guilty of high treason. Emmet produced no witnesses and offered no defence. The trial will best be remembered for Emmet's brilliant speech from the dock which included the words: 'Let no man dare, when I am dead, to charge me with dishonour; let no man attaint my memory by believing that I could have engaged in any cause but of my country's liberty and independence'. It ended with 'When my country takes her place among the nations of the earth, then, and not till then, let my epitaph be written. I have done'. He was then sentenced by Lord Norbury to be hanged and beheaded the next day. He spent his final night at Kilmainham Gaol. He was taken at 1 p.m. the next day to Thomas Street near St Catherine's Church at the intersection with Bridgefoot Street, where he was hanged, and after about thirty minutes, was beheaded. His final resting place has never been found. Of the nineteen others tried for high treason, seventeen were hanged. A bronze statue by Conor was erected 13 April 1966 at St Stephen's Green West, opposite his birthplace. One of three castings, the others are in Washington DC and San Francisco. The latter was bought by Mr and Mrs Francis J. Kane of the Robert Emmet Statue Committee of the USA. In 1897, Dr Thomas Addis Emmet, a grandnephew of Robert Emmet, commissioned the Irish painter, John George Mulvaney (c. 1766–1838), to paint the definitive portrait of the patriot. It hangs in the Irish Embassy in Rome.

Emorville Avenue

Portobello off South Circular Road

Part of the lands of St Sepulchre in the parish of St Peter. In 1869, Joseph Kelly of Thomas Street commenced building houses on a street not yet named, on the south by John Pierce's holding, and on the west a laneway, and partly by Joseph Jacob's premises. George Russell (Æ) (1867–1935),

poet, painter and mystic, lived with his parents at no. 33 until 1885. His sister, Mary Elizabeth, died there aged 18 years. Russell attended Power's School at no. 3 Harrington Street. James Joyce was allegedly conceived at no. 30. He was born on 2 February 1882 at 41 Brighton Square. *See* **Heytesbury Street** *and* **Portobello Gardens.**

Eolas

Glasnevin

On 1 January 1988, a new Irish science organisation was launched formally when the Institute for Industrial Research and Standards merged with the National Board for Science and Technology to form Eolas.

Essex Street

From Essex Gate to Fishamble Street

From Arthur Capel, Earl of Essex, Lord Lieutenant 1672–77, during whose viceroyalty the street was built.

At the Council Chamber in the street, the Lords Lieutenant on their arrival in Dublin were usually sworn into office. It was used by the government until it was destroyed by fire in 1711.

An elephant was accidentally burnt in 1681 where it had been brought for exhibition. It was dissected by Dr Allen Mullen, an eminent physician, whose treatise was one of the earliest anatomical accounts of the elephant. The Elephant tavern opened to commemorate the event and was frequented until about 1770. In 1707, a new customs house was built, adjoining the eastern side of Essex Bridge, the principal entrances being in Temple Bar and Essex Street. Nathaniel Gun had a publishing house in the 1690s and one of the largest shops dealing in second-hand books at the 'Bible'. According to Gilbert, 'at the southern end of Essex Street and Parliament Street there stood a house erected by George Faulkiner, a character of high Importance in his day'. In 1724, he commenced a newspaper called the *Dublin Journal** in his printing establishment at the corner of Christchurch Lane, but moved to Essex Street in 1730 and became the publisher of Jonathan Swift who described him as the printer most in vogue. Among other publishers in the street was Thomas Hume, next to the merchants' coffee house, publisher in 1727 of the *Dublin Gazette*. Thomas McDonnell at no. 50, publisher of the *Dublin Packet* or *Weekly Advertiser* from 1788; he also published the *Hibernian Journal*, which was contributed to by Wolfe Tone. Milton's epic poem, 'Paradise Lost', was printed by George Grierson in 1724. In the eighteenth century, there were many taverns and coffee houses, including one owned by Henry Donovan, head butler in Trinity College. The street was also occupied by people connected with shipping.

One of the mistakes of the Temple Bar project was the demolition of a nineteenth-century school, retaining only the gable front, and the complete stripping of the interior of SS Michael and John Church,* the vault of which was allegedly the pit of the Smock Alley Theatre,* to house the Viking Museum. Backed by Dublin Tourism, it cost between £5 and £6 million. It was popular for a few years but eventually closed. Dolphin House, formerly the Dolphin Hotel, a High Gothic red-brick and stone-exterior building designed by J. J. O'Callaghan in 1887 and opened in 1898. It was a popular venue with a variety of bars and restaurants which, along with the hotel, closed in 1966. In the 1980s, it was refitted for office accommodation and is used by the Family Law Public Office but the exterior remains.

See **Temple Bar, Cow Lane, Smock Alley.**

Eustace Street
From Dame Street to Wellington Quay
Named after Sir Maurice Eustace, Speaker of the House of Commons 1639, Lord Chancellor 1644, whose residence and gardens stood on the site of the street. Together with the Duke of Ormonde he was responsible for the creation of Phoenix Park. In 1692, the Quakers (Society of Friends) opened their Meeting House in Eustace Street. Cinema 1 of the Irish Film

Institute, 6 Eustace Street, is now based in the Meeting House. In 1728, the Presbyterian congregation of New Street moved to Eustace Street. It was described as the richest Presbyterian church in Ireland with an almshouse for twelve poor widows, a school for boys, partly supported by the collection from an annual charity sermon, and a female school nobly endowed. In the eighteenth century, there were several taverns, the most notable being The Eagle at which meetings of the Dublin Volunteers were held in 1782, and, on 9 November 1791, the first meeting of the United Irishmen of Dublin was held, with James Napper Tandy acting as secretary. St Winifred's, an ancient tidal well from the River Liffey, is encased in the street.

See **Film Institute of Ireland.**

Eucharistic Congress
The 31st Eucharistic Congress held 22–26 June 1932. Dublin was chosen because 1932 was then accepted as the 1,500th anniversary of St Patrick's lighting of the Paschal fire at Slane. The congress was sponsored by the Most Rev. Dr Byrne, Archbishop of Dublin, to promote devotion to the Blessed Sacrament. Cardinal Lorenzo Lauri, the Papal Legate, arrived in Dún Laoghaire from Holyhead on the *Cambria* on 20 June and was presented with an address of welcome by Alderman Devitt, chairman of Dún Laoghaire Borough Council. He then proceeded by train to Dublin, stopping at Merrion Gates to permit his Eminence to receive an address of welcome in Irish, English and Latin from the Lord Mayor of Dublin, Alderman Alfred Byrne. From the station his carriage was escorted into town by the Free State Hussars, a cavalry corps. He formally opened the congress in St Mary's Pro-Cathedral on 22 June in the presence of nine cardinals, over a hundred bishops and a thousand priests and religious. That night, Mass was celebrated in every church in the Dublin diocese and Dún Laoghaire. Seven ocean liners were moored in Dublin Port, bringing pilgrims from abroad and providing accommodation.

On Thursday, 23 June, over a quarter of a million men attended Mass in the Phoenix Park. Friday was ladies' day with an attendance of over 200,000, and Saturday was children's day with a special children's Mass in the park, where a choir of 2,000 from 88 Dublin schools sang. On Sunday, 26 June, over a million people attended the Pontifical High Mass in the park, 127 special trains having brought people from all over Ireland. Count John McCormack sang 'Panis Angelicus' and His Holiness Pope Pius XI broadcast his Apostolic Blessing to the large crowd. An altar was erected on O'Connell Bridge where, following a procession from the park with the Sacrament, Benediction was imparted by the Cardinal Legate. Trumpets rang out the royal salute as the monstrance was raised and later bugles sounded the Disperse. The director of organisation was Mr Frank O'Reilly, the first layperson ever to occupy this position. In the general strike and lockout of 1913,* he had organised stations where food was given to children of strikers. In 1922, he became secretary of the Catholic Truth Society and had organised the Catholic Emancipation Centenary celebrations of 1928. There was a tragic side to the congress when Rev. Fr Lindo de Touratio, a professor in a seminary at Viterlon, Italy, was fatally injured outside St Andrew's Church when he was knocked down by a motor car. Another Italian priest, Fr Francesco Alara of Turin, took ill in Lower O'Connell Street and died in Jervis Street hospital. The two priests were buried in Glasnevin Cemetery on 27 June. Two pilgrims were killed and twenty injured when the lorry, which was carrying them back to Tullamore, crashed into a bridge at Leixlip. In 1932, several ornamental cast-iron pissoirs were imported from France and erected on the Quays for the use of the men going to the meetings in the Phoenix Park. Long since condemned as unhygienic, the last one on Ormond Quay was sold in 1972 for £10.

Evening Herald
See Irish Independent.

Evening Mail
The first issue was offered to the Dublin public on Monday evening, 3 February 1823, and the first daily issue was in 1861. The enterprise was fathered by Thomas Sheehan who was the proprietor of a printing works at 27 Parliament Street, later numbered 37, where the paper was printed until it was taken over by *The Irish Times* in 1960. It was the first paper in the world to make use of wireless telegraphy for the reception of some of its news. In July 1898, the result of a regatta organised by the Royal St George Yacht Club in Dún Laoghaire was flashed by Marconi to one of its operators in the Mail offices in Parliament Street. The paper closed in 1962.

Exchange House
Lower Exchange Street
Formerly the presbytery of the Church of St Michael and St John, a drop-in day centre for Travellers, run under the auspices of the Committee for Travelling People. From 1980 until 1984, it was also used as a night shelter for Travelling People, many of whom were glue sniffers.

Exchange Street Lower
From Wood Quay to Essex Street West
The name comes from its proximity to the Royal Exchange.*
Originally Blind Quay (a quay not being on the river) when there were warehouses and storage depots for the Custom House* and traders, also Scarlet Lane in the thirteenth century. Roman Catholic Church of St Michael and St John, built in 1815 to a design of J. Taylor, is the oldest RC church in the city. Dr Maurice Craig notes that it had the first Catholic bell to sound in the city since the Reformation. The church had fallen into disuse and was for a time used to celebrate the Tridentine Rite. As part of the Temple Bar Project, the interior was stripped to house the Viking museum, now closed. The vault of the church was allegedly the pit of the Smock Alley Theatre.* In 1681, Frances Loveth, widow, petitioned the Corporation 'that she must

be forced to pull down her house on Blind Quay and rebuild the same, by reason of a great crack and breach there lately made by the shott of a great gunn; that the citty wall from Essex Gate to Issolls Tower and alsoe the said tower were soe much decayed that they were of noe use or safety to the citty, but endangered those that lived under it, and alsoe straightened and deformed the streete, soe that coaches could hardly passe, and which wall and tower being only supported by the petitioners house must of necessity fall unlesse taken downe with the house'. This request was granted and the street widened by 2 feet on the understanding that 'Essex Gate be not prejudiced thereby'.

See **Essex Street.**

Exchange Street Upper
From Lord Edward Street to Essex Street
Name comes from its proximity to the Royal Exchange.
General trading street including the Paramount Hotel. In 2003, Cahill-O'Brien Associates, architects, designed Sky Lab at nos. 1 and 2, an office block of 961 square metres with extensive use of glass, exposed metal and cladding of Scottish sandstone. The four-storey building over a basement has a front elevation broken into three stepped sections, each approximately 1 metre behind the other.

Exchequer Street
From South Great George's Street to Wicklow Street
Named after the old Exchequer established by John, Lord of Ireland, in the late twelfth century. Gilbert mentions a record of 1592 which refers to 'Richard Stanihurst, Gent, farmer of a garden called Colletts Innes, alias le old Exchequer'. The Exchequer, which was moved to Christ Church within the city wall to secure it from the marauding Irish, was demolished in the sixteenth century. Originally the street extended to Grafton Street but, in October 1837, the inhabitants in the part from South William Street to Grafton Street petitioned the Wide Streets Commissioners to have the name changed to Wicklow Street, because the street had a bad name, making it difficult to obtain respectable tenants for the properties. This was granted on 18 October that year. Brooking's Map of 1728 shows the entire stretch as Chequer Lane.
At no. 37 is The Old Stand pub with its Victorian furnishings. A tavern has stood on this site since the seventeenth century. It was for many years called The Monico until it was renamed after the demolished stand at Lansdowne Road. This establishment, together with Davy Byrne's,* is owned by the Doran family who have been in the licensed trade for nearly 100 years.

F

Fade Street

From South Great George's Street to Drury Street

Joseph Fade, a banker, joined the firm of Isachar and John Willcox in 1728. Isachar died in 1744 and Fade in 1748. The bank closed on 1 March 1755. In 1876, a group of businessmen acquired properties on the left-hand side of the street in order to build the South City Markets,* and the street was widened 1880–81.

Fairview

Fairview Strand

From Clontarf Road to Clonliffe Road

Created in 1879 and separated from Clontarf. A roadway bordering the slob lands, now Fairview Park. Between St Joseph's Schools and the shops on Marino Mart stood the entrance gates to Marino Estate, the demesne and residence of the Earl of Charlemont. The gateway was described as modern and neat with a centre of hewn granite of the Doric order surmounted by dragons couchant in Portland stone supporting an escutcheon with the family arms bearing the motto, 'Deo duce ferro commintante' (with God as my guide my sword by my side). When Dublin Corporation carried out the first housing programme of an Irish government in the 1920s, the gateway was dismantled and re-erected at the entrance to the Christian Brothers' house on the newly made Griffith Avenue.

See **Casino at Marino** *and* **Marino.**

Fatima Mansions

Rialto

Built in the 1950s as a social housing complex in a low-density prairie style with a large paved area between the four-storey high blocks. An unkempt grassland area separated it from a boundary wall and a residential area to the southeast. It developed into an area of high security risk with a crime rate and drug culture creating a type of ghetto situation and isolating itself from the rest of the community. An effort was made in the 1990s to refurbish the existing flats but this was considered to be a failure. In 2003, An Bord Pleanála gave permission for the demolition of 364 flats on four hectares and the construction of 511 residential units of two-, three- and four-bed units, ranging from one to three storeys, with an emphasis on cul-de-sacs rather than through roads. In August 2004, the Government announced the signing of a five-year plan in conjunction with Elliot-Mortitz, a consortium of private developers. There would also be four- and five-storey buildings facing onto the Grand Canal and the Luas station. The area would include a crèche and a variety of shops, also new recreational facilities to include a large indoor sports centre with accommodation for a wide variety of community projects and an enterprise and training unit to assist with local employment. St Anthony's Road is to be extended and a new road opened between Reuben Street and St Anthony's Road. When the original complex opened in 1951, it accommodated 2,000 persons. The new development will have 85 per cent of the units as affordable private dwellings and the rest as social housing.

Feinaglian Institution
Portland Row

In 1813, Professor von Feinagle from Luxembourg took over Aldborough House* and renamed it Luxembourg. He opened a very successful school using a system for aiding or strengthening the memory. He added the chapel and extra classrooms to accommodate 300 pupils. He then opened a preparatory school in Buck Jones's House in Jones's Road and a further school in Kildare Street. He died in 1819 and a few years later the school closed.
See **Aldborough House** *and* **Jones's Road.**

Fenian Street
From Cumberland Street to Hogan Street

From the name taken by members of the Irish Republican Brotherhood, an organisation founded in New York on 17 March 1858. A street of artisan dwellings with Autocars' large garage on the corner, a listed property. This 1940s building was sold in 1971 and became EWL Electric. It was bought by Noel O'Callaghan, a hotelier, and, on the June bank holiday weekend of 1991, he demolished the building. He was forced to reinstate it to its original design. In 1977, a large seven-storey-over-basement office block, on 1.64 acres, known as Cumberland House, was built and let mainly to Eircom. It was sold in 2004 for a figure in the region of €65 million.

Fever Hospital and House of Recovery
Cork Street

The hospital opened on 14 May 1804 and embraced two objects: the immediate removal of the diseased person from his own dwelling place and the adoption of measures for counteracting the progress of infection in the habitations of the poor. It was extended in 1817–19 to cope with extra pressure from the national typhus epidemic. Three thousand cases were admitted in October 1818. A report of November 1826 states that since its opening, '67,570 have been admitted; of whom 62,918 have been discharged cured; 4,251 have died and 401 were in the house on that day.' Their

chaplain, Rev. James Whitelaw (*see* Braithwaite Street, Liberties and Slums), died of fever in 1813. In 1953, the Cherry Orchard Hospital, Ballyfermot, replaced the old Cork Street institution which was renamed Brú Chaoimhín and used as a geriatric hospital. Because of extensive overcrowding in the slums,* the city had several epidemics including cholera in 1831–32, 1848–49, 1853–54 and 1866; smallpox in 1865, 1871 and 1878; and measles in 1899 when 568 children died.
See **Bully's Acre.**

Field (John) Memorial
Golden Lane

A rough-hewn granite stone with an elliptical bronze inset depicting the head of John Field, the creator of the nocturne, who was born in Golden Lane, 26 July 1782. He came from a musical background. His grandfather was an organist and his father a theatre violinist. He toured Europe as a fashionable pianist and in the early nineteenth century, after a concert in St Petersburg, he settled in Russia. He wrote over twenty nocturnes, as well as concertos and other pieces. He died in Moscow on 11 January 1837. The memorial erected in October 1988 has a granite seat placed to its left and stands beside a Dublin Corporation inner-city housing development. There were descendants of his in Golden Lane to within living memory. A Mrs Field in a velvet dress with a starched collar taught piano lessons for a penny at the time of the civil war in 1922.

Film Institute of Ireland
6 Eustace Street

The national body charged with the promotion of film culture, it owns and operates the Irish Film Centre. The IFC houses the Irish Film Archive, two cinemas, a library, and an education and outreach department, along with a bar/restaurant and a specialist film bookshop. Cinemobile, Ireland's first mobile cinema, is a wholly owned subsidiary of the Institute. The IFC is housed in the old Quaker Meeting House, adapted by

O'Donnell and Tuomey Architects. It also enclosed a passageway and open courtyard with a glass roof, which is used as a waiting area and as an overflow from the bar/restaurant.

Findlater's Place
See **Cathal Brugha Street.**

Findlater Street
Off Infirmary Road
Red-brick houses built by the Dublin Artisans' Dwellings Company* and named after William Findlater, wine merchant and grocer, who was a director of the Company.
See also **Cathal Brugha Street** *and* **Presbyterian Church.**

Fish, Fruit and Vegetable Markets
Arran Street East/Mary's Lane
The wholesale fruit and vegetable market was opened on 6 December 1892 by the Lord Mayor ,the Rt Hon. Joseph M. Meade LL.D. JP. Alderman B. Dillon was the chairman of the construction committee. The fish market was opened in 1897. The markets were built on the site of half-ruined houses and were constructed of brick and limestone. The entrance is surmounted with the Arms of the city. Part of the market extends inside the walls of the old prison in Green Street. In 2005, Dublin City Council closed the fish market as part of a €70 million rejuvenation of the market area, and demolished the building. The fruit and vegetable market building was converted, with two floors of retail units dedicated to food, and offices, modelled on the English market in Cork. Fyffes' (formerly Fruit Importers of Ireland) large fruit warehouse stands in Mary's Lane.
See **Armorials.**

Fishamble Street
From Lord Edward Street to Essex Quay
It extended from Castle Street to Essex Quay until Lord Edward Street was opened when nos. 5–10 Fishamble Street were demolished for road widening. Known as 'Vicus Piscariorum' (fishmon-

Fish, Fruit and Vegetable Market, entrance.

gers' quarters) in 1467, Fish Street in 1470, Fisher Street in 1570. The Fishambles are shown on Speed's map of 1610 and the name would appear to date back as far as 1408. A church of St Olaf or Olave, possibly a Dane, stood here and some documents describe it as the Church of St Olave the King. The General Post Office stood here from about 1684 to 1709 and, during the wars between James II and William of Orange, letters were despatched from here to General Ginkel's Camp. In 1709, a newspaper, *The Flying Post*, was published in the post office yard. From about the middle of the eighteenth century, a musical society met in the Bull's Head Tavern and, in 1757, Lord Mornington, who was to become Professor of Music at Trinity College in 1764, established his academy for entertaining the aristocracy. On 1 October 1741, the first concert was held in a newly built Music Hall and it was here in March 1742 that Handel gave the

first performance of his *Messiah*. He arrived in Dublin on 18 November 1741 to hold six subscription concerts, the first of which opened on 23 December. Seven hundred people attended the first performance of the *Messiah*, while the second performance was held in June. The building stood near the entrance to no. 19, which now houses the Contemporary Music Centre, occupied prior to that by Kennan's Metal Works. Next door is the George Frederick Handel Hotel. James Clarence Mangan, the poet, was born at no. 3 on 1 May 1803. One eighteenth-century house remains in private ownership. The entrance to the new civic offices is approached from the street.
See **Contemporary Music Society.**

Fishamble Street. Old Music Hall and Kennan's Metal Works.

Fishers Lane
St Michan's Street
Between Chancery Street and Mary's Lane
See **Carmelite Nuns, Fish, Fruit and Vegetable Markets.**

Fitzgibbon Street
From Mountjoy Square East to Emmet Street
Named after John Fitzgibbon (1749–1802), Lord Chancellor.
Late eighteenth-century street. Garda

Station built 1910. James Joyce lived at no. 13 (now 34) for a short period, with his parents.

Fitzwilliam Estate
The Fitzwilliams were the largest developers south of the river. Beginning about 1750 and continuing over a period of around 100 years, they built Merrion Square and Street, Mount Street Upper and Lower, Holles Street and Denzille Lane, Fitzwilliam Square and Street, together with Baggot and Pembroke Streets, Herbert Street and Place, also Warrington Place. With the Leeson family, they widened and rebuilt Donnybrook Road. The family died out in 1816 and the entire estate passed to the Earl of Pembroke.

Fitzwilliam Place
Following a line from Upper Fitzwilliam Street to Lower Leeson Street
Forms part of the ¾ mile streetscape explained in the text referring to Fitzwilliam Street Upper and Lower. Houses occupied by the medical profession and business concerns. The first house at the Lower Leeson Street end is designed in the Gothic revival style complete with its stone railings recently restored.

Fitzwilliam Square
From Pembroke Street to Fitzwilliam Street
Named after Richard 7th Viscount Fitzwilliam of Merrion (Meryon). He died childless in 1816 and, through a marriage in 1736, the entire estate passed to the Earl of Pembroke and Montgomery. The first leases were granted in 1791 and 1792. Because of political uncertainty at the time, caused by the 1798 rebellion and the Act of Union, the square took thirty years to complete, from 1798 to 1828, with most of the building being carried out between 1814 and 1824. The houses were occupied mostly by professional people and have four storeys over a basement. The garden in the centre of the square, laid out in 1813, has always remained private, with each household having a key to the park. The first tennis championships were held there in 1879 and

the first ladies' singles were held at the same time, five years before the event was included at Wimbledon. Tennis is still played there during the summer months.

Fitzwilliam Street Upper and Lower
From Merrion Square to Lower Leeson Street
One of Dublin's finest streetscapes, almost ¾ of a mile in length. The street was commenced as part of the Square* in 1791 and continued into the nineteenth century. On 30 September 1964, planning permission was given for the demolition of ESB property at nos. 13–28 Lower Fitzwilliam Street. Amidst much controversy, the sixteen houses were demolished in May 1965. A modern office block, designed by Stephenson and Gibney, was built on the site. The freehold for the new block, which was erected in 1966–70, was purchased from the 16th Earl of Pembroke whose family had taken over the Fitzwilliam Estate in 1816. He donated half of the money received for the freehold of the 16 houses to the Irish Georgian Society. At 29

Lower Fitzwilliam Street, the ESB has completely restored a middle-class house of the late eighteenth century and, together with the National Museum of Ireland, has sought to recapture the atmosphere and furnishings of a typical comfortable home of the general period 1790–1820. The United Arts Club, 3 Upper Fitzwilliam Street, founded in 1907 by Ellen (Ellie) Duncan (c. 1850–1937) and Constance Markievicz for the support of the Arts. Duncan became the first curator of Sir Hugh Lane's Municipal Gallery of Modern Art at Harcourt Street* on 18 January 1908. The first exhibition at the club's premises was of Post Impressionist paintings in 1911 and included works by Van Gogh, Cézanne and others. The club has a bar and restaurant and holds exhibitions. In 1990, it instituted the Markievicz Medal to be awarded annually to a young artist.

Five Lamps
See **Amiens Street.**

Fitzwilliam Street Upper viewed from Baggot Street Lower, showing one of Dublin's finest streetscapes.

Fleet Street
From D'Olier Street to Anglesea Street

At the beginning of this century, there were many solicitors' offices in the street. The rere entrance to *The Irish Times* is at nos. 25–27 and this part of the street is used as a bus terminus. Numbers 19–20 house the side entrance to Bewley's Oriental Café, opened by Joshua Bewley, a Quaker, in 1916, as a place for men to meet without having to resort to a public house. All three cafés closed in December 2004 (*see* Sycamore Street). In 1958, the Northern Assurance Company demolished a building on the corner of Westmoreland Street, designed by George C. Ashlin (1837–1921), a student of Pugin who married Pugin's daughter. A Dublin regional office of the Electricity Supply Board dominates the street.

Kevin Barry (1902–20), medical student and member of the IRA who was hanged on 1 November 1920, was born at no. 8. The Palace Bar, at no. 21, has a Corporation preservation order on it. Because of its proximity to *The Irish Times* newspaper it has always had a large journalistic following. The pub opened in 1848.

Flying Post

A newspaper published in 1708 and printed by S. Powell and F. Dickson in the yard of the Chief Baron's house, at Cork Hill.* It advertised 'fresh news without imposing old trash on the publick'.

Foley Street
See **Monto.**

Fortfield House
Fortfield Road

The name comes from the fort constructed near the front of the house.

Built 1785 by Barry Yelverton, Chief Baron of the Exchequer and 1st Viscount Avonmore. On his death in 1805, Fortfield House was sold to Lord Clanmorris and eventually to a Miss Perrin who died in 1930. It was demolished in 1934 and the estate covers part of Fortfield Road, Park, Drive and Grove. It was built in the Adam style with fine plaster work and one of the largest drawing rooms in Dublin.

Fortick Road
See **Clonliffe Road.**

Foster Aqueduct
Phibsborough Road

Constructed by the Royal Canal Company across the junction of Phibsborough Road and Constitution Hill at the beginning of the nineteenth century, to allow its barges access to the canal harbour between the House of Industry and the King's Inns. It was 15 feet high with a span of 30 feet, with two arched passages on either side for foot passengers. A three-part stone tablet on the south side bore the inscription, *FOSTER AQUEDUCT SERUS IN COELUM REDAS, DIQUE, POPULO HIBERNIAE INTERSIS*. It was designed by Millar and Ruddery and removed in 1951 to make way for road widening.

Foster Place
College Green

A cul-de-sac formed when the Parliament House* was extended 1787–94. Named after the Rt Hon. John Foster (1740–1828), last Speaker of the Irish House of Commons. Facing the Bank of Ireland is the Royal Bank of Ireland building, a bank founded in 1835 when the private banking firm of Sir Robert Shaw and Company adopted corporate status. Together with the Munster & Leinster and Provincial Banks it became the Allied Irish Bank in 1966. In 2000, AIB closed this branch and the building is now used by Trinity College. The premises facing College Green were occupied by the Central Bank of Ireland until it moved to its new premises in Dame Street, in 1978. The Central Bank was founded in 1942 on the winding up of the Currency Commission. From 31 December 1956, it controlled the circulation of banknotes throughout the country.

Four Courts
Inns Quay

In 1608, during the reign of James I, a newly constructed building belonging to

Four Courts, Inns Quay and Richmond Bridge (now O'Donovan Rossa Bridge). Engraving 1813.

the deans of Christ Church, which was erected on the eleventh-century site of an episcopal residence, was appropriated to the use of the law courts, and named the King's Courts. Prior to that, the courts had been situated in a building known as the Inns, shown on Speed's map of 1610 on the north side of the River Liffey from Bridge Street.

An assessment was levied in 1686 for the purpose of enlarging the law courts, but, as the existing building beside Christ Church Cathedral was so decayed, the Surveyor General was directed in 1695 to rebuild the old Four Courts. These were approached through a passage called Hell,* and discussions had taken place for some years with a view to moving them to a suitable building on a more appropriate site. In 1776, Thomas Cooley had commenced work on the Public Records Office on Inns Quay, and the following year it was decided to integrate the new buildings for the Four Courts into Cooley's structure. Gandon commenced work on this great showpiece with its enormous domed central mass. The foundation stone was laid by the fourth Duke of Rutland, Lord Lieutenant, on 13 March 1786, and the work was completed in 1801. The building was sufficiently complete at the end of 1796 for

the courts to sit. The statues of Moses, Justice and Mercy with Wisdom and Authority are by Edward Smyth. The building held the courts of Exchequer, Common Pleas, King's Bench and Chancery, and these radiated towards the corners of a square.

The nineteenth-century Law Library is the area where barristers wait for business as they do not have chambers. Solicitors and clients wait outside in a hallway while the barrister's name is called from within the library. When the civil war broke out in 1922, the building was severely bombarded. The Public Records Office went up in flames and the records of the country were reduced to ashes. The building was restored by 1932 but the interior was planned on a different style at the time.

Four Courts Marshalsea
See **Marshalsea Debtors' Prison.**

Fownes Court
Named after Sir William Fownes of Woodstock, Kilkenny. One of the wealthiest merchants in Dublin, Sheriff during the mayoralty of Van Homrigh in 1697 and Lord Mayor 1708–09, created Baronet 1724, died 1735. In the Assembly rolls dated fourth Friday after 25 December 1699/1700

there is the following entry: 'It is ordered by the authority of the said Assembly on the petition of Alderman William Fownes that the petitioner surrendering the present lease, formerly made to Alderman George Jones, and giving the citty a piece of plate like to and of equall value with that given to the citty by Sir Joseph Williamson, Knight, shall have a lease of part of Hoggan Greene, alias College Greene.' (*See* Civic Plate.) In 1698, he was appointed, with Henry Lord Shelbourne, Ranger and Gamekeeper, or Master of Game, Ranger of the Phoenix Park and all of the parks, forests, chases and woods in Ireland. In his latter years, Fownes resided at Island Bridge and his large house in Fownes Court was taken from 1727 to 1730 by Madame Violante, a French rope dancer. For a short time, it was run as a theatre by Mr and Mrs Ward and then became a chocolate house run by the actor Peter Bardin.

In 1742, Dr Bartholomew Mosse, who had studied surgery and midwifery on the continent, opened the first maternity hospital in the British Isles in the same house. He was later to build the lying-in hospital known as the Rotunda. Between 1755 and 1783, Fownes Court housed the General Post Office which later moved to the south-eastern side of College Green, after which a charitable infirmary was established in the old post office yard. There were also two schools in the yard run by the Rev. Enoch MacMullen (1750) and Rev. Thomas Benson (1749).

The ground of Fownes Court was eventually taken by a group of merchants and traders for commercial purposes, and a fine classical grouping of buildings was commenced in 1796 and opened under the name of Commercial Buildings in 1799. The architect was Edward Parke. It became the meeting place of the Ouzel Galley Society founded in 1705, which dealt with ship insurance and commercial arbitration and was later subsumed into the Dublin Chamber of Commerce. The buildings surrounded a courtyard backing onto Cope Street which provided a short cut for pedestrians going to the footbridge across the Liffey. By 1970, the Central Bank had acquired this and adjoining sites for its new headquarters. Several Georgian and Victorian buildings were demolished and the stones from the old Commercial Buildings were numbered before being taken down, with a view to re-erecting the frontage as part of the new complex. This plan never materialised and a new building was eventually completed in 1978, facing towards Fownes Street.

Fownes Street
From Dame Street to Wellington Quay
From Sir William Fownes (*see* Fownes Court). Lower part from Temple Bar to Quay formerly Bagnio Slip.* Mostly commercial properties. Right-hand side to Cope Street demolished to make way for new Central Bank offices opened in 1978. Included in the demolition was no. 24 which housed the Royal Insurance chambers on the corner of Dame Street in an elaborately carved Italianate palazzo, erected in 1869 by John Nolan to a design of W. G. Murray. The interiors, according to *The Irish Builder*, had masterly plasterwork.

Foxrock
Named after Edward Fox, the developer. William Wellington Bentley was an auctioneer at Bride Street and, in 1821, married Ann Butler from Co. Galway. Bentley's circumstances improved and he sold his Bride Street premises to Boileau and Boyd, the chemists, and opened an auction room at 161 Capel Street. He also had another auction room at 12 Wood Quay. Bentley and his sons got into land agency, rent collecting, insurance and money lending and took offices at 110 Grafton Street, later to be taken by James North and Co., auctioneers.

Here Edward Fox enters the picture. He and his brother were wine merchants who moved into stockbroking and insurance, with offices in Dame Street. The Bentleys were Protestants and the Foxes Roman Catholics. In the 1850s, Edward Fox realised that the wide-open spaces around

Foxrock and Clonkeen were mostly scrub with a few mansions built — Burton Hall, Leopardstown House and Cabinteely House. All this land was owned by the Church of Ireland's Ecclesiastical Commissioners and that is probably why Catholic Edward Fox came to strike up a partnership with the Protestant Bentleys. It was in the Bentleys' name that 119 acres 4 roods and 4 perches of Clonkeen were leased from 25 March 1859. Bentley then acquired a further 142 acres 2 roods and 15 perches. He then added Kerrymount to the estate. The new Foxrock was given snobbish English names like Westminster, Brighton and Torquay. Within five years, 30 villas had been erected. Fox built a hotel and also Foxrock Golf Club. He arranged for a railway station to be built. He built a mart, a type of supermarket, in Mart Lane, and opened a post office. He also had a Protestant church (Tulla, now Tullow) opened at Brighton Road. The plans did not go well; Beatrice Lady Glenavy, writing in 1888, described it as a wild lonely place. Soon both partners were in serious trouble. William Bentley disappeared and Edward Fox died at Glenageary Hall in 1887. What was planned to be a fashionable estate became Leopardstown Racecourse.

Francis Street

From Cornmarket to The Coombe

The name comes from St Francis Abbey, the friary of the Franciscans founded in 1235 by Ralph de Porter. In 1535, when Thomas Fitzgerald made an attack upon the Newgate, he fled to the 'Graie Friers in S. Frances his street, there couched that night unknown to the citie, until the next morning he stale privilie to his armie not far off'. On the site of the friary now stands the church of St Nicholas of Myra (1829), by John Leeson, which was opened in 1834. The Ionic columns supporting a pediment with a bell tower and cupola were added in 1860 to a design of Patrick Byrne. At the dissolution of the monasteries in 1537, the grounds of the abbey were granted to William Hande. A street of extreme poverty in the seventeenth and

eighteenth centuries, it is now becoming the centre of the antique trade. Numbers 21–27 house the Iveagh Markets, opened in 1907 and dealing mostly in second-hand goods and clothes. The markets designed by Frederick Hicks are at present closed awaiting refurbishment. Difficulties re title issues have now been resolved and disposal terms and conditions were agreed at the June 2003 meeting of the City Council. Negotiations with the developer are ongoing. The Tivoli cinema was built of reinforced concrete in 1935. Long queues of children formed on Saturday and Sunday afternoons to occupy the wooden seats. It is now the Tivoli Theatre and used as a popular venue for plays and concerts. In 2004, Anthony Byrne applied for planning permission to demolish 135–143, which includes the theatre, and build a new one, together with 130 apartments, shops and offices. Many of the buildings date to the 1830s and nos. 41 and 43 have some of the earliest shop fronts to survive in the city.

Frederick Street North

From Cavendish Row to Upper Dorset Street

Named after Dr Frederick Jebb, Master of the Rotunda Hospital, 1773, and a regular contributor of political essays to *The Freeman's Journal* under the name of 'Guatimozin'. His father, Sir Henry Jebb, built the street. Jonah Barrington (1760–1834) writing of his own time in *Personal Sketches*, describes one of the houses 'where eight or ten select persons were most plentifully served in company by plain Mrs Kyle, wife of an ex-trooper a gentlewoman by birth'. This would give the impression that some of the houses catered for paying guests, possibly during the season. Harry Clarke (1889–1931), the stained-glass artist, had his thriving studios at nos. 6–7. His father Joshua, the ecclesiastical artist and church decorator, lived at no. 33 until his death in 1921.

Patrick J. Tuohy (1894–1930), the talented painter, lived at no. 15 with his father, Joseph Tuohy, a surgeon, his mother, Marie, and two sisters, Marie and Bride. An Gúm, the leading Irish language publishers since 1926, are at nos. 24–27. Their publications include textbooks, children's books, dictionaries and general reading material.

Frederick Street South
From Nassau Street to Molesworth Street
From Frederick, Prince of Wales (1701–51), eldest son of George II.
Opened in 1731 and intended to be called Library Street as it faced onto the new library at Trinity College.
In 1961, five houses built in the 1750s, with fine stucco-work ceilings, were pulled down and a modern office block erected for the New Ireland Assurance Company, now occupied by an assortment of tenants. In 1983, more similar-type houses were demolished.

Free Church (C of I)
96 North Great Charles Street
Built as a Wesleyan chapel in 1800, it was acquired by the Church of Ireland and reconstructed in 1828. Called the Free Church because, unlike many other churches, no pew rents were charged. Closed for public worship in May 1988.
In 1990, the C of I handed the building over to the Pavee Point Trust, a support group for the Travelling Community. It was converted by architect Niall McCullough as headquarters of the Dublin Travellers' Education and Development Group and is now called the Pavee Point Travellers' Centre.

Free Citizens of Dublin
The ancient freedom of Dublin can be traced to the late twelfth century and was eventually abolished in 1918. Admission to the freedom was usually through one of the 25 trade guilds where there were various ways in which a person could become a freeman. This could be obtained by serving an apprenticeship to a freeman, or by being the son of a freeman. Provided that Inner Council of the guild agreed, freedom could be purchased or admittance gained by special grace and favour. There were significant trading privileges to the holders

of this ancient freedom and they had the right to vote in civic elections. It could also advance a political career with election to the Dublin City Assembly. Each guild was entitled to a certain number of seats in the assembly which was the forerunner of the Dublin City Council. This procedure continued until the 1840 Municipal Reform (Ireland) Act became law; it was enforced from 15 October 1841. Under this legislation, entry to the assembly was replaced with a property qualification and all rate payers with a yearly valuation of £10, irrespective of their religious allegiance, were eligible to vote in civic elections and sit on councils. In the first local elections under the new act, Daniel O'Connell was elected a city councillor and, on 1 November 1841, was elected the first Roman Catholic Lord Mayor of Dublin since 1690.
See **Lord Mayor, Guilds.**

Freeman's Journal
Newspaper. First number published on Saturday, 10 September 1763, entitled 'The Public Register or Freemans Journal'. It cost one penny and consisted of four pages of three columns each and was published twice weekly. In October 1769, a fourth column was added and it issued on Tuesdays, Thursdays and Saturdays. The editors styled themselves as the 'committee for conducting the free press'. Charles Lucas (1713–71), patriot and medical doctor who campaigned against corruption in the city administration, was a frequent contributor from its founding. In 1829, the paper supported Daniel O'Connell (1775–1847) and Catholic Emancipation giving the right of Roman Catholics to sit as MPs without having to take the oath of supremacy. It was read by middle-class Roman Catholics and supported the Government of the Free State (1922). On 29 March 1922, the IRA burnt down the building, destroying all the presses and files. In spite of compensation of £2,600, the paper never recovered and it ceased publication in 1924 when it was purchased by its rival, the *Irish Independent.**

French Street
See **Mercer Street.**

Friends of Medieval Dublin
Established on 8 April 1976 as a study group to increase knowledge about medieval Dublin and to promote public interest in it. The group was founded following the events of the Wood Quay débâcle. In 1982, a sub-committee prepared a lengthy policy document concerning development in the medieval city. It was circulated to members of Dáil Éireann and Dublin Corporation and was favourably received by both bodies. The group, which provided financial support at the time of the Wood Quay campaign, assigned the bulk of the residue of the funds towards the cost of publishing 28 learned articles edited by Dr Howard Clarke and produced in two volumes, *Medieval Dublin, The Making of a Metropolis* and *Medieval Dublin, The Living City.*

Fumbally Lane
From New Street to Blackpitts
A lease of 1741 refers to a lane called Fombily Lane and two houses leased to David Fombily, skinner, and Anthony Fombily, skinner. In *Irish Names and Places*, P. W. Joyce suggests *Fum* as wet or boggy ground, *Baile* as townland on boggy ground. The City of Dublin Brewery stood on the corner of Blackpitts and Fumbally Lane which had some fine examples of 'Dutch Billy' houses. The area housed the silk, wool and poplin trades and, later, several shroud makers took up residence. Today it comprises industrial lettings and some small residential houses.

G

Gaiety Theatre
South King Street

On 1 July 1871, the Lord Mayor, John Campbell JP, laid the foundation stone on a site where a grocery and baker's shop had formerly stood. Earlier, John and Michael Gunn, who had a music business at 61 Grafton Street, were given letters patent to erect a 'well regulated theatre and therein at all times publicly to act, represent or perform any interlude, tragedy, comedy, prelude, opera, burletta, play, farce or pantomime'. Their father had been drowned in 1861 when a horse omnibus plunged into the Grand Canal at Portobello harbour (*see* Dublin Trams). The building was completed in six months, with workmen labouring through the nights with torchlight. There was seating for 2,000 people. On the opening night, 27 November 1871, Mrs Scott Siddons delivered the prologue. This was followed by Oliver Goldsmith's *She Stoops to Conquer* presented by the St James Theatre Company.

Over the years, many famous actors have trod the theatre's boards, including Sir Henry Irving, Ellen Terry, Sarah Bernhardt, Sir Ralph Richardson, Hilton Edwards, Micheál MacLiammóir and Anew McMaster. The long operatic tradition associated with the theatre began in 1872. Another tradition, that of producing Irish plays, commenced at the beginning of the twentieth century. Pantomime appears to have been staged from the start, and the tradition is still carried on. In the 1890s, the theatre was completely redesigned by the theatrical architect Frank Matcham, and his layout has survived to the present day. It closed for three months in 2003, reopening in July that year with more comfortable seating, better lighting and the removal of the centre aisle of the parterre. A three-storey night club operates from 11 p.m. to 4 a.m. on Fridays and Saturdays.

Gallows Hill
Between Pembroke Street and Upper Baggot Street

The hill opposite Baggotrath Castle was the place where robbers and criminals were hanged. The site was leased to Denny Kevan, a merchant, in 1562, for 61 years at a rent of 5 shillings a year. Archbishop Dermot O'Hurley of Cashel was hanged there on 21 June 1584 (*see* St Kevin's, Camden Row). Bodies were taken from Gallows Hill to Misery Hill where they were left hanging for from six to twelve months.

Garda Síochána
See Police.

Gardiner Estates

The Gardiner family was one of the principal developers north of the Liffey in the eighteenth century. The family spanned three generations of builders, commencing with Luke, a banker, who built Luke Street behind Townsend Street in 1712, together with other parcels of land stretching towards George's Quay. The Gardiners also developed Bolton Street, the impressive Sackville Mall, Dominick Street, Henrietta Street, Gardiner Street, Mountjoy Square, Buckingham Street and Summerhill. Part of the Eccles estate was purchased for new streets, together with part of the lands of St Mary's Abbey belonging to the Moore family. The Gardiners were later to become the Earls of Blessington, the family dying out in 1829. From 1846 onwards, the estate was sold in parcels and divided among various owners.

Gardiner Street (Lower, Middle and Upper)

From Beresford Place to Lower Dorset Street
Named after the Rt Hon. Luke Gardiner (1745–98), Viscount Mountjoy 1795. Killed leading his regiment, the Dublin Militia, at the Battle of New Ross 1798.

Dating from about 1787, it was one of the city's most fashionable streets. By about 1800, it had reached Beresford Place. It quickly deteriorated after the Act of Union, and the fine houses eventually became tenements. Many of the buildings were demolished in the 1940s and modern flats constructed in their place. Most of these have now been vacated. At the north end of the street stands St Francis Xavier's Church (RC), built for the Jesuits to a design of John B. Keane, begun in 1829 and opened in 1832. It is fronted with a four-column Ionic portico. In 1898, Father James Cullen SJ founded the Pioneer Total Abstinence Association here. Some early nineteenth-century red-brick houses face the church at the southern end. The large labour exchange was built as Trinity Church (C of I) in 1838, to a design of Frederick Darley, and was de-consecrated in the 1930s. In 2003, the building was sold for €4 million to a religious group which plans to turn it into a hive of Christian mission and service. Some small hotels also operate in the street; also some four-storey housing designed by Boyle and Delaney in the 1970s.

Gardiner's Row

Laid out in 1768 from the new gardens (Rutland Square) to Temple Street, first appearing on the map of 1773. The eastern portion was renamed Great Denmark Street in 1792 when Gardiner Place was opened to Mountjoy Square.
See **Belvedere House.**

Gardiner Place

From Great Denmark Street to Mountjoy Square
Named after the Rt Hon. Luke Gardiner (1745–98). Gardiner's Row was laid out in 1768 and the eastern portion renamed Great Denmark Street in 1792 when the street was extended to Mountjoy Square and this portion was named Gardiner's Place.

Gate Theatre

Cavendish Row
The supper room of the Rotunda, part of the Rotunda Hospital.
Founded in 1928 by Mícheál MacLiammóir (born Alfred Lee Willmore 1899–1978), who was brought to Ireland by Anew McMaster, the Shakespearean actor who was married to MacLiammóir's sister, and Hilton Robert Hugh Edwards (1903–82), who was introduced to MacLiammóir by McMaster. Their first production was of Ibsen's *Peer Gynt* on 14 October that year in the Peacock Theatre, attached to the Abbey Theatre. In 1930, enough money was raised by subscription for them to lease the concert rooms of the Rotunda Hospital. Lord Longford (6th Earl 1902–61) became a director in 1931. In 1936, his company, Longford Productions, leased the theatre for six months annually. His company was disbanded following his death.
See **Rutland Square, Theatres.**

Genealogical Office

Kildare Street
The Office of Arms was established in 1552 and the Genealogical Office, which incorporates the office of Chief Herald, is the oldest functioning office of state in Ireland, having operated without a break since the year of its foundation. On 1 April 1943, the name Office of Arms was changed to Genealogical Office, and Chief Herald of Ireland replaced the title King of Arms. A consultancy service on ancestry tracing is available. There is also a small public museum attached to the building which is housed in part of the old Kildare Street

Club.* The office relocated from Dublin Castle to Kildare Street in 1981.

General Post Office

About 1684, the General Post Office was transferred from High Street to Fishamble Street. From about 1709, it was located in Sycamore Alley until Bardin's Chocolate House in Fownes Court was taken over in 1755 and used until 1783. In that year, it moved to an extensive five-storey building in College Green. A new building to the design of Francis Johnston was built in Sackville Street (now O'Connell Street) 1814–1818, being 200 feet long and 56 feet high with Ionic columns and pilasters in the Graeco-Roman style, and a clock with a peal of bells, which was later installed in the new university building at Earlsfort Terrace. The three figures above the pediment represent Mercury, Hibernia and Fidelity and are by the sculptor Thomas Kirk. The building cost £50,000 and the interior was extensively refitted at the beginning of this century. Much of it was destroyed in the Rising of 1916 but restored by 1924. A bronze statue, 'The Fall of Cuchulainn', by Oliver Sheppard, stands in the hall to commemorate the rebellion.

George's Hill

From Anne Street North to Mary's Lane
Presentation Convent backing onto Halston Street opened in 1794. Order founded by Nano Nagle (1728–84) in Cork—established in 1775. Opposite the convent there are warehouses for storing fruit. Several fine red-brick houses now in ruins.

Gill Square c.1760, now demolished

A blind court opening by a narrow archway under one of the houses in Cole Alley, Meath Street. Built on three sides of a square of about 50 feet, it contained nine, three-storey houses.

Glasnevin

Glasnevin, a village in the parish of the same name, and situated on the river Tolka, amalgamated with the city of Dublin by Act of Parliament in 1900. *Glas Naíon*, meaning the stream of a local chieftain bearing that name. In the eighteenth and nineteenth centuries it was a favourite summer residence place of Swift, Addison, Sheridan and Parnell.

Sir John Rogerson, the shipping magnate after whom a quay is named, built Glasnevin House which was finally occupied by the Bishop of Kildare, Charles Lindsay, whose name is perpetuated in two local roads: Lindsay and Crawford (his father was the Earl of Crawford). His executors sold the house—and extensive gardens that had been laid out by a previous owner Henry Mitchell—to the Holy Faith nuns.

General Post Office c. 1813.

Delville* was the home of the Delanys where Swift is said to have composed and printed his satires on the Irish Parliament. It became the residence of Stephen Lanigan O'Keefe but was then demolished, and the Bons Secours Hospital now occupies the site. The Botanic Gardens,* founded by the Dublin Society in 1795 in order to assist Irish agriculture and horticulture by experiments with plants most suitable to the climate, is open to the public. Glasnevin or Prospect Cemetery* was opened in 1832 and is the resting place of Daniel O'Connell beneath a replica of an Irish round tower. The Church of St Mobhi (C of I) at Church Avenue was rebuilt by Sir John Rogerson in 1707; the tower is an earlier date. The (RC) Church of Our Lady of Dolours, consecrated in 1972, is in the form of a pyramid or triangle and replaced a church that was built in 1881. The Meteorological Services building on Glasnevin Hill, also in the shape of a pyramid, was built by Sisks in 1979 and designed by Liam McCormick.

At the top of Botanic Avenue there was a school in the shape of a circular ink-bottle, allegedly designed by Swift. It was demolished in 1901. The Institute for Industrial Research and Standards, founded in 1946 and reconstituted in 1961 to promote the application of science and technology in industry, is close by the Meteorological Services. In November 2003, John Player and Sons, Botanic Road, moved to Park West. This company comprises the former interests of the tobacco firms of Player and Wills (Irl.), W. D. and H. O. Wills, and Wm Clark and Sons, established in Cork 1830. Player's was founded in 1923 and Wills' in 1924.

See **Eolas** *and* **Dublin City University.**

Glasnevin Cemetery

A campaign led by Daniel O'Connell (1775–1844), the liberator, resulted in the opening of a large Roman Catholic cemetery in February 1832, originally named Prospect Cemetery. Many patriots are buried here, including O'Connell who is interred in a vault beneath a 160-foot

Glasnevin Cemetery. Monument by George Coppinger Ashlin to His Eminence Edward Cardinal McCabe D.D. Archbishop of Dublin and Primate of Ireland. Died February 1885.

high replica of an Irish round tower, completed in 1869. A granite slab commemorates Charles Stewart Parnell. There is also a memorial to those killed in the 1916 Rebellion. High crosses abound in the cemetery, with every form of interlaced ornament and carved scenes.

The mortuary chapel, designed by J. J. McCarthy in the 1870s, was completed in 1878. The monuments have an extra-ordinary mixture of religious and patriotic symbolism, including the Crucifixion, harps, shamrocks, wolfhounds, with a mixture of antiquarian and popular ornament. George Coppinger Ashlin (1837–1921) designed the enormous monument for Cardinal McCabe who died in 1885. It is cruciform in shape with a mosaic floor with symbols of the four Evangelists, while the figure of the Cardinal is guarded by angels. The elaborate carving was done by C. W. Harrison and Sons.

See **Glasnevin Crematorium** *and* **Millennium Plot.**

Glasnevin Crematorium Ltd

A statement issued by the Catholic Press Office in March 1982 prior to the opening of the new crematorium stated: 'The Holy Office in May 1886 opposed cremation not because it is against divine and natural law, but because it had become associated almost exclusively with the aims and spirit of unbelievers who used cremation to ridicule Christian teaching on the immortality of the soul and resurrection of the body. The code of Canon Law promulgated in 1919 continued to oppose cremation, but in 1963 there was a significant shift in the Church's approach, when an instruction asked local bishops to exhort the faithful to continue to observe the Christian burial, but the presumption of law changed with this document and now favoured the good faith of persons requesting cremation . . . This presumption of good faith was reinforced by another document of the Holy See in 1969.' The 1983 Code of Canon Law states: 'The Church earnestly recommends that the pious custom of burial be retained; but it does not forbid cremation, unless this is chosen for reasons which are contrary to Christian teaching.'

In 1981, over 600 corpses were taken from southern Ireland to Belfast for cremation. On 10 September 1980, Dublin City Council agreed to give planning permission for a crematorium, the first in the Republic of Ireland, in a section of Glasnevin cemetery. This was opened with an ecumenical service on 12 March 1982. From March to 31 December 1982, there were 219 cremations, 352 in 1983, 377 in 1984 and over 500 in 1985. There have been 20,000 cremations over 22 years. The Newlands Cross Cemetery and Crematorium opened in 1990, with 800 cremations to 2004. A doctor normally scrutinises the corpses for pacemakers for fear of an explosion, as the Solihull crematorium in England blew up in 1976. The ashes are either placed in an urn or buried in an eight-acre garden of remembrance. There is also a wall to hold 2,000 mini-vaults for ashes, with accommodation for memorial tablets. Today all Christian denominations allow cremation.

Gloucester Street

From Cathal Brugha Street to Killarney Street
Named after William Henry, Duke of Gloucester 1764. Street laid out in 1772. Formerly Great Martin's Lane. Originally part of the Monto* until the Legion of Mary sought the help of the Garda Síochána, who arrested 120 people in the surrounding area. The street is dominated by a large Roman Catholic church, Our Lady of Lourdes, built in 1954, created a separate parish in 1970. The marble and glass memorial to Matt Talbot (1856–1925) describes him as a Servant of God. In 1975, he was declared Venerable. He is interred in Glasnevin and there is a memorial at 18 Rutland Street near where he lived. Patrick Kavanagh spent his first night in Dublin in Gloucester Street in the late 1930s. 'I paid sixpence for my bed. There were six other beds in the room. The stink of that room has never left my nostrils.'

The street is now called Sean MacDermott (1884–1916) Street after one of the seven signatories of the Proclamation of the Irish Republic. Sentenced to death and shot on 12 May 1916.

Golblac Lane (Lucy Lane, Mass Lane)
See **Chancery Place.**

Golden Lane

Part of the old medieval city, it was known as Crosse or Cherry Lane. Shown on John Speed's map of 1610 as Crosse Lane and Charles Brooking's map of 1728 as Golden Lane, as it is in the parish registers of St Nicholas Within in 1682. Little survives of the original lane. In 1812, the Company of Goldsmiths housed the assay office* at no. 22 until they moved to the Custom House in 1838. Birthplace of John Field,* the creator of the nocturne. Today there are houses and flats built by Dublin Corporation, and office blocks.

On Thursday, 9 April 1885, the Prince of Wales and his son, the Duke of Clarence, visited the slums in Golden Lane as part of a tour connected with the Prince's visit to Ireland to attend a meeting of the Royal Commission on the state of the working classes. As the young Duke descended from the carriage, a woman from one of the tenements discharged a bucket of foul-smelling liquid into the gutter. The Duke slipped and fell into the mess. One of the party, Sir Dighton Proby, gave his coat to the young Prince. The coat was much too large for the Prince, but he had to wear it during the rest of the day's tour. A local enquiry was later conducted by Sir Charles Cameron, Medical Officer for Health, as to whether the woman's action was deliberate. Nothing came of it.

See **Dublin Artisans' Dwellings Company.**

Goldenbridge and Inchicore
Dublin 8

Described in a contemporary record as 'a village in the parish of St James, Barony of Newcastle, County of Dublin and Province of Leinster, two miles west of Dublin on the road to Naas'. Known for centuries as Glydon Bridge, it spans the River Camac at Inchicore. In the sixteenth century, there was a cloth-fulling mill later owned by Richard Rawson, and by the eighteenth century local mills were producing such useful products as paper, flour and pearl barley. The paper mill was later to become a large saw mill owned by the Brassington family. This was sold in the 1960s and is now an industrial estate.

Here was also a popular spa to which the citizens of Dublin travelled in the hope of ridding themselves of biliousness, liver complaints and sundry other diseases. A modern street name plate attached to a wall near what were the old tram sheds is the only reminder we have of the old spa, all traces of which seem to have vanished completely. The girl's convent school, opened by the Sisters of Mercy in 1855, probably occupies the site. With the coming of the Richmond Barracks,* and later the railway, the whole area greatly expanded. The village also had a Methodist church known as 'the Bethel', having been

leased to the Methodists on 7 July 1828 at a rent of £2-10-0 per annum. This lease stipulated that they could not sell or let for any manufacture or trade that might be a nuisance to the lessor or to William Smith, Gentleman. The building was sold in 1884 and the proceeds were used towards the building of the new church and schools on Tyrconnell Road. Up until recently these were used by a business fitting car exhausts and are now awaiting further commercial development.

A school was erected in 1827 near the Richmond Barracks, the cost of which was met by military and civilian subscription and a government grant of £250. Across the road, between the Barracks and the canal, the Catholic Association founded by Daniel O'Connell (1775–1847) had, with the help of a kindly Protestant, as the record puts it, secured a plot of ground which was to become the first Roman Catholic cemetery in Dublin. It was opened in 1829 and was the principal RC burying ground until Glasnevin was opened in 1832. Among those interred there was W. T. Cosgrave, President of the Executive Council of the Irish Free State. It is known as Goldenbridge Cemetery.

The Church of Mary Immaculate, Tyrconnell Road, attached to the Oblate retreat house, was commenced in 1878 with the towers and spires being added in the 1920s. The carillon was completed for the Eucharistic Congress in 1932. At the rere is a replica of the Lourdes grotto. In 1814, Obadiah Willan, a Yorkshire man, opened a mill on Inchicore Road using the water from the River Camac. He built a house, Susandale (later Silverdale), now demolished and a row of houses for his workers. He also built the Congregational Church, originally named Salem Chapel after the name for Jerusalem found in Psalm 76: v.2. This building zoned 21 (to protect, provide and improve residential amenities) was sold in April 2004. St Jude's (C of I) also on Inchicore Road was opened for public worship on 2 January 1864 as a direct result of the efforts of the Rev. Thomas Mills who was minister of a small church at Goldenbridge attached to St James. Mainly because of the increase in numbers in the locality as a result of the coming of the Great Southern and Western railway works at Inchicore, there was a need for a parish church to be built near at hand. The church was demolished in 1988, together with the parochial hall and the old rectory, 'Fairfield', to make way for modern housing. The spire remains and the stones and windows from the church were re-erected at Stradbally to house part of the steam museum.

In 2003, An Bord Pleanála gave permission to a division of Treasury Holdings to demolish the former Nestlé/Rowntree Mackintosh chocolate factory opposite Kilmainham Gaol.* Designed by Anthony Reddy and Associates, architects, the new development will have five buildings ranging in height from three to nine storeys covering 7184 sq. m (77,328 sq. ft). it will include 173 apartments, a hotel, fitness centre, restaurant and eight shops.

Goldenbridge Cemetery
See **Goldenbridge.**

Grafton Arcade
A covered shopping precinct, from Grafton Street to Duke Lane.

Grafton Street (1708)
From College Green to St Stephen's Green North

From Charles Fitzroy, 2nd Duke of Grafton (Viceroy), whose father was the illegitimate son of King Charles II by the Duchess of Cleveland. Part of a development of fields belonging to Vincent Molesworth of Swords and the lands of 'Tib and Tom' which were set as wheat land at an annual rent of 2s 6d per acre. The earliest printed official reference occurs in a statute of 1708 but the street had been partially formed towards the end of the seventeenth century. In 1712, the Corporation allocated money for making a crown causeway through the street. A fashionable residential street in the eighteenth century but with the opening of

Carlisle Bridge in 1798, which opened a new cross-city route, the street changed to a commercial centre. There is only one remaining private residence, no. 1, the Provost's house. Samuel Whyte opened his English Grammar School at no. 75 in 1758 at the corner of and into Johnston's Court. He was a first cousin of Frances Chamberlain, the wife of the theatre impresario, Thomas Sheridan, who encouraged him to open a school. Among his first pupils were Richard Brinsley and Alicia Sheridan. His pupils also included the playwright John O'Keefe and the poet Thomas Moore. Robert Emmet also received his education here and it was where he learnt public speaking. In August 1849, the *Evening Mail*, reporting on Queen Victoria's visit, observed: 'The greater number of good houses in Dame Street, Grafton Street and other principal thoroughfares are in a dirty and dilapidated

In 1982, Grafton Street was zoned for pedestrians only, and in 1988 it was paved with brick sets. With the coming of the Luas to St Stephen's Green, the volume of pedestrian traffic has greatly increased.

condition, the windows broken, patched with brown paper . . .' The first electric mains were laid in 1890.

In 1982, the street was zoned for pedestrians only and, in 1988, it was paved with brick sets and new street lighting was installed; this was followed by the upgrading of many shop fronts. A fashionable shopping area with well-established stores and jewellers. A supermarket opened in 1988.

Opposite the Provost's house, a bronze sculpture, 'Molly Malone' by Jeanne Rynhart, was unveiled in November 1988. It was sponsored by Jury's Hotel. It depicts the seventeenth-century street vendor with her barrow containing cockles and mussels.

Grand Canal Sewer
See **Greater Dublin Drainage Scheme.**

Grand Canal Street Upper and Lower (1792)
From Hogan Place to Haddington Road

This forms the thoroughfare known as the road to Beggar's Bush. In 1736, John Villiboise obtained a lease for 99 years from Richard, 5th Viscount Fitzwilliam. It consisted of one rood at a rent of £30 per year. Villiboise erected a house and, in the garden, cultivated artichokes. The house was called 'the Artichoke' by the local inhabitants, and eventually the name was applied to the road. In 1792, the portion from the canal to Grantham Street was named Grand Canal Street. In 1836, a further lease of 99 years on the house and garden known as 'the Artichoke' was given to John Swift Emerson who built houses on the site and named them Wentworth Terrace. The original house ('the Artichoke') was no. 37.

A small portion of Grand Canal Street had previously been named Wentworth Place. Emerson, an attorney at law, was one of Major Sirr's bodyguards and had assisted in the arrest of Lord Edward Fitzgerald in Thomas Street.

Sir Patrick Dun's Hospital was founded under a will of Sir Patrick Dun, a Scottish doctor who practised in Dublin. It was

Grand Canal Street. This entire area including the Grand Canal Docks has been totally revitalised with modern apartments and improved living conditions, as part of the Dublin Docklands Development Act.

moved from Essex Quay in 1808 to the present site at Grand Canal Street. Building designed by Sir Richard Morrison. Closed 1986. Morrison's semi-circular lecture hall, based on Gondoin's school of medicine in Paris, was demolished in the late nineteenth century. The completely restored hospital buildings have been adapted for commercial use. Boland's bakery and mill were converted into a modern office block in 1990. High up on the end of the building is a bronze sculpture of a figure climbing, 'Human Endeavour' by Rowan Gillespie. Clanwilliam Square, another lower-rise office scheme, is beside it.

Grand Lyric Hall
See **Conciliation Hall.**

Grangegorman Road
From Brunswick Street to the North Circular Road

The priory of Holy Trinity possessed the manor of Glasnevin and Gorman. The name of the priory grange is perpetuated in

Grangegorman. The enclosed farm consisted of a large hall with additional rooms, a hay barn with a malt house and a workshop. There was also a yard for cattle and the haggard.

The Richmond Lunatic Asylum (1814) and the Richmond General Penitentiary (1812), together with Grangegorman Mental Hospital (1816), form a large complex of buildings designed by Francis Johnston. The old entrance to the Midland Great Western Railway Company was at nos. 39–59 Grangegorman Road.

On Phibsborough Road stands Grangegorman Parish Church with a window of Ruth and Naomi by Catherine O'Brien. Also the RC Church of St Peter built in 1911 to replace an earlier church by Patrick Byrne.

Gray Street
Off Pimlico

Named after Edmond Dwyer Gray MP (1845–88). Built by the Dublin Artisans' Dwellings Company* in January 1882.

On the corner of Reginald Street stands a

Gray Street. The statue and the date 1929 commemorate the centenary of Catholic Emancipation. Originally a water fountain with cattle trough attached, cast by McFarlane and Co. of Glasgow in 1898.

cast-iron centrepiece that was built as a fresh-water fountain in 1898. The dome was surmounted by an eagle until the Black and Tans shot it off. The fountain was replaced with a statue of Christ, erected by the parishioners of St Catherine's in commemoration of the centenary of Catholic Emancipation in 1929. It was restored to mark the visit of Pope John Paul II to the Liberties on 29 September 1979.

Great Denmark Street
From Parnell Square to Gardiner's Place

Parnell Square end retains the title of Gardiner's Row* from which the eastern end was renamed in 1792. Belvedere House,* facing down North Great George's Street, completed in 1786, occupied by the Society of Jesus since 1841, is one of the finest houses in the city. Many of the Georgian houses on either side of the Jesuit Belvedere College have been demolished. In 1968, the home of stuccodore Michael Stapleton was knocked down and replaced by an extension to the College.

Great Industrial Exhibition 1853

An international exhibition organised by William Dargan (see National Gallery). On 25 October 1852, the Earl of Eglinton and Winton, the Lord Lieutenant, visited the site on Leinster Lawn which was then the property of the Royal Dublin Society,* and raised the first pillar of the building designed by Sir John Benson. The exhibition was opened on 12 May 1853 by the new Lord Lieutenant, the Earl of St Germans. On 29 August, Queen Victoria and Prince Albert visited the exhibition which closed on 31 October 1853. Among the exhibits listed in the official catalogue is 'the original Tara Brooch which was found in Meath in 1850'. This refers to the now internationally known brooch that was found on 24 August 1850 by a poor woman who stated that her children had found it on the seashore near Bettystown. She offered it to a scrap merchant in Drogheda who refused it, and then to a watchmaker who took it to Dublin and sold it to Waterhouse and Company in Dame Street.

Great Industrial Exhibition of 1853.

Waterhouse made many copies of the brooch, eventually parting with it in 1868 when the Royal Irish Academy* received £200 government aid for the purchase of the brooch. It is now in the National Museum of Ireland.* Replicas of the brooch on a reduced scale were exhibited for sale at the Great Exhibition in London in 1851.

The exhibition building itself was inspired by the Crystal Palace in London and was built of glass, timber and cast iron. The design, which was immensely popular with the citizens of Dublin, was the result of a competition won by the Cork architect, John Benson, who was later granted a knighthood by Queen Victoria.

See also **Dublin International Exhibition 1865 *and* Irish International Exhibition 1907.**

Greater Dublin Drainage Scheme

Since 1975, the Dublin local authorities have been constructing the scheme. This work, costing more than £60 million, is the finest feat of engineering accomplished in the Dublin area in the past thirty years. It was designed to provide drainage for the new housing schemes at Blanchardstown, Lucan and Clondalkin, to relieve the overloaded south-city foul and surface-water sewers, and to control the gross pollution of the River Camac. Large trunk sewers were laid from the new areas to the city at Inchicore where they formed together and continued as a large diameter sewer in a tunnel beside the Grand Canal. The sewer from Herberton Bridge to Maquay Bridge, Grand Canal Street, is divided into two compartments for the conveyance of foul and surface-water sewage. The surface-water conduit is required for the relief of flood-prone areas in Crumlin, Mount Brown, Dolphin's Barn and Harold's Cross. The original proposal for constructing the culverts in the bed of the canal met with considerable public opposition since it would have meant closing the canal for a period of about three years. It was then decided to proceed with the more expensive tunnel alternative, as it meant less traffic disruption and no interference with the canal waterway. The surface-water conduit discharges storm water to the Grand Canal dock and then via an entrained siphon to

the estuary of the River Liffey. A second tunnel was constructed from Grand Canal Street through Bath Avenue under the River Dodder at London Bridge Road and the Ringsend housing scheme, to contain the foul sewage to the new Ringsend Treatment Works.
See also **Main Drainage System** *and* **Ringsend Treatment Works.** *Also* **Rathmines and Pembroke Drainage.**

Green Street
From Little Britain Street to King Street North
Originally Abbey Green (1558) from the Green of St Mary's Abbey.
Number 25 originally housed the old Sheriff's prison, sessions house and Newgate Prison,* the foundations of which now mark St Michan's Park.
The courthouse, built in 1792–97 to a design of Whitmore Davis, was the scene of many famous trials, including those of Wolfe Tone, Robert Emmet and the Fenian leaders. Lord Edward Fitzgerald died here. It is now used as the Special Criminal Court, with heavy security in the area.

Green Street Little
From Mary's Lane to Little Britain Street
Originally known as Bradogue Lane from the river of that name that rises near Cabra and enters the River Liffey at Arran Street East; also as Little Green from the larger Abbey Green (1568) of St Mary's Abbey.

Guilds
The Norman invasion began in 1170 and ended in 1175 and a guild system entered Ireland in its wake. The guilds were associations of artisans, founded for mutual protection of members and for adherence to the standards established for their crafts. The Charter of Prince John of 1192 to the City of Dublin states that the citizens should have all their reasonable guilds, and the earliest record of a named guild is a list of these admitted in 1226–27 to a body known as the Dublin Guild Merchants. Over the centuries, the number of guilds varied from about 16 to 25, each one making its own laws which were then

enforced by sanction. A Craft Guild consisted of a master, three wardens, freemen, quarter brothers, journeymen and apprentices. In addition, there was the Inner Council and the Common Council of members. Each guild was entitled to a certain number of seats in Dublin Corporation. This method of electing the city fathers probably went back as far as 1229 when Dublin had the privilege of electing its first Mayor. This practice of electing the Corporation of Dublin continued until 1840 when the Westminster Parliament passed an Act for the regulation of municipal corporations in Ireland (324 Victoriae Chapter 108), which granted for the first time the public elections of members to corporations. With this Act, the guild structure collapsed. The one exception was the Company of Goldsmiths which has continued to assay and hallmark goods made of precious metals to the present day. The following were the 25 Dublin trade guilds:

Merchants or Holy Trinity Guild
Tailors or Guild of St John the Baptist
Smiths or Guild of St Loy
Barbers and Surgeons or Guild of St Mary
  Magdalen
Bakers or Guild of St Clement and St Anne
Butchers or Guild of the Virgin Mary
Carpenters, Millers, Masons and Heliers or
  Fraternity of the Blessed Virgin Mary of
  the House of St Thomas the Martyr
Shoemakers or Guild of the Blessed Virgin
  Mary
Saddlers, Upholders, Coach and Coach-
  Harness Makers or Guild of the Blessed
  Virgin Mary
Cooks and Vintners or Guild of St James
  the Apostle
Tanners or Guild of St Nicholas
Tallow Chandlers or Guild of St George
Glovers and Skinners or Guild of the
  Blessed Virgin Mary
Weavers or Guild of the Blessed Virgin
  Mary
Sheermen and Dyers or Guild of St
  Nicholas

Goldsmiths or Guild of All Saints
Coopers or Guild of St Patrick
Feltmakers
Cutlers, Painters, Paper Stainers and
Stationers or Guild of St Luke
Bricklayers and Plasterers or Guild of St
Bartholomew
Hosiers and Knitters or Guild of St George
Curriers or Guild of St Nicholas
Brewers and Maltsters or Guild of St
Andrew
Joiners
Apothecaries or Guild of St Luke the
Evangelist
See **Assay Office.**

Guildhall
Winetavern Street
Business in Dublin was dominated by craft
and trade guilds whose selected members
ran the administration of the city, presided
over by the Mayor or Lord Mayor.* They
met in the Guildhall at Winetavern Street.*
Its date of construction is not known but it
was in existence in 1253. A move was made
to the new Tholsel* prior to 1311.

Guinness Trust
This was founded in 1890 by Sir Arthur
Edward Guinness who gave £50,000 in
permanent trust to supply improved living
accommodation for the poorer classes of
Dublin. The Iveagh Trust Act, 1903, which
received Royal Assent on 30 June 1903,
amalgamated the Guinness Trust (Dublin)
with the Dublin Improvement (Bull Alley
Area) Scheme and gave the Trustees
enlarged and extended powers. This
scheme was to include extra tenements for
the artisan and labouring classes, a lodging
house known as Iveagh House, costing
£35,000, and a swimming bath and private

Sir Arthur Guinness (Lord Ardilaun). Erected in St Stephen's Green in 1892.

baths with hot water in Bridge Street.
The Guinness Trust's first enterprise was
the building of the Bellvue complex at
Thomas Court in 1891.
This was followed in 1894 by four red-brick
blocks of flats off Kevin Street, with a gate
entrance in Heytesbury Street, designed by
the London architects, Joseph and
Smithem, with Parry and Ross.
See **Bull Alley.**

H

⸺⸺

Haddington Road
From Mespil Road to Bath Avenue
Named after the Earl of Haddington, Lord
Lieutenant 1834–35.
Part of the Pembroke Estates.
A fashionable nineteenth-century area. St
Mary's (RC) Church commenced in 1839
with various additions over the years, the
side aisles and the tower being completed
in 1894. Within the grounds is a school
built in 1870. There are also entrances to
the grounds from St Mary's Road. Because
of an expanding population, The 51 pub
was opened in 1889. It was frequented by
Patrick Kavanagh, the poet, who lived in
Pembroke Road. Beggars Bush military
barracks, built in 1827, houses the archives
of the Geological Survey which is a place of
deposit under section 14 of the National
Archives* Act. The Labour Court and the
Labour Relations Commission are housed
in Tom Johnson House, named after
Johnson (1872–1963), the leader of the
Parliamentary Labour Party until 1928. In
1980, several large houses on Haddington
Road, together with some in Percy Place,
were replaced with four large red-brick
office blocks, having a total of 100,000
square feet. Rawson Court, Haddington
Road, fronting onto Percy Place, built in
2003, consists of twelve three-bedroom
duplex units and five two-bedroom
apartments. Developer: Hibernian
Insurance Company; builder: Walsh,
Maguire and O'Shea; architect: Group
design Partners.

Haig's Avenue
See **Newbridge Avenue.**

*Architect's drawing of front elevation of St Mary's
Church, Haddington Road.*

Haig's Lane
See **Lansdowne Road.**

Hallmarking
See **Assay Office.**

Halpin's Row
North Wall

Halpin's Pool
North Wall
Named after George Halpin who was

Inspector of Works to the Ballast Board. He was involved with the building of the North Wall, various lighthouses, the Richmond and Whitworth bridges and possibly the Corn Exchange on Burgh Quay.

Halston Street
From Mary's Lane to King Street North
St Michan's Church, built in 1817, facing onto Anne Street North, redesigned in 1891 by George Ashlin with a tower in granite facing onto Halston Street. In the entrance through the tower an inscription on the holy water font reads, 'from the chapel of St Mary's Lane 1705–1817. Re-erected 1893.' Fine plasterwork ceiling with long gallery. Green Street Court House faces the church, and there is a playground where the Newgate Prison stood. The presbytery stands to the right of the church.
See **Newgate Gaol.**

Hanover Lane
Francis Street to Bull Alley Street
A housing complex built in 1873.

Harcourt Road
From Harrington Street to Adelaide Road
Named after Simon, 1st Earl of Harcourt, Lord Lieutenant 1772–76.
A short street with towering office blocks. Montrose House was completed in 1981 and given a face lift in 1989, having remained empty all those years. Iveagh Court was completed in 1973 and also given a face lift in 1989. In between the two, Dodder House was built in 1979. The area continues to expand with additional office blocks.

Harcourt Street
From Harcourt Road to St Stephen's Green
Named after Simon, 1st Earl of Harcourt, Lord Lieutenant 1772–76.
Created about 1775 by John Hatch. Clonmell House was built 1778 for the Earl of Clonmell. It was later divided into two and the larger section housed Sir Hugh Lane's Municipal Gallery of Modern Art 1908–32. On the corner of Montague Street lived Sir Jonah Barrington. A temporary

railway station was opened in 1854 and, in February 1859, a railway station was built to a design of George Wilkinson for the Dublin and South Eastern Railway. He was the designer of many of the poor houses in Ireland and designed several other railway stations plus extensions to Broadstone* and Westland Row. The station and the railway line to Bray were closed on 1 January 1959. Notices at the time described the losses being incurred on the line and that £71,000 would be saved by its closure, and referred to the remoteness of the station from the city centre. It was auctioned to ACC Bank in June 1959 and is now a restaurant. The vaults now house a nightclub and the space where the platforms once were, together with the old turntable, are home to another nightclub. It remains an impressive gently curving street in spite of the fact that many of the houses have been replaced by office blocks with Georgian façades. The technical bureau and headquarters of the Garda Síochána (*see* police) are housed at Harcourt Court on the site of the High School, opened in 1870 and which moved to Rathgar in 1971.

Harcourt Terrace
From Adelaide Road to the Grand Canal
Built in the Regency style by Charles Joly, from 1831, whose family had first arrived in Ireland in 1769. First Lieutenant in the Volunteers, property owner with lands at Charlemont Place and St Stephen's Green, he lived in a house on the site of no. 6. The terrace was enclosed with railings and a gate which were removed when the Garda Station was built. Many of the houses have been restored, including the one-time impressive nos. 6–7 with four Ionic columns surmounted by a Greek-style frieze with colonnades supporting the double building. The fronts near the canal have been retained with modern flats built at the rear, including no. 11, the home of Sarah Purser the painter. Hilton Edwards and Micheál MacLiammóir, the theatre personalities, lived at no. 4. On 2 January 1901, the world premiére of George Russell's *Deirdre* took place in the garden of no. 5.

Hardwicke Place

From Temple Street to Hardwicke Street
Named after the 3rd Earl of Hardwicke,
Lord Lieutenant 1801–06.

Hardwicke Place terminates with St
George's Church in the centre. It was to
have been a Royal Circus, designed by
Francis Johnston, with Eccles Street* at the
other end, but this never materialised.
Today Hardwicke Street and Place have
been replaced by modern Corporation flats
built in 1954. Number 38, a free-standing
house, was occupied by the Sisters of St
Clare from 1752 until they moved to new
premises in Harold's Cross in 1803. The
Dun Emer Guild* was the last to occupy it,
and it is there, in 1914, Thomas
McDonagh, George Moore and Edward
Martyn founded their Irish Theatre
Movement productions.

Harold's Cross

The name is probably of Viking origin and
relates to a cross that stood near Terenure
Road. At one time a village 2¼ miles S.W.
from the General Post Office, it stretches
from the Grand Canal on the road to
Rathfarnham. The canal reached Dublin in
1759 but a connection from what is now
Suir Road to the Grand Canal harbour was
completed in 1790. The original road from
the city had to be altered to provide for the
building of Clanbrassil Bridge, named after
the second Earl of Clanbrassil. This was
demolished in 1936 and replaced with the
present Robert Emmet Bridge, named after
the patriot and United Irishman
(1778–1803) who was arrested on 25 August
1803 in a house in nearby Mount
Drummond Avenue.

Harold's Cross now occupies a wide area in
the centre of which is the park laid out by
the Rathmines Commissioners (see
Rathmines). The convent and school of the
Sisters of St Clare: the sisters came from
Hardwicke Place in 1803 and established
their convent and an orphanage. In 1926,
some businessmen purchased Buckley's
orchard and built a greyhound track.
Mount Jerome Cemetery* is to the right of
the park, beside which is the C of I parish

church which, when built in 1837, was run
by a Board of Trustees from St
Catherine's.* There was a need for a church
in the area to cater for the soldiers and
officers from Portobello Barracks, built in
1810–15. In 1903, the Representative
Church Body took over the ownership; it
was grouped with Holy Trinity Rathmines
in 1977 and ceased to be used for worship
in 2001. On Sunday, 9 February 2003, it
was consecrated as a Russian Orthodox
Church and is now known as St Peter and
St Paul's. On the same side is Our Lady's
Hospice, established in 1834 by the Irish
Sisters of Charity. The impressive RC
church to the left of the park, Our Lady of
the Rosary, was consecrated in 1938. Mount
Harold House was purchased in 1931 by
Canon Fleming, Parish Priest of
Rathmines, on the instructions of
Archbishop Edward Byrne. In 1935, the old
tin church from Foxrock parish was erected
on the site and Harold's Cross was declared
a new parish from 30 September that year.
It had been part of Rathmines parish since
1823.

The Passionist fathers' house, St Paul's
Retreat at Mount Argus, was consecrated
in 1863, and the adjoining church in 1878.
The Church of St Paul of the Cross has two
high square towers between which a
pediment supports the gilt statue of St
Michael the Archangel. An artificial lake
reflects the buildings. Part of the grounds
was sold for a housing development in
1989. The church became a parish church
in 1974. The granite (C of I) Hall, built in
1882, was sold in 1982 and is now used by a
firm of accountants. The area near the
canal, where there is an office complex and
Boyne Court, was an old distillery until the
end of the nineteenth century when it was
taken over by a Belgian, Le Brocquy, who
started an oil refinery. Also on the site was
the Greenmount Linen Mill, dating from
1832 and owned by Pims the drapers; in the
1920s it amalgamated with the Boyne
Linen Company in Drogheda to become
the Greenmount and Boyne Linen
Company.

At the head of the park, a tall cross with

interlacing design, erected in 1954, bears the inscription in Irish and English, 'This cross was erected by the surviving members of the fourth battalion Dublin Brigade IRA in memory of all who served with it since Easter 1916.'

Harrington Street
From South Circular Road to Harcourt Road
A short street of nineteenth-century houses, mostly in a good state of repair and others being restored. The impressive St Kevin's (RC) Church, within a railed garden, and the presbytery facing onto Heytesbury Street were designed by George Ashlin. The church was opened for public worship on 3 June 1872.

George Russell (AE, 1867–1935) the poet, painter and mystic, attended Power's School at no. 3. The Methodist Female Orphan School at 36 and 37, funded by a legacy of Solomon Walker, silk manufacturer, at Bridge Street, who died after being thrown from a horse, and who left £2,150 for maintaining, educating, clothing and apprenticing destitute Protestant female orphan children, not necessarily of Methodist parents. The school opened in Whitefriar Street and moved to Harrington Street in 1852. it moved to Northbrook Road in 1938 and closed in 1943

Harry Street
In 1756, Harry Street also included what is now Balfe Street. Up to recently no. 4 housed the Weights and Measures Department of Dublin Corporation. Dublin City Council transferred the responsibility of this department to FORFÁS, the National Policy and Advisory Board for enterprise, trade, science, technology and innovation, Wilton Place. The premises are at present occupied by a wine merchant but the memorabilia of the department are on loan at no. 4 and may be inspected there.

In 1877, the Weights and Measures Department was housed in unsuitable premises in Fishamble Street. A new site was sought which would be convenient to the Lord Mayor's Court so that, 'the Lord Mayor as sole clerk of the market has the whole department of Weights and Measures under his control'. A tenement was purchased and the new building was opened to the public on 8 December 1880 by the Lord Mayor, E. Dwyer Grey.

By the end of the eighteenth century, deputy clerks of the market were in operation and the 1834 Weights and Measures Act ordered the appointment of inspectors of weights and measures. In Dublin, the existing clerks of the markets were appointed inspectors,, and to the present day, weights and measures legislation has been enforced by the Inspector of Weights and Measures. Until 1877, the Lord Mayor with his deputies toured the city, inspecting trading premises, and confiscated and broke fraudulent scales.

Hugh Tarpey was the last Lord Mayor to perform this duty.

McDaid's public house is on the site of a former city morgue and later a Moravian church which moved to Kevin Street Lower about 1760. Brendan Behan, Patrick Kavanagh and Brian O'Nolan (Myles na gCopaleen) were frequent visitors in the 1950s.

Hatch Street
From Harcourt Street to Leeson Street
Possibly from John Hatch, a barrister and director of the Royal Canal Company who resided in Harcourt Street. In 1759, five plots of land were leased to John Hatch on the corner of the street at Leeson Street. Hatch Street was built about 1810.

The foundation stone of St Matthias's Church was laid on 24 February 1842 and a square named Wellington Square was to be laid out beside it. The square came to nothing and part of it was included in the church grounds while the railway company bought the remainder in 1850. St Matthias's was demolished in 1952. University Hall of Residence, known as Hatch Hall, belonging to the Jesuits, was designed in 1911 by William Powell, with an internal courtyard and a small chapel with five altar windows by Evie Hone. Opened in 1913, and closed in 2004 after 91 years offering accommodation to male students. The decision to close was a result of the reducing number and increased age of the members of the order, together with financial pressures. The Court Laundry on the corner of Harcourt Street had planning permission for an office block since 1966. This opened in 1972 and was occupied by the Agriculture Credit Corporation until the late twentieth century when the building was redesigned with a new glass frontage and named Styne House. The old Gilbey bonded warehouse now has two nightclubs. Shell House, an office block, was completed in 1969.

Hawkins Street

In 1663, Alderman William Hawkins built a sea wall from the present Townsend Street to Burgh Quay, enclosing the River Liffey and thus encouraging speculators to build on reclaimed land in the area. The Dublin Society had its headquarters in the street 1796–1814. The Mendicity Institution, founded in 1818 to repress as far as possible obtrusive street beggary and to relieve pressing casual want in our city, used the same building until 1820 when it was taken over by the Theatre Royal.* This building was demolished by November 1962 and an office block, Hawkins House, with 122,000 square feet of office space, was erected on the site to a design of Sir Thomas Bennett. It is the headquarters of the Department of Health and Children.

Helix Centre for the Performing Arts

Dublin City University, Collins Avenue
Designed by Andrzej Wejchert and opened in 2002.

Its location was chosen to act as an intermediary between the academic world and the general public but giving easy access to both students and the community. The entrance to the foyer with its glass roof has a series of sweeping staircases which lead to the three main auditoria: the Aula Maxima/concert hall on two levels, with a seating capacity of

1,250. It has a large stage with balconies behind, suitable for choirs or extra seating for the public. The seating at ground-floor level is removable, making the hall available for large receptions. A kitchen is situated off the stage for use if catering is required. The main theatre, with a seating capacity of 450, is based on a proscenium arch theatre on two levels with clear visibility from all areas. There is an orchestral pit which may be closed over to give additional stage area or enabling this front space to be used for lectures. It is also designed for cinema use with a projection room. The studio theatre sits 150 and has retractable seating. It may be used for small theatre productions and has a wide variety of uses. There is an underground car park with pedestrian access undercover to the centre.

Hell

Nothing remains of a small gated laneway which bore this arresting title. It was a partially arched passage which led from Christchurch Lane to an open space called Christchurch Yard. In 1629, there is mention of a cellar called Hell. Many wine merchants had their cellars in the neighbourhood. During its latter years, it was occupied chiefly by trunk makers and toy makers who also sold fireworks. The name was in common usage: nineteenth-century advertisements offer lettings of furnished apartments in Hell. When Fishamble Street and the adjacent area was widened, the passage disappeared.

Hell Fire Club

Founded by Richard Parsons, the 1st Earl of Rosse, in 1735, in the Eagle Tavern, Cork Hill. He was described as having 'an infinite fund of wit, great spirits and liberal heart; was fond of all the vices which the beau monde call pleasures, and by those means first impaired his fortune as much as he possibly could do; and finally, his health beyond repair.' The club also used a stone building on the top of Montpelier Hill in the Dublin mountains. This had been built by William Conolly, elected speaker of the

Irish Parliament in 1727, probably as a hunting lodge. The building remains standing although all the cut stone has disappeared.

Hendrick Street
From Blackhall Place to Queen Street
Named after its builder, William Hendrick, 1773–74.
General housing, at one time a Methodist church, and at nos. 16–17 the premises of Judd Brothers, the hide and sheep skin tanners who recently ceased business.

Henrietta Street
Off Bolton Street
From Henrietta, wife of Charles II, Duke of Grafton, Lord Lieutenant.
Originally portion of the property of the Cistercian Abbey of St Mary which was surrendered in 1537 to Henry VIII and eventually passed to Robert Piphoe. After the death of Piphoe's widow in 1669, a portion was purchased by Sir Richard Reynell whose son, Sir Thomas, sold it in 1721 to Luke Gardiner MP, Vice-Treasurer

of Ireland. Work would appear to have commenced almost immediately on the construction of houses, the first three being on the site of the present King's Inns Library. These were leased on 5 March 1724 to Hugh Boulter, Archbishop of Armagh, who built a mansion for himself on the site of the three houses. In the lease, the street is referred to as 'a new street lately set out and called or intended to be called Henrietta Street near Bolton Street alias Drumcondra Lane'. It became a fashionable residential street in the eighteenth century.

After the site of the King's Inns at Inns Quay was acquired for the erection of the new Four Courts, the Honorable Society of the King's Inns eventually purchased the grounds from Lord Mountjoy in 1794. The foundation stone was laid on 1 August 1795. Further ground was purchased in 1802 from the Dean and Chapter of Christ Church and additional buildings were commenced. These were taken over and finished in 1817 by the government to house part of the public records and are now the Registry of Deeds. The buildings

Henrietta Street. King's Inns foundation stone laid 1 August 1795. Designed by James Gandon and Henry Aaron Baker.

Henry Street. Bill head dated 1930 from Arnott & Co. Ltd.

designed by James Gandon and his pupil, Henry Aaron Baker, back onto the street and face Constitution Hill. The library, built in 1827, is by Frederick Darley. Numbers 8, 9 and 10 now house the convent of the Sisters of Charity of St Vincent de Paul. No. 10, Mountjoy House, was built in 1730 for Luke Gardiner MP.

Henry Street
From O'Connell Street to Mary Street
Named after Viscount Henry Moore, Earl of Drogheda. Part of the lands of St Mary's Abbey granted to James Fitzgerald, Earl of Desmond, after the dissolution of the Irish monasteries in 1537 and purchased by Moore in 1614. The estate was sold 100 years later to Luke Gardiner, whose family was to become one of the largest developers in the city. The street began to develop in the 1760s, with a variety of business and retail outlets. Today a busy shopping area and pedestrian zone following complete tiling of the street in the 1980s. Numbers 9–15 house the firm of Arnott and Company, wholesale and retail drapers, upholsterers and carpet warehouse, named after John Arnott (1814–98), a Scot, who, in 1848, invested £6,000 in an existing store, Cannock and White, founded in Henry Street in 1843. The name was changed to Arnott, John and Co. in 1865. Numbers 11–15 of the original block of buildings,

extending from Prince's Street to Henry Street, were totally destroyed by fire on 4 May 1894. According to a report in the *Evening Mail* that evening, the fire was so intense that about 500 soldiers from Ship Street Barracks were called in to help the firemen. The premises were quickly rebuilt to a design of George Beater. The present building was designed by architect Geoffrey Henry in 1958, and in 1993 a new octagonal glass dome was added to brighten the store. In 2004, Arnotts expanded by buying four premises from the Royal Sun Alliance, occupied by HMV, Boots, Clinton Cards and Extrovert. They also purchased the *Irish Independent* and *Evening Herald* buildings on Middle Abbey Street. Roches Stores was redeveloped in 2004 to a design of Newenham Mulligan Architects and won an RIAI award; it now incorporates the Spanish fashion house Zara and other concessionaires.
***See also* Moore Street, Earl Street, Drogheda Street.**

Herbert Street
From Lower Baggot Street to Mount Street Crescent
Named after the Rt Hon. Sidney Herbert, second son of the 11th Earl of Pembroke. Built about 1830. Impressive red-brick houses built in pairs. Sir Charles Villiers Stanford (1852–1924), the composer, was

born at no. 2 on 30 September 1852. He was knighted in 1902 and his ashes are buried in Westminster Abbey. The Barrett Cheshire Home is at no. 21.

Heuston Station
See **Kingsbridge Station.**

Heytesbury Street
From South Circular Road to New Street
Name comes from the first Baron Heytesbury (1779–1860), Lord Lieutenant (1844–46).
Built and developed as an artery to join Portobello Harbour about 1820. The area of assorted red-brick houses bordering the Meath Hospital, South Circular Road and Clanbrassil Street was constructed in the 1840s through to the 1880s by three property developers, Sir John Arnott, James Fitzgerald Lombard and Edward McMahon, and three streets were called after their several names. Other streets in the complex include Carlisle, Emor and Emorville Avenue. In the 1860/70s, there was a building boom when houses were built by speculators for the purpose of renting, which gave them a lucrative return on their investment
See also **Emorville Avenue, Pleasants Street, Portobello Gardens.**

Hibernian Marine School
Sir John Rogerson's Quay
In 1766, a number of benevolent gentlemen including the banker, David La Touche, founded the Hibernian Marine Nursery at Ringsend for the education of orphans and children of Protestant seamen in distressed circumstances. In 1767, twenty pupils were admitted and, in 1770, a school was erected on Sir John Rogerson's Quay, at a cost of £6,600, to a design of Thomas Cooley. James Malton, the architectural draftsman who in 1791 completed a set of drawings of Dublin, attributes the design to Thomas Ivory. The school consisted of a main building with two wings and housed about 180 boys between the ages of nine and fourteen, who received an education that qualified them

for the British Navy or Mercantile Marine. The interior was damaged by fire in 1872. The school moved later to Seafield Avenue, Clontarf, and in the 1960s amalgamated with Mountjoy, Bertrand and Rutland schools to become Mount Temple Comprehensive. In 1875, Sir Richard Martin, a timber merchant, moved to Sir John Rogerson's Quay and occupied the out-offices of the old school until about 1920. The building was occupied by the B+I and then by an ice and cold-storage firm. It was demolished in 1979.

High Street
From Christchurch Place to Cornmarket
As the name implies, High Street was the principal street in the medieval period. In 1962 and 1963, archaeological investigations were carried out on a plot bordering High Street, Nicholas Street and Back Lane. The quantity and quality of the objects discovered were justification for the excavation of a larger site bordering High Street. Begun in 1967, it was completed by 1972. Results showed that the original ground surface lay 14 feet beneath the present street level and that the earliest occupation of this area occurred in Viking times. Articles recovered include brooches decorated in the tenth century and deer antlers used by the Vikings in comb making. An amount of leather was also recovered, including over 1,000 soles of shoes of Viking origin. The houses were built using the post and wattle technique: posts were hammered into the ground and horizontal layers of rods of hazel, ash and elm were woven in basketry to form the walls. In the sixteenth and seventeenth centuries, the high cross of the city stood at the junction of Skinners' Row. It was here that public proclamations were read, including papal bulls and sentences of excommunication. Persons convicted of certain crimes were also obliged to stand in a penitential manner, barefoot before the cross.
Two Norse parish churches stand at either end of the street, St Michael's* whose tower is incorporated in the disused synod hall,

and St Audoen's* with its transitional doorway dating from 1190. St Audoen's (RC) Church,* erected in 1841–47, was one of the last churches to be built in the classical tradition.

In 1668, the Post Office had a large timber house in the street with a garden plot reaching to Back Lane.* Following the death of Wolfe Tone on Sunday, 11 November 1798, Lord Castlereagh released the body to friends on the condition 'that no assemblage of people shall be permitted and that it be interred in the most private manner'. Tone's body was taken on 20 November to 52 High Street where his parents were living in reduced circumstances. He was buried in the family grave at Bodenstown the next day.

In 1989, phase one of an urban renewal development office block named Christchurch Square was opened, consisting of red-brick buildings on granite bases, with a clock tower designed by Horan, Cotter and Associates for Hillview Securities Limited. At the Three Candlesticks (1730–50) was a thriving printing and booksellers, Colm O'Lochlainn (1892–1972) would adopt the title when he opened his printing works, specialising in Irish printing types, in 1926.
See **Market Cross, Sign of the Three Candles.**

Hill Street
From Parnell Street to Temple Street
Formerly Temple Street Lower, but because of bad repute resulting in difficulty getting suitable lettings, the Corporation changed the name in 1887. All that remains is the tower of St George's Church,* founded in 1714, the main building being demolished in 1894. The graveyard is now a supervised playground.

Hoey's Court
From Werburgh Street to the Castle Steps
Sir John Hoey, serjeant at arms (died 1664), came from England in 1599 with Charles Blount, Lord Mountjoy. Lived at Dunganstown, Co. Wicklow, and became MP for Naas. On a portion of the site of Austin's Lane and the site of Sir James

Ware's house, he erected a series of houses, in one of which lived a Parsons Hoey in the early 1800s. Jonathan Swift was born on 30 November 1667 at the house of his uncle, Counsellor Godwin Swift, no. 7 Hoey's Court. Today all that remains is a plaque at the foot of the steps, commemorating Swift's birthplace.
See **Cole's Alley.**

Hog Hill
The name comes from the Blessed Virgin Mary del Hogges. In 1728, it was the western end of St Andrew Street* and, by 1756, the whole street was known as Hog Hill. Renamed St Andrew Street 1776.

Holles Street
From Merrion Square to Erne Street
Named after Denzille Holles, Earl of Clare. Part of the Fitzwilliam and Pembroke Estates.
The South Dublin Lying-in Hospital, founded on 17 March 1894 and grant aided by the RC Archbishop of Dublin in 1894, received a Royal Charter in 1903 and was renamed the National Maternity Hospital. It occupies most of the street.
See **National Maternity Hospital.**

Home's Hotel
18, 19, 20, Usher's Quay
In 1826, George Home, a Scotsman, built a 200-room hotel and cloth warehouse known as the Wellesley Market. By 1840, the large Doric-column porticoed hotel had become a weaving manufactory run by the White Quakers. That lasted only a few years. In 1848, it had become the premises of James Ganly, Auctioneers. The hotel was demolished in 1977 when Ganly's moved to new premises.
See **Royal Arcade.**

Hospital of St John the Baptist
This was on the site of John's Lane distillery and the present Church of St John the Baptist and St Augustine. It was in the care of a religious community of hospitallers who followed the rule of St Augustine. They wore a red cross on their

habit. It was the only hospital in Dublin, and Anglo-Norman families supported it. Reginald Hugo Barnewall (*see* Terenure) gave 60 acres to the hospital on ground known as St John's Leas opposite Mount Argus between the Swan and Poddle rivers AD 1250.

House of Industry
Channel Row
The workhouse in James's Street, originally built to house the vagabond or sturdy beggar, had been transformed by 1729 into a foundling hospital for unwanted children. On 8 November 1773, a house of industry was opened. According to Watson's *Almanack*, it was 'supported hitherto by parochial collections made from house to house, parliamentary aid, and by profits arising from the labour of the poor. There are commodious wards set apart for the aged and infirm, a large hospital for the sick remote from the habitations of the healthy and a few cells for lunaticks. Admitted from November 1779 to November 1780, 1436: compelled 457, total 2,716'. There were three categories of inmate: those who were destitute and entered voluntarily, fettered lunatics from the Bridewell and a third lot who were rounded up at night by the beadles touring in their black cart. Many a vicious battle took place with those wishing to avoid compulsory internment. A soup kitchen was opened in 1826 where one quart of nutritive soup and twelve ounces of wheaten bread were distributed daily to upwards of 300 convalescent fever patients discharged from the hospitals. The Talbot dispensary was opened on 24 April 1820 for the relief of the sick poor of the north-west district: bounded east by Capel Street, Bolton Street and Dorset Street; south by the river; north by the Circular Road. Those who were unable to appear at the dispensary were visited at their own residences. At certain times, outsiders were fed, provided that they could produce a certificate to show that they were starving. They were given a herring, some bread and a pint of beer.

The house eventually became part of the St Laurence's Hospital complex and the Morning Star Hostel took over some of the premises.
See **Workhouse, James's Street.**

Howth Castle
Howth, Co. Dublin
Howth Castle is built into the shelter of Howth Hill. It is the seat of the St Lawrence family which has held it for almost 800 years. A legend of Granuaile (or Grace O'Malley, the pirate queen) states that she put into Howth Harbour and while provisions were being loaded on board her ships, she knocked on the gates of the Castle and was refused hospitality. She allegedly snatched the infant son and

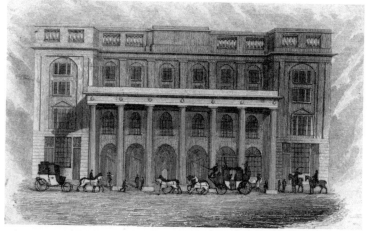

Home's Hotel, Usher's Quay, c. 1830.

Howth Harbour c. 1905.

heir to the title and took him to Co. Mayo. The child was returned on condition that the gates would always remain open at meal times. The Castle was rebuilt in 1738. Thomas was created Lord Howth in 1748, and Viscount St Lawrence and 1st Earl of Howth in 1767 after a brilliant political career. Sir Edwin Lutyens designed the western tower, a loggia, a Roman Catholic church, and enlarged the dining room.

Howth Summit and Village

Howth Head is one of the most striking features of north Dublin's coastline. Its rounded contours rising from the sea and the low outline of the isthmus give it the appearance of an island. The history and archaeology of Howth peninsula have been studied in numerous surveys and many of the areas are national monuments; a great many of these are now within An Taisce property, including Ireland's Eye with a lease from Mr Gaisford St Lawrence.

Ireland's Eye is about 1¼ miles from the harbour of Howth and once belonged to the Archbishop of Dublin. The landing bay is at Carrigeen Bay on the western side. The island contains approximately 58 acres of wild rocky mountain sheep pasture. The only buildings are a Martello tower* and the ruins of a church.

The ancient name of Howth was *Beann Étair*. There are many legends attached to the name. One of them claims that the name was derived from the Firbolgs who succeeded the Parthalonians. The wife of one of the five chieftains was named Étar and was supposed to have died on *Beann Étair*.

In 1800, Howth became the official mail-packet station and having a safe harbour was of vital importance. In 1807, the building of the harbour commenced. There was much disagreement on the positioning of the haven. In 1809, when the works had been in progress for eighteen months under the direction of Mr Rennie, the engineer, the Rev. Mr Dawson called the work a mockery of harbour making and foretold that the harbour would be a sand trap. The result was such a terrible failure that the construction of Dún Laoghaire harbour was immediately begun. About £350,000 was spent on Howth harbour which enclosed an area of 52 acres. When excavations were being carried out at the Baily lighthouse before building the engine rooms, an extensive kitchen midden was discovered at the base of the cliff. In the early Christian era, a monarch of Ireland named Criomhthan came to Howth on the site where the Baily lighthouse now stands, and, according to tradition, his bones lie buried in a valley near the Howth Golf Club between Shielmartin and Dunhill ridge, an area of low heather.

An Taisce now controls approximately 300 acres with pleasant walks to the summit, Lighthouse Road, the Hut Lane and Balscadden Road. Howth contains a fishing village, a large marina, some good restaurants, a hotel, and several churches of various denominations. Howth Golf Club is also situated on the peninsula. Howth Castle,* a cemetery, and part of the area around Carrickbrack and adjoining roads contain quality residential housing.

On 31 May 1973, Dublin Corporation ordered that burials should be wholly discontinued in the old Abbey burial ground.

In 1999, the Cosgrave Group purchased the Howth Lodge Hotel which stood on an elevated site with views of Ireland's Eye and Lambay Island and, in 2004, opened 54 luxury apartments, designed by architects Conroy Crowe Kelly, on the site.

Huguenots

The origins of the term *huguenot* remain obscure. Down through the centuries, various explanations have been offered, but none are conclusive. The word is known to have existed as a French surname in the fourteenth and fifteenth centuries. Some sources connect the term with King Huguet's gate at Tours which was a local meeting place for Protestants, while others suggest that huguenot came from the German *Eidgenossen* suggesting people bound by oath; still others maintain that the Huguenots were disciples of a French King Hugues Capet who had died nearly 600 years earlier. Many other explanations of the term exist, some more plausible than others, and, whatever the correct explanation, the word was in common use in the 1560s and was used to describe French-speaking Protestants—or, more precisely, Calvinists.

From 1661, after Louis XIV became King, Huguenot privileges were steadily eroded: by 1679, it was forbidden for midwives to attend at confinements; washerwomen could no longer take their places at river banks; education in Huguenot schools was prohibited; doctors and lawyers could no longer practice and most administrative jobs were closed to Huguenots. Louis could no longer tolerate the idea of a state within a state, which these people represented, and the persecution culminated in the Revocation of the Edict of Nantes on 22 October 1685. The reason he gave was that there were insufficient numbers of Huguenots within the state to warrant the privileges granted to them.

From 1630 on, there are records of Huguenots settling in Ireland. Every new wave of persecution brought hundreds across the Channel, but the greatest influxes were in 1662 and from 1686 onwards. There are also records of French Protestants fleeing from persecution under Catherine de Medici during the second half of the sixteenth century.

The notion that there was a universal welcome and support given to the Huguenots by all levels of Irish and English Protestant society is false. In England, the Privy Council, seeing the considerable advantages to be gleaned by the emerging industries from Huguenot skills, and the likelihood of increased European trading contacts through their persecuted fellow Protestants, actively made provision in legislative terms for their welcome. But in practice it was somewhat different. The Privy Council constantly had to counteract resistance from local corporations, guilds of jealous artisans and craftsmen who resented an influx of foreigners. Such also was the case in Ireland. They were seen as aliens and regarded with suspicion and downright hostility at times by the local tradesmen who feared the effects of imported labour on their livelihood. In 1682, there was an instance in Dublin, just one of many, when the Earl of Arran called on the King's guard to disperse a May Day riot of some 300 people who had come together especially to attack the refugees.

The feeling of security that Huguenots felt by 1686 was undermined a year later when King James appointed his supporter, the Roman Catholic Richard Talbot, Earl of Tyrconnell, to the Lord Lieutenantship. Under his instructions, the military made several search-and-seize forays in Dublin for horses and arms, no doubt reviving memories of the French dragonnades. Fears of persecution mounted pending the arrival in Ireland of the now-deposed James II from France and, by 1688, the Huguenots fully supported William of Orange.

In 1690, at the Battle of the Boyne, the Huguenot infantry were the first of the Williamites to cross the river at Oldbridge where Schomberg was killed. His son, Meinhard, led the diversionary force that attacked at Rossnaree.

Following the Treaty of Limerick, the Huguenot regiments returned to France and remained in service until the Peace of Ryswick, when the army was reduced and the French returned to Ireland where five regiments were disbanded in 1699.

Those who stayed in Ireland were given pensions, various offices and grants of forfeited lands. Marshall Schomberg's son, Meinhard, was made Duke of Leinster, while the Marquis de Rivigny was created Earl of Galway and given the 36,000-acre Portarlington estate where he settled many of his ex-officers.

It is almost impossible to state how many men from these disbanded regiments came to live in Dublin. Under Irish law, it was impossible for the Huguenots to worship in their own tradition of non-conformism and the register of the French Conformed Churches in the city contains the names of 165 officers who had permanent residence, many of them bringing their wives and families. Only the conformists enjoyed the freedom of public worship. Approaches to both Protestant and Roman Catholic administrations on freedom of worship had met with blank refusal. It was under James II and the Irish parliament that liberty of worship was granted, simply because James was intent on re-establishing freedom of worship for Roman Catholics, but it was not really until 1692 that full freedom to worship in their own tradition was granted to the Huguenots. By the first quarter of the eighteenth century, the Huguenot community in Dublin was firmly established and contributed much to both the business and cultural life of the city. A weaving industry was founded in the Liberties of St Patrick and the Earl of Meath, and many of the street names that are extant to the present day, such as

Pimlico and Spitalfields, prove that many of these refugees had first settled in London before travelling on to Ireland. A Weavers' Guild Hall which was in existence by 1682 was replaced by a more impressive structure in the Lower Coombe in 1745, £200 being advanced for this purpose by the then Master of the Guild, James Digges La Touche.

There appears to have been a silk and poplin weaving industry in Dublin by the time that David La Touche joined the Guild of Weavers in Dublin in 1701. By 1717, he was prominent in business affairs and eventually, with another weaver, Nathaniel Kane, founded the La Touche Bank. In 1752, a further influx of Protestants arrived in Dublin from France. Many of these were absorbed into the weaving industry, but many of them remained unemployed, as it was a time when the industry was beginning to decline, hampered with strikes, and the eventual withdrawal of the Bounties (duties levied on certain goods imported from England) in 1786 sounded the death knell for the industry. What was once a prosperous locality, the Coombe, had become one of the poorest slums in Dublin by the nineteenth century.

The gold and silver trades were also enriched by a great many immigrant craftsmen who brought new skills and current European designs to an already well established trade. The records of the Company of Goldsmiths are filled with the names of Huguenot apprentices and their masters. The D'Olier family came from Toulouse. Isaac entered the service of William of Orange and settled in Dublin. His son and grandson, both named Isaac, were goldsmiths. Jeremiah D'Olier, his great-grandson, also a goldsmith, became one of the founders and governors of the Bank of Ireland. His name is perpetuated in a street named after him. Huguenots were also actively involved as shop merchants, pewterers, wine and woollen merchants and sugar refiners. They seemed, on the whole, to have had a strong business acumen and took advantage of

any opportunity that was offered. Their contribution is written into the success of Dublin as a trading city.

As a community, they enriched the cultural life of the city. Elias Bouhéreau was the first public librarian of the library founded by Archbishop Narcissus Marsh beside St Patrick's Cathedral. On his death, he left his own important collection of books to the library. Huguenot names appear in the realms of music, painting and the theatre. By the end of the eighteenth century, the colony as a separate unit had ceased to exist.

Huguenot Cemetery
Merrion Row

In 1693, lot number 10 fronting onto St Stephen's Green and Baggot Rath* was opened as a Huguenot Cemetery. It was originally leased to Peter Ward, brewer, who sold his interest for £16. Probably as many as 600 corpses were buried there up to 1901 when the last interment took place. The present gateway, which may have come from the Chapel in Lucy Lane,* together with the wall and railings, was taken back four feet by Dublin Corporation in 1936. The memorial porch in the rere wall was erected by the Huguenot Society in 1880.

The graveyard now belongs to the French Huguenot Fund which restored it in 1988 through a grant from the French Ministry of Foreign Affairs in association with FÁS. The carved Roman lettering HUGHENOT on the entrance has the name misspelled.

Huguenot Cemetery
Peter Street

A new cemetery was opened in 1711 beside the newly completed Chapel of St Peter's* in Peter Street. It closed in 1879 when the site was acquired by Jacob's Biscuit Factory. In 1966, the remains were re-interred in Mount Jerome in a plot with a kerbstone bearing their names.

Huguenot Chapel
Lucy Lane

A small chapel occupied by the Jesuits was forfeited to the crown and a custodial grant given to Sir Charles Meredith on 30 July 1697. Shortly afterwards, a Huguenot congregation was established there. It was known as the French Church of the Inns. It was sold to the Presbyterian congregation of Skinners' Row in 1773 and demolished in 1825.

Huguenot Chapel of St Brigide's

In 1693, a group of Huguenots who preferred the Calvinist liturgy rented a private house in Wood Street off Bride Street. They were self-supporting as no grants were forthcoming from the State. Freedom of worship was granted to them in 1692 on the condition that their services were conducted in the French language. In 1711, they removed to Peter Street.
See also **Huguenot Chapel of St Peter's.**

Huguenot Chapel of St Mary

(St Patrick's Cathedral)
The Lady Chapel in St Patrick's Cathedral was used by the Huguenots 1665–1817 on condition of their being bound by the discipline and canons of the Church of Ireland.

Huguenot Chapel of St Mary (St Mary's Abbey)

Because of an expanding congregation, a chapel of ease was established in the crypt of St Mary's Abbey* in 1701 at Meeting House Lane, to relieve the crowding in the Lady Chapel in St Patrick's Cathedral. From 1704 to 1716, the congregation had separate ministers when the two congregations reunited until the chapel closed in 1740.

Huguenot Chapel of St Peter's

A new chapel was completed in 1711 in Peter Street after a problem arose with the St Brigide's congregation and their lease in Wood Street. Worship continued until 1814. Unsuccessful attempts were made to reopen it in 1815 and 1828. It was demolished in 1840.
See also **Huguenot Chapel of St Brigide's.**

Hume Street

From Ely Place to St Stephen's Green
Named after Sir Gustavus Hume MP who belonged to the Fermanagh gentry and whose daughter married Nicholas Loftus, Earl of Ely. Their houses, Ely Lodge and Castle Hume, are near Enniskillen. Hume was responsible for bringing the German-born architect Richard Cassels from London to Dublin in 1727 to design Castle Hume. Cassels was to develop a large practice in Ireland. Hume Street, like Ely Place, was laid out in 1770 on part of the Blue Coat Estate. In 1971, two properties belonging to the state were sold at auction for £86,000 to the Green Property Company which already owned houses at the other side of the street. These were demolished and two office blocks now mark the entrance. The City of Dublin Skin and Cancer Hospital, founded in 1911, occupies part of the street.

I

Independent News and Media
See **Irish Independent.**

Infirmary Road (1886)
Named after the Military Infirmary in the adjoining Phoenix Park which was designed by Gandon and executed by W. Gibson, architect to the Board of Works. The area known as Parkgate is now the main offices of the Department of Defence, including the Minister's Office and the Secretary General's Office. The road was built by the Dublin Artisans' Dwellings Company, together with the side streets, Aberdeen Street and Terrace. The entire complex of houses was opened by John Gordon, Earl of Aberdeen, Lord Lieutenant 1886–91.

Institute for Industrial Research and Standards
Glasnevin
Founded in 1946 to promote the application of science and technology in industry. Reconstituted in 1961, it is also responsible for drawing up standard specifications. The board is appointed by the Minister of State for Science and Technology. On 1 January 1988, the Institute merged with the National Board for Science and Technology to form Eolas. *See also* **Eolas.**

International Financial Services Centre
Custom House Docks
This was a project undertaken by the Irish Government in 1987, with European Community approval, to generate employment and prevent educated young people and financial experts from leaving the country. The entire thinking behind the project was to create employment. To encourage investors, certain institutions would qualify for a 10 per cent tax rate, 200 per cent tax deduction for ten years for rents paid for properties in the IFSC, 100 per cent deduction for the capital cost of properties purchased, and ten years' exemption from local authority rates. Those benefiting include banking services, financing activities, insurance and the re-insurance industry. The area originally covered an eleven-hectare site at the west end of the Dublin Docklands Development Authority* but continues to expand. Among the first buildings were the West building, 100,000 square feet, sold to Allied Irish Banks for a figure in the region of £28 million, the North building with 106,500 square feet sold to the Bank of Ireland for approximately £31 million. The similar-type South building, but having 109,200 square feet, has general occupancy as has the IFSC centre building of eight storeys with 137,000 square feet. There are over 380 business firms employing more than 14,000 people in the IFSC. After eighteen years, the net value of funds managed amounts to over US $430 billion.
In January 2001, the IFSC took over a conserved warehouse building, Stack A, from the Custom House Docks Development Company. Built in 1821 and designed by John Rennie to house wine and tobacco, these 15,000 square metres of accommodation were completely restored

and refurbished at a cost of €40 million in 2003. On 22 October 1856, a vast banquet was held in this building to celebrate Irish regiments returning from the Crimean war, when 3,000 people attended, it being the only building large enough to hold such a large gathering in the city. Also in 2001, two further storeys were added on to the Commons Street car-park building, giving an extra 5,000 square metres of offices. £300,000 was invested in the building, together with serviced pontoons in George's dock for trading boats with restaurants and other facilities in the hope that this would add to the attractions of the IFSC. In March that year, the four-star Clarion Hotel opened on Excise Walk, North Wall. This 147-bed hotel brings the total bed space provision in the IFSC to 386. A year later, in 2002, the Authority commissioned a €1.2 million refurbishment of the arches adjoining Connolly Central Station at Harbourmaster Place, providing one unit of 70 square metres and a larger one of 1,000 square metres which houses a sports bar/restaurant. The Clarion Quay residential development, a joint venture between the Authority and the Campshire Partnership, built three block towers towards the river and a social housing block at Mayor Street, providing in total 184 new apartments. This was awarded the RIAI Best Housing project in 2003 for its architects, Urban Projects. The Mayor Street project was continued along the demolished Sheriff Street flats, the area being renamed Custom House Square, with 580 apartments in eight attractive blocks, having a landscaped area backing onto three-storey houses built for the previous occupants of the Sheriff Street flats. A further development by Chester Bridge Development on Mayor Street, comprising 49 apartments and 2,005 square metres of shops and bar/restaurants, was completed at the end of 2002. Phases 1 and 2 of the IFSC are complete. This includes 100,000 square metres of offices, 1,100 apartments, 3,000 square metres of retail and restaurants, two hotels and a new university of 4,000 students, the National College of Ireland, covering 21,000 square metres with 162 permanent student residences and 124 temporary residences. *See* **Ballast Board, Dublin Dockland Development Authority, Dublin Port, Quays North Wall Quay** *and* **Custom House Quay.**

Irish Architectural Archive
44 and 45 Merrion Square
Incorporated as a company limited by guarantee in 1976, it houses a collection of photographs, drawings and documentation of Irish architectural interest, including manuscripts and books. Recognised as a starting point for anyone seeking information on any Irish building of note. Originally in no. 73, the Archive re-located in 2004 to nos. 44 and 45, which were redesigned by the Office of Public Works, with Patrick Brock and Sons, main contractor. Open to the public.

Irish Film Centre
See **Film Institute of Ireland.**

Irish Independent
Originally *Irish Daily Independent*, founded by Charles Stewart Parnell, with first issue appearing 18 December 1891, shortly after his death. It became the *Irish Independent* in 1905, five years after it had merged with the *Daily Nation*, owned by a prominent businessman and anti-union activist, William Martin Murphy, who was also the proprietor of the *Irish Catholic*, the first halfpenny daily journal. A sister newspaper, the *Evening Herald*, commenced publication in 1891 from the same offices as the *Independent* in Middle Abbey Street. In 2001, the paper moved to Independent House, designed by Robinson Keefe Devane at Citywest Business Campus. Another paper of the same name as the *Evening Herald* was published between 1805 and 1814, when it became the *Sentinel*. It closed a year later in 1815.

Irish Industrial Exhibition 1853
See **Great Industrial Exhibition 1853.**

Irish International Exhibition 1907

A guaranteed fund of over £150,000 was raised and it was built on a site of 52 acres with the entrance at Ballsbridge. The large central industrial hall covered over two acres, consisting of a central octagonal court surmounted by a dome 80 feet in diameter and surrounded by a corridor from which four radial buildings, each measuring 164 feet by 80 feet, housed Irish industries, a dairy and art gallery. There was a pavilion for British, colonial and foreign exhibits. Also electricity and machinery annexes. King Edward VII visited the Exhibition which was located in Herbert Park.
See also **Dublin International Exhibition 1865** *and* **Great Industrial Exhibition 1853.**

Irish Museum of Modern Art (IMMA)
See **Royal Hospital, Kilmainham.**

Irish Press

Founded on 5 September 1931 by the politician Eamon de Valera, leader of Fianna Fáil and later President of the Republic of Ireland, as a republican daily paper. De Valera travelled twice to America in 1928 and 1929 to raise funds for its launch. It ceased publication on 25 May 1995. The company also published the *Sunday Press*, founded in 1949, and the *Evening Press*, founded in September 1954.

Irish Times

Daily newspaper founded by Major Laurence E. Knox in 1859. Its core of readership at one time was among the Protestant middle and upper classes and it had been described as 'that jaundiced journal of West Britonism'; it was Ireland's first daily penny paper. On Knox's death, in 1873, it was bought by the industrialist John Arnott and, in 1974, a trust company was founded to control the paper. It has changed considerably over the years, with a large readership, and is known for its liberal views and coverage of international events. Geraldine Kennedy, its first woman editor, was appointed in 2002.

Irish Worker

A weekly newspaper founded in May 1911 by James Larkin (1876–1947), the socialist, trade unionist and later labour politician, to represent the views of the Irish Transport and General Workers' Union, founded by him in December 1908. Contributors included James Connolly (1868–1916), the Scottish Marxist and socialist who, with Larkin and O'Brien, was co-founder of the Labour Party in Ireland in 1912. He was the organiser of the IT&GWU in Belfast, along with William O'Brien (1881–1968), a master tailor and a founder member of the United Socialist Party. The paper's extreme views on nationalism, its support for the Lockout 1913* and its opposition to the Irish joining the British army for the 1914 war with Germany led to its being suppressed by Dublin Castle. The paper was revived by Larkin in 1930 and edited by his son until 1932.
See **Lockout 1913.**

Irishtown

On 11 February 1451, Richard Duke of York's appointment as Lord Lieutenant for ten years from 9 December 1447 was renewed. He had to return to England to fight the Lancastrians and left the 5th Duke of Ormonde and Wiltshire as his Deputy. On 12 May 1453, Ormonde was appointed Lord Lieutenant for ten years from 6 March of the previous year, without reference to York. Amidst all this political upheaval, both here and in England, Dublin Corporation issued a decree in 1454 ordering 'all men and women of Irish blood whether nuns, clerics, journeymen apprentices, servants or beggars to vacate the city within four weeks and anyone found within the city gates after that time shall forfeit their goods, chattels and be cast into prison and suffer other penalties.' These unfortunate people departed eastwards towards the coast and founded a community at what is now called Irishtown, 2 miles east from the General Post Office and within a few hundred yards of Ringsend. Until recently it was much resorted to for sea bathing. St Matthew's

Islandbridge, looking towards Kilmainham, c. 1885. Note the gas lamps on the bridge.

Church (C of I) was built for Dublin Corporation in 1703–06 for the use of mariners and fishermen. A square tower was added in 1713. The church was completely rebuilt in 1878–79.
See also **Pigeon House Road.**

Islandbridge
Amalgamated with the city of Dublin by Act of Parliament 1900.
Partly in the parish of St James and partly in the parish of St Jude, but chiefly in Dublin city, 2 miles west from the General Post Office, it takes its name from an old bridge that spanned the Liffey prior to the present one, with an arch of 105 feet span, erected in 1791 when the first stone was laid by Sarah Countess of Westmoreland. The bridge connects the South Circular Road with Conyngham Road. The Liffey is a tidal river to the weir at Islandbridge. There is an entrance to the Phoenix Park within which portion are the old magazine fort and the Wellington monument. At the South Circular Road and at Con Colbert Road are entrances to the war memorial gardens designed by Sir Edwin Lutyens to commemorate the Irishmen who fell in the First World War. This was an area occupied by the Vikings and, when the gardens were being laid out, several graves with skeletons and artefacts were found.

Island Street
From Watling Street to Bridgefoot Street
From an island formed by a branch of the River Camac which divided at the north end of Watling Street, one portion emptying into the Liffey at the bridge and the other running parallel to the Liffey and emptying into an inlet at Usher's Pill. The Mendicity Institution, formed in 1818 for the alleviation of street beggary, moved from Usher's Island in 1954. Also a street of Corporation flats.
See **Quays, Usher's Island.**

Iveagh Trust
See **Bull Alley** *and* **Guinness Trust.**

J

James's Street
From Mount Brown to Watling Street
St James's Gate 1555, one of Dublin's outer defences, crossed the street near Watling Street. It was taken down at the end of the eighteenth century. A workhouse,* built to house the vagabond or sturdy beggar, was transformed by 1729 into a foundling hospital for unwanted children and, in 1773, a House of Industry* was opened.
In 1721, the city basin, supplied by the River Poddle, provided ninety days' storage of drinking water for the city. Arthur Guinness opened a brewery in 1759 at St James's Gate, and this now covers a large area of the street. The drinking fountain, designed by Francis Sandys, was erected in 1790 in the form of an obelisk with four sundials at the top. The stonework was replaced in 1932 to include a drinking trough for horses and cattle. A complete restoration was carried out in 1995 at a cost of £85,000. St James (C of I)* designed by Joseph Welland was built in 1858–60. It is the third church on the site. Prior to the suppression of the monasteries in 1537, it was the site of the RC Church. The present St James (RC) Church, designed by Patrick Byrne, was opened in 1852.
See **Lowsie Hill.**

Jammet's Hotel and Restaurant
In 1900, two Frenchmen, Michel and François Jammet, bought the Burlington dining rooms and restaurant at 27 St Andrew Street, whose speciality was oysters from the red-bank oyster beds of the Burren. The brothers traded at 26–27 Andrew Street and 6 Church Lane until their lease reverted back to the Hibernian Bank in 1926. They then acquired Kidd's Restaurant at 45–46 Nassau Street and brought some of the fittings from their original premises. It became the haunt of the artists and the literary set. The Jammets took pride in the fact that theirs was Dublin's only French restaurant. François returned to Paris in 1908 and Michel gave the business to his son, Louis, who ran it until its closure in 1967. The oyster bar and smoking room had a rere entrance through Adam Court.

Jervis Street
From Parnell Street to Abbey Street
Planned development on the north side of the river began when Sir Humphrey Jervis, Sheriff 1674, Lord Mayor 1681, obtained portion of the land belonging to St Mary's Abbey in 1674 and built a street system on the estate which became a fashionable residential centre. The Charitable Infirmary* moved from Inns Quay in 1796. The first Earl of Charlemont's house at no. 14 was rebuilt in 1877 to become Jervis Street Hospital and Charitable Infirmary. The hospital finally closed in 1987. George Simpson who lived at no. 24 left money for an asylum for men in reduced circumstances. Simpson's Hospital* was opened in Parnell Street in 1781. John Thomas Gilbert, author of *A History of the City of Dublin*, was born 23 January 1829 at no. 23, later renumbered and since demolished.

Jervis Street Hospital
See **Charitable Infirmary** *and* **Beaumont Hospital.**

Jewish Museum
Walworth Road
Between Victoria Street and Stamer Street. Off South Circular Road. Opened by President Herzog of Israel in 1985 in what was originally a synagogue built in 1917. President Herzog was the son of Isaac Herzog, first Chief Rabbi of Ireland, who lived in nearby Bloomfield Avenue. On the same day, President Herzog unveiled a plaque on his father's home.

John Dillon Street
From Patrick Street (Hanover Lane) to Back Lane
Named after John Blake Dillon (1814–66), nationalist and co-founder of *The Nation* with Thomas Davis and Gavan Duffy. His son, John Dillon (1851–1927), surgeon and politician, was chairman of the anti-Parnellite group. In 1987, the residents in this grouping of approximately 125 houses, built about 1886 in the Liberties off Back Lane, formed a tenants' association following the publication of the Draft City Plan. They then drew up a proposal, which included a walking environment and an open area for children to play in, which was submitted to the Corporation. In 1989, the City Fathers rejected the proposal.

John's Lane, East
Named after St John's Church, Fishamble Street.
A pedestrian way at the rere of Christ Church Cathedral, from Fishamble Street to Winetavern Street.

Jones's Road
From North Circular Road to Clonliffe Road
Frederick E. Jones opened the road in 1799 to make travelling easier to his theatre in Crow Street. He lived at the Redd (now Red) House on Clonliffe Road.
In 1913, the city and suburban grounds were purchased by the Gaelic Athletic Association and named Croke Memorial Park after Archbishop Thomas William Croke (1824–1902) who promoted the GAA in rural Ireland. The All-Ireland Gaelic football and hurling championships are held there. A major reconstruction of the stadium took place 1997–2002, designed by Gilroy McMahon, making it the fourth largest stadium in Europe, with a capacity of 80,000.
See **Croke Park.**

K

Kelly's Corner
Junction Upper Camden Street and Harrington Street
Named after James J. Kelly, a tobacco grower and one-time city Sheriff. He owned the National Tobacco Company which had premises at nos. 35–36 Camden Street and also at no. 8 Great Brunswick Street.

Keogh Barracks
Keogh Square
See **Barracks, Richmond.**

Kevin Street, Lower
From Redmond's Hill to Bride Street
Name comes from St Kevin's Church.*
Very little remains of the original street because of road widening. The technical school designed by W. M. Mitchell in 1887 was replaced with a new building to form the College of Technology in 1968. Designed by Hooper and Mayne, the college was extended in 1987 when a second block by McKenna Brock was added. The Moravian Church of the United Brethren was built about 1755. In 1915, a new front, designed by Rudolph Maximilian Butler, himself a Moravian, was added to the existing building, with a pediment enclosing a carving of the Paschal lamb with a flag. It was closed for public worship some years ago. The building is now used for commercial purposes. Opposite is a red-brick public library built in 1904. The Moravian graveyard may be seen on Whitechurch Road. The Good Times bar, a fine example of a Victorian public house, was demolished in 1987 to allow a feeder road

to be built for traffic entering Redmond's Hill. Corporation flats corner onto Bride Street.

Kevin Street, Upper
From Bride Street to New Street
In 1212, Archbishop Henry of London built the palace of St Sepulchre which is now part of Kevin Street Garda Station. The medieval vault remains, together with a sixteenth-century window. The seventeenth-century gate piers are in danger of being demolished if a plan to widen the street by a further 12 feet goes ahead. On the other side of St Patrick's Close, formerly Chapter Lane, leading to Marsh's Library* and St Patrick's Cathedral,* is the Deanery House of the Cathedral, built in 1781. At the end of Cathedral Lane opposite, Oliver Cromwell ordered cabbages to be planted in the garden of Philip Fernley in 1649.
See **Cabbage Garden** *and* **Cathedral Lane.**

Keyzar's Lane
From Cornmarket to Cook Street
According to Gilbert, the lane is described in 1587 as 'steepe and sliperie in which otherwhiles, they make more haste then good speed, clinke their backs to the stones.' Jenico Marks, Mayor of Dublin in 1486, was killed in the lane in 1496 while endeavouring to quell a riot of the citizens. The hall of the Guild of Carpenters stood at the Cornmarket end and, extending from this building to Cook Street, was a meat market. There was also a poor house here about 1610. Nothing remains of the lane.

Kildare Place

Off Kildare Street

In 1885, no. 1 was demolished to make way for part of the new National Museum. It would appear that in the 1750s, two houses designed by Richard Cassels stood on the site. Amid much controversy, nos. 2 and 3 were demolished in August 1957 by the Office of Public Works, and a wall was built in their place. In 1811, the Society for the Education of the Poor was founded; it was normally known as the Kildare Place Society. Between 1816 and 1825, new premises for the Society were built, and buildings designed by T. N. Deane were opened in 1890 by the Lord Lieutenant, the Marquis of Zetland. These were demolished in 1970.

After nos. 2 and 3 were demolished, the campanile was a landmark. It was used as a smoke stack for Government Buildings but had been the clock tower for the Royal University in Earlsfort Terrace until the college was redesigned in 1915, when it was erected at Government Buildings. It had a clock dial and bell which had been fitted in 1887 and had come from the GPO. In the centre of the square stands the bronze statue of William Conyngham, Baron Plunket, Protestant Archbishop of Dublin 1884–97, from the studio of Sir Hamo Thornycroft BA, which was unveiled by the Lord Lieutenant on 16 April 1901.

Kildare Street

From Leinster Street South to St Stephen's Green

Part of the Molesworth Fields and known as Coote Lane* or Street until 1753. James Fitzgerald, 20th Earl of Kildare, soon after his accession to his father's title in 1744 decided to erect a family mansion in the Molesworth Fields. It was designed by Richard Cassels, and the foundation stone was laid in 1745. The building has two formal fronts and a central corridor. In 1815, Leinster House was sold to the Dublin Society* and, on 14 August 1924, the government took over the house and the Society received £68,000. The upper house or Senate sits in the eighteenth-century saloon, while Dáil Éireann meets in the octagonal lecture theatre built by the Royal Dublin Society. On either side are the National Library* and the National Museum, erected in 1885–90, designed by Sir Thomas N. Deane. On the corner of the street overlooking College Park is the old Kildare Street Club* building, and at no. 6 is the Royal College of Physicians of Ireland.* On the opposite side of the street: a hotel, modern office blocks and a building designed by J. R. Boyd Barrett, erected in the late 1930s, with stone carvings by Gabriel Hayes, to house the Department of Industry and Commerce.

Kildare Street Club

Kildare Street

In November 1782, David La Touche purchased the interest in a house in Kildare Street from Sir Henry Cavendish on behalf of the newly formed Kildare Street Club. In 1786, La Touche bought a second house from Cavendish for the club. In 1860, a fire destroyed the greater part of the two buildings. A new club house was then designed by Benjamin Woodward. Woodward died in May 1861 before its completion which was supervised by his partner, Thomas Newenham Deane. It was described in 1967 by Dr Maurice Craig as one of Dublin's 'most distinguished 19th century buildings, faultlessly handled in scale and texture and enriched with highly characteristic craftsmanship of Charles Harrison and the O'Shea brothers'. In 1967, planning permission was refused to an insurance company to demolish half the building. The insurance company having sold its interest in 1971, the interior was gutted and the staircase with its stone balustrades was removed, together with the hall and its vaulted arcades, drawing room and morning room, and in their place was constructed 15,500 square feet of office space. In 1982, the Office of Public Works undertook the work of restoring and preserving the building which was taken over by the Genealogical Office and opened to the public March 1987. The entire ground floor houses the Heraldic

Museum. The exterior carvings by C. W. Harrison and the O'Shea brothers survive. *See* **Royal College of Physicians of Ireland.**

Killarney Street
From Portland Row to Buckingham Street
In 1939, Dublin Corporation built a four-storey cement flats complex called St Joseph's Mansions, with deck access and open staircases with a brick-work entrance. An area of high unemployment and urban decay. As part of Dublin City Council's plan to rejuvenate one of Dublin's most deprived areas, a design team, headed by architects Anthony Reddy Associates (ARA), carried out a survey listing the problems associated with the original complex including a need to de-institutionalise it. With a budget of €18 million the buildings have been completely redesigned. The decks are now enclosed, units knocked together, providing 105 flats including 57 units for elderly people, with a residents' lounge, laundry room and assisted bathing facilities with a warden in charge. Now called Killarney Court and opened by An Taoiseach, Bertie Ahern, in May 2003. The centre area has been regrassed with seating and a play area for children and bordered with silver birch trees. A focal point is a stone and bronze monument by Leo Higgins remembering those who died from heroin abuse. Three adjoining social enterprise units are also being revamped. Cluid, the Irish subsidiary of the St Pancras Housing Association, a British voluntary sector agency, has its headquarters in the street and is involved in community activity here.

Killiney and Ballybrack
These places, including the village of Loughlinstown, were formed into a township on 18 July 1866 and are now part of Dún Laoghaire/Rathdown County Council. The Vico Road, a scenic area with fine views, skirts Dalkey Hill and Killiney Hill. The name comes from Cill Iníon Léinín, the church of the daughters of Léinín. The ruins of this building remain. On the hill (Victoria Park), a public area, is an obelisk erected in the middle of the eighteenth century by Mr Malpas to give relief in a season of great distress. The bay sweeps in one unbroken curve as far as the headland of Bray. It has a stony beach. At Ballybrack near the Shankill Road there is the Shanganagh dolmen, a portal tomb.

On Killiney Hill Road, Holy Trinity (C of I) Church, erected in 1858, stands behind a stepped wall with stone entrance. On the same road is St Stephen's (RC) Church, designed by Pearse McKenna and opened in 1982, with a font by Imogen Stuart. St Matthias's (C of I) Church in Ballybrack, opened in 1842, stands precariously near the dual carriageway; it has a square clock tower. The Church of the Apostles in Willow Vale, Ballybrack, is to a design of Richard Hurley and was opened in 1982. The Stations of the Cross are by Benedict Tutty and the metal vessels by Niall O'Neill.

There is a golf course with an entrance off Ballinclea Road. In 1815, a monument was erected to the memory of the Duke of Dorset at Killiney Hill, on the spot where his death was caused by a fall from his horse. Killiney Hill was opened as a public park on 30 June 1887 by Prince Albert Victor.

Kilmainham
Incorporated with the city of Dublin by Act of Parliament 1900.
Formerly a township, comprising the villages of Kilmainham, Goldenbridge,* Inchicore and Islandbridge,* situated on the road to Naas. Named after a seventh-century monastery, *Cill Mhaighneann.* According to the *Annals of the Four Masters,* one of the monks who was known as the philosopher of Kilmainham died here AD 782. The monastery flourished for many years until the coming of the Danes, when the work of this Christian community came to an end. The fields were used as a camping ground for the Irish forces in their raids against the Vikings. It was here in 1014 that Brian Borumha set up his headquarters. After the Anglo-Norman invasion, the grounds were given by

Strongbow to the Order of Knights Templars in 1175. They established an almshouse and hospital. These knights were followed by the Knights Hospitallers of St John of Jerusalem who occupied the area until the dissolution of the monasteries.

In his *History of Dublin*, Dalton states that, in 1530, Archbishop Allen enumerated Kilmainham among the churches of the Deanery of Dublin. This church was suppressed when the monastery was dissolved in 1542. The old order was restored with Queen Mary in 1553 but an Act of Parliament under Elizabeth I in 1558 vested the estates of Kilmainham in the Crown. After that, the priory house was used as a summer residence by the Lords, Deputies and other English officials of high rank. A census taken in 1659 records that the new town of Kilmainham had six English and ten Irish persons. Inchicore had three English and five Irish, while Islandbridge had ten English and sixteen Irish.

The foundation stone of the Royal Hospital* was laid in 1680. According to the Charter of Charles II, the hospital was for the reception and entertainment of ancient, maimed and infirm officers and soldiers. The other historic building in the area is Kilmainham Gaol,* opened in August 1796 on that part of the commons known as Gallows Hill on the road leading to the Black Lion Turnpike (Inchicore Road).

See also **St John's Well, Richmond Tower, Bully's Acre.**

N.B. As there is a certain overlap of townlands, it is advisable to read this together with the above and Goldenbridge and Inchicore.

Kilmainham Gaol

Inchicore Road

When the Knights of St John of Jerusalem established their castle and manor house at Kilmainham in 1210, included among the buildings was a jail. Their priory was confiscated in 1542 after the suppression of the monasteries and eventually Charles II

Robert Emmet by Jerome Connor. Erected St Stephen's Green 1966.

established the Royal Hospital* on the site. The jail was situated at Old Kilmainham near the entrance to Brookfield Road on the banks of the River Camac. By the eighteenth century, the old prison was in a dangerous state with the inmates living in deplorable conditions. In 1786, a Bill was passed providing for the erection of a new jail. This came about as a result of John Howard's publication of *The State of the Prisons*. He was Sheriff of Bedford and visited the old jail on a couple of occasions. Luke Gardiner, the wealthy developer and member of parliament, was instrumental in getting Sir Edward Newenham to put the Bill through parliament. Four years later, Newenham was to find himself an inmate of the prison for failure of payment of a debt. The new prison, designed by John Traile, was situated on an area known as Gallows Hill, bordering the South Circular Road. It opened on 12 August 1796 having 52 individual cells. After the failed insurrection of 1798, the cells were filled with political prisoners as well as with the usual run of prisoners.

Again in 1803, when Robert Emmet's* rebellion failed, he and 200 others were to be interned, including Anne Devlin. Emmet was executed outside St Catherine's Church* in Thomas Street on 20 September 1803.

In 1857, John McCurdy, architect, won a prize for the enlargement and redesign of Kilmainham Gaol; this was completed in 1863, and the present building differs very little from McCurdy's original design.

Charles Stewart Parnell was committed to Kilmainham Gaol on 13 October 1881 after his election as president of the Land League; he was released on 2 May 1882.

Following the Easter Week rising of 1916, fourteen leaders were executed there; in 1922, there were also executions. Eamon de Valera was held in Kilmainham in 1923 and the prison was closed in 1924. The building has been restored by a group of volunteers and is now a public monument kept by the Office of Public Works. It is open to the public.

See also **Phoenix Park Murders.**

Kimmage Manor
Whitehall Road East
Sir Robert Shaw (*see* Bushy Park and Templeogue Road) died in 1869 and was succeeded by his brother, Frederick. Frederick built Kimmage Manor, now the Holy Ghost Missionary College. The fine window of St Columcille by Hubert McGoldrick was erected in 1940. Shaw's house was built in the Tudor style with spiral turrets and an interior designed in the Elizabethan revival style. It passed through several owners until Mrs Mary Clayton purchased it in 1898 and sold it in 1911 to the Holy Ghost order whose students had previously been educated in France.

King Street North
From Stoneybatter to Bolton Street
A sixteenth-century street which formed part of an area that became populated enough by 1697 for a separate parish to be

created from part of the parish of St Michan's. St Paul's Church* (C of I) closed for public worship in 1987 and was converted into a youth enterprise centre in what has become a poverty-stricken area. In a report of 1731, the Poor Clares had a school for daughters of wealthy citizens, and fashionable houses were built when the area was opened up with the building of Bolton Street.

King Street South
From St Stephen's Green to Mercer Street
Probably best known for the Gaiety Theatre* opened in 1871 and used for plays, opera, musicals and the Christmas pantomime. Most of the houses on the other side of the street were demolished between 1966 and 1981 to make way for the 4.5-acre St Stephen's Green shopping complex opened in 1989. The adjoining site to the Gaiety Theatre was sold in July 1984 to Telecom Éireann for £7 million.

In 2001, the street was closed to through traffic. The granite pavement at the Gaiety Theatre was widened and the opaque glass canopy extended to protect the public from the elements. Polished granite benches also adorn the area. At the Mercer Street end, a multi-jet small fountain completes the streetscape.

Kingsbridge (Heuston) Station
The 1844 Act of Incorporation of the Great Southern and Western Railway includes the words '. . . and it be enacted that the railway hereby authorised to be made shall commence in a field at or near King's Bridge in the county of the city of Dublin between Military Road and the River Liffey'. The station was built of local stone to the design of Sancton Wood of London; the work was executed by Gilbert Cockburn, 179 Brunswick Street (Pearse Street), and Arthur Williams, 41 Talbot Street. The three coats of arms carved on the front of the building are those of Dublin, Cork and Limerick.

Erected in a rural area, it faced various difficulties which had to be surmounted. The grounds of the Royal Hospital which

Kingsbridge (Heuston) Station.

were affected by the railway became a bone of contention between the governors of the Royal Hospital and the directors of the railway. In 1874, the road known as Long Lane, which ran across the railway towards Islandbridge, was largely obliterated and the present thoroughfare, St John's Road West, was formed. The Irish Army barracks (Clancy) was sited on an area needed by the railway company, and the directors offered the Board of Ordnance £5,000 for the area, or the alternative that the railway company would build a new barracks in a different situation. Nothing came of this as the authorities took too long to make a decision and the track layout was already planned by the time they offered the barracks to the Railway Company for £2,000. Later, a connecting line was run to the Guinness Brewery.

Renamed Heuston Station in 1966 after Sean Heuston (1891–1916), an employee of the Great Southern and Western Railway Company who was executed after the Easter Week Rising of 1916, for commanding the Volunteers in the Mendicity Institute.*

King's Hospital (alias Blue Coat School)
Blackhall Place

Charles Lucas in his narrative concerning the hospital states: 'According to a resolution thus taken and declared on the eighth day of May in the year of our Lord 1669 this work was begun. . . . The fabrick consists of three isles or Rows of Buildings meeting in one front. In the whole it contains very many apartments; the greatest Number of which are designed for Lodgings and may without annoyance or Incumbrance receive 250 or 300 persons. . . . There are four large school rooms . . . one for the perfect reading of English, another for writing and arithmetick, a third for the Latin and Greek tongues and the fourth for mathematicks. His majesty was graciously pleased as an honourary addition to his royal grant to give a name to this issue of public charity; commanding it henceforth to be called The Hospital and free school of King Charles the Second, Dublin.' It was to be held in 'free and common soccage, as a mansion house and place of abode for the sustentation and relief of poor children, [and] aged, maimed and impotent people inhabiting or residing in the said City of Dublin'.

The present building was erected from 1773 onwards, to the design of Thomas Ivory. The stonework and ornamental carving are by Simon Vierpyl and the plasterwork by Charles Thorp, Senior. In 1894, the unfinished central tower was removed and replaced with a cupola. When the school removed to Palmerstown near Lucan, an extensive renovation plan was commissioned by the Incorporated Law Society which now has the building as its headquarters. The original drawings by Ivory were presented to George III in 1776. His son, George IV, later presented them to the British Museum.

King's Inns
See **Henrietta Street.**

King's Hospital (alias Blue Coat School). Erected from 1773 onwards to a design of Thomas Ivory.

L

La Scala Theatre
4–7 Prince's Street
On 11 April 1919, Frank William Chambers and George Peter Fleming, two directors of the Carlton Cinema, were given full power and authority to establish and keep a well-regulated theatre with an expenditure of £30,000. T. F. McNamara was employed as architect, and permission was granted to alter the plans from two to three tiers. It was later renamed the Capitol Cinema when a joint film and live show was presented. It closed in March 1972 and, with the Prince's bar at no. 3, was demolished, together with the Metropole Ballroom and Cinema,* to make way for a new department store.

Langrishe Place
Cul-de-Sac off Summerhill
Named after the Rt Hon. Sir Hercules Langrishe, Bart. (1731–1811) MP for Knocktopher. Introduced the Catholic Relief Bill in 1792.
None of the eighteenth-century houses remain and the nineteenth-century end houses were knocked down to make way for the Summerhill dual carriageway commenced in 1989. The strange castellated stone-fronted building with its narrow windows was St Mary's Boys' National School. It now houses a motor firm.
See **Summerhill.**

Lansdowne Road (1855)
From Northumberland Road to Herbert Road
Named after the fourth Marquess of Lansdowne. Created 1784, died 1866.

Part of it originally called Haig's Lane (see also Newbridge Avenue) after a whiskey distiller whose buildings were situated on the banks of the River Dodder. After the loss of a legal battle with the Revenue Commissioners in the mid-nineteenth century, the distillery was demolished and the stones used as foundations for two new roads constructed across the site, namely Herbert Road and Newbridge Avenue. Numbers 1–47 contained the Trinity College Botanic Gardens on which now stands the Berkeley Court Hotel. Number 62b is the entrance to the Irish Rugby Football grounds where international and Triple Crown games are played. Also home of Wanderers' Football Club. The road consists mainly of large red-brick houses, also a railway station serving the DART network.

La Touche and Son
Castle Street
On a portion of the city wall on the south side of Castle Street stand the remains of the bank founded by David Digges La Touche who fought as an officer in the regiment of the Comte de Cailemotte at the Battle of the Boyne. After the war, as a Huguenot refugee on half pay in Galway, he entered into trade in worsteds. He removed to Dublin and went into partnership with Nathaniel Kane (later Alderman Kane, Lord Mayor 1734) and in 1693, established a cambric and poplin factory in the High Street. He also acted as the custodian of monies lodged with him by the French community and other traders, setting up a bank under the name

of Kane and La Touche.

About 1720, La Touche discontinued poplin manufacturing and concentrated on the business of banking. In the late 1750s, many small banks in Dublin failed. These were private concerns often run by merchants and traders who were authorised to issue notes. Public confidence in the banking system was undermined and only three banks survived the crisis: Gleadowe and Co., Finlay and Co., and La Touche.

In 1726, La Touche leased a 49-foot wide area in Castle Street from Dublin Corporation and built a bank that opened in 1735. It was four storeys high over a basement, with wings being added in 1802–03. David, a grandson of the founder, was elected first governor of the Bank of Ireland.* Another grandson, William George, married in 1784 the daughter of the London banker Puget and, with the aid of his London connections, greatly expanded the business. In 1788, the Irish Exchequer was completely exhausted due mainly to restrictions on native industry to maintain English monopolies. The La Touche bank loaned the State £20,000, and thus 'not only upheld the shattered credit of Government but prevented the dissolution of the State'. A request for a similar second loan was declined. William died of apoplexy, on the Stock Exchange in 1803.

James Digges La Touche, son of William, also entered the business and was active in the public life of the community, acting on the boards of several public companies. He steered the bank through the major crisis in 1820 when many provincial banks failed, causing a great run on the Dublin banks. His grand-nephew, William, was made resident director of the Munster Bank in 1870 on the dissolution of the La Touche bank. The Munster Bank used the premises until 1874 when it moved to new offices in Dame Street. It was later used by the veterinary department of the Privy Council. The building was demolished in 1945 except for the granite front wall. The archway was opened up in 1987 to make a new entrance into Dublin Castle and relocated at basement level to form a cloister alongside an ornamental pool. The Venus plaster ceiling from the back boudoir was installed in the directors' luncheon room of the Bank of Ireland.

See also **Bank of Ireland** *and* **Kildare Street Club.**

Lazar's Hill

*Now Townsend Street**

From the name Lazarus (Lk 16:20). In 1743, a hospital for incurables started in Fleet Street; it moved to Townsend Street in 1753 when it was renamed St Margaret of Cortona. Became Donnybrook Lock Hospital in 1792. The name is derived from the locks or rags which covered the patients' sores. Given a Royal Charter and now called the Royal Hospital, off Morehampton Road, Donnybrook.

It was at Lazar's Hill that Archbishop Henry of London founded the Steyne Hospital in 1220. It was built for lepers about to depart for the shrine of St James at Compostela and as a quarantine halt for immigrants with infectious skin diseases.

See **Townsend Street.**

Leeson Street

From Mespil Road to Morehampton Road

See **Magdalen Asylum and Chapel.**

Leeson Park

From Northbrook Road to Chelmsford Road

An area of mainly private dwellings with a strong residents' association formed in 1968 to fight rezoning of the area for office use. The Molyneux House* for female blind, which had been housed in Peter Street between 1815 and 1862, then moved to Leeson Street. Christ Church, Leeson Park, built about this time to a design of Rawson Carroll, was for many years used by the Church of Ireland community. When the Methodist church in St Stephen's Green was burnt down, it was agreed that the Methodists would share this church. The Methodists also built a conference centre in the 1970s behind the Litton parochial hall which was built in the 1870s.

Legion of Mary
De Montfort House, Morning Star Avenue, Brunswick Street

An apostolic movement founded in Dublin at 100 Francis Street, on 7 September 1921, by Frank Duff, Fr Michael Toher and Mrs Elizabeth Kirwan and which has spread phenomenally. Its mission is primarily spiritual. It has adopted some features from the organisation of the Roman army. Its units are called praesidia, a group of praesidia is a curia and the regional body is the senatus.

Leinster Hall
See **Theatre Royal.**

Leinster House
Architect Richard Cassels (1690–1751).

In 1744, James Fitzgerald succeeded to the 20th Earldom of Kildare at the age of 22. Considering the family house in Suffolk Street not to be adequate to his new rank, he acquired from Viscount Molesworth for £1,000 a site in Coote Lane in the Molesworth Fields on the then un-fashionable south side of the River Liffey. The construction of a new house on the site began in 1745 and took two years to complete. There is a tradition that the Earl had said that society would follow wherever he went, and he was proved correct when, within a few years, extensive residential properties had been built around the neighbourhood of the new Kildare House. As a result of this development, Coote Lane was widened and renamed Kildare Street. In 1766, the Earl was created 1st Duke of Leinster, and Kildare House was renamed Leinster House.

The family maintained an interest in the house until 1815 when the 3rd Duke of Leinster sold the mansion to the (Royal) Dublin Society* for £10,000 and a yearly rent of £600 which was later redeemed. Extensive additions were made to the house by the Society, notably the lecture theatre.

In 1922, after the establishment of the Irish Free State, the government obtained part of the building for parliamentary use, and the entire building was acquired in 1924. It is now the seat of Dáil Éireann (House of Representatives) and Seanad Éireann (Senate), the two houses of the Oireachtas (National Parliament).

A statue of Queen Victoria by John Hughes (1865–1941) was erected on the forecourt in 1908, removed in 1948 and placed in storage until 1986, when the Irish Government 'in a spirit of goodwill and friendship' presented it to the Australian people to mark the bicentenary of that country. It stands at the entrance to the Queen Victoria Building shopping mall, Sydney.

Leinster Street South
From Nassau Street to Clare Street

Named after Viscount Leinster 1744 and Duke of Leinster 1766. It was formerly included with Nassau Street and Lincoln Place in St Patrick's Well Lane. About 1750, five impressive houses were built, one of which was the residence of Philip Tistall, Solicitor General 1750 and Attorney General 1760, University of Dublin MP 1739–77. Apart from the side of Benjamin Woodward's Kildare Street Club, the street today consists mainly of office blocks.

At no. 1–2 stood Finn's private hotel and restaurant. It was here in 1904 that James Joyce met Nora Barnacle. She had come from Galway and was working as a chambermaid in the hotel. They left Dublin together later that year and settled in Trieste.

Lemon Street
Grafton Street through to Hibernian Way

Named after Graham Lemon, a confectioner who bought property in the street 1871. Formerly called Span's Lane 1728, Grafton Lane 1795. The Marks and Spencer store has a side entrance onto the street. Originally a cul-de-sac but was opened up in 1988 to join with the large-scale office and shopping complex named the Hibernian Way, leading to Dawson Street and replacing the Hibernian Hotel.
See **Dawson Street.**

Leinster House viewed from Leinster Lawn. Built for the Earl of Kildare, it is now the seat of the two houses of the Oireachtas (National Parliament). It was from this lawn that Richard Crosbie, on 19 July 1785, became the first Irish aeronaut by ascending in a balloon.

Leopold Bloom Sculpture Trail

A set of fourteen bronze plaques set into the pavement, following the route taken by Leopold Bloom, the principal character in James Joyce's novel, *Ulysses*, on 16 June 1904. Starting at Middle Abbey Street, it passes Lemon's Sweet Shop, crosses O'Connell Bridge to the Ballast Office, Westmoreland Street; then across the road to Harrison's Restaurant, past the statue of Thomas Moore in College Green to Trinity College, crossing at the corner of Nassau Street to Jammet's Restaurant; halting at Brown Thomas in Grafton Street, the route proceeds along Duke Street to Burton's Restaurant, then goes back to Davy Byrne's pub;* from there to Dawson Street along Molesworth Street to the National Library,* and ends at the National Museum.*

Each plaque has a quote from the eighth chapter of *Ulysses* and a figure of Leopold Bloom. Sculptor Robin Buick, sponsored by Cantrell and Cochrane in 1988.
See **Martello Towers.**

Liberties

Adjoining the area under the jurisdiction of the Mayor of the city were several jurisdictions known as the Liberties, of which the most important were the Liberty of St Sepulchre, under the Archbishop of Dublin, and the Liberties of Thomas Court and Donore, belonging to the Abbey of St Thomas, as well as the Liberty of St Patrick's. All are mentioned in Archbishop Allen's register of 1529 which states that the Liberty of St Thomas begins beyond the island of the Coombe behind the former gallows of the Archbishop and on the side of the well of St Francis.

During the sixteenth century, when the dissolution of the monasteries by Henry VIII led to the suppression of a large number of religious houses, the Liberties of Thomas Court and Donore were granted to William Brabazon, ancestor of the Earls of Meath. Charles Brooking's three street maps of 1728 give an incomplete area of the 'Archbishop and Earl of Meath's Liberties with the bounds of each parish'. Brooking's map gives a line for the Archbishop's Liberty along the south side of St Stephen's Green to Wexford Street, Redmond's Hill, Bishop Street across to Bride Street and Bull Alley, Francis Street and Blackpitts. According to Brooking, the Liberty was bounded by a water course from Blackpitts to the Poddle. The Liberty of St Thomas Court, now the Earl of Meath's Liberty, proceeded along the Coombe to Ardee Street, Echlin Street, Grand Canal Place over to James's Street to the junction of Meath Street and Thomas Street, then on to Ash Street and into the Coombe. St Patrick's was the smallest Liberty, nine acres in all, which offered sanctuary to defaulting debtors into the nineteenth century.

In 1798, the Rev. James Whitelaw, rector of St Catherine's described the Liberties: 'The streets are generally narrow; the houses crowded together; the rears or back yards of very small extent, and some without accommodation of any kind. Of these streets a few are the residence of the upper class of shopkeepers or others engaged in trade; but a far greater proportion of them, with their numerous lanes and alleys, are occupied by working manufacturers, by petty shopkeepers, the labouring poor, and beggars, crowded together to a degree distressing to humanity. A single apartment in one of these truly wretched habitations rates from one to two shillings per week, and to lighten this rent two or even four families become joint tenants. Under such circumstances it is not extraordinary that I should have frequently found from thirty to forty individuals in a house.' Another Liberty, that of Christchurch, consisted of one acre and two roods. The administration of the city was radically altered by the Municipal Corporations (Ireland) Act of 1841, and, during the following 20 years, the area of the Corporation was increased by the abolition of the Liberties.

In 1835, there were five manorial jurisdictions or Liberties: St Sepulchre's, Thomas Court and Donore, the Liberty of the Dean of St Patrick's, the Manor of Glasnevin or Grangegorman and the Manor of Kilmainham.

See also **Pimlico, Gray Street, Thomas Court, Dublin Artisans' Dwellings Company.**

Liberty Hall
Corner of Eden Quay and Beresford Place

On 12 May 1961, the forty-fifth anniversary of James Connolly's execution, the foundation stone was laid for Dublin's first skyscraper building, designed by Desmond Rea O'Kelly. The Irish Transport and General Workers' Union demolished its old headquarters (see Eden Quay) and erected a 17-storey tower, 197 feet high. When it opened in 1965, it included an observation terrace open to the public who could view almost the entire city from such a great height. In 1972, a bomb blew out most of the windows, and clear glass was then replaced with reflective glass.

There is a theatre in the Liberty Hall Centre.

Liffey Street Lower
From Bachelor's Walk to Middle Abbey Street

Name comes from its proximity to the river. A general trading street. On the pedestrian way outside the Dublin Woollen Mills stands a bronze and granite sculpture, 'Meeting Place', by Jakki McKenna, erected in 1988.

Lincoln Place
From Leinster Street to Westland Row

Originally part of St Patrick's Well Lane, was Park Street East from 1792 until 1862 when the name changed following complaints from landlords that they were unable to obtain suitable rents for their properties as the street had such a bad reputation. An interesting feature until it was demolished in 1969 was the Turkish Baths designed by Richard Barter with a 50-foot high onion dome and a large ornamental chimney. On the opposite side of the street are the Dental Hospital and one of the entrances to Trinity College. Lincoln's Inn at no. 18, originally part of Finn's Hotel (see South Leinster Street), opened as a separate public house in 1926 and closed in 2002. It was owned by Trinity

College who in 2004 sought planning permission to extend into no. 19, giving the appearance of one building.

Linen Hall
Off North King Street
An Act of Parliament of 1711 made provision for the establishment of a board of linen manufacture, necessitated by an increase in that trade. In 1722, a site was purchased that originally belonged to Thomas Pooley, a wealthy land owner who was involved in the Castle market among other developments. A large edifice bordering onto North Anne Street and George's Hill was completed in 1728. Several additions were made over the next 30 years, with the complex extending as far as Coleraine Street, Derry Street and Lurgan Street, with the main frontage onto Lisburn Street. As the street names imply, there was a close association with the linen trade in Ulster, much of the produce being manufactured there and sold by agents who rented warehouse space in the hall. The buildings were further enlarged in 1781, with a yarn hall being extended to join with the linen hall. During the nineteenth century, trade declined and the board of linen manufacture ceased as overseers in 1829. The military, who had leased part of the premises since 1851, took over the entire hall in 1867. In 1911, nos. 6, 7 and 8 Lisburn Street, described as Linen Hall barracks, were vacant. The same applied to nos. 5–9 Coleraine Street. The yarn hall was eventually taken by a pharmaceutical firm.

Lockout 1913
The lockout was probably the most climactic moment in Irish labour history and spawned the creation of modern work practices through the trade union movement.
In January 1909, James Larkin (1876–1947), the socialist, trade unionist independent labour politician, founded the Irish Transport and General Workers' Union. He organised strikes among the stevedores and casual labourers on Dublin's docks. He also organised walk-outs involving railwaymen and tram workers and bitterly attacked employers in his newspaper the *Irish Worker,** which he had founded in May 1911. The employers were led by William Martin Murphy (1844–1919), a wealthy businessman and Nationalist politician who, as owner of both the *Irish Catholic* newspaper and the *Irish Independent,** had a strong influence in swaying public opinion and had formed a 400-strong Employers' Federation. In August 1913, he informed the workers in the Dublin United Tramway Company that the directors had no objection to their forming a legitimate union but demanded a written undertaking that they would not join the disreputable organisation of the 'strike monger' Larkin. Larkin called on the tramway workers to strike and in September, Murphy called on the members of the Federation to lock out their employees, resulting in the Lockout of 1913. On 29 August, the Dublin Metropolitan Police baton charged a crowd in Sackville Street (O'Connell Street). Two men, James Nolan and John Byrne, died of fractured skulls, 500 civilians were injured as were 50 DMP members after Larkin, disguised in a false beard and frock coat, in defiance of a ban on a public meeting planned for 31 August, addressed the crowd from the balcony of the Imperial Hotel owned by W. M. Murphy (Clery's department store now stands on the site). Larkin was arrested but released shortly afterwards.
The *Irish Worker* also gave details of police brutality during the riots at Beresford Place, Inchicore, Kilmainham, North Strand, Ringsend and Talbot Street. By September, 25,000 workers were locked out and on 29th September, a government inquiry opened under the direction of Sir George Askwith. Timothy Michael Healy, the nationalist politician, who was to become the first Governor-General of the Irish Free State, represented the employers and Larkin spoke for the workers. The report condemned the strike but found that the employers were in error in trying

to impose anti-union restrictions. The findings of the inquiry were rejected by the employers. *The Irish Times** of 4 September 1913 observed that members of the ITGWU lived for the most part in slums* which were responsible not only for disease and crime but for much of the industrial unrest. Again, *The Irish Times* of 7 October 1913 published a lengthy letter from George William Russell (1867–1935), the poet, artist and mystic, condemning the employers and signed with his pen name, AE. Part of it stated; 'you do not seem to read history so as to learn its lessons. That you are an uncultivated class was obvious from recent utterances of some of you upon art. That you are incompetent men in the sphere in which you arrogate imperial powers is certain, because for many years long before the present uprising of labour, your enterprises have been dwindling in the regard of investors, and this while you carried them on in the cheapest labour market in these islands, with a labour reserve always hungry and ready to accept any pittance. You are bad citizens for we rarely, if ever, hear of the wealthy among you endowing your city with the munificent gifts, which it is the pride of merchant princes in other cities to offer, and Irishmen not of your city who offer to supply the wants left by your lack of generosity are met with derision and abuse. [. . .] you have allowed the poor to be herded together so that one thinks of certain places in Dublin as of a pestilence. There are twenty thousand rooms, in each of which live entire families, and sometimes more where no functions of the body can be concealed and delicacy and modesty are creatures that are stifled ere they are born. [. . .]
The conception of yourselves as altogether virtuous and wronged is, I assure you, not at all the one which onlookers hold to you. [. . .] Your insolence and ignorance of the rights conceded to workers universally in the modern world were incredible, and as great as your inhumanity. [. . .] You may succeed in your policy and ensure your own damnation by your victory. The men

whose manhood you have broken will loathe you, and will always be brooding and scheming to strike a fresh blow. The children will be taught to curse you. The infant being moulded in the womb will have breathed into its starved body the vitality of hate . . . .'
Larkin was again imprisoned for seven months on 27 October but was soon released. The situation was beginning to cause much concern as many families were without money to buy food and clothing. At one stage in October, arrangements were made to take the workers' children to England, but the Archbishop of Dublin, William Walsh, objected and the clergy of the diocese organised the distribution of relief to the needy. Larkin, on being released from jail, organised food and clothing to be sent from England and America.
This aid came to a halt after Larkin had a disagreement with the British Trade Union Congress over wanting to close the docks in sympathy with the Irish workers. By the end of January 1914, many of the strikers had returned to work, encouraged by vitriolic sermons preached at Sunday Masses. By the end of February, the lockout was over. Larkin's union had been greatly depleted, and in October he left for America to raise funds. He was to remain there for nine years, getting involved in workers' movements and, in 1920, was sentenced to ten years' penal servitude in Sing Sing. He was released in 1923 and returned to Ireland to a tumultuous welcome. Larkin's aim was for the underprivileged not just to have material sufficiency but to have access to culture and the graces of living as well. The strike was organised from the old Northumberland building which the ITGWU bought and renamed in 1912 as its headquarters. Liberty Hall,* its current headquarters, now stands on the site on the corner of Eden Quay and Beresford Place. The Irish Citizen Army, founded by Larkin and Connolly on 23 November 1913 as a defence corps to protect the striking workers and their families from the Dublin

Metropolitan Police, continued to operate after the lockout and was involved in the Easter Rising of 1916 and the civil war of 1922. It was disbanded the following year.

Longford Street (Little, Great)
Crosses Aungier Street
Name comes from Francis Aungier, 1st Earl of Longford 1677, who developed the lands of the White Friars which his ancestors had obtained by grant in 1621. He laid out Aungier Street, Cuffe Street and Longford Street. The title became extinct in 1704.

Lord Mayor
The office of mayor was established in 1229 when Richard Muton or Moulton was chosen first Mayor of Dublin, but the first Lord Mayor was Sir Daniel Bellingham (c. 1622–71) who was elected in 1665. He was a silversmith who became a freeman in 1644, Sheriff in 1655, knighted in 1662, Deputy Receiver General and Vice-Treasurer for Ireland 1663–66, re-elected Lord Mayor in 1666 but declined the office and obtained a letter from the Duke of Ormonde to the Corporation stating that it would be a great hindrance to his Majesty's service if he should be continued Lord Mayor for another year as he was Deputy Receiver in the Exchequer. Created baronet in 1666. In 1665, he provided himself with a great mace* to be borne in procession along with the city sword.

The Lord Mayor is the first citizen of the city and is elected each year by the City Council from among its members. The term normally lasts for one year but Thomas Cusack held the office 19 times between 1390 and 1430. More recently, Alfie Byrne was elected for nine consecutive years, 1930–39, and again in 1954–55. The Lord Mayor presides at the meetings of the City Council and signs the record of the proceedings, and must also be present when the city seal is affixed to municipal documents.
See also **Civic Regalia, Guilds, Free Citizens of Dublin, Riding the Franchises.**

Lord Mayor's State Coach
The city did not possess a state coach until the latter half of the eighteenth century. Prior to that, the Lord Mayor either went on foot in public processions or provided his own carriage. Humphrey French supplied his own coach at the celebration of the birthday of King George II and Pue's *Occurrences* described '. . . the greatest appearance that ever was known on such an occasion. His Lordship rode in his state coach, drawn by six horses, whose tails and manes were tied with blue ribbons, their ear knots the same, and before him his body coach, with two horses, attended by several footmen on each side of the coach, with blue cockades in their hats.'

According to the Assembly roll of 22 July 1763, 'certain of the Commons setting forth that supporting the grandeur of the Chief Magistrate of the city must necessarily reflect honour upon the Corporation and respect by the public, that there is nothing more wanting than a state coach to add dignity to the Lord Mayor's appearance in public days, it was ordered that a committee be appointed to provide a state coach for succeeding Lord Mayors, the expense whereof, with a suitable set of harness, not to exceed £400'. Nothing appears to have been done regarding this resolution but an entry on 18 July 1766 records payment of £100 for repairs to a Berlin made a present to the city of Dublin 'by the most noble Marquis of Kildare' (created Duke of Leinster 1766). Another entry of 1768 shows a payment of £50 'to reimburse the late Lord Mayor, Edward Sankey, for his expenses in providing horses and servants on public days for the state coach presented to the City by the most noble James, Duke of Leinster'.

By 1789, it was agreed that the existing coach was beyond repair and an entry in Faulkner's *Dublin Journal* of 1 August 1789 reads: 'Notice—The Committee appointed by the Corporation of the City of Dublin for purchasing a state coach for the Chief Magistrate hereby give notice that they will receive drawings and estimates for the same to be lodged in the Town Clerk's office on or before the 1st Monday in September next—The committee will meet at the Tholsel at one o'clock on Monday next when such Irish artists as choose to undertake the same will receive every necessary information on the subject.' William Whitton of Dominick Street won the order, and £1,200 was set aside for a vehicle that would be completed '. . . in a manner becoming the consequence, grandeur and dignity of their great city'.

The coach was to be ready for a procession on 4 November 1790, but this was delayed due to the arrival in September of a London-built coach by Godsal of Long Acre at a cost of nearly £7,000 for the Lord Chancellor, John Fitzgibbon, Earl of Clare. It was exhibited to the public in the Chancellor's stables in Baggot Street at the rere of his house in Ely Place. The whole design of the new coach for the Lord Mayor was revised and the ornamentation made more elaborate at a cost of £2,690-13-5, in order to show that Dublin could produce as fine work as London. A year later, on 4 November 1791, it made its first appearance on the occasion of the annual celebration of the birthday of King William, which the Lord Mayor attended in state. The Lord Chancellor's coach was also in procession. It was a wet day and the streets were thick with mud. *Magee's Weekly Packet* of 12 November 1791 records: 'To convey a just idea of its elegance by words would be impossible—the City Berlin and the Chancellor's coach from their situation in the train came immediately into competition; the former certainly lost nothing by this circumstance; the latter, if nothing else, gained an uninterrupted hiss.' The *Hibernian Magazine* went further in its praise: '. . . It more than corresponded with the expectations of the most sanguine friends of Irish genius and afforded ocular demonstration that it must be of choice, not necessity, that a neighbouring Kingdom has been resorted to for a vehicle to suit the pomp of a newly-acquired dignity. The superior excellence of Irish workmanship, when contrasted with the most boasted productions of art and genius

imported into this country was never more conspicuous than the comparison impartially made between the Lord Chancellor's and the Lord Mayor's superb carriages, though the latter did not cost half the sum'.

In 1975, the coach was completely restored by craftsmen employed in the mechanical section of Dublin Corporation and made its reappearance on St Patrick's Day, 17 March 1976. Prior to that, it had been in storage in the National Museum since its last appearance at the Eucharistic Congress in 1932. At some stage in its history, the original wheels were replaced. It is elaborately decorated on all panels with paintings. On the near door is a female figure representing the City of Dublin, who offers a prize medal as an encouragement to the arts, which are represented by female figures bearing emblems pressing forward eagerly to obtain the reward. On the front panel, Commerce recommending to the patronage and protection of the Chief Magistrate the manufacturers of Ireland. On the off door panel, Apollo instructs the muses to sing the praises of Hibernia while the genii of immortality hold the imperial crown of Ireland over the head of this favoured nation. The back panel depicts Minerva, the Goddess of Wisdom, directing the Corporation of Dublin on the road to fame and honours. On the carriage are four allegorical figures: Justice, Mercy, Plenty and Liberality. It is 24 feet in length, 8 feet in breadth and in height 11½ feet.

Lord Edward Street

From Cork Hill to Christchurch Place

Lord Edward Fitzgerald (1763–98), United Irishman, twelfth child of the 1st Duke of Leinster, died of gunshot wounds in Newgate Prison on 4 June 1798. A new street opened and named 27 July 1886 by the Rt Hon. T. D. Sullivan MP, Lord Mayor. Prior to its opening, traffic had to proceed along Castle Street to Christchurch Place.

Numbers 2–12 housed the Dublin Working Boys' Home and Harding Technical

George Roe & Co. Distillery established in 1757. The large windmill used for grinding corn was built in 1805. The sails were removed in 1860.

School, founded in 1876. The object of the institution was to provide comfortable board and lodgings for boys in employment in the city who were not resident with their parents. The present building dates from 1892 and was designed by Albert Murray. In 1886, money left by Miss Harding was given on the understanding that the home should include a technical and night school. Now a hostel.

Lots

Living Over The Shop

In 1994, a scheme was launched to try to create up to 2,000 residential units where owners of shops left the areas above their shops vacant. The project did not take off, probably through lack of proper or adequate advertising. It was again launched in April 2001 and, to encourage proprietors to participate, Dublin City Council restored apartments in no. 3 and no. 4 Capel Street, followed by an extensive advertising campaign. Again, there was very little interest in rooms lying idle on upper floors as many of the buildings are owned by landlords collecting large rents from ground-floor premises. Entrances would have to be redesigned to give dual access, which might take valuable space

from the retail outlet, and security may have been another one of the issues. Dublin City Council's Economic and Development Unit now has a team of architects and quantity surveyors who will inspect properties and advise on their suitability for conversion and a possible cost, in the hope that it would encourage more owners to consider making so much derelict space available.

Lowsie Hill

St James's Gate

St James's Gate, 1555, one of old Dublin's outer defences, was taken down at the end of the eighteenth century.

The Dublin Assembly rolls of 1623 read, 'to appoint surveyors to survey the passage going to Lowsie Hill, St James's Gate at the back of the pipes. Mr Mayor to direct his warrant to the city treasurer for such monies as shall be thought necessary to be disbursed in repairing the defects.' In 1670, the area was leased to Alderman Giles Mee who had a brew house on the hill. In 1709, his son-in-law, Alderman Sir Mark Rainsford, took the lease and, in 1715, leased it for 44 years to Paul Espinasse. In 1759, the hill and the ground called 'the Pipes' were leased for 9,000 years to Arthur

Guinness at a rent of £45 a year and, by 1935, it would have 3,000 persons employed. The James's Gate Brewery continues on the site to the present day. *See* **James Street.**

Luas

The Dublin Transportation Initiative report of April 1994 recommended the establishment of a three-line light rail transit system linking Tallaght, Ballymun and Cabinteely to the city centre. In October 1994, reflecting the availability of funding, the phasing of two lines, one linking Sandyford with St Stephen's Green and the other linking Tallaght with Connolly Station, was recommended. A consultant's report of April 1998 concluded that a surface system would be the most appropriate and cost-effective option to meet long-term passenger demands. In May 1998, the Government decided to proceed with the two lines, which have no physical connection between them. In October 2000, the Dublin Transportation Office published 'A Platform for Change' —Outline of an integrated transportation strategy for the Greater Dublin Area— 2000–2016. The Government approved the broad thrust of the strategy, which provides an overall planning framework for the development of the transport system in the Greater Dublin Area. In December 2001, the Transport (Railway Infrastructure) Act 2001 was enacted, providing for the establishment of the Railway Procurement Agency as an independent statutory agency responsible for the procurement of railway infrastructure systems. In May 2002, Connex was appointed to operate the Luas system. In March 2003, the Minister for Transport, Mr Seamus Brennan, travelled on a test run of the first tram to serve the line from Sandyford to St Stephen's Green. On 15 March 2004, testing commenced along the full extent of this line. On 11 February 2004, safety and engineering tests began on the Dundrum to Ranelagh (Beechwood) section. The line opened to the public on 30 June 2004 with five days of free travel. Another test run took place

from the Red Cow roundabout in November 2003 and, on Sunday 7 March 2004, testing commenced on the Tallaght to Heuston section of the Tallaght to Connolly line. The line was opened by the Taoiseach, Mr Bertie Ahern, on 28 September 2004, with five days of free travel. Forty trams manufactured by GEC-Alstom in France were ordered and the first show tram went on view in November 2001. Each tram can carry up to approximately 235 passengers—60 of whom will be seated. Twenty-six trams are 30 metres long and 14 are 40 metres long. Tram extensions can offer a wide range of line capacities.

Lucan

On part of the great Slí Mór which ran from the High Street in Dublin to Galway An inland parish and suburban village 8 miles west of Dublin on the Leixlip–Maynooth Road. In the eighteenth century, it was a fashionable sulphur spa, discovered in 1758. About 1910, a new hotel and sanatorium were completed on the site by the Lucan Hydropathic Spa Co. Limited. All that remains is the hotel. Situated on the River Liffey, the village was important from medieval times for its salmon weirs and for its fishing. Adjoining the village is Lucan demesne which became the home of an English family, the Sarsfields, who had arrived in Ireland in the wake of the Anglo-Norman invasion. William Sarsfield was knighted in 1566. Patrick Sarsfield was a military commander in the Williamite Wars and was created Earl of Lucan by James II. He followed the King into exile in France and was killed at the battle of Landen (in Flanders) in 1693. The estates eventually passed through marriage to the Vesey family, and Agmondisham Vesey designed the Palladian Lucan house in 1772. The house was later refurbished and Michael Stapleton the stuccodore artist worked on the ceilings. The medallions are attributed to Angelica Kauffmann. It is now the residence of the Italian Ambassador. Vesey was also responsible for the erection at his

Lucan village as it appeared in 1903.

own expense of the bridge at Lucan. James Gandon, the architect, died at his own home, Canonbrook, in 1823, and is buried in Drumcondra. St Edmundsbury, built by Edmund Sexton Pery, speaker of the Irish House of Commons (1771–85), was taken over in the late 1890s to form a new hospital attached to St Patrick's Hospital* which had been founded by Dean Swift. Another large land owner was the Shackleton family. The Shackletons purchased the Petty Canon lands from the representatives of the late J. Ganon. Here they built a flour mill.

The historic village atmosphere has now disappeared with a vast ungraceful form of low-density housing covering a large area of countryside, all built within the last 35 years.

Lucas's Coffee House
Cork Hill
Part of Cork House* was fitted out as a coffee house towards the end of the seventeenth century and became a fashionable resort for gentlemen about town seeking admiration. The yard at the back was frequently used for fighting duels, which were watched from the rear windows by the occupants partaking of their coffee. Cork House and Lucas's Coffee House closed in July 1758 and were eventually demolished to make way for the new wide and convenient passage called Parliament Street,* opened in 1762.
See **Cork House.**

Lucy Lane
Now Chancery Place*
Also called Mass Lane after the Jesuit Church there until 1697. Also Golblac Lane.
See **Huguenot Chapel.**

Luke Street
Off Townsend Street
Name comes from Luke Gardiner, a banker in Castle Street who bought land in this area in 1712.
See also **O'Connell Street** *and* **Gardiner's Mall.**

Lying-in Hospital
See **Rotunda Hospital.**

M

Macgiolla Mocholmóg Street

An entrance gate in the old city wall stood here named after the tribe of Mac Giolla Mocholmóg who were lords of the territory in the immediate vicinity of Dublin. AD 291, Mac Giolla Mocholmóg dispossessed the Uí Dercmaisig for the Lordship of Dublin. Donnchadh, the first king of the race, assumed the sovereignty of Leinster. About the beginning of the fifteenth century, the name was changed to the street or lane of St Michael. Many of the mayors of the city lived here in the sixteenth century. By the seventeenth century, it was occupied chiefly by lawyers. The law or plea office of the Exchequer was here until 1738. Now St Michael's Close.

Magdalen Asylum and Chapel

8 Lower Leeson Street

Lady Arabella Denny, a descendant of Sir William Petty who produced *The Down Survey*, the first scientific mapping out of Ireland in the time of Cromwell, was widowed in 1740 and became involved in many charitable works including the foundling hospital in James's Street. While working there with destitute children, she founded the Magdalen Asylum which opened in Lower Leeson Street on 11 June 1766, 'for unfortunate females abandoned by their seducers, and rejected by their friends, who preferred a life of penitence and virtue to one of guilt, infamy and prostitution'. A chapel was opened in 1768 and an annual charity sermon was preached there in aid of the asylum. Over the years, the chapel was enlarged to increase the accommodation from 500 to 700. In 1868, it was completely renovated

and a new front in the fashionable Romanesque style with a spire was added. Comhlucht Siúicre Éireann (Greencore Plc), the state-owned sugar company, eventually acquired the Asylum building. In 1960, an award-winning design by Liam Boyle and Seamus Delaney for an eight-storey building on a plinth got planning permission. The new building was completed by 1964 and is at present being refurbished. The Sugar Club, a regular live music centre, is on the ground floor. *See* **Workhouse, James's Street.**

Main Drainage System

The medieval walled city of Dublin was a congested warren of narrow lanes, passages and courts with no sanitation of any form, and frequent visitations of plague and epidemics caused by water-borne organisms. During the seventeenth century, the city expanded outside the walls, resulting in what is now termed the inner-city area. New areas of industrial development were founded and, with a concentration of population in these regions, large quantities of untreated domestic sewage were discharged into streams which often flooded, causing great misery from disease and a high death rate. The Poddle river* was described as an immense sewer and, as there were no privies, middens or cesspits, all sorts of filth was flung into the yard or street, often reaching the first-floor windows. Even though the origins of sewer systems with water-borne drainage can be traced to Greek and Roman times, it was not until the Georgian city that we know today was completed that the provision of sewers was considered. The first step towards the systematic provision of sewers in Dublin was the appointment in 1807 of paid Commissioners for Paving and Lighting* who also had the power to construct sewers. Their work did not extend to the poorer districts where it was impossible to levy rates, and in these areas the only drains were rivers and streams.

By 1848, the Commissioners had constructed 35½ miles of sewers. These had rubble masonry walls and were covered by brick arches and had earthen inverts or beds. Between 1853 and 1879, the Corporation built 65 miles of new sewers and improved about 30 miles of old sewers. The completion of the Vartry water supply scheme in 1868 made possible a system of sewage disposal by water-carriage using the sewers which had been built for street drainage. This was then discharged through 54 openings into the River Liffey.

The enactment of the 1878 Public Health Act gave the authorities greater powers to remedy the unsanitary conditions in the city. The first major drainage scheme was begun in 1896 and completed in 1906. Provision was made in the design for the drainage of the suburbs of Clontarf, Drumcondra, Glasnevin and Kilmainham, which at that time lay outside the city boundary. Sewers were laid along the north and south quays and were linked together by an inverted siphon which crossed the Liffey between Eden Quay and Burgh Quay. These sewers intercepted the flow from the local sewers which up to then had been discharging crude sewage directly into the Liffey. An 8-foot-diameter low-level sewer in tunnel conveyed the sewage from Hawkins Street to the main pumping station at Ringsend, where it was lifted to an 8-foot-diameter high-level sewer and passed on to the treatment works at the Pigeon House. Primary treatment was provided there and the treated effluent after settlement was discharged to the estuary. The settled sludge was conveyed in the sludge boat T.S.M.V. *Shamrock* and discharged in the deep water and fast current northeast of the Baily lighthouse.

This dumping of sludge into the sea ceased with the opening of the Ringsend Treatment Works* in 2003.

In consequence of the Dublin Boundaries Act of 1900, all the suburbs provided for in the design were incorporated in the city. In the 1901 census, the population of the city was 245,000 and the area some 3,807 acres. A design population of 324,000 was adapted for this scheme which cost £508,000. Terenure joined its sewers to the system in 1910, as did Kilmainham and Cabra; Rathdrum (Dundrum) in 1911; North Lotts was drained in 1912; Rathfarnham linked to Rathdrum in 1913; Clontarf joined in 1915; Chapelizod North in 1928; Crumlin in 1929; Chapelizod South in 1937; Whitehall and Donnycarney in 1937; Finglas in 1941. Howth had its own limited scheme in 1909 as did Coolock and Raheny in 1938.

The North Dublin drainage scheme designed to cater for a population of 265,000 cost £2 million when completed in 1958. It was designed to relieve overloading in the north city sewers and to provide drainage facilities for the expanding suburbs north and northeast of the city, including Sutton, Baldoyle and Howth. A gravity trunk sewer was laid from Navan Road via Finglas Bridge, Glasnevin, Griffith Avenue, Killester, Raheny and Sutton through a tunnel to a deep-sea outfall 200 feet off the nose of Howth, the sewage being discharged to the sea with no prior treatment other than coarse and fine screenings. The Dodder Valley or South Dublin drainage scheme was undertaken by Dublin County Council in 1975 to relieve the branch sewers extending outwards from the city by intercepting the sewage from Rathfarnham, Willbrook, Churchtown, Dundrum, Ballinteer and Goatstown. Provision was also made for the new town of Tallaght. The trunk sewer follows the course of the Dodder river from Tallaght to Milltown and proceeds via Belfield and Nutley Lane to Beach Road and across Sandymount strand to the new treatment works at Ringsend. The scheme was designed to cater for an area of 8,000 acres with an ultimate population of 240,000.

See also **Rathmines and Pembroke Drainage 1881, Grand Canal Sewer** *and* **Ringsend Treatment Works**.

Malahide

A maritime town 9 miles north of Dublin. A pre-Christian settlement, proved by the excavations of many flint axe heads and tools. It became a Viking stronghold from the eighth century until the Anglo-Norman invasion of 1170 by King Henry II. In 1176, Henry gave a grant of land to one of his knights, Sir Richard Talbot, who built a castle that remained in the same family until 1976, apart from a short time during the Cromwellian period. It is now the property of Dublin County Council and leased to Dublin Tourism. The present post-medieval structure and the grounds which contain many rare plants are open to the public. In the grounds are the ruins of a fifteenth/sixteenth-century church. One of the tombs is allegedly that of Maud Plunket whose husband, Sir Walter Hussey, was killed on their wedding day by a raiding party in the village. She later married Sir Richard Talbot.

As well as being a fishing port in the eighteenth and nineteenth centuries it was an area of silk and poplin mills, and Yellow Walls Road derives its name from an area where the wools were dyed and hung out to dry. The Dublin–Drogheda railway viaduct, opened in 1844, was built by Robert McEntire, a prominent mill owner, and caused the decline of the local fishing fleet. Between Malahide and Portmarnock stands Robswall Castle, owned by the Cistercians of St Mary's Abbey in Dublin (see also Dalkey). St Sylvester's (RC) Church was consecrated on 5 July 1846. The preacher that day was Father Theobald Mathew (1790–1856), the Apostle of Temperance. St Andrew's (C of I) Church was opened on 21 November 1822. A set of plans, dated 1824, by John Semple, states that these are a copy of Mr Read's drawings.

The Grand Hotel was built in 1835 and has recently been refurbished and extended to include a conference centre. Near the golf course and sand hills is a Martello Tower.* The area has greatly expanded in recent years with the building of a marina, providing berths for 300 yachts, and the construction of luxury apartments and houses.

See also **Carmelite Nuns**.

Manor Street

From Stoneybatter to Prussia Street

Until 1781 part of Stoneybatter,* possibly named after the manor of Glasnevin and Gorman (*see* Grangegorman Road). The Stanhope Street convent schools of the Religious Sisters of Charity (previously known as the Irish Sisters of Charity), an order founded in 1815, have an entrance in Manor Street.

Mansion House

See **Dawson Street**.

Mansion House Fund for Relief of Distress in Ireland

Ireland was beset by harvest failure during the 1870s and, in 1880, famine threatened the country. To prevent this, the Mansion House Fund was set up to collect money from Irish emigrants all over the world. The records of the Fund are held in the Dublin City Council archives and are important for local history because they contain reports from 800 local committees which distributed relief in every county in Ireland.

Marino

Originally part of the parish and townland of Donnycarney.

James Caulfield, 1st Earl of Charlemont (1763), inherited the title of 4th Viscount Charlemont at the age of six in 1734, and with it large estates in Co. Tyrone and Co. Armagh. He was a delicate child and was educated by a series of tutors including Rev. Edward Murphy, a classical scholar of considerable attainment, with whom he set out on the grand tour in 1746. This was to last almost nine years, five of which were

Marino. St Vincent de Paul Church.

spent in Italy. He returned to Marino and purchased some surrounding farms and it was here that he was to build the beautiful habitable Casino.* While this work was in progress, he was living at Marino House, which was demolished about 1925. It was surrounded by fine gardens designed by Matthew Peters. A public meeting held at Clontarf Town Hall in 1910 put forward a proposal for a garden city. By 1915, the Corporation had obtained control of the lands of Marino House and lands from the Christian Brothers and, over the years, an area from Fairview to Griffith Avenue was acquired, including land that was known as the 'Bloody fields' because of its association with the Battle of Clontarf. Eventually 1,283 houses were constructed and, in 1925, a tenant purchase scheme was agreed. Because of the large population a Roman Catholic church was built on the north side of the 100 Foot Road, renamed Griffith Avenue in April 1927. In 1926, agreement was reached to build two schools, one for 1,300 girls and the other for 1,000 boys.
See also **Fairview.**

Marino Crescent
Connecting Malahide Road and Howth Road
In 1792, a builder, Charles Ffolliot of Aungier Street, proceeded to erect a crescent of houses. Lord Charlemont accused the builder of obscuring the view from his house of Dublin Bay and obliged the builder to pay heavy dues on goods passing through his toll gate. Ffolliot then brought his materials across the bay by barge and built his houses in a style which blotted out the view from Marino House entirely. Bram Stoker (1847–1912), the author of *Dracula*, was born at no. 15 on 8 November 1847. William Carleton (1794–1869), author of *Willy Reilly and His Dear Colleen Bawn*, lived for some time at no. 2.

Market Cross or High Cross
High Street
This cross stood at the junction of Skinners' Row and the High Street at the entrance to Nicholas Street. It was here that public proclamations were read, including papal bulls and sentences of excommunication. Banns of marriage were read from the steps during the Commonwealth period and persons convicted of certain crimes were also obliged to stand in a penitential manner, barefoot before the cross. Others were obliged to wear white sheets with a placard around their necks

stating their offence. The cross, which was approximately 18 feet high, was in the form of a square carved tower supported on three high steps. It was topped with a bun-shape capital having a cross on top. Its location is shown on Speed's Map of 1610. *See* **High Street.**

Markets
See **Fish, Fruit and Vegetable Market.**

Marlborough Street (1728)
From North Earl Street to Cathal Brugha Street
Probably built around the time of Marlborough's wars.

In 1740, Tyrone House, designed by Richard Cassels for Sir Marcus Beresford, later to become Earl of Tyrone, a large house seven bays wide, was built. The house became known as Beresford's Riding House establishment where his own corp of yeomanry practised. In 1835, it was bought by the government and is now used by the Department of Education and Science. The government built a replica on the other side of the Central Model Schools which Bernard Shaw attended. The street is probably most famous for St Mary's Pro-Cathedral,* opened in 1825. In 1969, 13 tenement buildings and shops were demolished to make way for a pre-cast eight-storey concrete block of 83,000 square feet. In 1772, Williams' Glasshouse on Marlborough Green advertised that any colour glass could be made.

St Thomas's Church (C of I)* was extensively damaged by gunfire in 1922 and was re-erected in 1931–32 on an island in the extended Sean MacDermott Street.

Marshalsea Debtors' Prison
About 1580, the entrance to a lane opposite St Werburgh's Church, named Le Hynd Street, was enclosed with the new prison of the Four Courts Marshalsea. The office of Marshal was from 1546 associated with the constableship of Dublin Castle. In 1671, Sir Daniel Bellingham bequeathed lands valued at about £50 for the relief of poor debtors in the city and Marshalsea Gaol.

An Act of Parliament of 1697 separated the two jails which were then housed in Bridge Street about 20 yards from Brown's Castle. The Marshalsea was also known as the 'Black Dog'. According to Gilbert, 'there were twelve rooms for the reception of prisoners, two of which contained five beds each; the others were no better than closets but had one bed each. The general rent was one shilling per night but in particular cases a much higher price was charged'. It frequently happened that four or five men slept together in one bed, each individual still paying the rent of one shilling. The Four Courts Marshalsea moved to Molesworth Court on the western side of Fishamble Street in 1704.

A new Marshalsea was built in 1739 at the rere of Bridgefoot Street near Bonham Street. This was again rebuilt in 1775. It was a prison for debtors who were often confined with their families, having taken refuge from their creditors. The majority paid rent for their lodgings, while those who were destitute were supplied with bread. Robert Emmet* used the Marshalsea as an arsenal. The Dublin militia used it as a barracks in the latter half of the nineteenth century, and officers' quarters were added near the entrance gates. After the British troops left in 1922, Dublin Corporation used it as a tenement and for a few years before it was closed in 1970, drop-outs from other Corporation housing lived there. It was demolished in 1975.
See **Newgate Gaol.**

Marshalsea Lane
Joining Bonham Street
Named after the Marshalsea debtors' prison which stood there from 1739 to 1975.

Marsh's Library
St Patrick's Close
Designed by Sir William Robinson who had been architect for the Royal Hospital Kilmainham.* Built in 1701 for Archbishop Marsh (1638–1713), it was the first public library in Ireland and one of the earliest in these islands. It is a fine example of an early scholars' library, with oak bookcases having

carved and lettered gables topped by a mitre. There are three wired alcoves or cages where readers were locked in with rare books. Originally many of the books were on chains which ran on wooden rods attached to each shelf. In 1707, the Irish parliament passed an act, 'settling and preserving a public library for ever'.

There are four main collections consisting of 25,000 books relating to the sixteenth, seventeenth and early part of the eighteenth centuries. In 1705, Narcissus Marsh paid £2,500 for a library of 10,000 books belonging to Edward Stillingfleet (1635–1699), Bishop of Worcester. It contains books printed by some of the earliest English printers. Archbishop Marsh left his own books to the library, as did Dr Elias Bouhéreau, a Huguenot who fled from France in 1685 and was appointed the first librarian. John Stearne (1660–1745), Bishop of Clogher, bequeathed his books in 1745; these included Cicero's *Letters to his Friends*, printed in Milan in 1472. The library also contains a large number of manuscripts, including a volume on the lives of the Irish saints dating from about 1400. There are also mementos of Jonathan Swift who was a governor of the library.

Martello Towers

Named after a tower in Cape Mortella in Corsica, captured by the British in 1793–94.

Twenty-one of these circular tapering towers of stone were built on the coast, 1804–06 to oppose a possible landing of Napoleonic troops. They cost £1,800 each and stand at Balbriggan, Bray, Bullock Harbour, Carrickhill, Dalkey Island, Dún Laoghaire, Howth, Ireland's Eye, Killiney, Loughshinny, two at Portrane, Robert's Wall, Rush, Sandycove, Sandymount, Seapoint, Shanganagh, Shenick's Island, Skerries and Williamstown. From 9 to 15 September 1904 James Joyce (1882–1941) lived at the tower in Sandycove. The first chapter of *Ulysses* is set in the tower. It opened as a Joyce Museum in 1962.

Mary Street
From Capel Street to Henry Street

Name comes from St Mary's Church 1702* and the new parish of St Mary formed out of St Michan's parish in 1697 and named from St Mary's Abbey.* Langford House, a late seventeenth-century dwelling, stood in its own grounds. It was named after Viscount Langford whose father had bought it in 1743. It was demolished in 1931 and replaced with the Nurses' Home for Jervis Street Hospital. In 1909, James Joyce opened the Volta Cinema at no. 45, with financial support from Trieste businessmen. It did not prosper and was sold to a British group who renamed it the Lyceum but later reverted back to the name Volta Electric Theatre. Primark Limited, trading as Penneys' Stores, occupies the large Victorian building with its copper dome built for Todd Burns and Company, the general outfitters at no. 47, which extends back to nos. 24–30 Jervis Street. Todd Burns was completely rebuilt after a fire in 1902, when under the chairmanship of John Boyd Dunlop, son of Dr Boyd Dunlop, inventor of the pneumatic tyre (*see* Stephen Street). Burns was a nephew of the Scottish poet, Robert Burns.

Michael Collins (1890–1922) had offices at no. 22 and later at no. 28.

Mary's Abbey
From Capel Street to Arran Street East

Name comes from Abbey of St Mary, foundation affiliated to the monastery of Savigny founded in 1139. The remains of the Chapter House may be viewed at Meeting House Lane, together with the slype of 1190. The monks owned extensive lands around the monastery which were extended by Henry II in 1172 to include the land of Clonliffe as far as the Tolka. In 1147, the Abbeys of St Mary and of Savigny (in Normandy) came under the Cistercian order. In the Middle Ages, the Abbey's guesthouse was the finest in Dublin and was sometimes used as the meeting place of the English Council. It was in the Chapter House that Silken Thomas Fitzgerald renounced his allegiance to Henry VIII and

Coombe Lying-in Hospital. Built as the Meath Hospital in 1770; became the County Dublin Infirmary in 1774; was taken over by Margaret Boyle and became the Coombe Lying-in Hospital in 1826.

began his unsuccessful rebellion of 1534. The Abbey was closed in 1539 after the suppression of the monasteries. The statue of the Blessed Virgin which belonged to the Abbey and was discovered in the eighteenth century, is in the Carmelite Church in Whitefriar Street.

Mater Hospital
Eccles Street

The hospital was opened in September 1861 by the Sisters of Mercy. On the opening day, it had accommodation for 40 patients. Five years later, during a cholera epidemic in 1866, it treated 248 patients in six weeks. It is now one of the largest hospitals in the country.

Among the most recent developments in a hospital which has continued to develop and expand its services: a mobile breast screening unit with back-up ancillary structures; major expansion of the national cardiac surgery unit at the Mater; opening of new library and lecture theatre for students; commencement of work on the provision of major clinical sciences laboratories; formal recognition by the Department of Health of the Mater's information technology programme.

Mayor
See **Lord Mayor.**

Meath Hospital
Long Lane

Founded on 2 March 1753 by gentlemen who took a house on the Upper Coombe near Meath Street 'because the Charitable surgery at Spring gardens in Dame Street was so far away'. The surgeons agreed to 'attend without fee or reward from 8.00–10.00 a.m.' John Watson writing in *The Gentlemen's and Citizens' Almanack* in 1754 states: 'The Meath Hospital on the Coombe was opened on 2 March 1753. Supported hitherto by a benefit play, some benefactions and annual subscriptions of several of the principal inhabitants of the Earl of Meath's Liberty, and other well disposed persons, who judged that an institution of this nature was much wanted in a part of the town remote from the city hospital and greatly thronged by the industrious poor.' In 1756, the lease expired and the hospital moved to Skinners'Alley. A further move was made in 1760 to Meath Street, and again in 1764 to larger premises in Earl Street. The premises were declared to be in a dangerous state by 1769 when it was decided to build a proper hospital.

On 10 October 1770, Lord Brabazon laid the foundation stone of the Meath Hospital, which subsequently became the old Coombe Lying-in Hospital, now demolished. It was opened in 1773 and changed its name by Act of Parliament in 1774 to The County Dublin Infirmary. Finally a site was purchased for £1,120 rent free, on 22 December 1815. This was known as the Dean's Vineyard in Long Lane, the property of the Dean and Chapter of St Patrick's Cathedral. That year, Thomas Pleasants, the philanthropist, gave the governors £6,000. Patients were transferred from the Coombe to the New Meath Hospital on 24 December 1822. In 1952, a new red-brick Nurses' Home was built facing onto Heytesbury Street.

The Federated Dublin Voluntary Hospitals group established on 6 November 1961, with the following members: the Adelaide, the Meath, Harcourt Street, Mercer's, Dr Steevens', Sir Patrick Dun's, Royal City of Dublin (Baggot Street). The group moved to a new hospital at Tallaght. The hospital was bought by the South West Health Board in 1999 (formerly Eastern Health Board) and now houses a primary care unit with occupational therapists and physiotherapists, speech and language therapy, minor injury unit and basic dental service. There is also a public health nurse, an area medical officer, a social worker and personnel from the supplementary welfare services. The hospital currently operates a unit of 66 beds for older people, in the newly refurbished Nurses' Home, designed in 1949 by Robinson Keefe, architects, following an €8 million capital funding from the Eastern Health Board in 2003. The building is user friendly for residents, all the floors being serviced by a lift. The centre also accommodates the practices of seven local GPs who transferred here, where their 8,000 patients are able to attend.
See **Tallaght Hospital.**

Meath Street
From The Coombe to Thomas Street
Named after William Brabazon 2nd Baron

of Ardee, created Earl of Meath on 28 March 1627.

A busy trading street with markets at the weekends. Towards the end of the eighteenth century, it was the centre of a brewing area. The old archway at no. 26 was the entrance to the meeting house of the Quakers* (Society of Friends), and a soup kitchen operated there in the early part of the twentieth century. Church of St Catherine of Alexandria (RC); the parish church originally situated in Dirty Lane (Bridgefoot Street) moved here in 1782. The present church opened in 1858 and was designed by J. J. McCarthy. It is one of the churches serving the Liberties area of Dublin. In 1978, a brick complex of housing and shops was completed to a design of Delany McVeigh and Pike.

Mecklenburgh Street
See **Railway Street.**

Media Lab Europe
See **Digital Hub (The).**

Meeting House Lane
Mary's Abbey
Name comes from the meeting house of the Presbyterian Congregation which met there from 1667 to 1864, when it removed to Rutland Square.
See also **Huguenot Chapel of St Mary.**

Memorial Road
Part of the crescent in front of the Custom House, from Beresford Place to Custom House Quay.
Originally part of Beresford Place, renamed after 1922 in honour of the Dublin Brigade, and a memorial by the Breton sculptor, Yann Renard-Goulet, was erected at the west end of the Custom House.

Mercer's Hospital
Stephen Street
In 1734, Mrs Mary Mercer gave a large house at the end of Stephen Street for a hospital for the reception of sick poor, and appointed governors and directors. The

ground was given by Dr Whittingham, Archdeacon. The city gave £50 towards fitting the house and, soon after, several further contributions were made. On 17 August, ten beds were filled. The physicians and surgeons gave their attendance gratis. In 1738, aided by a legacy from Captain Hayes, a considerable addition was built and the number of beds increased to 62. The hospital still retains some of its original stonework with additions over the years. Built on the thirteenth-century site of St Stephen's leper hospital, it closed in 1983 and was taken over as a hostel and library for the Royal College of Surgeons. The front of the building houses Mercer's Health Centre, a general medical practice, travel health centre and international immunisation clinic. In 1989, apart from the façade, it was completely demolished and a new building erected with the existing frontage. The Royal College of Surgeons,* which was founded in 1784, used the hospital as part of its training school until it moved to St Stephen's Green in 1810.

Mercer Street Upper and Lower

Mrs Mary Mercer opened a hospital for the sick poor in 1734 on the site of the ancient St Stephen's Church where at one time stood a leper hospital. Mercer's Hospital closed in 1983 and was taken over by the Royal College of Surgeons. Apart from the façade it was rebuilt for use as student accommodation with a library and Mercer's Health Centre.

Until 1734 the street was named Love Lane, and the upper part was known as French Street (after French settlers) until 1860. The name was changed on account of the bad reputation of the street.

Merrion Row

From St Stephen's Green North to Upper Merrion Street

Named after the 2nd Viscount Fitzwilliam of Merrion.

Recently restored Huguenot graveyard* beside a modern office block built in 1977 which replaced the Swiss Chalet Café and

Bakery at nos. 2–3, Duigan's, the tobacconist, and Norman Allen, the painters and decorators. Several shops and public houses including O'Donoghue's, the original haunt of the Dubliners, the well-known ballad group.

At the junction with St Stephen's Green North, on the traffic island, a stone sculpture, 'Trace' by Grace Weir, was erected by the Sculptors' Society of Ireland in 1988. It consists of two and a half arches in different-coloured stonework with bronze insets.

Merrion Square

North of St Stephen's Green and Upper Merrion Street

Named after the 2nd Viscount Fitzwilliam of Merrion.

Laid out in 1752 by John Ensor for the Fitzwilliam Estate and completed towards the end of the century. All the original eighteenth-century houses remain, some of them having very fine stucco ceilings. The Rutland memorial in the form of a drinking fountain was designed by Francis Sandys in 1791 to commemorate Charles Manners, 4th Duke of Rutland, Lord Lieutenant 1784–87. The National Gallery,* built by subscription as a testimonial to William Dargan (1799–1867), the railway engineer, was designed by Francis Fowke; it was opened in 1864. On the west side of the building is Leinster Lawn (see Royal Dublin Society).

Number 1 Merrion Square was the home of Sir William and Lady Wilde, the parents of Oscar. Sir Philip Crampton, surgeon, lived at no. 14, and at no. 42 Sir Jonah Barrington, diarist. Daniel O'Connell lived at no. 58, Joseph Sheridan Le Fanu at what is now the Arts Council, no. 70, and William Butler Yeats at no. 82. George William Russell (AE) worked at no. 84. Number 63 houses the Royal Society of Antiquaries of Ireland,* and the Irish Architectural Archive* is at nos. 44 and 45. The park in the centre of the Square had been held for many years by the RC archbishops as a possible site for a cathedral. In 1974, Archbishop Ryan handed it back to the people of Dublin and it is now an attractive public park. Sculptures within the park include a bust of George William Russell; Henry Grattan by Peter Grant; and the seated figure of Éire by Jerome Connor. 'Tribute Head' by Dame Elizabeth Frink was donated in 1982 by Artists for Amnesty. It was unveiled by the Lord Mayor of Dublin, Cllr Dan Browne, on South Africa Freedom Day, 25 June 1983, in the twentieth year of imprisonment of Nelson Mandela. Bronze bust of Michael Collins by Dick Joynt. Bronze chair in memory of Dermot Morgan ('Father Ted'), writer and actor. A granite slab with a poem, 'Tree of Life' by Eavan Boland, erected 1994.

The Rt Hon. Richard Viscount Fitzwilliam was an important instigator in the move to coax the gentry from north of the river to fashionable town houses on the south side, although much of the credit has gone to the Earl of Kildare with his much-quoted phrase, 'They will follow me wherever I go'. Merrion Square was probably the first totally residential square of this period. While John Ensor had already laid out part

of Rutland (Parnell) Square in 1751, a large area had been taken over for Dr Mosse's lying-in hospital and Rotunda.

Merrion Street Lower
From Fenian Street to Upper Merrion Street
Merrion Hall, an Evangelical church, was designed by Alfred G. Jones in 1863. It had served a large congregation for many years, but attendance had dropped recently and the building was sold in 1990. It was extensively damaged by fire on 2 May 1991. The building was demolished and rebuilt as the Davenport Hotel, retaining the original Jones façade.

Merrion Street Upper
From Merrion Square to Merrion Row
In 1867, the Royal College of Science was founded as part of the Royal Dublin Society. In 1911–15, it moved to impressive new buildings designed by Sir Aston Webb and Sir Thomas Manly Dean. The building now houses government offices which were completed in 1922. The exteriors of all the buildings, including those in the

Merrion Square. Restored doorways and fanlights at nos. 74 and 75. The square was laid out in 1752.

Merrion Hotel, Upper Merrion Street. A listed property of 18th-century town houses restored with great attention to detail. It is one of the city's most elegant hotels, located opposite the Dáil.

impressive courtyard, were cleaned in 1990 and the offices adapted for modern usage.

In 1926, the Royal College of Science became part of University College Dublin. The foundation stone of the college was laid by King Edward VII on 28 April 1903, and the college was officially opened by King George V and Queen Mary on 8 July 1911. The building housing the Museum of Natural History, designed by Frederick V. Clarendon, opened in 1857.

Mespil Road

A tree-lined road along the Grand Canal from Leeson Street Upper to Baggot Street Upper. In 1962, four Georgian buildings were demolished to make way for the Irish Life Assurance Company's five-storey L-shaped office block, with a landscaped courtyard and fountain designed by Downes Meehan and Robson. In 1751, Dr Barry built Mespil House with fine plaster-work ceilings. It was demolished to make way for the Irish Life Mespil flats, a series of red-brick blocks.

Davitt House, built in 1965, replaced two Victorian houses

Metropole Ballroom, Cinema and Restaurant
O'Connell Street

Built in Aberdeen granite to a design of Aubrey V. O'Rourke (1885–1928) and opened in 1922. As well as a cinema and restaurant, it housed one of the most popular ballrooms in Dublin, in which various functions were held each year, including the Arts Ball. It was demolished in 1973 to make way for a new department store. It was built on the site of the Metropole Hotel which was destroyed in the Easter Rising of 1916. It had been a hotel since the middle of the nineteenth century when it was known as 'Spadaccini's' and then 'the Prince of Wales'. The Jury family had it until 1892 when it was sold to the Mitchell family who named it the Metropole and embellished it with iron-work balconies and verandahs.

Mill Street
From New Row to Clarence Mangan Row

Name comes from a malt mill, a wood mill and two double mills, originally part of St Thomas's Abbey, which were granted to Sir William Brabazon at the dissolution in

1538. Also from the mill pond, part of the Poddle, that fed the mills situated between Warrenmount* convent and Mill Street. Today it is mostly warehouses and industrial buildings, but the bricked-up front of no. 10 still stands; this was at one time the dower house of the Brabazon family. It was redesigned by the Victorian architect, George Beater.

Millennium Garden, Dame Street
Between Palace Street and Exchange Court
Opened in 1988 by the Parks Department of Dublin Corporation. Behind a fountain stand three statues provided by the Office of Public Works, representing the crafts of wood, metal and stone. They were originally on exhibition at Earlsfort Terrace (now the National Concert Hall) in 1872. The Liscannor stone surrounding the grass areas was sponsored by Guinness and Mahon, Bankers, to mark their 150th anniversary.

Millennium Plot, Glasnevin Cemetery
Until very recently, Dublin Corporation was the last-known local authority in Ireland to send bodies to 'the poor ground'. These pauper plots were used to bury the unclaimed bodies of the poor. It was known that some old people forsook medical care, proper heat and nutrition out of fear of being placed in a pauper's grave, where it was not permitted to erect grave markers, thus making it impossible to determine exactly where in 'the poor ground' they had been buried. The ALONE* organisation acquired a plot at Glasnevin Cemetery in 1988 and Dublin Corporation approved the use of this 'Millennium Plot' for those who might otherwise have been relegated to the paupers' section. The large inscribed granite headstone and limestone nameplates and surrounds were donated by members of the Architectural and Monumental Stone Association. Other sundry expenses were taken care of by the singers of the 'Molly Malone' millennium record, who donated their royalties to the

cause. The staff of Glasnevin Cemetery prepared the site and laid the foundations for the stonework.

The first person to be buried in the plot was Edward Montgomery who, because of initial difficulty in tracing next of kin, was taken under contract by Staffords to the city morgue, from where he would have been taken for burial early in the morning without a church service on 24 March 1988. His daughter was contacted and he was given a funeral Mass and graveside prayers when he was buried on 25 March. The dedication of the plot took place on Thursday, 28 October 1988, at 2.15 p.m.
See **ALONE.**

Milltown
Named after the Leeson family who made their money in brewing and buying up parcels of land. Joseph Leeson was created Earl of Milltown in 1763. The village became part of the Rathmines and Rathgar urban district* in 1880 and remained so until the Local Government (Dublin) Act of 1930, when it became part of the Dublin Corporation area. The Sisters of Charity are at Mount St Anne's where they have a secondary school and a social service centre. There is also a fine golf course bordering Milltown and Churchtown Road Lower. The Institute of Theology and Philosophy is at Milltown Park, which was once a pleasure resort for Dubliners.

The area also includes Palmerston Park and Temple Road, named after Henry John Temple (1784–1865), 3rd Viscount Palmerston. St Philip's Church (C of I) on Temple Road, designed by Sir Thomas Drew, was opened for worship on 1 May 1867 to serve the needs of a rapidly expanding wealthy middle-class community. In marked contrast is the long RC church in the centre of which is a pediment supported by four pilasters, while over the side entrance is written 'the Church of the Assumption Parish of Milltown'. Legend has it that it was originally a barn used for Mass in penal times. It was rebuilt in 1819, altered several times through the years and now has a modern frontage and interior.

On 16 March 1990, An Bord Pleanála gave permission for houses to be built on the Shamrock Rovers Football Ground.

Misery Hill
Between Hanover Street and Hanover Quay at end of Townsend Street
In 1220, a leper hospital stood at the end of Townsend Street at the Hawkins Street entrance. Many of the unfortunate sufferers unable to gain admission to the hospital would spend the night on the hill, where a bell was rung to warn citizens of their presence. The hill was also used as a place of execution where criminals were hanged. There was also a custom of bringing those already hanged on Gallows Hill* to Misery Hill, where their bodies were left hanging for anything from six to twelve months.

Molesworth Street
From Dawson Street to Kildare Street
Dating from an Enabling Act of 1725 and laid out in 1727 by Richard, 3rd Viscount Molesworth. It necessitated pulling down four houses, the property of Joshua Dawson, in order to connect with Dawson Street. Of the 23 Georgian houses, built of brick over mountain-granite bases, only four survive. The two buildings on either side of the Masonic Hall were designed by Edward Holmes in 1868. An interesting feature of this building with its great portico supported by columns: the brass fittings on the entrance steps that held the rods for the red carpet laid for the frequent visits of Edward, Prince of Wales. In 1978, St Ann's School and Molesworth Hall were demolished and a modern office block to house the Commission of the European Communities was erected in its stead. The Government Publications Sales Office, the Passport Office, general offices and Buswell's Hotel are also on Molesworth Street.

Molyneux House
34 Peter Street
Built in 1711 by Thomas Molyneux, Physician General to the army in Ireland

and younger brother of William Molyneux, the philosopher and patriot who in 1698 published *The Case of Ireland's being bound by Acts of Parliament in England Stated.* Thomas published a pamphlet asserting that the Giant's Causeway was a natural phenomenon and not man made. He also published an account of the Irish elk. He moved from the family home in New South Row, Thomas Street, to the new house where his second son lived until 1778. It then passed to Philip Astley, the circus promoter, who built an amphitheatre behind the house, in Bride Street, where many forms of entertainment were presented, including pantomime and horsemanship. He sold out in 1809 to Henry Erskine Johnstone who ran the Royal Hibernian Theatre until 1812 when he absconded, heavily in debt. Between 1815 and 1862, no. 34 Peter Street housed the Molyneux Asylum for Blind Women, which subsequently moved to Leeson Street. The house then became a home for aged women until about 1907, and was finally taken over by the Salvation Army until 1941. It was demolished in 1943. The chapel at the back, which replaced the amphitheatre, was adapted in 1947 as a recreation hall for Messrs Jacobs. In 1974, Stephenson Gibney and Associates re-faced the building with brick, built a courtyard with a fountain and converted the building for use as premises for their architectural practice until the partnership was dissolved in 1975.

Monto (Montgomery Street) (1776)
From Mabbot Street to Amiens Street
Named after Elizabeth Montgomery who married the Rt Hon. Luke Gardiner. Now Foley Street. The area included Railway Street, formerly Tyrone Street and prior to that Mecklenburgh Street after Charlotte Sophia, Princess of Mecklenburgh-Strelitz, wife of George III. Known as one of the most dreadful dens of immorality in Europe.
From 1800 to 1900, it was recorded that the Monto contained some 1,600 prostitutes. While the area spread over several streets,

Lower Mecklenburgh Street was the most notorious. Following a police raid in 1925 when 120 persons were arrested, the Monto ceased operating. Edward Smyth (1749–1812), sculptor, who carved much of the decoration including the heads of the river gods on the new Custom House,* died at no. 36 on 2 August 1812.

With the coming of the nearby IFSC,* the area has been rejuvenated with the help of the section 23 tax-relief scheme. Apartment blocks have been built, similar to the Steelworks at Foley Street and Gloucester Square, with frontage onto James Joyce Street and Foley Street, with 88 apartments, penthouses and shops designed by Anthony Reddy and Associates. Liberty Corner on James Joyce Street, a project in Dublin City Council's Integrated Area plan, opened in 2004 and consists of 58 apartments, on four floors over ground-floor level, with offices and retail units. The development includes a dance centre, arts centre and a crèche. A penthouse floor is set back from the front.

Moore Street
From Henry Street to Parnell Street
Named after Viscount Moore who came into possession of part of the lands of St Mary's Abbey in 1614. This area was granted to James Fitzgerald, Earl of Desmond, on the dissolution of the Irish monasteries by Henry VIII in 1537. The estate was purchased in 1714 by Luke Gardiner.

A general trading street with some street stalls selling fruit, vegetables and flowers. From 1964, a development company had been buying up property in the area between Moore Street and Chapel Lane. These sites were eventually bought out by Dublin Corporation on a compulsory purchase order. By 1973, Coles Alley, Gregg's Lane, Horseman's Row and Riddles Row had disappeared. Also part of Parnell Street was demolished. All of this demolition was to make way for the Ilac Centre and Irish Life Mall. This was designed by Keane Murphy Duff and was opened in 1981 as a large undercover shopping complex with a multi-storey car park. In 1985, Dublin Corporation opened a fine library in the Centre.

See also **Henry Street, North Earl Street, Drogheda Street.**

Moore Street, from Henry Street to Parnell Street. A general trading street with street stalls selling fruit, vegetables and flowers. Recently a new immigrant ethnic community has moved into the area and this is reflected in the type of shop and produce being offered for sale.

Mount Jerome Cemetery

On a 47-acre site established by the General Cemetery Company of Dublin, constituted by an Act of Parliament in 1834. Its statutory duty was to maintain and keep the cemetery, together with the walls and fences. It operated profitably for many years and paid dividends to its share-holders, as did a closely linked company, Mount Jerome Monumental Company Limited. In September 1983, Cemetery Holdings Ltd registered as a company, and the shares of the General Cemetery Company were transferred to it. In December 1984, the Massey firm of undertakers bought the cemetery. Those interred there include Sir William Wilde, father of Oscar; John Synge the playwright, Reverend Stephen Jerome, vicar of St Kevin's Parish 1639; some ancestors of Lord Longford; there is a plot for members of the Royal Irish Constabulary and a vault of the Guinness family. The cemetery has an impressive collection of funerary monu-ments and now has a crematorium at the north walk. The chapel facing the main walkway was designed by William Atkins.

Mount Street Lower

From Merrion Square to Northumberland Road
Halliday suggests that the name is derived from the mount of Gallows Hill shown on Roque's map of 1756 between Lower Baggot Street (Gallows Road 1757) and Mount Street. A street of mixed-quality eighteenth- and nineteenth-century houses built until about 1820. John Millington Synge (1871–1909) died at no. 130. Over the past few years, 60 houses have been demolished to make way for office blocks. Prize Bond House at no. 33 was completed in 1970, then Grattan House, and now the entire street consists of office accom-modation. The Prize Bond office moved to College House, Townsend Street, in 1990.

Mount Street Upper

From Merrion Square to Mount Street Crescent
Built about 1820, although nos. 58–62 may be earlier. The tall red-brick houses make a splendid vista, with St Stephen's Church* by John Bowden facing towards Merrion Square. In 1988, the Electricity Supply Board decided to restore eight houses, together with the two adjoining ones on Lower Fitzwilliam Street. A year later, while work was in progress, a large section collapsed into the street. The interiors of all these houses have now been replaced with modern office accommodation. In 1988, Ivor Fitzpatrick and Company, Solicitors, commissioned Derek A. Fitzsimons' lovely bronze statue, 'Memories of Mount Street', depicting a child swinging out of a lamp standard from a rope. It stands in front of Pepper Canister House.

Mountjoy Prison

Built in 1847 and completed in 1850. Designed by J. Owen, architect of the Board of Works, with five wings of cells that extend from a central block. It replaced the Marshalsea Debtors' prison* and the Newgate Gaol.* the large towers are air vents. There is no sanitation in the overcrowded cells, and prisoners have to 'slop out' each morning. It is the setting for Brendan Behan's (1923–1964) play, *The Quare Fellow*, and where he served four years of a 14-year sentence from 1942 for shooting at a garda. In 2005, the government bought a 150-acre site at Thorntown, between Ashbourne and Swords, at a cost of €29.9 million. It proposes to build a new prison complex that will eventually replace Mountjoy in 2008.

Mountjoy Square

From Gardiner Street to Belvedere Place
From Luke Gardiner, Baron Mountjoy 1789, Viscount 1795.
Wilson's directory for 1791 names the square as Gardiner's Square. In 1792, the building of houses commenced and it became Mountjoy Square. The building of the east side from Fitzgibbon Street to Great Charles Street was not finally completed until 1818. The west side was the first to be completed in 1793, and the first

three residents were William Pemberton, John Russell—both builders—and Michael Stapleton, stucco worker. Water mains were laid in 1799, following a letter from the residents to Dublin Corporation read on 18 October 1799. In 1801, it was decided that the waste space in the square itself should be levelled and laid out. An Act of Parliament received royal assent on 30 April 1802: to ornament and enclose the square with a railing. A garden was laid out and completed in June 1805, each resident receiving a key. By 1818, Mountjoy Square had 82 lamps, 'fitted in plain but neat lamp irons at the distance of about 21 feet asunder'. A military marquee was erected in 1836 as ladies of the square, 'are often incommoded by a sudden shower'. Military bands used to perform in the marquee during the summer. In 1889, responsibility for the footpaths on Mountjoy Square passed to the Corporation of Dublin. After the Act of Union in 1801, the square and surrounding streets went into a steep decline. In the late 1960s and early 1970s, several efforts were made by conservation groups to try to save the square. The PMPA motor group built a modern office block behind nos. 40–45 in the 1970s, with mock Georgian fronts (now the College of Marketing & Design), which helped to save part of the south side. The Church of Ireland divinity hostel occupied nos. 25–26 from 1924 to 1963. These were then bought by Edward Dillon, Wine Merchants, who did an impressive restoration job. Since 1974, no. 26 houses the National Council for Educational Awards. Some new apartments, but a lot of the square requires rejuvenation.

Mountrath Street
See **Charles Street West.**

Mullinahack
*From the lower end of John Street to Meeting House Lane. Near Gormund's Gate (Wormwood Gate) now part of Oliver Bond Street**
From the Irish *Muileann an chaca,* a dung mill. A large pipe from the mill discharged its foul-smelling contents here. Today there is a block of corporation flats to the left side. Another explanation for the name is that in 1571 it was agreed that two privies should be built, one near Mr Fyan's new tower and the other over the stream at Gormund's (Gormond's) Gate.

Music Hall, New
Fishamble Street
The eighteenth century was a time when a great many Dublin charities were founded. Among these was a charitable musical society that used to meet in the Bull's Head Tavern in Fishamble Street. Included in the members of the group were some of the Vicars-choral of St Patrick's Cathedral. The society decided to build a new music hall to the design of Cassels. It was opened in October 1741. On 13 April 1742, Handel's *Messiah* was first performed for the relief of the prisoners in the several jails and for the support of Mercer's Hospital* — and of the Charitable Infirmary.* The choirs of both the cathedrals took part in the performance at which 700 persons attended. According to the *Dublin Journal's** account of 15 April, 'the most grand, polite and crowded audience witnessed a triumph'. Following Handel's visit, there was a great increase in musical activity in Dublin. John Neal, the music publisher, and his son, William, were the managers of this thriving venture which housed every kind of theatrical entertainment, including Lord Mornington's 'Musical Academy' in the 1750–60 period. The hall survived into the nineteenth century, being used at considerable intervals. The building stood near the entrance to no. 19, which now houses the Contemporary Music Centre,* occupied prior to that by Kennan and Sons Metal Works.
See **Fishamble Street.**

N

Nassau Street

From Grafton Street to South Leinster Street
Name comes from William III, Prince of Orange and Count of Nassau.

Originally St Patrick's Well Lane, from a twelfth-century well or fountain. Legend has it that St Patrick, complaining of the dearth of fresh water, struck the ground with the point of the staff of Jesus and produced fresh water. It dried up in 1729 and was cleaned out and restored by the Corporation in June 1731. The well was situated within the grounds of Trinity College. When the Thingmote* (Norse assembly mound) was demolished on College Green in 1685, the earth was moved to St Patrick's Well Lane, raising the level by about 8 feet as the area had been subject to flooding. In 1842, the street was widened and the old wall enclosing Trinity was replaced with a lower one surmounted by railings. In the 1960s, 15 eighteenth- and nineteenth-century buildings owned by the Norwich Union group were demolished and three new office blocks with shops at street level were built to a design of Lardner and Partners. Further down the street, the Kilkenny Design shop is housed in the two-and-a-half-acre development, Setanta Centre, opened in 1975.

National Archives

Bishop Street
Established on 1 June 1988, when most sections of the National Archives Act, 1986, came into operation, it is an amalgamation of the Public Record Office (established in 1867) and the State Paper Office (established in 1702). It is situated on the site of the original Jacob's Biscuit Factory in Bishop Street. The main function of the National Archives is to preserve the records of central government and the courts. Court and probate records are transferred to the Archives after 20 years, while the records of central government are transferred after 30 years. The National Archives also contain papers from other sources including Church of Ireland parochial registers, state-sponsored bodies, business firms, solicitors' and estate offices and private individuals. The reading room at Bishop Street is open to the public and records are available for inspection to those holding a valid Reader's Ticket.

In 1991, the former State Paper Office and the Public Record Office moved offices to Bishop Street. By the autumn of that year, the Four Courts premises (PROI) and the Dublin Castle premises (SPO) had been vacated. The reading room at Bishop Street was opened in January 1992 and won a major architectural award later in the year. In July 1993, it was dedicated to the memory of the first Chairman of the National Archives Advisory Council, Niall McCarthy, in a ceremony carried out by the President of Ireland, Mary Robinson. A bust of Niall McCarthy by Marjorie Fitzgibbon was unveiled on that occasion and is on display in the Reading Room. Other art works are also displayed.

Military Archives, Cathal Brugha Barracks, Rathmines: Archives of the Department of Defence, the Defence Forces and the Bureau of Military History are held in the Military Archives, which is a place of deposit under section 14 of the National Archives Act, 1986.

Part of the National College of Art and Design complex at Thomas Street. Originally affiliated to the RDS, the College was re-constituted as the Dublin Metropolitan School of Art in 1877. It moved from its premises in Kildare Street to the premises formerly occupied by Power's Distillery, its present home, in the 1970s.

Geological Survey, Beggars Bush, Haddington Road: Archives of the Geological Survey are held at the offices of the Geological Survey, which is a place of deposit under section 14 of the National Archives Act, 1986.

National College of Art and Design
Thomas Street

The Dublin Society, founded on 25 June 1731, had been paying Robert West since 1746 to take students at his drawing academy in George's Lane. By 1750, West's drawing academy had become the Society's school of figure drawing at Shaw's Court, Dame Street. After several moves, the school was situated in Kildare Street. The Board of Trade took control in 1849 until 1854 when it came under the Department of Science and Art. The Dublin Metropolitan School of Art was founded by an Act of 1877. It became the National College of Art in 1936. In 1971, the college came under the control of the Higher Education Authority and was renamed The National College of Art and Design. In 1980, the college moved from Kildare

Street to extensive premises originally part of an old distillery at Thomas Street.

National Gallery of Ireland
Merrion Square

William Dargan, the railway engineer, who had contributed a large sum of money to the organisers of the 1853 Industrial Exhibition, had stipulated that the inclusion of pictures was to be a feature of the Exhibition. A fund was set up to commemorate Dargan in the form of an art gallery to be called the Dargan Institute. This never materialised but a site was acquired from the Royal Dublin Society on Leinster Lawn, and Francis Fowke, a captain in the Royal Engineers, was commissioned to design a building in keeping with the Museum of Natural History which had been erected recently on the opposite side of the lawn. The foundation stone was laid by the Lord Lieutenant, the Earl of Eglinton, on 29 January 1859, and the building was opened on 10 August 1864. Its first director was George Mulvany, the portrait painter who had been actively involved in the establishment of the gallery. A statue of Dargan by Thomas Farrell (1827–1900) is on the lawn outside the gallery. It was unveiled by the Lord Lieutenant, the Earl of Carlisle, on 30 January 1864. Over the years, an important collection of Italian, Spanish, Dutch and French paintings has been added, plus a representative group of Irish paintings. Hugh Lane gave 21 pictures during his period as curator. He left his house and property, apart from 39 continental pictures, to the National Gallery. The old masters in his possession at the time of his death were to be sold and the proceeds used to purchase works for the gallery. The Courts agreed that 41 of the pictures might be retained for the gallery. Five hundred oils and water colours were received as a bequest from Nathaniel Hone after his death. The gallery has a restoration studio for the care and preservation of pictures, opened in 1968, a fine library and lecture hall in the basement, and a restaurant on the ground floor. In 1996, a competition was held for a design to extend the Gallery into Clare Street and was won by Benson and Forsyth. Following objections about the demolition of an eighteenth-century building at 5 South Leinster Street, revised plans were submitted in 1998, retaining the listed building, and the new extension opened two years later at a cost of £17 million.

National Library of Ireland
Kildare Street
The Royal Dublin Society Library was taken over by the State in 1877 and renamed the National Library of Ireland. The library had been explicitly a public library free to respectable persons introduced by members of the Royal Dublin Society since 1836. From 1877 to 1900, the library was administered by the Department of Science and Art. In 1890, the library entered its new building which was designed in 1883 by Sir Thomas N. Deane in consultation with Mr William Archer FRS. Its special points are the isolation of the large circular central reading room, shelved to receive a large

number of books, and the adoption of the stack system of book cases in the book store. The National Library and National Museum* are matching buildings on either side of Leinster House.* In 2003, the Office of Public Works got permission to demolish a 1920s extension and a 1960s flat-roof extension, and to construct a new five-storey block to the rere of the building.

National Maternity Hospital
Holles Street
In 1884, Dr William Roe, a professor of midwifery at the Royal College of Surgeons, had a small lying-in hospital at 32 Holles Street. However, when he died in 1893, the hospital ran out of funds and closed. At that time, the two main maternity hospitals were the Rotunda and the Coombe but there was a need for an inner-city Roman Catholic hospital serving areas as far out as Ringsend and Sandymount. On 17 March 1894, the South Dublin Lying-in Hospital was founded at no. 32 and the first baby was born there the next day, 18 March. It was normal for women to have their babies at home but the concept of a lying-in hospital gave working-class mothers the chance of a few days' rest after childbirth, as well as having expert attention. In his address at the opening of the hospital, the chairman said it was 'for the Catholic people under Catholic management wholly and solely'. A letter was read from the Archbishop, promising a contribution of £1,000. The hospital received a Royal Charter in 1903 and was renamed the National Maternity Hospital. By 1931, the governors had purchased 32, 33 and 34 Merrion Square, including the large three-storey home of Lord Antrim, and the Pembroke Estate had granted a 1,000-year lease on 29–36 Holles Street. The architect Ralph Byrne was employed to design a new building, Cramptons winning the building contract. The first stage was opened on 17 December 1934 and the second and final part in 1938. The hospital is mentioned in James Joyce's *Ulysses*, and Oliver St John Gogarty who had completed his midwifery course there

refers to it in *Tumbling in the Hay*.

As part of the centenary of the hospital, in 1994, a granite stone was erected in Merrion Square, carved with a poem by Eavan Boland entitled 'Tree of Light'.

National Museum of Ireland
Kildare Street

In February 1876, the Royal Irish Academy* was informed that the government intended to build a National Science and Arts Museum to house the Academy's great collection of antiquities. In 1883, three houses, nos. 7–9 Kildare Street, were demolished and, in 1884, the foundation stone was laid for a new building designed by Sir Thomas Deane. The building opened in 1890 and the entire collection transferred to the government on the condition that it should be retained in Ireland. The National Library* and Museum are matching buildings on either side of Leinster House.* Major structural repairs were carried out in 1988–90. The Treasury Room, refurbished with a generous grant from Allied Irish Banks Plc, contains a collection of antiquities, including pennanular brooches, the Tara Brooch, the Ardagh Chalice, the Derrynaflan hoard and the Cross of Cong. After many years, the museum reverted to its original function as Museum of Archaeology and History, when, in 1997, the newly restored and redesigned Collins Barracks opened as Museum of Decorative Arts and History, to house the collection of silver, glass, furniture, musical instruments and porcelain. In 2001, the National Museum of Ireland—Country Life opened in a new building at Turlough Park, Castlebar. The Museum of Natural History at Merrion Street Upper opened in 1857.

National Photographic Archive
Meeting House Square, Temple Bar

Houses the photographic collections of the National Library of Ireland. The collection comprises approximately 300,000 photographs, the majority of which are Irish. These are catalogued onto the library's OPAC system and it is possible to access the images through the Internet. Indexes and catalogues are available in the National Library's main reading room and in the reading room of the Archive.

Neighbourhood Watch

A crime-prevention programme designed by the Community Relations section of the Garda Síochána to encourage the public to co-operate with the gardaí in reducing crime and vandalism. The underlying objective is that people would watch over each other's property and personal

National Museum of Ireland. In 1997 the newly restored and redesigned Collins Barracks opened as the Museum of Decorative Arts and History.

Sackville Street Upper, showing in the foreground William Curry & Co. booksellers and music publishers at no. 9, part of Drogheda House. In the centre Nelson Pillar, to the right the General Post Office.

well-being. The scheme is managed by an area co-ordinator who serves as a liaison between the gardaí, the street co-ordinators and individual members. Each street or block has its own co-ordinator who delivers a newsletter which keeps members up-to-date on the latest trends in crime and methods used by criminals. Members are asked to be on the alert for any unusual or suspicious behaviour and to report immediately to the gardaí.

Nelson Pillar
O'Connell Street

Undertaken by a committee of Dublin traders and bankers after the Battle of Trafalgar. The foundation stone was laid in the middle of O'Connell Street by the Lord Lieutenant, the Duke of Richmond, on 15 February 1808. The consulting architect was Francis Johnston (1760–1829), though preliminary designs were submitted by William Wilkins, a London architect (1778–1839). The Doric column was 134 feet high and was topped by a 13-foot Portland-stone statue of Admiral Nelson by Thomas Kirk (1781–1845), the Cork sculptor, who was paid £300. The column

cost £6,857 to erect. A porch at street level, designed by G. P. Beater, was added in 1894. Prior to this, the entrance was underground. Over the years, various attempts were made to have it removed and re-erected elsewhere. On the night of 7 March 1966, the column was seriously damaged by an explosion and, two days later, Army engineers demolished the remains. Prior to the explosion, the students at the National College of Art held a ball in the Clarence Hotel, which ran at a loss as a great number of the tickets were never paid for. In order to repay the hotel, some students arranged to have the head of Nelson stolen from the Corporation store. Amid much publicity, it was sold to Benny Gray, a London antique dealer, who drove to Belfast with it. The two-hundred-weight head was then flown to London where Gray used it as a publicity stunt to open his new antique market. It was then returned to Dublin where a street party was held with the musicians, 'The Dubliners', accompanying it on the back of a lorry. A representative from Dublin Corporation then took it away. The head of Nelson is now in Dublin

City Hall Multimedia Exhibition. In 1998, 32 years after the explosion, a small group of breakaway republicans admitted responsibility for the damage to the pillar. *See* **The Spire of Light.**

New Row South
From Blackpitts to Dean Street
Originally a street of 'Dutch Billy' brick houses with triangular gables, where the silk and poplin makers worked, and where there was also one of the many breweries in the area. Charles Brooking published his two- and three-sheet maps of the city and suburbs of Dublin in 1728. Hanna Madricks at the Sign of the Red Lion, New Row, together with Thomas Benson of Castle Street, sold the street map for 3/6d. Until comparatively recently, the offensive smells from Keefe's knackers' yard dominated the air.

New Street
From Clanbrassil Street to Patrick Street
One of Dublin's oldest streets, dating from the early part of the thirteenth century, it forms part of a dual carriageway from Clanbrassil Street to Patrick Street. A new housing scheme, extending from Cathedral Lane along Upper Kevin Street into New Street, was officially opened by the Corporation on 30 April 1982.

Newbridge Avenue
From Herbert Road to Sandymount Road
Originally known as Haig's Lane after a whiskey distiller whose buildings were situated on the River Dodder at this point. After losing a legal battle with the Revenue Commissioners in the mid-nineteenth century, the distillery was demolished and the stones used for two new roads constructed across the site, Herbert Road and Newbridge Avenue. The family of Patrick Pearse lived at no. 3 from 1886 to 1900.

Newbridge House
Donabate
Built in 1737, probably to a design of Richard Cassels. The estate was purchased in 1736 by the Rev. Charles Cobbe, later to become Archbishop of Dublin. The elaborate stucco plasterwork is by Robert West, and the drawing room is a later addition of about 1760, also with plasterwork by Robert West. It was opened to the public in 1986.

Newcomen's Bank
Castle Street
Designed by the architect Thomas Ivory and opened in 1781. In 1722, William Gleadowe married into the Newcomen family from Carriglass, Co. Longford, and assumed their name. He was knighted in 1781 and represented Co. Longford in the Irish parliament. Unlike his banking competitors, the La Touches,* four of whom sat in the House of Commons, he voted in favour of the Act of Union. A peerage was granted to his wife in return for the favour, much to the disgust of the print sellers who described him as a new-come-in. He died in 1807 and his son, Thomas Viscount Newcomen, inherited his mother's title and the bank. Thomas was educated at Eton and Oxford, where he read law, and was admitted to the English Bar in 1794. The bank had been in difficulties since the 1820s when many provincial banks closed. Eventually it also failed in 1825 and Newcomen shot himself, aged 48. As he was unmarried, the title became extinct. The building now houses the Rates Department.

Newgate Gaol
Newgate Gaol had been one of the gates of the city wall situated at the corner of the Cornmarket. It had four drum towers, one at each corner, with a gate and portcullis. In 1285, under Richard II, the city jail was established here; it was built in black calp with a granite pediment in the centre, and an iron balcony for public executions. By 1620, much of the jail had collapsed, and frequent repairs were necessary. The gate and portcullis were removed in 1705, and the passage widened. At an inquiry held in 1729, it was found that while John Hawkins who ran the Newgate and

Marshalsea jails was paid an annual salary of £10, he received £1,150 through bribery and corruption, forcing the unfortunate inmates to pay high rates for bed, food and drink. Those who could not pay were stripped and beaten and kept on a side of the building that had only loopholes for light, while others were kept in cellars, naked and in chains, with the only light coming from a sewer.

Oliver Plunkett, Archbishop of Armagh, was confined there from December 1679 to October 1680. John Wesley paid several visits in 1747. 'I preached in Newgate [he says] in the common hall, the jailor refusing us the room where we used to preach; but that is not the worst. I am afraid our Lord refuses his blessing on this place, all the seed seems to fall to the wayside.'

The foundation stone of the modern Newgate at Green Street was laid in 1773 and it opened for the reception of prisoners in 1780. It was built to a design of Thomas Cooley. The old prison was partly demolished but was used for two years as a lock-up for any night-strolling females who were caught by the old parish watch. Many supporters of the 1798 rebellion were jailed in Green Street, including Oliver Bond, William Jackson, Hamilton Rowan; also Napper Tandy and Robert Emmet in 1803. The prison was demolished in 1839 and is now part of a children's playground.

See **Marshalsea Debtors' Prison.**

Newman House
See **Catholic University of Ireland.**

Newmarket
From Bride Street to Ward's Hill
In 1674, the Earl of Meath applied for a Charter to hold bi-weekly markets and biannual fairs, and the area was developing by 1676 with several builders acquiring leases. The raw wool for the weavers was traded in the area and country produce was also on sale. Robert Emmet used these traders to make contact with the insurrectionists in rural areas. The Earl of Meath frequently dined in Matt White's tavern, demolished in 1892. There were many breweries and malthouses in the surrounding areas. The area has recently been developed with apartment blocks, a large IDA Crafts and Small Industries centre, and a FÁS Community Training, Education, Rehabilitation Centre, funded by South Inner City Task Force. There is a public house on the corner of Brabazon Place where the IDA extends to a small business centre.

Nicholas Street
From Christ Church to Patrick Street
Name comes from the Church of St Nicholas Within* built in the mid-eleventh century at Winetavern Street. Sometime in the twelfth century, it was rebuilt on its present site. The walls of the church may be seen beside the Peace Garden on the corner of Christchurch Place. Nicholas Street was originally separated from Patrick Street by a gate in the city wall which had two round towers without, a square tower within and a portcullis. (*See* Walls, Towers and Gates of the City.) Humphrey Powell, printer appointed for the realm of Ireland, lived in the street in 1566. Primate James Ussher was born in the parish in 1580 and by the seventeenth century it had become a fashionable street. Dr John Whalley, publisher of prophetic almanacks on the stars, moved to a house next to the Fleece Tavern in 1698. In 1709, he had moved to Blew Ball, Arundel Court without St Nicholas Gate. Here he published *Whalley's News Letter* in 1714. By the nineteenth century, the area had become one of the worst slums in Dublin. In April 1890, Sir Arthur Guinness founded the Guinness Trust* which became the Iveagh Trust in 1903, and seven acres of slums were cleared and new flats were built in the area.

See **Bull Alley.**

North Bull Island
A large island in the form of a sand bank and joined to the mainland at Clontarf by the Bull Wall,* completed in 1820 and by an extension of Watermill Road at the junction of James Larkin Road. Probably

Dublin's finest bird sanctuary. It is also the home of two golf courses, the Royal Dublin and St Anne's.

North Great George's Street
From Great Denmark Street to Parnell Street
Built by the Archdall family who lived in nearby Mount Eccles. Building commenced about 1775 but most of the remaining buildings date from the late 1780s. Sir Samuel Ferguson (1810–86), the poet and antiquary, lived at no. 20, Lord Kenmare at no. 35, and at no. 38 John Pentland Mahaffy (1839–1918), Provost of Trinity College. His house was designed by Charles Thorp Senior who lived at no. 45; nos. 34 and 35 are by Michael Stapleton. Many of the houses, including no. 38, are now in private ownership, with major restoration programmes taking place. The James Joyce Cultural Centre is at no. 35.

Northbrook Road
From Ranelagh Road to Leeson Park
Residential area. The Old Men's Home founded in 1811 to provide a comfortable home for respectable aged men of good character. It is managed and regulated under a scheme approved by the Rt Hon. The Master of the Rolls, 22 March 1894.
With the completion of Northbrook House, a complex of 20 apartments on Strand Road, Sandymount, in 1991, this charity and the Brabazon Trust merged and the remaining residents of the Old Men's Home were moved to the new accommodation.
St Anne's Hospital, founded in Beresford Place 1899, moved to Pearse Street in 1904, to Holles Street in 1911, and to Northbrook Road in 1926. In October 2003, the hospital was converted by architect O'Mahony Pike into a row of five houses, each of 172 sq.m. (1,854 sq. ft) and four apartments.
The Swastika laundry, founded in 1912, traded until 1989.

Northumberland Road
From Lower Mount Street to Pembroke Road.
Named after Hugh Percy, 3rd Duke of Northumberland, Lord Lieutenant 1829–30. The road was opened in 1830 and impressive red-brick houses were constructed from 1832 onwards. The Protestant hall at no. 4 was built in 1899 for the Loyal Orange Lodge. The Irish Cancer Society has used it as headquarters since 1983. In 1861, St Stephen's Parochial Schools, attached to St Stephen's Church* at Mount Street Crescent, were built on a site given by the Earl of Pembroke, who made a major contribution towards the cost. In 1878, the schools came under the control of the Board of National Education. They closed in 1969 when the Department of Education decided to close a number of two-teacher schools. The buildings were used for a short time by the City of Dublin Vocational Education Committee until they were sold and extended. Now the School House Hotel.

Northumberland Square
Off Lower Abbey Street
Named after Hugh Percy, 3rd Duke of Northumberland, Lord Lieutenant 1829–30. Originally part of Blenheim Street which continued through to Talbot Street until Carolin's buildings were erected in 1810.
With the building of the Irish Life Mall (*see* Abbey Street Lower), Brooks Thomas and 16 brick artisan dwellings were demolished to make way for the new complex.

Nutley Lane
From Stillorgan Road to Merrion Road
A new road designed by James Wall, architect, in 1947.
Approval was granted on 13 July 1956 for the building of houses designed by associated architects Munden & Purcell and John E. Collins, with work being carried out by Borough Builders Ltd. RTÉ* studios are at the Stillorgan Road end on a six-acre site, formerly the playing fields of St Andrew's College, with Elm Park Golf Course opposite. St Vincent's Hospital faces onto Merrion Road, with a large supermarket complex on the other corner.

Observatory Lane
15–31 Rathmines Road
At the end of this cul-de-sac was the world famous astronomical and instrument-manufacturing firm owned by Sir Howard Grubb F.R.S., F.R.A.S. It manufactured telescopes including a 4-foot reflector for Melbourne, Australia, and two for the Russian government at the end of the Tsarist regime. The Bolsheviks paid for the telescopes after the revolution. During the First World War (1914–18), the firm made precision instruments for the army and navy, including gun-sights. After the war, the business was transferred to its English works and the Dublin factory closed. Sir Howard lived at Aberfoyle, Orwell Road, Rathgar.

O'Connell Street
See **Sackville Street.**

Old Circular Road
See **Adelaide Road.**

Old Dublin Society
Founded in 1934 to promote the study of the history and antiquities of Dublin. In furtherance of its aims, the Society arranges for: a series of papers during the winter session in the Lecture Theatre, Dublin City Library,* Pearse Street; a series of visits during the summer session to places of historic interest, and the publication of *The Dublin Historical Record*, which appears quarterly.

Oliver Bond Street
From Bridgefoot Street to St Augustine Street
Formerly part of Mullinahack.

Winged figure of courage by John Henry Foley on the O'Connell monument, O'Connell Street.

Oliver Bond (1760–98), a woollen merchant, joined the United Irishmen. Sentenced to be hanged but died suddenly in prison. He is buried in St Michan's Church.*
See **Mullinahack for details.**

Opera Ireland
See **Dublin Grand Opera Society.**

Orbital Routes and Signage System

In 2003, Dublin City Council introduced a major new directional signage system for the city to help redirect unnecessary traffic away from the city centre. The system is colour coded for the inner and outer orbital routes. Each junction has a unique number. The outer orbital route has purple signs, giving the junction, which are numbered J51–J81, a directional sign for straight ahead, plus left and right arrows for alternative routes. The inner orbital route has blue signs at major junctions, which are numbered J1–J42. The blue signs also indicate the nearest parking area plus directional arrows. When approaching either of the orbital routes, the signs have a white background with the top panel colour coded to indicate an approach is being made to the inner or outer route.

Order of St Patrick

See 'Crown Jewels' of the Order of St Patrick.

Orphan House for Destitute Boys

Prussia Street

Opened in 1793 'for receiving, maintaining, educating, apprenticing and bringing up in habits of industry, destitute boys who have lost both father and mother and are between the age of four and ten years.'

Orphan House for Destitute Female Children

Prussia Street

Opened on 1 January 1791 'for receiving, maintaining, educating and apprenticing or bringing up as useful servants, destitute female children who have lost both father and mother and are between five and ten years.'

Oxford Road

From Ranelagh Road to Charleston Road

Mostly red-brick houses and some shops. In 1988, the old Mount Pleasant Buildings were demolished and Dublin Corporation opened a new complex for the elderly: Oxford Grove with single- and double-room accommodation together with a common room. In front of the building is a bronze sculpture, 'Coexistence' by Michael Burke, which was unveiled in June 1989. It depicts an elderly lady seated on a granite slab with her cat, while around them bronze birds perch.

Oxmantown Green

Names comes from Ostmantown, a place where the Anglo-Normans compulsorily resettled the Vikings living in the city.

A Viking settlement north of the river (*see* Blackhall Place) stretching beyond the river to King Street and Smithfield. In 1635, together with College Green and St Stephen's Green, the area was to be 'kept for the use of citizens to walke and take the open air by reason this cittie is at present growing very populous'. At a meeting of Dublin City Assembly in 1664, a proposal was agreed to divide Oxmanton Green into 96 portions, leaving a convenient highway and a large market place at Smithfield,* where cattle had been sold since 1541. By the second half of the seventeenth century, the area was becoming popular, with the building of King's Hospital* in 1669, and fashionable houses.

See **Smithfield.**

P

Page's Court

This passage led from Cornmarket to Cook Street. Fagan's Castle within the old city wall stood there until 1788. No trace remains.

See **Walls, Towers and Gates of the City.**

Palmer's Hospital

See **St John's Hospital.**

Palmerstown or Palmerston

Five miles west from the General Post Office
Situated on the River Liffey and on the road to Lucan.

Named after Ailred the Palmer, a Norse citizen of Dublin who founded the hospital of St John* near Thomas Street in the twelfth century. He lived on the road leading to Kilmainham and owned about 1,500 acres at Teach Ghuaire or Palmerstown. Palmerstown House was built by John Hely Hutchinson, Prime Serjeant-at-Law, about 1763. His descendants, the Earls of Donoughmore, occupied it until it was taken over in 1869 by the Stewart Institution for Imbecile Children (now Stewart's Hospital). In 1911, the population of the parish was 1,511 and it was described as a village of small humble dwellings, irregularly built, and a Roman Catholic chapel. Today it is a large suburb of Dublin.

St Loman's was opened as a sanatorium in 1952. It was handed over to Grangegorman Mental Hospital Board in 1958 and is now a psychiatric hospital.

Palmerstown Cemetery

The first lawn cemetery was opened on 1 July 1978 at Palmerstown, Co. Dublin. The expanse of green lawns is broken only by rows of headstones and paths set level with the grass. There are no kerbs, railings or other obstructions. It was acquired and developed by Dublin County Council for the west area of Dublin.

See **Dublin Cemeteries Committee.**

Park Street East

See **St Patrick's Well Lane** *and* **Lincoln Place.**

Parkgate Street

From Conyngham Road to Wolfe Tone Quay
At the Conyngham Road entrance to the Phoenix Park there were four circular limestone piers with three iron vehicular gates and pedestrian entrances through the walls. This entire nineteenth-century structure was removed in 1932 to make way for the enormous crowds entering the park for the Eucharistic Congress. After 56 years the four limestone piers were restored without the gates as in 1932. For many years, Ross Hotel at 10–13 Parkgate Street was a favourite stopping point for persons disembarking at Kingsbridge (Heuston) Station. Numbers 17–22 housed the pantechnicon and works of Robert Strahan, the well-known furniture manufacturers, while the central depot for the Lucan Dairy was at nos. 23–24.

Parliament House

College Green
Erected on the site of an old parliament house that was originally built as a hospital and later became Chichester House,* the residence of Sir Arthur Chichester, which by 1727 was in a state of collapse. The Surveyor General, Captain Burgh, was

asked by parliament to draw up plans for a new parliament building. He gave the commission to Edward Lovett Pearce and this beautiful building was erected between 1729 and 1739. It was extended in 1785 by James Gandon and enlarged again in 1794 by Robert Parke. During the construction of the new building, the parliament met in the King's Hospital* (Blue Coat School), but moved into the partially finished new premises in 1732. Pearce did not live to see his work completed.

In 1727, Robert Baillie, upholsterer, presented a petition that he had himself at great expense brought into this kingdom from Great Britain, France and Flanders, a sufficient number of exceedingly good tapestry weavers!

A committee that was appointed to deal with the building and furnishing of the new Irish House of Lords referred to a second petition of Baillie's, proposing that there should be six tapestries in the new house:

1. The valiant defence of Londonderry, from the opening of the trenches to the raising of the siege, by the arrival of the English Army.
2. The landing of King William and his army at Carrickfergus.
3. The glorious battle and victory of the Boyne, with the rout of the Irish Army.
4. The splendid and joyful entry of King William into Dublin.
5. The Battle of Aughrim.
6. The taking of Cork and Kinsale by the late victorious Duke of Marlborough.

In May 1728, Baillie received the order for such tapestry and other furniture as should be wanting for the new House of Lords. It would appear, however, that the final order limited the tapestries to two in number — the defence of Londonderry and the Battle of the Boyne — and these were completed between 1728 and 1732. These may be seen in the old House of Lords room in the Bank of Ireland.

Also to be seen is the silver gilt House of Commons Mace, 59 inches long and made by John Swift of London, in 1765. Another important item is the purse of the Lord Chancellor. The Lord High Chancellor held the highest official rank in Ireland until independence. The purse of the Lord Chancellor, which was worn like an apron by the purse bearer, had been in France in the safekeeping of Lady Vivienne Glenavy whose late husband was the grandson of the last Lord Chancellor in Ireland. In January 1991, Lady Glenavy donated the purse to the Bank of Ireland for custody and public display.

The most important pieces of monumental grandeur to have survived are the great gallery-pavilions facing College Green, together with the old House of Lords and the long passageway enclosing what was the House of Commons. Gandon was responsible for the large Corinthian columns and portico at the Westmoreland Street end, while Parke extended the building towards Foster Place to accommodate the House of Commons. This domed chamber was badly destroyed by fire in 1792 and was rebuilt to a design of Vincent Waldré. After the Act of Union in 1800, the country was governed from Westminster, and the building was sold in 1803 to the Bank of Ireland* for £40,000.

Parliament Street (1762)
From Dame Street to Wellington Quay

A map dated 1753, published in the journal of the Royal Society of Antiquaries of Ireland, shows the proposed new Parliament Street. Described as 'a design for opening proper streets or avenues to His Majesty's Royal Palace in Dublin'. After completion of the plans, it was found that the street could not be carried in a direct line with an entrance into the Castle Yard without the destruction of many valuable buildings. In 1757, an act was passed for 'making a wide and convenient way, street or passage from Essex Bridge to the Castle of Dublin'. The Commissioners appointed for the task were known as the Wide Streets Commissioners.*

George Semple who designed Essex Bridge was probably responsible for the plan of 1753 which was to open onto a square (*see* Bedford Square), with the equestrian statue of George I in the centre. Nothing came of this; Semple quarrelled with the Commissioners and the design was finally given to a surveyor called Purfield. It was proposed that, instead of a square, a chapel for government, with a high cupola, should face down the new street. The merchants of Dublin raised an objection and presented a petition to parliament requesting an Exchange to enable further trade in the city.

Four doors from Essex Gate, James Hoey published a newspaper, *The Mercury*, which became the organ of the Irish government between 1767 and 1772. The Hibernian silk warehouse was opened in February 1765, founded by the Corporation of Weavers. George Faulkner, the eminent publisher, had a house on the corner of Essex Street. The *Evening Mail,** founded in 1861, had its offices at nos. 38–40. This was a popular paper and survived for over 100 years. In its latter years, it was published by *The Irish Times*. A general trading street with a large variety of shops including Sunlight Chambers at no. 21, with its painted terracotta frieze depicting the history of soap, the building at one time being used by Lever Brothers.

Parnell Square
See Rutland Square.

Parnell Street
From Capel Street to Summerhill
Formerly Great Britain Street. Renamed on 1 October 1911, following the unveiling by John Redmond MP of a statue of Charles Stewart Parnell (1846–91), political leader, in Sackville Street.

A fine street laid out in the first half of the eighteenth century. In 1748, Bartholomew Mosse acquired a lease of four acres and one rood plantation measure from William Naper on the north side of the Street for the building of his new hospital. (*See* Rotunda Hospital). William Corbett of no. 57 bought the copyright of *Wilson's Dublin Directory* in 1802. This was the first directory to be published on Dublin, appearing in 1752. It was eventually taken

over by Thom's,* bought by The Irish Presss Plc in 1999. Simpson's Hospital* was built in 1787 and demolished in 1978. None of the eighteenth- or nineteenth-century houses remain. A new dual carriageway was built recently, ending what had been a busy shopping area. The ILAC Shopping Centre backs onto the street, and an extensive car park now takes up a large part of the north side where red-brick houses and shops once stood. At the junction with O'Connell Street stands the Parnell Monument (*see* Statues), erected 1906–07 and unveiled by John Redmond. The section from the monument to Summerhill retains shops, a small hotel and some pubs, with an assortment of architecture.

Patrick Street
From Nicholas Street to New Street
A church has stood here since AD 450. It is said that St Patrick baptised converts to the Christian faith in a well beside the present St Patrick's Cathedral which was built in 1191. The first university in Ireland was here from 1320 to 1520. Extensive demolition has taken place recently, of houses, shops and bars, to make way for the Corporation's dual carriageway scheme affecting Patrick Street, New Street and Lower Clanbrassil Street.
See Bull Alley *and* St Patrick's Cathedral.

Paving Board
This body was established by statute in 1774 and reconstituted in 1807. It was accountable for the paving, draining, cleaning and lighting within the area of the city enclosed by the Circular Road.* In 1851, these duties were transferred to Dublin Corporation.

Peace Garden
Corner Christ Church Place and Nicholas Street
A Dublin Corporation Millennium project officially opened by the Rt Hon. the Lord Mayor Cllr B. Briscoe TD on 12 September 1988, generously assisted by CRH plc (Computer Services). A sunken garden with a fountain, having quotations in

bronze relief from the Books of Proverbs and Isaiah, also quotations by Kavanagh and Yeats. In the background is a tree sculpture against a wooden framework. On the pavement outside Barnardos, celebrating children of the new millennium, a bronze sculpture of three children, 'Millennium Child' by artist John Behan (supported by Tipperary Crystal), unveiled by President Mary McAleese on 8 November 2000.

Pearse Street
From College Street to Ringsend Road
Formerly Great Brunswick Street.
James H. Pearse, father of the patriot brothers, Patrick and Willie, was a sculptor who had his premises at no. 27. Patrick was born here on 10 November 1879. He was prominent in the Gaelic League and edited its journal, *An Claidheamh Soluis.* He founded a school at Cullenswood House, Ranelagh, which moved in 1910 to the Hermitage at Rathfarnham. In the Rising of 1916, he was commander of the forces of the Irish Republic. Tried by court-martial and executed in Kilmainham Gaol on 3 May 1916.
The Dublin Oil Gas Company, founded in 1824 by Act of Parliament 'to light the city of Dublin and environs with oil gas', had its elaborate premises which was taken over by the Academy Cinema, shortly to become an office block. The Brunswick and Shamrock Pneumatic Cycle Factory* was at no. 2. The Queen's Theatre* stood on the site of what is now an office block, finished in 1971, named Áras an Phiarsaigh and occupied by the Revenue Commissioners. In 1884, plans were submitted by the Lyceum Theatre for a theatre with seating for 2,500, on ground at the junction with Tara Street where the former fire station stood, but this elaborate venture came to nothing. Pearse railway station is on the corner with Westland Row. Near the Garda station, a replica marks the place on which the Vikings had erected a standing stone where the River Steyne entered the sea near this spot at D'Olier Street. St Mark's Church was built

in the classical style in 1729. Oscar Wilde was baptised here in 1854 when the family was living at no. 21 Westland Row. The church was purchased in 1971 by Trinity College and used as an overflow library. In 1987, it was again sold, this time to an American-based group, the Assemblies of God. It has recently been renovated with the aid of a FÁS youth-training project. The large Garda station, which forms part of the corner with Hawkins Street, was designed by Andrew Robinson in 1912 for the Dublin Metropolitan Police. The large eight-storey complex that houses the IDA Enterprise centre was built in 1862 for Bewley, Moss and Co. Sugar Refiners, to William Fairbairn's design. On 13 December 1907, the new central station of the Dublin Fire Brigade was opened. Designed by C. J. McCarthy in the Italian-Romanesque style, in red-brick with a high tower, it was erected by James Donovan and Sons builders at a cost of £21,840. It closed in 1988 and is now part of a nightclub and hotel. The fire brigade relocated to a new building at the rere on Townsend Street but retained four run-outs on Pearse Street. Numbers 138–144 Pearse Street (then Great Brunswick Street) house the library designed by C. J. McCarthy and completed in 1909. Built in the classical style, it is a symmetrical nine-bay composition of Mount Charles sandstone and Ballinasloe limestone, its principal features—a portico and Venetian window with a triangular pediment, together with two adjoining houses—completing the layout. Several alterations have taken place over the years including a major redesign of the interior at the beginning of the twenty-first century. It reopened on Wednesday 2 July 2003 as the Dublin City Library and Archive.* St Andrew's Resource Centre, designed by William Hague, was built as an RC school for the Parish of St Andrew and, when opened in 1897, there were 1,200 children on roll. It closed in 1972 and reopened as a resource centre in 1989. It runs adult education programmes and has a day centre for the elderly, it also holds organic food markets on Saturdays. In 1999, a four-storey eleven-bay Holiday Inn hotel opened on the street.

Pembroke Memorial Cottages
Between St Mary's Road and Northumberland Road
A delightful complex of red-brick cottages with a playing field. On 3 April 1914, an objection was raised by the residents of St Mary's Road to the application of the Earl of Pembroke and Montgomery Estate for planning permission, as dwellings for artisans would seriously affect the value of property in the area. A similar objection was raised on 1 May 1914 by the householders on Northumberland Road, on the same grounds. An agreement was drawn up on 12 August 1919, and this beautifully designed scheme was completed.

Peter Row
From Aungier Street to Whitefriar Street
A laneway at the back of the now demolished St Peter's Church. Mostly disused warehouses and car park.

Peter Street
From Bride Street to Whitefriar Street
Facing Church of St Peter.* Rebuilt in Gothic manner, 1863–67. The Adelaide Hospital was built in 1839 in Bride Street and closed in 1847. Reopened in Peter Street, 1858, where it occupied most of one side of the street until, together with the other members of the Federated Dublin Voluntary Hospitals Group, it moved to a new hospital complex in Tallaght. The building which had a preservation order on the staircase was refurbished, extended and opened as an apartment block in 2002. A Huguenot cemetery* was opened in 1711; it closed in 1879 when the site was acquired by Jacob's biscuit factory. In 1966, the remains taken from the Huguenot cemetery were reinterred in Mount Jerome Cemetery. Molyneux House,* built in 1711 by Thomas Molyneux, was demolished in 1943.

Pharmaceutical Society of Ireland
37 Northumberland Road
Established in 1875 by the Pharmacy Act (Ireland), which embodied the constitution of the Society and governed the practice of pharmacy in Ireland. In that year, the Society consisted of twenty-one members, all of whom were named in the Act as comprising its first council. Those who commenced practice subsequent to the act were obliged to sit an examination before gaining registration as registered druggists. By 1932, pharmacy was entering upon a new era, and education was gradually orientated in a different direction. Lectures were increased and, with educational developments in view, a large property was converted into laboratories and lecture halls. An extended course was introduced in 1952 and the College of Pharmacy was recognised as an institution for third-level education. This method of education continued until 1963 when the college became associated with University College Dublin and a three-year BSc. (Pharm.) degree was established. In

Gas lamp: Phoenix Park.

1977, full responsibility for education to degree level was transferred to Trinity College Dublin and a four-year BSc. (Pharm.) degree course instituted. In 1984, the degree course was made an all-honours degree.
See **Apothecaries' Hall.**

Phoenix House

Built for Sir Edward Fisher in 1611 where the Magazine Fort now stands. Phoenix Park is named after the house. Henry Cromwell, Oliver's fourth son, lived there from 1655. The Magazine Fort was built in 1734.

Phoenix Park

Main entrances: Parkgate Street, North Circular Road and Conyngham Road
The name was probably derived from *Fionnuisce*, a spring of clear water.
Formed in 1662 when the lands of over 2,000 acres surrounding the Viceregal residence, the Phoenix Manor which stood on the site of the Magazine Fort, were acquired to form a royal deer park. Over 400 acres belonged to Sir Maurice Eustace (*see* Eustace Street). By 1669, the Park had cost £31,000 and was stocked with deer, partridges and pheasants. It was popularised as a recreation centre for the citizens of Dublin in 1745, during the time when the Earl of Chesterfield was Lord Lieutenant (1744–47); shrubs were planted and gravel paths laid, similar to the present layout. The Phoenix Monument was erected in 1747. Today the Phoenix Park covers 1,752 acres. It contains the People's Gardens,* the Royal Zoological Gardens,* and the Royal Military Infirmary by James Gandon, now the Department of Defence. Other buildings include Áras an Uachtaráin, the residence of the President of Ireland; the residence of the United States Ambassador; St Mary's Hospital built as the Royal Hibernian Military School.* Mountjoy House, home of Luke Gardiner, Viscount Mountjoy, Keeper of the Phoenix Park, killed at the Battle of New Ross in 1798, became in 1825 the Ordnance Survey Office. The Wellington Monument,* commenced in 1817, dominates the area. A large part of the Park is reserved as playing fields, and a tall steel cross was erected to commemorate the visit of Pope John Paul II in 1979.
The Phoenix Monument was restored to its original position in the centre of the main road on 30 January 1990. It had been moved some years previously to a side road on the occasion of a closed circuit motor race.

Phoenix Park Murders. The informer James Carey, murdered in 1883.

Phoenix Park Murders

On 6 May 1882, the new Chief Secretary, Lord Frederick Cavendish (1836–82), who had replaced William Edward Forster, and the Under Secretary, Thomas Henry Burke (1829–82), while walking in the Phoenix Park were murdered outside the Viceregal Lodge by a Fenian splinter group, the Invincibles, using surgical knives. James Carey (1845–83), a Dublin bricklayer and member of the group, turned informer, resulting in the execution of five associates, Joseph Brady, Timothy Kelly, Thomas Caffrey, Michael Fagan and Daniel Curley. Others were sentenced to penal servitude; these included James Fitzharris, known as Skin the Goat, who drove the party to the Park. James Carey was murdered in 1883 aboard the *Melrose Castle* off Capetown, by Patrick O'Donnell, one of the Invincibles.

Pigeon House Road

From York Road, Ringsend, to the South Wall
John Pigeon was a workman and caretaker employed during the building of the South Wall. His home was a large wooden structure, built at this time for storing wreck and builders' materials. A seven-bay three-storey hotel, designed by Robert Pool, was erected between 1793 and 1795 for persons crossing to or from England. John Pigeon had several pleasure boats that took trippers around the bay from the hotel. The hotel became a barracks in 1798 and a fort from 1814 to 1897, for storing State papers and bullion in times of disturbance. The half-moon bathing place originally housed a gun turret for the fort. During the height of the tuberculosis epidemic of the 1940s and 1950s a former cholera isolation hospital on Pigeon House Road was used for terminal TB cases. A large generating station, commenced in 1902, but now derelict and due for demolition, dominates the area. The Poolbeg Yacht and Boat Club, founded in 1971 with a current membership in excess of 200, has its location at the South Bank, Pigeon House Road. The Club is in consultation with the local River Amenity Group regarding a redevelopment plan to improve clubhouse facilities and the building of a 100-berth marina.

Pike Theatre

18A Herbert Lane
Pike Theatre Club
A bohemian theatre, founded in 1953 by Alan Simpson and Carolyn (Solomon) Swift after they had both been dismissed by Anew McMaster, the actor manager of the Gate Theatre.* The theatre was small with a seating capacity of around 70 but, by 1955, had a club membership of three thousand. It produced international drama including Beckett's *Waiting For Godot* and the first staging of Behan's *The Quare Fellow*.
During the An Tóstal Dublin Theatre Festival of 1957, a huge controversy arose over the staging of *The Rose Tattoo* by a

Pigeon House Hotel. Designed by Robert Pool and erected 1793–5.

young American author, Tennessee Williams. The Garda Superintendent demanded that the production should cease because of objectionable passages, which were not qualified. When Simpson refused, he was arrested and spent the night in the Bridewell. He was the only theatre producer in Ireland ever to spend a night in prison. The charge of producing an indecent and profane play for gain opened in the District Court on 4 July and was then appealed to the High Court. The charges were dismissed but the adverse and damaging publicity had a serious effect on both Simpson and the theatre, with membership dropping to a few hundred. The Pike continued for several more productions but eventually closed as the momentum of the early years was not there. Alan Simpson died in 1980 and Carolyn Swift in 2002. Carolyn Swift's surname was Solomon but Simpson advised her to change it to Swift for theatrical purposes.

Pill Lane (now Chancery Street)
From Arran Street East to Church Street
Name possibly comes from a creek or pool. In an estuary at the confluence of the Liffey and the Bradogue river, which flows along East Arran Street and into the Liffey at Ormond Quay, the Abbey of St Mary had a pier for the use of its fleet which traded with England and France. Chancery Street, as the lane is now called, stands on the site of the estuary. The old name of the street was Pill Lane. In 1641, Charles I granted to the city by Charter the ground called the Pill. The present street runs at the back of the Four Courts. Numbers 28–60 include the Bridewell Garda Station and Land Registry Office cornering onto Greek Street. On the other corner is River House, built in 1972 to house the Motor Taxation Department. The street continues along by the former Corporation wholesale food markets.

Pimlico
Off the Coombe in the Liberties to Thomas Court and Marrowbone Lane
Named after a street in London SW1

between Chelsea Bridge Road, Ebury Street and Vauxhall Bridge Road. The name was brought by woollen merchants who settled here at the start of the eighteenth century. The Earl of Meath leased part of the medieval street known as Donore Street to them. In 1177, Henry II of England founded an abbey near here and, in 1210, his son, John, created the lands the liberty of Thomas Court and Donore. A large metal sculpture by Peter Fink, 'Parable Island', sponsored by Allied Irish Banks for the Sculptors' Society of Ireland, was erected in 1988 but removed some years later. The area consists largely of houses erected by the Dublin Artisans' Dwellings Company,* many of which are occupied by Guinness employees. The first public playground for children was opened on 3 September 1887 by the Lord Lieutenant, Lord Londonderry. It was closed in 1955.

Pitt Street
From Harry Street to Chatham Street (now part of Harry Street)
Name comes from William Pitt (1759–1806), Tory prime minister 1783–1801 and 1804–06. Pitt forced the Irish parliament to bring in a Catholic Relief Act in 1793. Became first prime minister of the Imperial Parliament of Great Britain and Ireland after the Act of Union (22 January 1801). In 1850, nos. 8–9 housed the Institution for Diseases of Children.
See **Balfe Street.**

Pleasants Street
From Camden Street to Heytesbury Street
Named after Thomas Pleasants (1728–1818), Carlow-born philanthropist who gave away £100,000 in his lifetime. His asylum for female orphans stands almost opposite in Camden Street. The street opened in 1821 but the greater part of the area, from Synge Street along Heytesbury Street and into Camden Row, consisting of cottage-style terraced houses, was built in 1838. Youth Reach opened in 1989; an organisation funded by the European Social Fund and now part of the

National Development plan 2001–2006, it caters for 75 people, with classes including computer skills, assorted crafts and junior certificate subjects.

For Thomas Pleasants *see also* **Botanic Gardens, Camden Street, Stove Tenter House.**

Poddle (River)

Rising north of Tallaght, it proceeds through Greenhills, Whitehall Park, Kimmage Manor, Kimmage Road, Sundrive, Mount Argus, Mount Jerome Cemetery, along Parnell Road to Harold's Cross Bridge, crossing the South Circular Road, then to Blackpitts, Patrick Street, Ship Street through the Lower Castle Gate, into Dublin Castle, across Dame Street, entering the River Liffey near Grattan Bridge. It divides in several places.

With the coming of the Anglo-Normans in 1170, the river was diverted in a moat that surrounded the city on the south and east sides and became the main water supply. It eventually developed an economic role, powering watermills for tanneries in the Nicholas Street area and down past St Patrick's Cathedral into the Coombe and Pimlico, where it powered an assortment of mills including those used in the making of malt, linen and for the wool, wood and leather industries. There was also a mill at Great Ship Street which was attached to the monastery founded in the sixth century by Aonghas, Bishop of Kilcullen, plus a further nine mills from New Street until it entered the River Liffey. At Crosspoddle Street at the junction of Patrick Street, women washed their clothes in the river. It was always subject to flooding, causing high risk of disease from the dumping of domestic refuse and the extensive use of bleach in the linen mills, which was discharged into the watercourse. By the 1750s the river regularly overflowed into the chapel of St Nicholas Without in St Patrick's Cathedral.

From medieval times, the river was under the control of the Mayor and Commonalty of the City of Dublin, and the dean of St Patrick's Cathedral. This continued until 1840 when the responsibility for the river

passed to the Paving Board Committee of Dublin Corporation. In the eighteenth century, a start was made to culvert sections of the river, including a barrel of brickwork down Great Ship Street and into Dublin Castle. Small sections are visible at Kimmage Manor, Poddle Park, Mount Argus and Mount Jerome.

Point Depot
North Wall Quay

Built for the Midland and Great Western Railway Company as a train terminus, in 1878. (*See* Royal Canal). It has been converted into an exhibition and concert hall with bars and a restaurant, by architects Stephen Tierney and Shay Cleary, for entrepreneur Harry Crosbie who invested £5.5 million in the project, while Apollo Leisure, the British entertainment consortium, injected a further £3 million.

Pole Mill Street
See **Ship Street, Great and Little.**

Police

After the restoration of the monarchy in 1660, the English government established the first police force known in Dublin; it was called the Dublin Watch. The majority of the recruits were old and decrepit, most of them over 60 years of age and some over 70. They had been servants and retainers, and the new force was regarded as a means of providing for aged servitors. The members of the Watch were dressed in long greatcoats, reaching to the toes of their boots, and low-crowned broad-brimmed hats. This clumsy dress rendered them ineffective, and their only weapon was a long pole with a spear at one end and a crook at the other, which was very often used on the watch member himself.

In 1715, the Dublin Parish Watch was formed under the power of the Lord Mayor and aldermen of the city to watch every night from eleven o'clock in the evening until five o'clock in the morning. Each parish had its own Watch, supervised by the clergyman and the churchwardens.

Various Acts of 1778, 1786, 1788 and 1799 put the police force on a more professional level.

On 1 August 1807, an Insurrection Act was passed during the period Sir Arthur Wellesley (1789–1852), later 1st Duke of Wellington, spent as Chief Secretary. This included compulsory registration of arms and the right to search the dwellings of suspects. In 1808, the Watch system was abolished and a proper police force was formed, made up of younger men who were armed with short swords, and at night carried heavy pistols. The city was divided into departments under the supervision of divisional justices. The system proved unruly and unsatisfactory and, by 1835, the police were again being described as old and worn-out men. Crime was on the increase, brothels flourished and were being described as hot beds of depravity, while unlicensed public houses operated without supervision.

On 4 July 1836, the Dublin Police Act reorganised the police in the same manner as that of the London police and, on 6 July 1837, the first members of the new Dublin Metropolitan Police were enrolled. Each one was given a frock coat, trousers and a top hat in navy blue. They were provided with handcuffs, a wooden baton and a whistle. The 850 members of the force paraded at Dublin Castle and were inspected by the Lord Lieutenant, the Earl of Mulgrave. Two four-wheel horse-drawn enclosed vans were purchased in 1838 for conveying prisoners and convicts.

Following the signing of the Anglo Irish treaty and the removal of British Rule from Ireland, the control of the DMP was removed from the British government. The force continued to operate until amalgamated with the Garda Síochána on 5 April 1925. After Independence on 16 January 1922, a new police force, the Civic Guard, was formed, with a strength of 4,000; it became the Garda Síochána (guardians of the peace) in 1924, when the number was raised to 6,300. An Act of 1958 provided for the entry of women, Ban Gardaí, to the force. The headquarters of the force is

located at Phoenix Park, with a technical bureau at Harcourt Court, on the site of the High School, and a national drugs unit at Dublin Castle. The Garda training college is at Templemore, Co. Tipperary.

Poolbeg Lighthouse by John Smith 1768. This was the first lighthouse built to replace a lightship and the first to use candles instead of a coal fire.

Poolbeg Street
From Hawkins Street to Moss Street
In the fifteenth century, it was a long lane that led to *Poll Beag* (little pool), one of the deep anchorages in the harbour of Dublin. Gilbert refers to an official being appointed to see that the south bank of the Poolbeg was properly kept. This road was extended along Ringsend* and Irishtown* in 1735. It was to become Pigeon House Road.* A sea wall was built in 1761 and the Poolbeg lighthouse, designed by John Smith in 1761 and completed in 1768, was the first in the world to use candles rather than a beacon of coals. The massive south wall that was to replace the old sea wall was begun in 1785.

Pooly's Alley
From Dame Street to the Wood Yard
Shown on Bernard de Gomme's Map of 1673. Possibly from Dr John Pooley, rector of St Michan's and later Bishop of Raphoe and Cloyne.

Port Tunnel
See **Dublin Port Tunnel.**

Portland Row
From Amiens Street to Summerhill
Named after the 3rd Duke of Portland, Lord Lieutenant 1782.
Aldborough House,* built as a private residence in 1796 for Viscount Amiens, stands at the Amiens Street end. It was the last of the great eighteenth-century houses to be erected. The original gardens and much of the Row are occupied by Council flats. At the opposite end is St Joseph's Home for aged single ladies. At the junction of Portland Row and Amiens Street stands the Five Lamps, a monument to General Henry Hall of the Indian Army.
See also **Aldborough House and Feinaglian Institution.**

Portobello Gardens
Off South Circular Road
Mention of Portobello in 1760s. Popular park for city dwellers, opened in 1839. The ground was sold to Frederick Stokes, a Yorkshire-born developer, who built Kingsland Park in 1867. Because of the proximity of Portobello Military Barracks, prostitution spread as far as the Park, and Stokes was responsible for ridding the area of this problem and renaming the park Victoria Street, after additional building in 1876.
The district derives its name from Admiral Vernon's capture of Porto Bello from the Spaniards in the Gulf of Mexico in 1739. Vernon Street is a nineteenth-century street in the area. Porto Bello was also where Sir Francis Drake succumbed to fever, while his expedition was fighting the Spaniards, and where he was buried at sea on 28 January 1596.
See **Emorville Avenue *and* Heytesbury Street.**

Portobello Harbour
On the Dublin to Rathmines Road
A row of nineteenth-century yellow-brick houses survives, including the Lower Deck public house. The harbour was built by the Grand Canal Company* to accommodate barges and boats moored at Portobello House.* It was largely filled in during 1948 and the Ever Ready battery factory was built on the site. This was sold in 1987 for £200,000 and demolished in 1989 to make way for a development of 12 two-bedroom apartments, plus offices and a restaurant, by Oak Valley Property Company. On the opposite bank of the canal, at Grove Road, an impressive construction of 54 two-bedroom townhouses, stretching over 400 feet, was opened in 1990 by Zoe Developments.

Portobello House
Beside the Dublin to Rathmines road on the banks of the Grand Canal
Built by the Grand Canal Company* as one of its five hotels between Dublin and the Shannon, it opened on 13 July 1807. It was leased by the Company in 1813. The passenger boats had ceased to operate by 1852, but Portobello House continued as a hotel until 1860 when it was taken over by the Sisters of Charity as an asylum for female blind, until they moved to Merrion Gates in 1868. Various tenants had it for periods of ten years until it was opened in 1898 by Miss Hampson as a private nursing home which operated until 1971. Jack B. Yeats (1871–1957), painter and novelist, spent his last years there. It was sold by Lisney's in 1971 and was completely restored by G. & T. Crampton for office accommodation. Listed as a Class B building, it is a brick-front composition with a pediment over the central bays and a portico at ground-floor level. A cupola formed part of the restoration.

Powerscourt House
South William Street
Built from the designs of Robert Mack, a mason living in James's Street, by Richard, 3rd Viscount Powerscourt, who succeeded

his brother to the title in 1764. The house was begun in 1771. An extract from the builder's day book commences: 'On the six and seventh of April Lord Powerscourt approved of the plan and elevation for his house drawn by Robert Mack, and agreed to pay the said Mack at the rate of five per cent for conducting the whole of sd works and also that sd Mack execute all the stone cutting parts of the house.' The house, built of granite from the Powerscourt estate in Co. Wicklow, was completed in 1774. The carpentry was done by J. Doyle and the carving by Ignatius McDonagh. Richard, the 4th Viscount, who succeeded his father in 1788, sold the mansion for £15,000 to the government in 1807. From 1811 until 1832, it was used by the Commissioners of Stamp Duties; then it was sold to Messrs Ferrier and Pollock, wholesale warehousemen. In 1981, it was converted into a speciality shopping centre of 80 units. The project was nominated by the government as a demonstration project for the Council of Europe's Urban Renaissance Year in 1980–81.

Presbyterian Church
Parnell Square (Rutland Square)
The foundation stone was laid on 26 November 1862 and, on 17 November 1864, the church, designed by Andrew Heiton (Heaton) of Perth and built by Samuel H. Bolton, was opened for public worship by the Rev. Dr Cooke LL.D., of Belfast. The site was purchased by the Presbyterian congregation worshipping in St Mary's Abbey, at a cost of £2,600. The church, the gift of the philanthropic grocer Alexander Findlater, cost £14,000 and is commonly called Findlater's Church.

Prince's Street
Cul-de-sac off O'Connell Street
The La Scala Theatre* and Opera House, with its three tiers of private boxes and two galleries, was opened in 1919 and could seat 1,400 spectators. It included a ballroom and café and was later to become the Capitol Cinema. The property extended to the La Scala buildings in Middle Abbey Street. The Capitol enjoyed a great deal of popularity with a live show, having Jack Kirwan as resident comedian, followed by a film, until it closed in March 1972. Together with the Prince's Bar next door at no. 3 and the Metropole Ballroom, it was demolished to make way for a new department store. Opposite is the side of the GPO.

Prussia Street
From Manor Street to North Circular Road
At one time named Cabragh Lane, and Prussia Street in 1765 after Frederick II (1712–86), King of Prussia. At the time of renaming the street, he was known as the Protestant hero. About this time, fashionable houses were built for persons wanting to live in a rural-type setting near the Phoenix Park, where they could drive their carriages along the North Circular Road* laid down in 1763. Until recent years, the area was associated with the sale of cattle, with the market situated at nos. 51–54. Gavin Low, the livestock agents, were at nos. 48–50. The old yards have now been taken over for modern housing.
See Abattoir.

Public Lighting
Street lighting on any scale was unheard of in Dublin before the middle of the seventeenth century, and persons travelling after dark carried their own lights. The first record of public lighting appears to date from 1616 when the Corporation ordered that every fifth house should have 'lantern and candlelight set forth from 6 o'clock to 9 o'clock every dark night from hallow tide until after Candlemass'. In 1697, Michael Cole, merchant, was the first person to obtain a contract for lighting in the city. He was ordered to place lights on both sides of the main thoroughfares, eight houses apart, and on byways staggered lights six houses apart, to burn from 6 o'clock until midnight 'if it be so long dark all the tyme between 29th of September and 25th of March'. To finance this scheme he was allowed to levy a charge of three shillings per annum on each householder.

While there were many complaints, this method of collecting the light bill remained unchanged into the nineteenth century.

Gas lighting was introduced in 1825 using a lantern similar to that operating in oil lamps. A number of gas companies participated in this scheme until their amalgamation in 1866. The use of the gas mantle, in 1887, was a dramatic step forward in improving the luminosity of the gas flame. Twenty-five lamplighters lit and quenched 3,750 lamps every day. Electric lighting by arc appeared with the opening of the Fleet Street generating station when 81 electric arc lamps were erected to light the principal streets. A new generating station at Pigeon House fort was opened in 1903 and, apart from the arc lamp, the city continued to be lit by gas.

The ESB, which was set up in 1927, took over the arc lamps in 1929 and converted to filament-type lamps; about this time, Fleet Street generating station finally closed. Maintenance of the city's lighting reverted to Dublin Corporation before the Second World War, by which time 500- and 750-tungsten filaments were in use. A new system was introduced in O'Connell Street in 1938 when the cast-iron columns were replaced by polished concrete, each one having two lanterns with 1,500-tungsten filament lamps. Mercury and sodium lamps were adopted for all road-lighting schemes in 1960 to the exclusion of tungsten, solely on economic grounds: mercury in the centre city and residential areas and sodium on main roads outside the North and South Circular Roads.
See **Dublin Electric Light Company.**

Public Records Office of Ireland
See **National Archives.**

Q

Quakers
See **Society of Friends.**

QUAYS

In 1674, Sir Humphrey Jervis, a city merchant, Sheriff 1674, Lord Mayor 1681, purchased for £3,000, 20 acres, portion of the lands belonging to the former St Mary's Abbey, for development. He planned to build warehouses and residences with their backs facing the river, without any quay. On the advice of the Duke of Ormonde, the new Viceroy to Charles II, the houses were built onto a stone quay. In 1676, he built Essex Bridge (Grattan) and Capel Street, and the first quay, named Ormond Quay, would serve as an example for the development of the entire quays. He then developed Bachelor's Walk, making the area with adjoining streets the most fashionable in the city. Over many decades during the eighteenth and nineteenth centuries, the buildings along the quayside had deteriorated through neglect and, in the 1980s, much of the area was threatened with road-widening schemes. However, with the introduction of the Section 23 tax-incentive scheme, many new apartment blocks replaced the old structures and were purchased by investors, which allowed them to write off the entire capital cost against income

North Side
North Wall Quay Commenced in 1729 at the mouth of the river. The reclamation and laying of the North Lotts occurred between 1717 and 1729, with the eventual construction of the North Wall Quay. Detached, 16-bay, two-storey railway point

depot built in 1878. Extensively refurbished and converted to a theatre and exhibition hall in 1985 and named the Point Theatre. The railway tracks were removed to provide a car park to the side and rere. Campion's public house at no. 47, now derelict, is a protected structure as are the North Wall passenger station (1877), the wool store and the former eight-bay, three-storey with attic, London Midlands and North Western Railway hotel (1883). If the National Conference Centre proceeds at

George's Quay from Custom House Quay, showing Keane Murphy Duff's scheme approved by An Bord Pleanála in 1991. In the foreground is part of the bronze sculpture, 'Famine', by Rowan Gillespie.

Spencer Dock, permission may be given to demolish no. 47. Two other red-brick commercial properties between Wapping Street and Castleforbes Road are also protected buildings.

Custom House Quay In front of the new Custom House,* for which John Beresford laid the first stone on 8 August 1781, and which was completed in 1791 at a cost of nearly £400,000. A new pedestrian walkway along the river is the site of a bronze sculpture, 'Famine', by Rowan Gillespie, consisting of six separate figures, one carrying a child; a dog also stands by. It was commissioned and donated to the people of Ireland by Norma Smurfit and unveiled by President Mary Robinson on 29 May 1997. In January 2001, the International Financial Services Centre* took over a conserved warehouse, 'Stack A', built in 1821 and designed by John Rennie to house wine and tobacco. The €40 million refurbishment is let commercially.

Eden Quay Name comes from the Rt Hon. William Eden, Chief Secretary 1780–92. In a letter from him, dated 27 October 1782, addressed to the Rt Hon. John Beresford,

he says, '. . . if our great plans should ever go into execution for the improvement of Dublin, I beg that you will contrive to edge my name into some street or into some square opening to a bridge, the bank or the Four Courts'. The present 197-foot-high Liberty Hall,* the headquarters of the Irish Transport and General Workers' Union, stands on the site of the Northumberland buildings, premises already owned by the ITGWU. When they were built in the 1820s, they included a hotel and coffee rooms and a shopping complex; later, part was converted to Turkish Baths, known as Northumberland Baths, with an entrance at 19–20 Abbey Street. In 1912, the buildings were purchased by the ITGWU as its headquarters.

Bachelor's Walk After the building of Ormond Quay, what had become a fashionable residential area was extended eastwards. As part of the government's millennium projects, a boardwalk, designed by McGarry Ní Eanaigh, costing £2 million, was erected from Bachelor's Walk, extending along Ormond Quay Upper and Lower.* Because of the

The Boardwalk, Bachelor's Walk. As part of the government's millennium projects, a boardwalk designed by McGarry Ní Ianaigh was erected from Bachelor's Walk extending along Ormond Quay Upper and Lower. In 2004, it was extended along Eden Quay to the Point Depot.

Quartier Bloom, Lower Ormond Quay. A new Italian shopping and eating district including Italian food shop, cafés and bars.

popularity and success of this project, it was decided in 2004 to extend the boardwalk along Eden Quay from Grattan Bridge to the Point Depot, at a further cost of €3 million. The Dublin Docklands Development Authority* also created a boardwalk from Matt Talbot Bridge in 2004.

Ormond Quay Lower and Upper During the time of the Viceroy Lord Essex in 1676 a wealthy merchant, Sir Humphrey Jervis, later to become Lord Mayor, agreed to build a bridge and a street named after the Viceroy's family (Capel). When the Duke of Ormonde replaced Jervis in 1677, he suggested that the warehouses and residences which backed onto the river should have a stone quay along the river. The entire system of quays on both sides of the Liffey owes its origin to the prototype built on this Quay. The Armory Grant of 1674 included arrangements for the laying out of Eden Quay, Bachelor's Walk and Ormond Quay.

Inns Quay Named after the King's Inns, which occupied the site where there had been a Dominican friary from 1541 to 1775. The Quay is dominated by James Gandon's Four Courts building with its large dome. The Law Library and the Land Registry are housed behind the Four Courts.

Arran Quay Named after Lord Arran, son of James Duke of Ormonde, who arrived in Ireland, 27 July 1662, as Lord Lieutenant. Arran Bridge (Mellows) was built in 1683 and the Quay was developed about this time. St Paul's Church (RC), built 1835–42 to a design by Patrick Byrne, is a feature of the riverside.

Sarsfield Quay From Wolfe Tone Quay to Ellis Quay, formerly Pembroke Quay. Named after Patrick Sarsfield, Earl of Lucan, Brigadier General in the army of King James II. In 1984, most of the 13 houses comprising a nineteenth-century development that once housed the Salvation Army Hall and later the Simon Community were demolished by the

Upper Ormond Quay, showing the Presbyterian Church designed by E. P. Griffin, built in 1846 and closed in 1938. The church was demolished apart from the façade, which was incorporated in 1989 into an office block as part of the urban renewal, to a design of Grafton Architects.

Corporation. There is a proposal to build 44 duplex apartments to a design of Frank Hall, architect.

Ellis Quay Named after William Ellis whose grant in 1682 included Ellis Quay and Arran Quay and a portion of Inns Quay which was to be laid out for the advantage, ornament and beauty of the city.

Wolfe Tone Quay Formerly Pembroke and Albert Quays. Named after Theobald Wolfe Tone (1763–98), United Irishman. The North Quays end here at Parkgate Street and, across the river at Frank Sherwin Bridge, the South Quays commence.

South Side

Victoria Quay Named after Queen Victoria when she opened the new iron bridge in 1863 across from Watling Street to Albert Quay (Wolfe Tone Quay).

Usher's Island From an island formed by a branch of the River Camac which divided at the northern end of Watling Street, one portion emptying into the Liffey at the bridge and the other running parallel to the Liffey and emptying into an inlet at Usher's Pill. John Usher built a house near here on ground which he leased from the Corporation in 1597. The area was drained in 1683. Moira House was built in 1752 by Sir John Rawdon, 1st Earl of Moira (1762).

Wesley visited the house in 1775 'and was surprised to observe though not a more grand, yet, a far more elegant room than any that he had seen in England'. Lady Pamela Fitzgerald was there the night that her husband Lord Edward was arrested. The house was acquired in 1826 by the Association for the Suppression of Mendicancy in Dublin, which had been formed in 1818 for the alleviation of street beggary and to relieve pressing casual want in the city. The Association greatly extended the building and renamed it the Mendicity Institute.

The Mendicity Institute was occupied by Seán Heuston in 1916. It continued to be used until 1954 when the Institute moved to Island Street. The building was demolished in 1962. At no. 15 the newly restored building where James Joyce set his story 'The Dead'.

See Bridges — James Joyce.

Usher's Quay Named after John Usher (or Ussher) and his descendants who had a house and a garden at Bridgefoot Street. Laid out in the early part of the eighteenth century, it became a fashionable residential area.

Merchant's Quay The first reference to the quay is in 1565. There were medieval cobbled slipways here and at Wood Quay for the loading and unloading of merchant ships and foreign cargoes. In 2002, archaeologists discovered one of these slipways, together with a jetty leading to the river. The quay is on a modern street front but in the medieval period it would have fronted directly onto the river. On 10 July 2002, Dublin City Council unveiled the newly restored eighteenth-century building at no. 9, with decorative plaster-work, thought to be possibly by Michael Stapleton. After the building of the new Customs House,* the area became residential. St Francis' Church, built in 1834 to a design of James Bolger, commonly called Adam and Eve's, after a tavern, behind which the earlier church was concealed in Penal times.

Wood Quay (1451) Probably the oldest of the quays. The name probably derives from being formerly made of wood. It was completely rebuilt in stone in 1676. In 1969, the National Museum of Ireland commenced an archaeological dig and unearthed evidence of a Viking settlement. By 1973, about 5 per cent of the site had been excavated when Dublin Corporation ordered a halt to the excavations, as it was about to commence work on building the new municipal offices. As far back as January 1956, the City Council had agreed plans for the offices on a four-acre site from Christ Church Cathedral to the Quay. Following a public outcry at the amount of

levelling being done by bulldozers, the government issued a statement on 13 November 1973: 'The government has decided that development of the Winetavern Street site . . . should cease pending consultation and further investigation.' On 13 February 1974, the government announced that, having reconsidered its decision, the scheme could proceed with the building of four office blocks. Archaeological excavations resumed on the site and Sam Stephenson, the architect for the project, commenced redesigning his competition-winning

Civic offices at Wood Quay. Scott Tallon Walker's winning architectural competition design serves to mask Sam Stephenson's earlier 'bunker' buildings.

Clarence Hotel, Wellington Quay. Built in 1852, it was a sedate hotel until 1996 when it was purchased by a consortium including some members of U2 and refurbished to become one of the top boutique hotels.

entry, and submitted new designs in May 1976. In that year, a new organisation was formed, The Friends of Medieval Dublin, under the chairmanship of the learned Augustinian, Fr F. X. Martin, Professor of Medieval History at UCD. He persuaded the High Court to declare much of the area a national monument. In September 1978, 20,000 people marched through Dublin as a protest against the building of the new office blocks, but to no avail, as a contract had already been signed in October 1977 for the first two blocks. A large sculpture of Red American cedar wood on a steel frame, by Michael Warren, representing the prow of a Viking ship, was erected in 1995.

Essex Quay Named after Arthur Capel, Earl of Essex, Lord Lieutenant 1672–77. *See also* Exchange Street Lower (Blind Quay) where the Smock Alley Theatre stood (1662) close to the church of St Michael and St John. On the grass verge is a sculpture, 'Báite' by Betty Maguire, organised by the Sculptors' Society of

Ireland in collaboration with Dublin Corporation and An Foras Áiseanna Saothair (FÁS).

Wellington Quay Named after Arthur Wellesley (1769–1852), Duke of Wellington. Western end formerly Custom House Quay, site of the old custom house (1621–1791).

Crampton Quay Now part of Aston Quay. Six houses from Asdill's Row to Bedford Row. Name comes from Philip Crampton, bookseller.

See Crampton Court.

Aston Quay From Bedford Row to Westmoreland Street. City land that was let to Mayor Henry Aston in 1672. He enclosed the area from the sea and built a quay. His son, Henry, was to rebuild most of the houses on the Quay and Fleet Street in 1760. The Ballast Office, which was erected by the Corporation in Westmoreland Street, had an elevation of five bays onto the Quay.

Burgh Quay (1808) Named after Margaret Amelia Burgh, wife of John Foster, last speaker of the Irish House of Commons. The impressive stone-built Carlisle building (*see* D'Olier Street) was demolished in the 1960s and the towering O'Connell Bridge House was opened in 1965. Alex Findlater, the wine merchant and grocer, opened his first shop at no. 8. The Dublin Library Society, instituted on 10 May 1791 for the establishment of a library of expensive books beyond the reach of private individuals, moved in 1809 from Eustace Street to Mr Connolly's house, the second door from the corner of Westmoreland Street at the foot of Carlisle Bridge. Daniel O'Connell's Conciliation Hall, built in 1840 (*see* Conciliation Hall) later housed the *Irish Press*. Next door was the Dublin Corn Exchange an early nineteenth-century building which was sold in 1963 for £23,000 and the interior gutted. It was acquired by the *Irish Press* in 1979 for office use but nothing came of this. The bricked-up frontage remains.

George's Quay Named after King George I. A general trading quay. Before the building of the new Custom House on the opposite bank, most of the corn and rock salt was unloaded here.

City Quay This is shown on Rocque's map of 1756 as part of Sir John Rogerson's Quay. Up to 1715, when the Corporation extended the wall, 606 feet remained unbuilt between Mercer's Dock and George's Quay. The three-storey Victorian red-brick building on 0.065 hectares (0.16 acres), formerly used by the City Arts Centre, was purchased in 2003 by a consortium for a figure in the region of €4.4 million. The same company paid €8 million in 2002 for a site of a third of an acre to the rere of the building, originally a coal yard, and facing onto Gloucester Street.

Sir John Rogerson's Quay In 1713, Alderman Sir John Rogerson, a former Lord Mayor (1693) and MP, secured a fee farm grant of 133 acres of the South Strand 'on the high road to Ringsend' and commenced reclamation starting from City Quay. By 1729, the river was embanked almost to Ringsend, and plots known as South Lotts were leased out. He built a tavern called the Fountain in 1718. It was not until the 1760s that many houses were built on the Quay and, by the 1790s, it had become a fashionable suburb which also housed the Hibernian Marine School from 1770.* On the quayside there stands Bindon Blood Stoney's (1828–1909) diving bell. This revolutionary engineering mechanism enabled men to enter the chamber and replace the existing stone quayside with concrete blocks, some weighing 350 tonnes. Under Stoney's supervision, a large part of the quay walls were rebuilt from c. 1860 to c. 1900. He also designed Butt Bridge.* Butler's Pier, designed by architect Anthony Reddy, consists of 32 units with apartments for residential use only on the upper floors, and on the lower floors apartments with work/office space.

South Wall A wooden construction extending 7,983 feet seaward was commenced in 1717. The present wall was begun in 1735 and completed ten years later. It consists of a double block wall with

an infill of rocks. The Poolbeg lighthouse, designed by John Smith, was built 1761–68. The wall divided the bay for 3 miles and every vessel had to pass within this boundary. It was organised by the Ballast Office* set up in 1708.

See **Dublin Port and Docks Board, Pigeon House Road** *and* **Poolbeg Street.**

Queen's Square
Pearse Street (Great Brunswick Street)
An advertisement in Henry Shaw's directory of 1850 reads: 'it was commenced in 1839 and by indefatigable zeal brought nearly to a close. The houses are all of a uniform appearance at the front; some containing seven apartments and a kitchen, whilst others are formed of five rooms and a kitchen; each house having a scullery, coal vault etc. To the credit of the reformed Corporation, they lost no time in sending a plentiful supply of pipe water. In the street opposite the houses and running parallel with them there is a main sewer which discharges into the Liffey with every receding tide and into which sewer there is a private one for each house, thus according cleanliness and health to the inhabitants.' It faced onto Pearse Street near Pearse Square and Macken Street (Great Clarence Street).

Queen Street
From Arran Quay to North King Street
Named after Catherine of Braganza, wife of King Charles II.
Part of a Viking settlement including Oxmantown Green,* which in 1635 was to be kept for the use of citizens to walk and take the open air. By 1665, the area was being divided into lots, apart from Smithfield* and a convenient highway which is Queen Street. The King's Hospital* or Blue Coat School was founded by Charles II in Queen Street at Oxmantown Green before moving to Blackhall Place in 1669. Some Georgian houses still stand but nothing else remains of a once-fashionable area.

Queen's Theatre
Pearse Street

The theatre was built in 1844 at no. 209 by J. C. Josephs who took a lease from Trinity College, dated 29 June 1844 and renewable up to July 1893. It was on the site of the Adelphi, an older theatre opened in 1823. A Mr Ellis Jones had a further lease, which expired after 21 years in 1907. The Queen's Theatre had been redesigned in 1893 by W. Stirling. On 15 June 1908, Frederick Wentworth Marriot Watson entered into an agreement that, from 1 October that year, he would demolish houses on either side of the theatre, and within nine months would construct a first-class theatre on the site of nos. 207–211 Great Brunswick Street. He agreed to expend £5,000 and was given a lease for 99 years at a rent of £300. In November 1915, the lease was altered to permit smoking in the auditorium. The Abbey Theatre* Company used it from 1951 to 1966 while its new theatre was being constructed following a fire. Áras an Phiarsaigh, an office block opened in 1971, now occupies the site.

Quit Rent Office

This was created in 1669 to organise the collection of rents on lands forfeited after the 1641 rebellion. It was under the jurisdiction of the Commissioners of Excise in Ireland until 1823, when it was placed under the control of the Commissioners of Woods and Forests. From 1903, it acted on behalf of the Board of Trade in connection with the foreshores, harbours and railways. In 1924, it was taken over by the Department of Finance. A large collection of letters and books is available in the National Archives.*

Railway Street
From Lower Gardiner Street to Lower Buckingham Street
Formerly Great Martin's Lane, renamed Mecklenburgh Street, where the Dublin Society had a premises and botanic garden, in 1733. Renamed Tyrone Street 1887.
See also **Monto.**

Ram (Rame) Lane
The title should really be plural, as from Anglo-Norman times there were three lanes, all bearing this title, leading off the High Street.
See **Schoolhouse Lane** *and* **Skipper Alley.**

Ranelagh
A suburban district two miles S.E. from the General Post Office. It is situated on the road to Dundrum. Until about 1920, about half a mile further on, there was the village of Cullenswood, named after an extensive forest area. At one time, the whole district appears to have been called Colon. In the seventeenth century, Lord Ranelagh, who was Paymaster General to the Forces and whose family name was Jones, took the title from Ranelagh in Wicklow. He moved to London in about 1690 and built a house there to the east of Chelsea Hospital. After his death, a syndicate bought his London property and, in 1742, opened the famous Ranelagh pleasure gardens. Near Cullenswood lived William Barnard, Bishop of Raphoe and Derry, in a mansion called Willbrook. After his death, this house was bought by the Hollister family who converted the grounds into a pleasure garden and renamed the house Ranelagh after the London pleasure gardens. The garden was opened to the public in 1768. Eventually the entire area became known as Ranelagh. On 19 January 1785, Richard Crosbie made a balloon ascent from the gardens, with the Arms of Ireland painted on the covering of the balloon. Sandford Church (C of I) on Sandford Road (named after Baron Mountsandford who provided the site) was built in 1826; the present front with its rose window, bell tower and double doorway, was erected in 1860. The side aisles were added about twenty years later. There is a two-light window by Harry Clarke, consecrated in 1921. The Methodist church on Charleston Road was sold and converted into office accommodation in 1983, in which year the design won the Dublin Corporation Environmental Award. Charles Jones, 4th Viscount Ranelagh, resided in Molesworth Street in 1786.

Rathfarnham
Four miles S.W. of the General Post Office
A dual carriageway now bypasses the village, which consists of one long irregular street. Following in the wake of the Anglo-Norman invasion, the de Brett family came into ownership of the lands of Rathfarnham and leased them to the Harolds who were tenants until the fifteenth century, when the lands were sold to the Eustace Estate. In 1585, they passed by royal decree of Elizabeth I to Adam Loftus, who was responsible for building Rathfarnham Castle.*
Loreto Abbey, in the vicinity at Grange Road, was established in 1822 and incorporates an eighteenth-century house

built in 1725 for William Palliser, son of the Archbishop of Cashel. It was bought in 1821 by Archbishop Daniel Murray (1768–1852) as a school for girls. In 2001, the Loreto order sold the convent and school (its most famous novice was Mother Teresa of Calcutta, beatified in October 2003) to Danniger the developer, together with the 12.1-acre site, for just under €18 million. The site included the Victorian chapel, an eighteenth-century house, the Victorian concert hall and dormitory blocks, one of which is castellated. Ten residential blocks with a total of 271 apartments designed by John Fleming for Riversmith, a subsidiary of Zoe Developments, were built in the grounds. The first phase was completed in 2004. South of the Abbey is The Priory, Grange Road, now demolished, where Robert Emmet courted Sarah Curran. St Enda's a bilingual school founded by Patrick H. Pearse (1879–1916) at Cullenswood House, Ranelagh, in September 1908, moved to larger premises at The Hermitage, Rathfarnham, in 1910. St Enda's is now the Pearse Museum.

Marlay, an eighteenth-century manor, has stucco work by Michael Stapleton. The grounds are now a public park and the outbuildings are used by craftworkers in various skills. St Columba's College, founded in Co. Meath in 1842 as a Church of Ireland boarding school, moved to Holly Park in 1849. This house was built in 1780 for Lundy Foot, the snuff and tobacco manufacturer. St Columba's College chapel of St Mark was built in 1880 to a design by William Butterfield, the furnishings being a gift from Magdalen College, Oxford. The Church of the Annunciation (RC) was consecrated in 1878. The Stations of the Cross are represented in the stained-glass windows. The (C of I) church at Whitechurch is typical of the work of John Semple (c. 1801–c. 1873) who designed about fifteen churches for the dioceses of Dublin, Kildare, Ossory, Ferns and Leighlin. A feature of all his churches is narrow lancet windows between buttresses and a narrow tower supporting a slender spire. John Philpot Curran (1750–1817), the advocate of Catholic emancipation, lived at The Priory. His daughter, Sarah, was forced to leave her home when her father discovered that she was secretly engaged to Robert Emmet. Taking the road through Ballyboden and Woodtown to the summit of Mountpelier, one comes to the ruins of the 'Hell Fire Club'.*

The Church of the Holy Spirit (RC) at Ballyroan was designed by Raymond McDonnell in 1967, with decorative work by Sean Keating and Imogen Stuart. Rathfarnham Golf Club is off Stocking Lane. The Castle Golf Club is approached from Hillside Drive.

In 2003, a large Victorian mansion, Ballinteer Hall, on 24.3 acres at Ballinteer Avenue, was sold for €51 million to Glenkerrin Homes, with 401 homes planned for the site.

Rathfarnham Castle

Four miles from Dublin, near the village of Rathfarnham

A castle has stood on this site since the twelfth century. The present building was erected by Adam Loftus, Protestant Archbishop of Dublin, in 1583. It is a rectangular building with four corner towers with three storeys over a basement. The very fine eighteenth-century interior decoration is by William Chambers and James Stuart and was commissioned by the first Earl of Ely. In 1913, the castle was bought by the Society of Jesus, who maintained it in good order until they sold it in 1985. Because of the risk that it might be demolished, the State purchased it a year later, and a permanent preservation order was issued by the Commissioners of Public Works.

Rathmines and Pembroke Drainage (1881)

In 1881, these townships, which had a population of 50,000 people, lay outside the city and were administered by their own authority. This scheme for the removal of sewage was the first of its kind in the Dublin area. A high-level sewer along the old Swan river from Harold's Cross via Rathmines and Ballsbridge, which drained to the Dodder river near Londonbridge Road, was extended to the outfall at Whitebanks on the Great South Wall between the Pigeon House and the Poolbeg lighthouse. At the outfall, crude sewage was discharged to the estuary of the Liffey on the ebb tide. The low-level sewers in the Pembroke area around Sandymount were served by a pumping station at Londonbridge Road, where the sewage was lifted into the high-level sewer.

See also **Main Drainage System, Greater Dublin Drainage Scheme, Rivers, Rills etc.** *and* **Ringsend Treatment Works.**

Rathmines Road and Surrounding Area

The name comes from the de Meones family who came to Dublin in 1279. Gilbert de Meones held land in the area from the newly appointed Archbishop de Derlington who had recently arrived from England. The area expanded during the eighteenth century, and the village green was gradually reduced at what is now

Upper and Lower Rathmines Road. Rathmines and Rathgar were joined with the new Highfield Road in 1756 and became the separate Rathmines and Rathgar Urban District in 1840. The name *Rath Garbh* is mentioned as early as the twelfth century. In 1146, Dermot McMurrogh, King of Leinster, granted lands in the area to the convent of Augustinian nuns. After the suppression of the monasteries in 1539, the land came into the possession of Nicholas Seagraves and, in 1609, it passed to John Cusack, Lord Mayor of Dublin, and remained in the family possession throughout the eighteenth century. In 1785, Rathgar House was built; this was taken over as the Cancer Research Centre in 1950 and is now called St Luke's Hospital. It was an extensive district in the parish of St Peter, Uppercross and Rathdowne Baronies, two miles south from the General Post Office.

Situated on the road to Rathfarnham and Tallaght, in one continuous line of buildings upwards of 1½ miles in length, intersected by numerous terraces with detached villas, and separated from the city

Rathmines Road showing the large copper dome of the Church of Mary Immaculate Refuge of Sinners, built in 1854. Photograph taken in the 1950s.

at Portobello only by the Grand Canal. In 1847, a local act created the part of the parish which was in the barony of Uppercross into a township. The townland of Sallymount was added in 1862. The townlands of St Catherine and St Nicholas Without were added in 1866, and Milltown was added in 1880.

The Rathmines and Rathgar Water Act 1880 constructed a waterworks at a cost of about £200,000 at Glen na Smól Valley. The impressive town hall was built in 1887 to a design by Sir Thomas Drew, with a clock tower from which, in 1896, Marconi demonstrated his wireless telegraph. The Church of Mary Immaculate Refuge of Sinners (RC) was built in 1854 to a design of Patrick Byrne, with a pediment supported by Corinthian columns. Its large copper dome is a distinctive landmark and was enlarged following a fire in 1920. The church replaces a smaller one built in 1830. Holy Trinity Church (C of I), Church Avenue, was designed by John Semple and opened in 1833; it stands in the centre of the road at the junction with Belgrave Road. It has a central spire and cornered pinnacles. In 1885, it was rebuilt at a cost of £6,000. In 1990, the building was completely reroofed and the interior redesigned to provide a modern church and a suite of halls and rooms all under one roof.

With the Local Government (Dublin) Act of 1930, the Rathmines urban district became part of the Dublin Corporation area. The library cornering onto Leinster Road was designed by Batchelor and Hicks and was opened in 1913. It was funded like so many other libraries by the Scottish steel millionaire, Andrew Carnegie. The area began to expand in the nineteenth century; Leinster Road was commenced in 1835, Grosvenor and Kenilworth Roads in the 1850s and Orwell Road in 1864. James Joyce (1882–1941) was born on 2 February 1882 at 41 Brighton Square. (*See* also Martello Tower, Sandycove.) John Millington Synge (1871–1909) spent 16 years of his childhood at 4 Orwell Park. In 1906, George Russell (AE, 1867–1935) moved to 17 Rathgar Avenue and lived

there for 25 years (see also Emorville Avenue). A scheme is at present under consideration to upgrade the swimming pool, built in 1970. It would have 90 apartments overhead and set back from Rathmines Road to create a public square. The area to the rere of the pool, which is at present used as a route by children going to St Louis' school, would be landscaped. The project would also include social housing and a crèche. Donnelly Turpin are the architects and work could commence in 2005 at an estimated cost of €30 million. *See* **Observatory Lane, Milltown** *and* **Zion Church.**

Records of Urban District Councils

Each of the areas of Rathmines and Rathgar and of Pembroke had its own local government until 1930. The records are preserved in the Dublin City Council archives,* describing the development of these suburbs from the mid-nineteenth century. The records of the Howth Urban District Council from 1918 to 1940 are also available.

Redmond's Alley
Off Wood Quay
Denis Lambert Redmond, patriot, lived at no. 14 Wood Quay. His home was used as a hiding place during the 1798 rebellion. On 14 July each year, Bastille day, he lit a large bonfire in memory of the French revolution. He was hanged in front of his home on 6 October 1803.

Richmond Tower
South Circular Road, Kilmainham
Originally stood at the foot of Watling Street but had to be removed to make way for the extra traffic which used the southern quays after the new railway came into operation in 1844. The work of removing it to its present position at the western entrance to the Royal Hospital grounds was undertaken at the expense of the railway company, which had it carefully taken down and re-erected in 1846. The structure was designed for the original site by Francis Johnston (1760–1829).

Riding the Franchises

One of the great highlights of Dublin life and certainly the most spectacular was the display by the guilds called the riding of the franchises, or fringes. This was a triennial parade, headed by the Lord Mayor and City Fathers in full regalia, all mounted on horseback, parading the boundaries of the city. In July, each of the 25 guilds represented in the common council was summoned to ride the franchises. The parade was held at the beginning of August, each member having to appear on horseback with complete arms and furniture. Every guild had an immense carriage with a great platform on which its wares were advertised. The parade served two purposes: it commemorated the city's defiance against its enemies outside the walls or confines, and it also acted as an outward and visible sign for the benefit of the unfree of the city, that the guilds were determined to hold and perpetuate the privileges they enjoyed. This parade was under the jurisdiction of Dublin Corporation, which was bound by its charter to ride around the city limits once every three years. This ceased in 1841 with the Municipal Corporations (Ireland) Act (324 Victoriae Chapter 108) when Dublin Corporation members were elected by the rate-payers of the city. There are nineteenth-century records in some of the guilds showing that it was becoming difficult to find members who could ride a horse.

See **Guilds.**

Ringsend

A maritime village two miles east from the General Post Office

Some scholars attribute the name to *an rinn*, which means a point; thus the point of the tide, but a more likely interpretation would be the end of a point of land. It was here in 1649 that Oliver Cromwell arrived with 12,000 troops. St Matthew's Royal Chapel was built in 1704, with the tower an addition in 1713. Ringsend by this time had become the port of Dublin with the packet boats from England mooring below the Pigeon House.* The 'Ringsend cars' raced across the sands of the unwalled River Liffey and River Dodder, taking passengers

Author's drawing of a paddle steamer at Ringsend, waiting to be broken up for scrap in 1961.

Ringsend. St Matthew's built in 1704, with the tower an addition in 1713. The church was rebuilt in 1879, the tower remaining from the original building.

to and from Dublin. St Matthew's was rebuilt in 1878; the tower remains from the original building.

When the Grand Canal* docks were built, they covered an area of 25 acres with 2,000 yards of quayside. In recent years, several private housing developments qualifying for Section 23 relief have been constructed around the dock area. In 1989, Zoe Developments completed Fisherman's Wharf near the East Link Bridge and York Road. Following the success of this experiment, the next year they built Alexandra Quay on York Road: 35 units consisting of seven two-bed apartments on the ground floor, eight two-bed apartments on the first floor and sixteen two-bed, two storey duplex units on second and third floors, and four two-storey townhouses. Alexandra Quay faces the East Link toll bridge, and is beside Ringsend Mission Hall, built in 1896. In 1990–91 Cosgrave Brothers built Camden Lock on South Docks Road, with 72 units and 8,000 square feet of offices. The housing consists of four-storey blocks comprising two-bed

apartments and three-bed two-storey duplex units, designed by FitzGerald Reddy and Associates. St Patrick's (RC) Church was built in 1912 and backs onto the River Dodder. It replaces an earlier church constructed in 1859.

See **Designated Areas Scheme and Dublin Docklands Development Authority.**

Ringsend Treatment Works

On 30 June 2003, Europe's largest water-waste project came into full operation with the opening by the Taoiseach, Mr Bertie Ahern, of the new works at Ringsend, the 10.5 km submarine pipeline across the Bay and the new pumping station in Sutton. The project cost €300 million and was completed in just over three years. The new plant is controlled by high-tech software, and the treated water going into the Bay is similar in quality to clean river water. A unique combination of 100 per cent natural processes is used at the works. Following preliminary treatment at the new works, the waste water undergoes treatment in 12 lamella primary tanks, where sludge in the waste water settles out. This then undergoes biological treatment in 24 huge Sequencing Batch Reactors to further remove polluting matter and ammonia and nitrogen. In summer, during the bathing season, ultraviolet disinfection is provided as part of the tertiary treatment. Sludge from the waste water is de-watered and digested at Ringsend to produce biogas and reduce odours. The biogas provides over 50 per cent of the annual energy needs of the plant—making it cost-effective to run. The digest sludge is thermally dried to produce 20,000 tonnes of organic fertiliser each year. Marketed as Biofert, it is highly sought after by tillage and grass farmers alike. A natural fertiliser, it contains valuable nutrients and means fewer artificial fertilisers are used. The new treatment works was designed and built by Ascon, Black and Veatch and Anglian Water International, the Irish, US and UK consortium that will operate the plant for the next 20 years. Prior to the opening of the new works, the *Sir Joseph Bazalgette* sludge boat, named after the mastermind of the main central London drainage scheme, dumped its cargo north of a line due east of the Baily lighthouse

The 10.5 km submarine pipeline from Ringsend to Sutton, laid below the shipping channel, has pipes 16 m long and 1.4 m in diameter, made of steel and coated with 150 mm concrete surround, bringing them to 1.7 m diameter. The pipeline weighs 25,000 tonnes and is made up of more than 650 pipes welded together. The consortium responsible is Pierce, the Irish civil engineering company, McAlpine, a pipe specialist contractor from the UK, and Tideway, a Dutch/Belgian dredging contractor. The new pumping station at Sutton was built to intercept waste water from North Dublin, including Finglas, Ballymun, Baldoyle and Sutton, and pump it to the Ringsend Treatment Works. Prior to this, waste water was discharged untreated off the nose of Howth. The station was constructed by Ascon and Bowen Water Technology; it is fully automatic and the four main pumps are capable of pumping almost 3 cubic metres per second.

The Sutton Pumping Station was officially opened by the Taoiseach, Mr Bertie Ahern, on 9 September 2003. The Lord Mayor of Dublin, Cllr Royston Brady, and the Cathaoirleach of Fingal County Council, Cllr Sean Dolphin, also spoke at the ceremony.

Rivers, Rills, Rivulets and Streams

There are more than 50 rivers and streams in the city area, each with its own different characteristics: catchments, regimen, channel shape and grade, storm behaviour and local vulnerability in built-up areas. The principal ones are as follows:

Abbey stream
Colcur brook
Gray's brook
Tramway brook
Bloody stream
Santa Sabina stream
Carrickbrack stream
Balsaggart stream
Whitewater brook
Grange stream
Kilbarrack stream
Black Banks stream
Santry river
Nanniken river
Wad river
Tolka river
Claremont stream
Finglas river
Finglaswood stream
Scribblestown stream
Liffey river
Furry Glen stream
Mayne river
Magazine stream
Zoo stream
Bradogue river
Portland watercourse
Steyne river
Poddle river*
Old City watercourse
Tymon river
Tenter's water
Commons water
Camac river
Gallanstown stream
Blackditch stream
Walkinstown stream
Creosote stream
St Laurence stream
Pound Lane stream
Swan river
Dodder river
Dundrum river
Little Dargle stream
Castle stream
Owen Doher river
Lakelands overflow
Whitechurch stream
Nutley stream
Elm Park stream
Trimblestown stream
Cuckoo stream
Oldcourt stream
Glibwater
Coleman's brook
Greater Dublin Drainage Scheme S.W.
Tallaght stream

The drainage division of Dublin City Council keeps these rivers and streams in check as the run-off from storm water (rain) greatly exceeds that of the dry weather flow of raw sewage at a ratio as high as 200:1, resulting in the need for carefully designed pipes or river channels to accommodate heavy rainfall.

See also **Main Drainage System, also Water Supply.**

Rochel Lane, Rochell Street
See **Back Lane.**

Rosemary Lane
From Merchant's Quay to Cook Street
In 1270, it was called the King's Lane and Lowestock's Lane; in 1403, Lovestoke's Lane, a name subsequently changed to Longstick Lane. By 1600, it was known as Rosemary Lane. In 1607, the City Assembly agreed that a gate should be erected at each end of the lane 'to avoid the noisomeness thereof. . . to be locked every night and opened every morning'. The Church of St Michael and St John stood in the lane until it was moved in 1815 to its present site at Exchange Street. A contemporary drawing of 1930 shows derelict sites and tenements.

Rotunda Hospital
Bartholomew Mosse became a Licentiate in Midwifery of the King and Queen's College of Physicians on 22 May 1742 and devoted the rest of his life to midwifery. In the poorer houses in Dublin, he had discovered the pitiable conditions that resulted in the high mortality rate of mothers and babies. A committee of friends was formed and a house was acquired in George's Lane, now South Great George's Street. It had formerly housed Madame Violante's theatre. The first maternity patient was admitted on 15 March 1745 and the first Dublin Lying-in Hospital was launched. By 2 April 1746, 209 women had been admitted and 208 were delivered. One woman died from childbed fever and 190 infants were discharged alive.

Because the accommodation in George's Lane was inadequate, Mosse raised funds through lotteries, many of the winnings being returned to the Hospital Committee. The first Irish performance of Handel's *Judas Macabeus*, in February 1748, was for the benefit of the hospital. A lease of 'four acres and one rood plantation measure on the north side of Great Britain Street' was acquired from William Naper on 15 August 1748, 'for three lives, renewable forever at a fine of a peppercorn on the fall of each life'. Mosse surrounded the area with a wall and laid it out similarly to the Vauxhall Gardens, London. He also built a coffee stall and orchestral hall. There was an admission charge of one shilling to the

Rotunda Hospital. Engraving 1768.

entertainments that commenced a year later and which included famous cross-channel musicians. Banquets and other entertainments were also organised to fund the new hospital. Richard Cassels was employed as architect but died in 1750. The foundation stone was laid on 24 May 1751 by Thomas Taylor, Lord Mayor, and the supervision of the building was given to John Ensor a pupil of Richard Cassels. On 2 December 1756, a royal charter was granted, with Mosse as Master for life. The new hospital was opened on 8 December 1757 by the Lord Lieutenant and his wife, the Duchess of Bedford.

One of the features of the building is the chapel with ornamentation by Barthelemy Cramillion; this, with the exception of the centre panel, was completed in 1758. A contemporary account of the hospital states: 'The centre building 125 feet by 82 in depth has two fronts of excellent mountain granite; in the centre of this, four semi-columns of the Doric order on a basement story, support the entablature and pediment; at either end curved colonades serve to gain a courtyard in front which is secured by a handsome iron balustrade. The wards, which in the upper stories open off galleries running the entire length of the building, are airy and spacious. The hospital gardens are beautiful in a very eminent degree and contain a variety that is astonishing. A high wall was taken down in 1784 and a handsome iron railing on a dwarf wall, with lamps thickly placed, was put in its stead. The Rotunda and new rooms adjoining were built in the year 1757. In 1785 work was begun on an elegant suite of rooms to be added to the Rotunda and the Rotunda itself was much beautified by Mr Richard Johnston, architect. The rooms consist of two principal apartments one over the other 86 feet long by 40 broad; the lower is the ballroom or Assembly room and the upper the supper and tea rooms. There is a smaller ballroom on the ground floor. The entertainments of the Rotunda during the winter form the most elegant amusements of Dublin. The

receipts of the whole after defraying the incidental expenses go to support the hospital.' Bartholomew Mosse died in February 1759.

Royal Arcade
Suffolk Street
George Home, a Scotsman, built Dublin's first enclosed shopping arcade in 1819, linking Suffolk Street with College Green, at a cost of £16,000. It was beset with problems from the start and was eventually destroyed by fire in 1837. It stood on the site of the General Post Office that removed to Sackville Street in 1818.

Edward Clibborn, writing in *Saunders' Newsletter* on 26 December 1849, on the antiquities of the Royal Irish Academy states: 'in 1837, during the fire which destroyed the Arcade, immediately in the rere of the Academy house, that more of these curious articles were removed or stolen'.

Wilson's *Dublin Directory* notes that in the Royal Arcade, 'Arrangements were continually in operation in this establishment for supplying the Public and Strangers visiting the Metropolis with every Article that can please the eye . . . the various shops giving them a choice and facility in procuring every description of goods on fair terms. As the proprietor of each shop is bound to keep every article in his or her line, the best of its kind, as also to ask but one price for each article they sell under heavy penalty. Adjoining the Arcade is an extensive hotel, coffee room and taverna, for the accommodation of Families or Travellers.'
See **Home's Hotel.**

Royal College of Physicians of Ireland
6 Kildare Street
Sir Henry Cavendish, Teller of the Exchequer, erected two houses demised to him by James Fitzgerald, 20th Earl of Kildare. In November 1782, the interest in one of the houses was purchased on behalf of the Kildare Street Club* by David La

Touche who bought the second house in 1786 for the club. In 1860, Dominic Corrigan, who was president of the RCPI, urged the College to buy the vacant building. Before the College had taken possession, a fire occurred, resulting in the destruction of the greater part of the premises. William Murray, architect, was employed to redesign the building, and the classical designed portico with Doric and Corinthian columns dates from this time. The foundation stone of the new building was laid by the Earl of Carlisle, Lord Lieutenant, on 7 July 1862. In 1870, a second hall was built in the garden on the racquet courts of the old Kildare Street Club. The corridor linking the two halls pre-dates the fire. In 1982, further expansion took place, with the building of a 60-seat lecture theatre to be followed by a new conference and examination hall together with common rooms and offices. The classical pillared portico, built in the 1860s by Dominic Corrigan and his architect, William Murray, and covering the original façade of brick, had by 1963 begun to shed its sandstone. Desmond Fitzgerald, architect, was employed to supervise the restoration of the entire front in Portland stone at a cost of £18,500. The old façade of the college now stands as a folly at Woodbrook Golf Club.

See also **David La Touche.**

Royal College of Surgeons
St Stephen's Green

In 1805, a Quaker burial site on the corner of St Stephen's Green and York Street was purchased as a site for the new college. The building was designed by Edward Parke, architect to the Dublin Society, in 1806. By the time that the College had moved to St Stephen's Green, there were 18 private medical schools in the city, as well as the School of Physic in Trinity College and Sir Patrick Dun's teaching hospital. In 1827, William Murray re-centred the building and extended it by four bays. During the registrarship of Dr Harry O'Flanagan, the College was greatly extended along York Street. Recently the headquarters of the

Salvation Army* was purchased and demolished and a new building, designed by architects Brian O'Halloran and Associates, opened in 2004, further extending the College's presence in the street.

Royal Dublin Society

The RDS had its beginnings as 'The Dublin Society for improving Husbandry, Manufactures and other useful Arts' and held its first meeting on 25 June 1731 in Trinity College. The words 'and Sciences' were added to the title within a week. In April 1750, it was incorporated on being granted a charter. It became the Royal Dublin Society in 1821, following a royal visit to the city.

The work of the Society was inspired by the wretched conditions of the people at the time. For some years before 1731, men were writing pamphlets about the state of Ireland. These included Lord Molesworth's 'Some considerations for promoting agriculture and employing the poor', which appeared in 1723. The purpose of the Society was to improve the conditions of the people. It carried out research in agriculture, was responsible for the establishment of industries and encouraged the arts and sciences by creating institutions to promote these objects. These institutions include the Botanic Gardens* which have been located at Glasnevin since 1795 and were preceded by the Society's garden at Summerhill, established in 1733. The National College of Art* originated in the 1740s as the Drawing School of the Society. The National Library,* the National Gallery* and the Veterinary College* all owe their origins to the work of the Society in the nineteenth century.

After its inaugural in the rooms of the Philosophical Society in Trinity College,* it held its weekly meeting in the Parliament House.* It met in several other buildings also until 3 December 1767 when it met for the first time in its own premises in Grafton Street (now nos. 111–112). These premises were sold in 1796 for £3,000 when the Society moved to Hawkins Street.

Sums in the region of £60,000 were laid out on the Hawkins Street premises. On 14 December 1814, Augustus Frederick, 3rd Duke of Leinster, sold Leinster House* to the Society for £10,000. The Society tried, unsuccessfully, to sell its Hawkins Street premises and, in 1820, the lessees of the Theatre Royal* took them over gratis, subject to the ground rent of £610 p.a. which the Society was then paying. In 1877, an act transferred much of the Royal Dublin Society's work to the state and, after this, the Society was relegated to a suite of rooms in the house.

On 14 August 1924, the Minister for Finance announced the intention of the government to take over Leinster House. The Society received £68,000 and then moved to the present premises in Ballsbridge.

The activities with which the Society is most associated in the public mind today are the annual Dublin Spring Show, held in May, and the annual Horse Show, held in August. In the 1870s, the horse shows were held in the courtyard of Leinster House. In September 2004, An Bord Pleanála granted planning permission for a €100 million office development, on 16.05 hectares at Simmonscourt Road, consisting of four office blocks varying in height from four to six storeys over basement with 189 underground parking spaces. Permission was also granted for the upgrading of the Anglesea Stand, hospitality accommodation and refurbishment of the RDS offices.

Royal Exchange

According to Gilbert's *History of the City of Dublin*, the Royal Exchange of the city appears to have stood in Winetavern Street* in 1629. After the drawing-up of the plans for the new Parliament Street,* it was agreed that too many valuable buildings would be destroyed if the Exchange faced directly into the Castle Yard.* A new proposal suggested that a chapel of government with a high cupola should face the new street.

The merchants of Dublin, however,

objected and presented a petition to parliament 'setting forth their want of a proper lot of ground to erect an Exchange on; that the difficulties they laboured under for want of such ground was a detriment to trade, and that if a lot of ground was granted to them in Dame Street, opposite Parliament Street, it would be a great advantage to the commerce and trade of the city of Dublin'. Their petition was favourably received, and a plot of 100 feet square was reserved. The purchase money of £13,500 for the site was obtained from parliament by the zeal and activity of Dr Charles Lucas, one of the city representatives. To defray the cost of the building, the sum of almost £40,000 was raised by lotteries conducted by the merchants.

*The Dublin Journal*of 12 July 1768 has an entry stating that demolition work had started on Cork Hill* in order to widen the Avenue and make room for the New Exchange 'which we hear, the Trustees intend to be a covered Building as most suitable to our climate, and to the Dimensions of the Ground granted for the purpose'.

An advertisement in the *Freeman's Journal* of 27 July 1768 invited architects to submit designs for the new exchange, which were to be received by September 1768. Out of the 61 designs exhibited in the Assembly Rooms* in William Street, the prize was awarded to Thomas Cooley of London. The second premium was awarded to James Gandon and the third to T. Sandby. The Duke of Northumberland, while Lord Lieutenant of Ireland, obtained a charter incorporating the trustees and it was intended to erect his statue in marble in front of the building. He was, however, recalled from Ireland, and the laying of the first stone was performed on Wednesday, 2 August 1769, by his successor, Lord Townshend. The foundation stone was laid in a rock known locally as Standfast Dick.* The building took ten years to complete and was finished in 1779. In October 1851, the building was transferred from the Corporation of Merchants or the Guild of

the Holy Trinity to the Rt Hon. the Lord Mayor, Aldermen and Burgesses of Dublin.*
See also **City Hall.**

Royal Hibernian Academy
Ely Place
In May 1780, the Society of Artists in Ireland, founded in 1764, held its last exhibition. (*See* City Assembly House). About 20 years later, another society of the same name was founded and exhibited in the Dublin Society's premises in Hawkins Street. This facility ceased in 1818 when the Dublin Society moved to Leinster House in Kildare Street. On 5 August 1823, the Royal Hibernian Academy of Painters, Sculptors, Architects and Engravers was founded with a royal charter. It had 14 members and 10 associates; today the Academy is made up of 30 members and 10 associate members all of whom are professional artists. In 1824, Francis Johnston was made President on the death of William Ashford. He designed and built, at his own expense of £14,000, a home and gallery for the Society, in Abbey Street. It was opened in 1826 and extended in 1830. An extract from the *Dublin Penny Journal* gives the following information. 'This chaste and elegant edifice, situated in lower Abbey Street, consists of three stories; in the basement there is a loggia or recess, ornamented by two fluted columns, of the Doric order, supporting the first storey. Over the entrance is the head of Palladio, representing Architecture; over the window on the right, one of Michael Angelo, representing Sculpture, and on the left, of Raphael, emblematic of Painting. These are by J. Smyth Esq. an associate. Passing through an entrance-hall, and ascending a broad flight of steps, the first exhibition room, 40 feet by 20, and intended for water colour drawings, is entered. This communicates by an arch-way with the great saloon, for the exhibition of oil paintings, 50 feet by 40, lighted by a lantern. From this room a door-way leads to the new Sculpture gallery, which is a beautiful octagonal apartment.

'The Academy is possessed of a fine collection of casts from the Antique, a few pictures by the old masters, and a tolerable library of works, chiefly connected with the fine Arts, the greater number of which were presented by the late Edward Houghton Esq.

'A very ingeniously contrived staircase leads to the council-room, keeper's apartment, & which are all in the front building. The first stone of this edifice was laid on the 29th of April, 1824, by F. Johnston Esq.; and on a copper plate which was firmly bedded in the stone, was the following inscription: "Anno. Dom. MDCCCXXIV. His most Gracious Majesty, George the Fourth, King of the United Kingdoms of Great Britain and Ireland, Defender of the Faith, & having by his Royal Letters Patent, bearing date the 5th of August, 1823, incorporated the Artists of Ireland, under the name of 'The Royal Academy of Painting, Sculpture, and Architecture'. Francis Johnston, Esq. Architect, one of the members of that body munificently founded this building for their use, to form a National School of Art; and laid this the first stone, April 29th, 1824, the day appointed for the celebration of His Majesty's birth, in the presence of the Academy." Messrs. Carolan were the builders.'

The premises were completely destroyed in 1916. Everything belonging to the Society was lost in the flames. It was not until 1939 that new premises were bought at 15 Ely Place, formerly Oliver St John Gogarty's house, together with the adjacent garden. It was unsuitable for exhibitions and the hall of the School of Art in Kildare Street was used. In 1970, St Patrick's Hall in Dublin Castle was made available, and, from 1971 to 1984, the exhibitions were held in the National Gallery of Ireland.* In 1971, Matthew Gallagher, a builder, offered to erect a new gallery on the Ely Place site, entirely at his own expense. Raymond McGrath designed a building and work commenced in 1972. The Gallagher group collapsed in 1981 before the building was completed. The 156th Annual exhibition of

Royal Hibernian Military School, built for the orphans of soldiers, to a design of Francis Johnston.

the Royal Hibernian Academy opened on 19 June 1985, with 460 exhibits and a revived architectural section in the new building, which had received an injection of funds from the National Lottery.

Royal Hibernian Military School
Phoenix Park

A small book printed in Dublin in 1721, entitled 'Methods of erecting, supporting and governing charity schools with an account of the charity schools in Ireland and some observations thereon', contained the following paragraph: 'A charity school set up here in 1705 of twenty five girls, clothed, instructed in the principles of the Established Church, taught to read and work and when qualified put out to trades or services. The school is entirely supported by some pious ladies who live out of St Paul's parish. But as there are a number of inhabitants in it of great honour, affluence and charity, it is not doubted that a charity school will shortly be erected and maintained by them.' The Rev. Dr Carr bequeathed £100 in debentures on the 'Maryborough Turnpike' towards a similar day school for poor boys of the parish. An advertisement in the *Freeman's Journal,*

February 1765, implied that the governors of the school found mostly orphans of soldiers applying as 'there appeared to be, at that time in this parish above four hundred boys all orphans or destitute children of soldiers who had either died or were killed or absent in foreign parts in the service of the Crown'.

The Corporation of Carpenters granted the use of part of a house owned by them in Oxmantown Green to house twenty boys. Two charity sermons preached by Rev. Joseph Pratt aroused a great deal of interest and eventually, by royal approbation, the King's Garden at Chapelizod and three acres in the Phoenix Park were granted for a hospital, with a bounty of £1,000 per annum. Francis Johnston designed the new building and, according to the *Freeman's Journal,* 'on 31st October 1766 their excellencies the Lords Justices went to the Phoenix Park and laid the first stone of a building there to be erected pursuant to a grant of £3,000 made in the last session of parliament'. Money was raised from many sources, including one day's pay from each of the non-commissioned officers and men of various regiments. The school was given a royal charter on 15 July 1769. In 1788, a

Commission reported that there were 260 children (boys and girls) in the care of the hospital and the average cost of maintaining each child over the preceding seven years was £12–3–8½. Boys were apprenticed with fees of £5 and girls at £3–10–0.

The school closed with the ending of British administration and, in September 1922, the boys were removed to Kent and then to the Duke of York's Royal Military School at Dover. The buildings were then taken over by the army and by the Church of Ireland Teacher Training College. They were eventually fitted out as St Mary's Chest Hospital, which today is a geriatric hospital run by the Eastern Regional Health Authority; there is also a unit for young chronically disabled persons. It is now called St Mary's Hospital, Phoenix Park.

Royal Hospital
Donnybrook
See **Donnybrook** *and* **Townsend Street.**

Royal Hospital
Kilmainham

The hospital designed by the Irish Surveyor General, Sir William Robinson, was built for the reception and entertainment of ancient, maimed and infirm officers and soldiers. The foundation stone was laid by the Viceroy, James Duke of Ormonde, in April 1680 and took seven years to complete, the first soldiers being admitted in 1684. The building stood on the site of the Priory of the Knights Hospitallers, their castle being to the left of the present hospital. The plan for the building provided for a closed courtyard with ground-floor loggia on three of the sides and part of the fourth. It was designed to accommodate 300 pensioners on its three floors. The central tower and spire were added in 1701. The beautiful chapel consecrated in 1687 has a papier-mâché ceiling which is a facsimile of an original stucco ceiling. There is also some fine woodcarving by James Tabary, a Huguenot. When the chapel was in use,

Irish Museum of Modern Art (IMMA). A major restoration work was carried out at the Royal Hospital Kilmainham between 1980 and 1984 by the Office of Public Works as a centre for culture and the arts. In 1991 it became IMMA and houses modern collections of Irish and international art.

the music for the services was supplied by a military band as there was no organ.

The chapel closed for public worship on 17 January 1927. In the same year, the Garda Síochána took over the hospital, which it occupied until the building was declared unsafe in 1949. A major restoration work was carried out by the Office of Public Works in 1980–84 under the supervision of John Costello. The building opened as a centre for culture and the arts in 1988. It also houses the Irish Museum of Modern Art (IMMA) since 1991.

See also **Bully's Acre, Kilmainham, Richmond Tower** *and* **St John's Well.**

Royal Irish Academy
Dawson Street
Founded in 1785 in a house at no. 114 Grafton Street, with the Earl of Charlemont as its President. In 1852, it moved to Northland House in Dawson Street, built in 1770 for the Knox family of Dungannon. The rear of the house was extended to house the library. The objects of the Royal Irish Academy were the study and preservation of the national treasures, and its museum housed the Tara Brooch, the Ardagh Chalice, the Cross of Cong and many more of the country's antiquities. It was also involved in the advancement of science. Almost from its inception, academic research was published, and today all disciplines from archaeology to zoology are represented. The massive project initiated in the 1960s is the New History of Ireland. In 1890, the artefacts from the museum of the Academy were transferred to the government and moved to the new National Museum of Ireland,* opened that year in Kildare Street.

Royal Irish Academy of Music
36 Westland Row
Founded by royal charter in 1848 and restructured in 1856. It is the principal college in Ireland for teaching and examination at all levels. A perpetuating body with a board of governors, it was based first at 18 St Stephen's Green and moved to its present location in 1871. The

house was built in 1771 and has some plasterwork ceilings by Michael Stapleton. The academy was extended in 1911 when nos. 37 and 38 were purchased.

Royal Society of Antiquaries of Ireland
63 Merrion Square
Established from the Kilkenny Archaeological Society in 1849 to preserve, examine and illustrate the ancient monuments of the history, language, arts, manners and customs of the past as connected with Ireland. Given a Royal Charter in 1912.

Royal Zoological Society of Ireland
Phoenix Park
At a meeting called by advertisement and held on 10 May 1830 at the Rotunda, under the chairmanship of the Duke of Leinster, it was decided to establish the Zoological Society of Dublin. Its object was to form a collection of living animals on the plan of the Zoological Establishment of London. At the meeting, it was announced that the Lord Lieutenant had kindly consented to allow a portion of the Phoenix Park already enclosed to be used as a site, and a month later it was reported that His Excellency had been pleased to give the Surgeon General formal possession of the ground in the Phoenix Park (see Crampton Memorial). The same year, the Royal Menagerie at Windsor Great Park was disbanded and the animals given to the Zoological Society of London. Some surplus animals and birds, including deer, emus and ostriches, were sent over to Dublin in June 1831. Later in the year, a lioness, a hyena, a leopard, a Bengal sheep and a wolf also arrived from London. The first lion cub was born at the Zoo in 1857. An elephant was purchased in 1835 and a giraffe in 1844. The Society is a private voluntary body, governed by a council, and membership is by subscription.

The Zoological Society of Dublin became the Royal Zoological Society of Ireland in 1838 when Queen Victoria agreed to become its patron.

RTÉ (Radio Telefís Éireann)
Montrose, Donnybrook
Entrance from Nutley Lane

RTÉ occupies six acres, formerly the playing fields of St Andrew's College which was paid £17,500 for the site. Built to a design of Michael Scott and Associates, the studios were opened in 1961. Radio Éireann later moved from accommodation in the GPO building in Henry Street to the newly established Radio Telefís Éireann Centre. The national television service opened on 1 January 1961 and the new RTÉ authority came under the control of the Broadcasting Authority (Amendment) Act, 1966.

Russell Hotel
101–104 St Stephen's Green

Originally a temperance hotel founded at no. 102 by Thomas W. Russell (1841–1920), MP for Tyrone and actively involved in the prevention of intemperance. At the beginning of the century, nos. 103 and 104 formed part of the hotel. In 1947, Kenneth Besson purchased the hotel, together with no. 101, and ran it successfully as Dublin's finest hotel until it closed on 15 June 1974. It was demolished a year later. The site was sold to Irish Life in 1979 and a large seven- and nine-storey office block was erected, with an entrance from Harcourt Street, named Stokes Place after Stokes Kennedy Crowley, the firm of accountants.

Thomas William Russell put the Irish Sunday Closing Act through the Westminster Parliament in 1878. He was the author of *England and the Empire*.

See St Stephen's Green.

Russell Street (Originally Avenue)
From North Circular Road to Jones's Road

John Russell the builder, died 1825. General housing.

Russian Orthodox Church, St Peter and St Paul
See Harold's Cross.

Rutland Square
North of Upper O'Connell Street

Named after Charles Manners (1754–87), 4th Duke of Rutland, Lord Lieutenant, died in office. Later to be called Parnell Square after Charles Stewart Parnell (1846–1891), the political leader whose monument* was erected at the top of Sackville (O'Connell) Street in 1911.

This is the second earliest of the Dublin squares. It was commenced in 1751, the houses on the east side being designed by John Ensor and others. A fashionable square in the second half of the eighteenth century, its houses were occupied by members of parliament and several bishops.

On the north side is Charlemont House,* built in 1761–63 for James Caulfield, Earl of Charlemont, on what was named Palace Row. In 1932, this became the Municipal Gallery of Modern Art, founded on 18 January 1908 at Clonmel House, Harcourt Street, and later the Hugh Lane Gallery of Modern Art. Now the Dublin City Gallery, The Hugh Lane. Further along is a Presbyterian Church* designed by Andrew Heiton and commonly called Findlater's Church, after the philanthropic grocer.

On the east side, no. 4 was the town house of the Earl of Wicklow. In no. 5, Oliver St John Gogarty was born. The Galway scientist, Richard Kirwan, was born at no. 6; Dr Bartholomew Mosse lived at no. 9, and the Earl of Ormonde at no. 11. Parnell House, no. 14, is occupied by the Companies Registration Office and the Competition Authority, also the Registry of Friendly Societies, while no. 16 is the Office of the Director of Corporate Enforcement, all under the Department of Enterprise, Trade and Employment. Number 18, whose first owner was Lord Farnham, passed through various owners until George Jameson, a distiller, purchased it in 1891. He employed the Manchester architect, Alfred Darbyshire, to redesign the interior and the large salon with an ornamented colonnade and gilded frieze. The house also has a ceiling by Michael Stapleton. It now houses the Dublin Writers' Museum* and, at no. 19 is the Irish Writers' Centre. In 1785, an Act was passed for completing and effectually lighting and watching Rutland Square. Forty-eight houses are mentioned in the Act. This was financed by each house having to pay one pound per annum per foot running measure. This would cover £12 for fire and candles, £12 each for eight night watchmen (*see* Police), £16 for a constable and £4 for contingencies.

On the south side is the Rotunda Hospital,* designed for Dr Bartholomew Mosse by Richard Cassels and John Ensor, in 1757. The hospital was built at an angle to the square after Mosse had a disagreement with Luke Gardiner, the developer, who came into the ownership of the lands of St Mary's Abbey and was building and widening Drogheda Street* and the surrounding area (*see* Sackville Street). He also built houses in the square from no. 11 down to Drogheda Street. The Rotunda was erected in 1764 for entertainments, and is now a cinema; the supper room became the Dublin Gate Theatre.*

In the garden opposite Charlemont House* is the 1916–1922 Garden of Rembrance, designed by Daithi P. Hanly. Over the pool stands the gigantic bronze group of 'The Children of Lir' by Oisín Kelly. This was erected with the opening of the park in 1966. In 1790, the family of Sir Thomas Taylor (Taylour) moved from the family home, Bective House, built in 1738–39 at Oxmantown Green, to Rutland Square to a house owned by Archbishop Cobbe. This was demolished in 1863 to make way for Findlater's Church.

The National Ballroom opened on 17 March 1945; it was a popular venue for dances but closed in the late 1970s as it did not have an alcohol licence. In 2003, Dublin City Council voted in favour of the proposed extension to the Hugh Lane Gallery, which involved the demolition of the ballroom.

See also **Dublin Writers' Museum, Harcourt Street** *and* **United Arts Club.**

Rutland Street Upper
Off Summerhill

Named after Charles Manners (1754–87), 4th Duke of Rutland, Lord Lieutenant 1784–87, who, according to James Gandon, the architect, was the only Viceroy who could find the leisure to pay the least attention to the fine arts.

It was an area that had long since gone into decay but Shaw's directory of 1850 lists it as a street of solicitors and barristers. As part of a renewal scheme, the Corporation cleared it and built a complex of red-brick houses and renamed it Sean O'Casey Avenue after the playwright (1880–1964).

See also **Champion's Avenue.**

S

Sackville Place
From Lower O'Connell Street to Marlborough Street
Originally named Tucker's Row after George Tucker, Sheriff in 1731. Clery's department store sides onto it.

Sackville Street (O'Connell Street)
Named after Lionel Cranfield Sackville, 1st Duke of Dorset, and Lord Lieutenant 1731–37, 1751–55. The first mention of Sackville Street is in the 1750s when Luke Gardiner came into the ownership of the lands of St Mary's Abbey, which included Drogheda Street and extended from Great Britain Street (Parnell Street) to Abbey Street. Gardiner demolished the houses on the west side and widened the street by 150 feet. A new speculative housing development went up, together with a central mall, named Gardiner's Mall. A finer-quality house was built on the east side for professional people and members of parliament to live in. The only one of these remaining is no. 42 Upper O'Connell which was erected in 1752 and stands next to the Royal Dublin Hotel. In 2003, the Fitzwilliam Group, owners of the hotel, got permission for a complete revamp and extension of its premises at nos. 40 and 41. One of the conditions was that full closure works to openings in the party wall between no. 42 and the hotel would be carried out under the supervision of a conservation architect. The ground floor of no. 42 is part of the hotel foyer. In 2004, Ampleforth Ltd was granted permission for the restoration and change of use from hotel to office use of no. 42, development to consist of restoration and conservation

Sackville Place. Advertisement 1910.

of the entire existing Georgian townhouse, removal of modern concrete stairs to basement and reinstatement of timber stairs to historic detail, strengthening of historic floors and reinstatement of historic detail of sliding sash windows to rere, demolition of existing one- and two-storey twentieth-century extensions to rere to allow reinstatement of garden and of window apses at basement and ground-floor level. In 1752, the street did not extend to the river. In 1777, the Wide Streets Commissioners* were given a grant

Sackville Street (Lower O'Connell Street), showing the square tower of the Dublin Bread Company, built in 1901 to a design of George F. Beckett. The first floor served as a luncheon room. The building was severely damaged in 1916 and subsequently demolished.

to extend, and in 1782 a grant of £15,000 was given for a new bridge. In 1785, it was agreed to extend the street to join with the proposed new Carlisle Bridge (O'Connell Bridge) which was opened in 1795 while work was still in progress on the Sackville Street extension. The Commissioners published a map about this time, entitled, 'the improvement of the eastern end of the town by opening the streets and building a new bridge over the river'.

There have been many additions and alterations over the years. A statue of General Blakeney, by Van Nost, once stood at Gardiner's Mall. A fountain erected on the site of the Parnell Monument was removed in 1807 as the wind blew the water onto the road and the water froze in bad weather. Nelson Pillar* was erected in 1808 and destroyed in 1966. The General Post Office was built in 1814–18. Other statues to be erected were the O'Connell Monument in 1874; William Smith O'Brien in 1870; John Gray MP in 1879; Father Mathew in 1891, Charles Stewart Parnell Monument 1911; and James Larkin 1980. In 1916, the rebel troops occupied the General Post Office and, as a result of the

fighting, the lower end of the street (from the river to the Post Office) was devastated, causing about £2.5 million worth of damage to property. Rebuilding continued until 1923 but in June 1922 the civil war left the area from Cathedral Street to Parnell Square in ruins. Three quarters of the street had been demolished between 1916 and 1922. What had started as a fine residential street became a commercial street in the nineteenth century and ended up with cinemas, shops and banks. The 1960s saw the introduction of the fast-food chains that dominate the street to the present day. The 'Anna Livia' millennium fountain made in granite with the statue in bronze by Eamonn O'Doherty was unveiled on 17 June 1988. Known by Dubliners as the 'Floosie in the Jacuzzi', it was removed in 2002, its location being considered unsuitable for the revamping of the streetscape and the positioning of the new 'Spire of Light'. In 2005, it was relocated without its framework to a pond in the Croppies' Acre Memorial Park.

See **Drogheda Street, Spire of Light** *and* **Metropole Ballroom, Cinema and Restaurant.**

St Andrew's (C of I)
Suffolk Street

Parish founded probably in the eleventh century. The original church stood on the corner of Church Lane and Dame Street. This was united with St Werburgh's at the time of the Reformation and was used as a mint and a stable. It was recreated a parish in 1665. A new church was built 1670–74 to a design of William Dodson, near where the present church stands. It was the only Protestant church to have a statue over the door, that of St Andrew, the work of Edward Smyth. On the organ of this building, which was burned down on 8 January 1860, Handel played at the annual benefit for Mercer's Hospital, on 10 December 1741. The present church was built slightly to the south of the old building to a design of Lanyon, Lynn and Lanyon of Belfast, and opened in 1866. The building is now used by Dublin Tourism as an information centre.

St Andrew's (RC)
Westland Row

A twelfth-century parish. The present church of St Andrew or All Hallows was built 1832–37, replacing a smaller church in Townsend Street, to a design of James Bolger (Boulger), having a stepped front with two Doric columns supporting a pediment with a sculpture of St Andrew. The wooden crucifixion over the altar is by Oisín Kelly. Two paintings, 'The Martyrdom of St Thomas a Becket' by Alfred Elmore (1815–1881) and 'The Crucifixion', were both presented by Daniel O'Connell, together with the red marble baptismal font. There are 49 vaults in the church. During the Eucharistic Congress* in 1932, Father Lindo de Touratio, an Italian professor, was fatally injured when he was knocked down by a car outside. The church cost £13,000, and at the time was the largest Roman Catholic one in the city.

St Andrew Street (1776)
From Exchequer Street to Suffolk Street
Originally Hog Hill.*

St Andrew's Church,* built in 1866, replaces an older church. It is alleged that members of Daly's Club used the statue of St Andrew for pistol practice; this stands in the churchyard which is now used as a car park. The post office is a modern building, completed in the 1950s. A street of restaurants, public houses and offices, with the Environmental Information Service at no. 17.

St Ann's (C of I)
Dawson Street

The parish of St Ann was formed in 1707. An ecclesiastical register of that year states that 'An act was passed in this year for erecting a new parish by the name of St Ann, of which 200 feet in length and 100 feet in breadth were the gift of Joshua Dawson Esq. for erecting a church and vicarage house with garden and for enclosing a churchyard and garden for the Vicar's use.' The Act further directs 'that a considerable scope of ground lying between the road leading to St Patrick's Well (in Nassau Street) and the north side of St Stephen's Green, part of the parishes of St Peter and St Kevin, and now in the possession of Joshua Dawson Esq., will shortly be let out for building, and will contain more inhabitants than can be accommodated in the parishes aforesaid'. The Act then directs that 'the east side of William Street, part of Chequer Lane, Clarendon Street and the square in the back part [where Pitt Street at present stands] should be severed from the Parish of St Bridget, and added to the newly constituted parish of St Ann'.

The site referred to was on the west side of the street and, after the Act was passed, was exchanged for the site on which the church now stands. The church was designed by Isaac Wills, and building probably commenced in 1720, in Italian style of cut stone which was painted. The interior has a shallow rounded apse, a single-span vault and columns of unfluted Ionic support the galleries. In 1868, the present Romanesque front by Deane and Woodward was erected a few feet in front of the original façade.

Stained-glass windows were introduced in 1859–60, and one to the poetess Felicia Hemans (1793–1835) was erected in the chancel after an appeal raised £250. One who did not subscribe was Charles Dickens who wrote in reply '. . . I would rather read Mrs Hemans by her own light than through the colours of any painted window that ever was or will be contracted for'. She died at her home, 21 Dawson Street, on 16 May 1835.

Among those who had connections with the church was Dr Barnardo* who was a pupil in St Ann's Sunday school. Michael William Balfe, the composer, was baptised there. Wolfe Tone married Martha Witherington on 21 July 1785. Patrick Campbell, journalist and author, married Sylvia Alfreda Willoughby Lee on 7 August 1941, and Dr Douglas Hyde and Erskine Childers worshipped frequently in the church.

St Audoen's (C of I)
Cornmarket

The only medieval church in the city, founded at the end of the twelfth century by the men of Bristol. It was at one time a group of guild chapels. The nave dates from 1190 to 1250. Some interesting old monuments and a Romanesque font, with the date 1194. The floor is partly paved with medieval grave slabs.

St Audoen's (RC)
High Street

Work commenced in 1841 and the building was blessed and opened for public worship on 13 September 1846 by Archbishop Murray. The architect was Patrick Byrne of Talbot Street. Little is known of him except that he studied under Baker at the Dublin Society School,* and designed the Turf Gas Company's offices in Great Brunswick Street (Pearse Street). He died in 1864. The Very Rev. Patrick Mooney, Parish Priest 1850–67, completed the internal plaster-work and installed the Walker three manual organ. The dome collapsed in 1884 and was replaced with a flat plaster circle and, in 1899, the external portico was added. An unusual feature: the holy water

fonts in the form of large sea shells given by a retired sea captain. The Great Bell which was awarded a gold medal from the Royal Dublin Society* announced the liberation of Daniel O'Connell from the Bridewell Prison* and also tolled his funeral knell. It was dedicated and named the Liberator on All Saints Day 1848. The church was for many years the worshipping place for the Italian community in Dublin.

St Bartholomew's (C of I)
Clyde Road

A granite church with a hexagonal clock tower and turrets, completed in 1867 by Thomas Henry Wyatt for a congregation influenced by the Oxford movement, and Anglo-Catholic in its approach to the liturgy.

Until some years ago, article 36 of the Constitutions and Canons Ecclesiastical forbade the placing of a cross on the communion table. St Bartholomew's vicar, Rev. Travers Smith, carried on a bitter controversy through the ecclesiastical courts on this issue. The vicarage, built in 1872, was sold in 1965 to the Knights of Malta for use as their headquarters.

St Bride's (C of I)
Bride Street

One of the oldest and most important parishes in the city. The church was rebuilt in 1684 and the parish united with St Werburgh's in 1886. The church stood on the corner of Bride Street and Bride's Alley, now called Bride Road. It was demolished in 1898 as part of the Iveagh Scheme for laying out Bull Alley. The organ is in the National Museum and the bell in St Werburgh's.

St Catherine's (C of I)
Thomas Street

Built to a design of John Smyth in the Roman Doric style with mountain granite. The square tower was designed to carry a spire but this was never built. Robert Emmet* was executed in front of the church after his failed rebellion of 1803. A granite column commemorates the event.

The church was closed in 1966 and given to Dublin Corporation in 1969 on the understanding that it would be put to community use. The Corporation in turn transferred it to the Bell Tower Trust, a voluntary group which did a lot of restoration work and cleaned up the graveyard. Left vacant for some years, it is again in need of restoration. The graveyard was laid out as a park by Dublin Corporation in 1986. In 1990, Dublin Corporation offered the building for sale as part of the inner-city development plan. It is again being used as a church by City Outreach through Renewal and Evangelism (CORE).

St Catherine's Park
Thomas Street
The graveyard of St Catherine's Church was turned into a public park, maintained by Dublin Corporation since 1986. One of the features is a stone sculpture, 'Adult and Child Seat', by Jim Flavin, sponsored by Allied Irish Banks for the Sculptors' Society of Ireland.

St Doulagh's (C of I) (Doolagh's) (Doulough's)
Portmarnock
Situated in the parish of Balgriffin, 6 miles N.E. of the General Post Office on the road to Malahide. The principal object of attraction is the old pre-Norman church dating from c. 1160. Built in stone, some of the walls are 3 feet thick with narrow stairs leading to various rooms. The square tower with battlements is probably a fifteenth-century addition. The church was restored and extended in 1865. The original building was 48 feet long and 18 feet wide.

St George's (C of I)
Hardwicke Place
Because of a growing population, a new parish was formed in 1793, and the church begun in 1802. Francis Johnston, the architect, modelled the steeple on Gibb's design for St Martin in the Fields, the clock being a prominent feature. The total height of the spire is 180 feet. According to

Maurice Craig, the woodwork, decorations and fittings of the whole church bear the strong impress of the architect's personality and of the school of decoration which he founded. The clock and eight bells were housed in a tower at the rere of the architect's house in 64 Eccles Street until his death in 1829, when they were installed in the church. During the 1988 millennium year, the bells were removed and installed in Taney C of I, Dundrum. The spire is in a dangerous condition and has been enclosed for many years in scaffolding. The church closed for public worship in the 1980s and is at present occupied by a theatre group.

St George's (C of I)
Hill Street
Founded in 1714 by Archbishop King and Sir John Eccles as a chapel of ease. It was converted into an open space by Dublin Corporation at a cost of £700 and formally opened by the Lord Mayor in 1894. The tower remains standing and the graveyard is now a playground. The bell and one monument are to be found in St George's, Hardwicke Place.

St George's Lane
See South Great George's Street.

St James (C of I)
James's Street
Designed by Joseph Welland, architect of the Church Commissioners, and built 1858–60. The third church on the site, its spire was removed in the 1960s after the interior ironwork hoops had expanded with rust, causing it to lean. Closed for public worship in 1963 and is now used as a commercial showroom. The large graveyard was cleaned up in 1987/88 by a FÁS-funded community project and is maintained by the St Patrick's Cathedral group of parishes. Some interesting monuments including one to Sir Theobold Butler, 1721, Solicitor General for Ireland.

St James (RC)
James's Street
Prior to the Reformation, the church stood

in St James's churchyard on the site now occupied by St James C of I church. The parish was outside the wall of the city, starting at the junction of Thomas Street and Watling Street, with an entrance at St James's Gate. With the suppression of the monasteries in 1537, worship ceased in the church and services were held in secret. In 1710, the Protestant church was built on the site. In 1724, the chapel in Jennet's yard became an RC parish church. In 1745, Fr Fitzsimons obtained a site near St James's Gate at the east corner of Watling Street and built a chapel that served until the present church was built.

Patrick Byrne, architect, was commissioned to design a new church and the foundation stone was laid by Daniel O'Connell in March 1844, across the street from the old chapel. The church was opened in 1852 without its clock tower and spire as Fr Smyth, the Parish Priest, felt that the famine and the subsequent cholera epidemic had wreaked havoc among the people and resources were not available to finish the work. It was never completed.

St James's Gate
See **Lowsie Hill** *and* **James's Street.**

St John the Baptist and St Augustine (RC)
Thomas Street

An impressive city church designed by Edward Welby Pugin, son of the well-known Victorian architect. The foundation stone was laid in 1862. It was opened for public worship in 1874 but, following various setbacks, the exterior was completed in 1895 and the interior about 1911. Built in red sandstone for the Augustinian friars, the tower stands 50 feet high. An extensive restoration job was carried out in 1989. It was built on part of the Abbey of St John and is known locally as John's Lane church.

While the design of this church is generally attributed to Pugin, it is possible that George Coppinger Ashlin (1837–1921), who was articled to Pugin in 1856, may have been involved in the design, as drawings were

exhibited for the proposed building in 1861 under the authorship of Pugin and Ashlin.

St John the Evangelist (C of I)
Fishamble Street

The parish dated from the twelfth century. Various churches were erected on a site near Christ Church Cathedral until the final one was built to a design of George Ensor in 1766–69. This closed in 1878, the congregation having united with St Werburgh's the previous year. It was demolished in 1884 as part of a road-widening plan to join Dame Street and Christchurch Place.

Henry Grattan (1746–1820), the patriot and orator, was baptised here in July 1746. In a burst of enthusiasm during millennium year 1988, Molly Malone, the fishmonger immortalised in the ballad of that name, was found by one researcher to have been baptised in this church on 24 July 1663 and buried on 13 June 1699, while other sources record her burial in 1734. It is doubtful if either of the records relates to the cockles and mussels Molly. Over 12,500 burials took place in the graveyard, Elizabeth McCausland being the last to be interred in 1850. In the centre aisle of St Werburgh's Church, there is a bell with Napper Tandy's name cast in it, which came from St John's.

St John's Hospital
Thomas Street near John's Lane

Founded in the twelfth century by Ailred the Palmer, a Norse citizen of Dublin, who together with his wife took monastic vows. The hospital was made free from diocesan interference by Pope Clement III on 1 December 1188, and was for the care of both men and women in poor circumstances. The Palmers sold their lands at Palmerstown* to support the enterprise. There would appear to have been 155 beds until the hospital was burnt and razed to the ground during the war of Edward Bruce in 1317. It was rebuilt and survived until the suppression of the monasteries in 1537, when it went into private hands and lasted on a reduced scale as a charity or workhouse into the seventeenth century. Several documents refer to it as Palmer's Hospital.

St John's Lane East
Off Fishamble Street along the rere of Christ Church Cathedral

Name comes from the church of St John the Evangelist which formerly stood on the site. The houses on the right were at one time occupied by the Vicar Choral of Christ Church. Through the entrance of no. 4 was a racquet court, founded about 1620. The end wall of the racquet court remained until May 1978. It was in this laneway in 1842 that Dr Robert Madden (1798–1886) found the poverty-stricken Anne Devlin (1778–1851), the friend of Robert Emmet.* Madden was later to erect a monument over her grave at Glasnevin.

St John's Road West
From Heuston Station to the South Circular Road

Named after St John's Well* near St John's Terrace.

In 1874, the road known as Long Lane, which ran across the railway line towards Islandbridge, was largely obliterated and St John's Road West was formed on part of the grounds of the Royal Hospital to give traffic from the west easier access to Kingsbridge (Heuston) Station.* In September 2004, An Bord Pleanála approved of a 10-year €500 million development on a 9.5 acre site at the junction of St John's Road and Military Road opposite Heuston Station. The site is at present occupied by Eircom and the OPW. The plan, designed by architect Tony Reddy, when built will consist of over 250 apartments, offices, a hotel, shops and restaurants. A museum and art gallery is also planned, which may be run by the Irish Museum of Modern Art.

St John's Well
Kilmainham

According to the records, this well was sited in a number of positions near what is now St John's Terrace. It once stood further

down the hill on the eastern side of the road but the construction of the railway necessitated rebuilding the outlet of the well further up the hill. It was for a great many centuries an important place of pilgrimage and it is recorded that, in 1538, Dr Staples, Bishop of Meath, preached to the multitude assembled there, denouncing Archbishop Browne. In 1710, the House of Commons, in an effort to suppress these gatherings, described them as dangerous, tumultuous and unlawful assemblies. In June 1737, the officers of the Royal Hospital complained that their grazing fields were rendered almost useless owing to the traffic through them to a well near Kilmainham frequented by numbers of superstitious persons.

It would appear that a path had been constructed across the hospital fields for the convenience of the Earl of Galway, a Lord Justice who resided at Islandbridge, and this path was taken over by the populace from the city on 24 June each year for the feast of St John the Baptist, and at other times to visit Bully's Acre.* Many gates and fences were erected in the daytime to be levelled by the people at night, and after many struggles the pathway was adjudged in the courts as a right of way and the people were permitted to visit the graveyard and the well without any further interference from the hospital authorities. Many attempts were made by the clergy to have the celebrations suppressed during the eighteenth and nineteenth centuries but they continued in one form or another into the first half of the twentieth century. The stonework that surrounded the last appearance of the well may be seen in the grounds of St James's (RC) Church in Echlin Street. There is also part of a water fount from the same well in the grounds of St Bartholomew's (C of I) Church in Clyde Road.

St Joseph's (RC)
Berkeley Road

The foundation stone of this Gothic church was laid on Sunday, 6 September 1874, by Cardinal Paul Cullen, Archbishop of Dublin. James Canon McMahon was PP at the time. The architects were O'Neill and Byrne, and the builder James McCormack. The opening and dedication took place on Sunday 18 April 1880, with Edward McCabe, Archbishop of Dublin, officiating. In a triangle of ground with an entrance from Eccles Street are a cross commemorating the four masters and a small grotto to the Blessed Virgin.

St Kevin's (C of I)
Lower Kevin Street (Camden Row)
At the foundation of St Patrick's, this ancient parish was made part of the endowment. The present building was built about 1780 and finally unroofed about 1920. It remained in use after the opening of the new St Kevin's Church on the South Circular Road in 1889. The church was used as a place of pilgrimage as Archbishop Dermot O'Hurley, who was hanged at Gallows Hill, St Stephen's Green, in the reign of Queen Elizabeth in 1584, for being in possession of treasonable papers, is interred in the graveyard. The graveyard is now a public park and there are monuments to Fr John Austin SJ; John Keogh, a champion of Catholic Emancipation; and to the parents and sister of Thomas Moore, the bard. There is also a large altar tombstone, dated 1685, to the Leeson family.
See **Saul's Court.**

St Kevin's (C of I)
South Circular Road
Built 1888–89 of red sandstone and granite for a rapidly expanding Church of Ireland community. It was closed in 1983 and sold by the Representative Church Body in 1987. Planning permission obtained for office accommodation and, while vacant, used for RTÉ television 'Megamix' rock programme. Re-sold in November 1990 and converted into apartments on a three-floor level.

St Luke's (C of I)
The Coombe
Built in 1713–16 to accommodate large

congregations of the established church (C of I) requiring a place of worship. Prior to this, many of the congregation worshipped in the Church of St Nicholas Without in the north transept of St Patrick's Cathedral. The much-quoted Huguenot link with the church is debatable as no Huguenot names appear in the parish registers during the eighteenth century. Built in a severe rectangular shape with a gallery of which only the western part has survived. It was closed in 1975 and leased to a publishing company in 1981. A fire in 1986 left the building roofless. It is pleasantly situated in a tree-planted garden with widows' almshouses which are also derelict. The entire complex is subject to extreme vandalism. Dublin Corporation plans to drive a dual carriageway through the almshouses.

St Marie Del Dam
A twelfth-century or earlier church dedicated to the Virgin Mary at what is now known as Cork Hill.* Legend has it that the diadem used at the coronation of Lambert Simnel at Christ Church* in 1487 was taken from the statue of the Virgin Mary in this edifice. During the reign of Henry VIII, the parishes of St Mary del Dam and St Werburgh* were united by George Browne, first Protestant Archbishop of Dublin. The disused building then came into the possession of Richard Boyle, 1st Earl of Cork,* who built a mansion house for himself on the site. Dame Street* derives its name from the demolished church. The Dam was probably a mill dam.

St Mark's (C of I)
Pearse Street
A new parish was created in 1708 from part of St Andrew's. Building began on the church in 1729 and was assisted until 1757 by parliamentary grants. A plain un-interesting building with a gallery supported by Corinthian columns. Oscar Wilde was baptised there in 1854. The building was purchased in 1971 by Trinity College and used as an overflow library. In

1987, it was again sold to an American-based group, the Assemblies of God. It has been renovated recently with the aid of a FÁS youth training project.

St Mary, Chantry of

In 1469, Edward IV (1461–83) gave the Earl of Worcester permission to found a chantry in honour of God and the Blessed Virgin Mary and to have Masses said for the benefit of the founders and all the departed. It was established in St Nicholas Within and was under the authority of the Provincial of the Augustinian Friars of England. When the church of St Nicholas was being demolished and rebuilt in 1706 – 07, it was recorded that the chapel of St Mary 'which lies on the south side of the church next to Kennedys Lane contains in length from the east wall 26 feet 6 inches and from the north to south 17 feet'. When the church was rebuilt, the chapel extended in front of the Lord Mayor's seat, and in breadth to the middle of the church 'and a gate in the western wall which is called the priests gate'. After the dissolution of the monasteries, chantries in parish churches in England were abolished, but no act was passed to abolish them in this country and some continued to function according to the use of the Church of Ireland. The chantry of St Mary continued to function until 1882, being a sinecure in name only. (A chantry is an endowment for a priest to say Mass daily for some person or persons deceased).

St Mary's

Mary Street

Designed in 1697 by Sir William Robinson, architect of the Royal Hospital Kilmainham. Most important classical church to survive the seventeenth century. Because of a growing population, the ancient parish of St Michan's (1095) was divided into three: St Michan's, St Paul's and St Mary's. St Mary's was built in 1702 but the intended tower never materialised. First church in the city to have a gallery. Impressive wood carving on the pilasters and internal cornices and organ case. The

Earl of Charlemont and Wolfe Tone were baptised there, and John Wesley first preached in Ireland there. Philip Le Fanu (later Dean of Emly), the father of Joseph Sheridan Le Fanu (1814–73), the novelist and author of *The Cock and the Anchor*, was curate here until 1823. In the 1970s, the Church of Ireland ceased using it as a parish church and it was leased for a short time by the Greek Orthodox community until it was declared unsafe. Sold in 1988 to a Waterford retailer, it had an uncertain future for several years until it opened as a public house in 2005.

St Mary's Chapel of Ease (C of I)

St Mary's Place

Commonly called the Black Church.

Built in 1830 to a design of John Semple in the Gothic revival style, with a parabolic vaulted interior, it was sold to Dublin Corporation in 1967 and used in that year to exhibit the first draft of the development plan for the city. It was planned to lease it for a graphic studio to an artists' co-operative but this was abandoned when asbestos was found in the roof. In 1990, Dublin Corporation's planning and development committee agreed to sell the building for £100,000 to a businessman for conversion into offices.

St Mary's Pro-Cathedral

Marlborough Street

As a result of a competition held in 1814, John Sweetman of Raheny, formerly one of the owners of Sweetman's Brewery, won the prize for the most suitable design. One of the most active Catholic laymen in the city, he had been involved with the opening of other Catholic churches, notably the Carmelite Church of St Teresa, Clarendon Street. As a member of the United Irishmen and because of his participation in the insurrection of 1798, he had spent some years in prison at Fort George in Scotland. At the time of the competition, he was living in Paris. It is thought that he may have bought plans from a French architect as the exterior is similar to Notre Dame de Lorette in Paris, completed in

1824, while the interior is similar to the Church of St Philippe du Roule.

John Sweetman's brother, William, was the competition organiser, and the foundation stone was laid on 8 March 1815 by the sponsor, Archbishop Troy. Among those present were Daniel O'Connell and John Philpot Curran. The opening took place on 14 November 1825 and was conducted by Most Rev. Dr Murray, Archbishop of Dublin. The building had been in use two years previously, though still in the hands of the builders. The first service held within its walls was a requiem for its sponsor, Archbishop Troy, who died in 1823. The high altar was executed by the Belfast-born sculptor Peter Turnerelli (1774–1839). The building-fund committee room was allocated to him as a studio and workshop. The altar was afterwards dismantled and the panels depicting two angels in bas relief on either side of a monstrance were rearranged as a base for the tabernacle. Above the altar is an alto-relievo representing the Ascension of Christ, by Smyth, whose work may also be seen in the Church of St Nicholas of Myra, Francis Street. A feature worth noting: the 'half-moon galleries' above and on either side of the sanctuary. The original structure also had an oratory known as St Kevin's Chapel, situated near the main entrance. This was removed in the last century although the altar remains. The exterior is built in the classical style with a pediment supported on six Doric columns. Two large marble seated figures are visible on entering the aisles of the building: one of Cardinal Cullen (1803–78), which cost £2,000, and one of Archbishop Murray (1768–1852), which cost £1,300. Both are by Thomas Farrell (1827–1900).

St Michael and St John
Essex Quay

Built in 1815 to a design of J. Taylor, it is the oldest RC church in the city. Dr Maurice Craig notes that it had the first Catholic bell to sound in the city since the Reformation. The church had fallen into disuse in recent years and it appeared likely that it would be the first Catholic Church in the inner city to close. For a short time, it was used to celebrate the Tridentine Rite. One of the mistakes of the Temple Bar* project was the stripping of the interior to house the Viking museum. Backed by Dublin Tourism, it cost between £5 and £6 million. It was popular for a few years but eventually closed. The burial vault of the church was allegedly the pit of the Smock Alley Theatre.*

St Michael's Christchurch

Probably built during the episcopate of Archbishop Laurence O'Toole (1162–1182), it served as a chapel to the palace which was beside what is now Christ Church Cathedral. In 1447, it was established as a parish church. Demolished in 1676 and rebuilt in 1679. This building was demolished in 1787 and an auction was held to sell the church fittings, roof timbers and slates. The tower remained intact. The congregation met in the Lady Chapel of the Cathedral until 1815 when a new church was built at a cost of £4,430. The church was closed in 1872 to make way for the building of the new Synod Hall, and the parish was united with that of St Audoen. The new Synod Hall was opened on 6 April 1875. The seventeenth-century tower of St Michael's is incorporated in the Synod Hall building.

St Michael's Close
See **Macgiolla Mocholmóg Street.**

St Michael's Hill
From Christ Church to Winetavern Street

Name comes from its proximity to St Michael's Church,* which was demolished in 1787. The tower remained intact. The archway across the road was built in 1875 as part of the Synod Hall* which was incorporated into the tower of St Michael's.

St Michan's (C of I)
Church Street

The parish was for 600 years the only city parish on the north side of the river. The church was dedicated on 14 May 1095 to St

Michan the martyr. It was rebuilt in 1685–86 and the vaults date from this time. The church was re-roofed and extensively repaired in 1828, at which time the old chancel was removed. Little remains of the original organ installed in 1725, except the fine outer case work. It was rebuilt in 1952. There is an unsubstantiated tradition associated with Handel but there is no evidence that he ever played on the organ. Edmund Burke (born at 12 Arran Quay in 1729) was baptised in the church. The brothers Sheares were buried in the vaults in 1798, and Oliver Bond in the churchyard where there is also the grave of Charles Lucas, the physician and patriot who died in 1771. The vaults constructed from magnesium limestone absorb moisture, resulting in the mummified corpses which are a popular tourist attraction.

St Michan's (RC)
See **Halston Street.**

St Nicholas Within
Nicholas Street
Built in the mid-eleventh century by Bishop Donat and dedicated to St Nicholas of Myra, it stood in Winetavern Street. Sometime in the twelfth century, a church was built on the present site in Nicholas Street and, during the fourteenth century, the parish was extended beyond the city walls. The church was rebuilt in 1573 and again in 1707. It was found to be in an unsafe condition in 1835 and demolished. The parish consisted of five acres and, in the 1860s, contained a population of 1,838, of whom 184 belonged to the established church. A Sunday service continued to be held in an upper room of an adjoining schoolhouse until 1867 when the parish united with St Audoen's. The walls of the church may be seen beside the Peace Garden on the corner of Christchurch Place and Nicholas Street.

St Nicholas Without
St Patrick's Cathedral
During the episcopate of Archbishop Alexander de Bicknor (1317–49), the parish of St Nicholas was extended beyond the walls of the city to include the Liberties of St Sepulchre's Palace, the residence of the Archbishop of Dublin and the Liberties of St Patrick's Deanery. The parish was then divided into two parts, within the walls and without the walls. The north transept of St Patrick's Cathedral became the parish church of St Nicholas Without, and a wall separated the transept from the rest of the Cathedral. By the 1750s, the River Poddle* regularly overflowed into the chapel, which was finally abandoned by the congregation in 1780. They signed an agreement with the French Huguenot community to rent St Mary's Chapel, or the Lady Chapel of the Cathedral, where services had been held in French since 1666.

In 1707, the southern part of the parish was divided to form the new parish of St Luke, and a new church was built between the Coombe and Newmarket in 1713–16. The congregations joined for worship in St Luke's in 1789 but again separated a few years later, when the St Nicholas congregation returned to the French Church. Major rebuilding commenced on the church in 1822 and was completed in 1826, but by 1860 the transept was again in poor condition and the final service was held on 20 October 1861 when the parish was again united with that of St Luke.

St Olaf's
On Fishamble Street near Wood Quay
Olaf Haraldsson was a Christian king of Norway from 1015 to 1030 and was being venerated as a saint soon after his death in battle. The church here may date from about this period and was built on what became nos. 40–41 Fishamble Street. About 1949, workmen digging foundations for a petrol station found skeletons beneath a stone floor and further traces were found during the Wood Quay excavations between 1977 and 1981.

St Patrick's Cathedral
St Patrick's Cathedral stands on the oldest Christian site in Dublin where, it is said, Patrick baptised converts to the Christian

faith in a well beside the building. Because of this sacred association with St Patrick, a church has stood here since AD 450. In 1191, that old church was replaced by the present building, the largest church in Ireland, which as well as being a cathedral became later the first University of Ireland (1320–1520).

The famous Jonathan Swift, who was Dean of St Patrick's (1713–1745), is buried in St Patrick's Cathedral beside Stella. Swift's pulpit, table and chair and the scroll he received when honoured as a Freeman of the City of Dublin are here. Also to be found here are old Celtic gravestones, medieval brasses and tiles, the medieval Chapter House door with a hole in it, dating from 1492, which gave the phrase 'chancing your arm' to the English language. The Earl of Kildare cut the hole and stretched out his arm to grasp the hand of his enemy, the Earl of Ormonde, who had taken refuge in the Chapter House. By his taking the initiative reconciliation was achieved. In the choir are the banners and stalls of the Knights of St Patrick (1783) and in the transepts the old Irish regimental banners and monuments. Memorials to famous Irishmen abound in the Cathedral, including Carolan, last of the Irish bards; Philpot Curran; Balfe the composer; Douglas Hyde, first President of Ireland. The Huguenots worshipped in the Cathedral from 1666 to 1861. A memorial tablet to them has been placed in the Lady Chapel. There are also many fine stained-glass windows in the Cathedral.

A massive west tower which houses the Cathedral bells, the largest ringing peal in Ireland, was built by Archbishop Minot in 1370, and the first public clock in Dublin was placed here in 1560.

St Patrick's Cathedral, more than any other building in Ireland, embodies within itself the history and heritage of the Irish people from the earliest times to the present day. The Celtic, Anglo-Norman, medieval, and Anglo-Irish traditions are all reflected within its walls.

The Organ

There is evidence of an organ in the Cathedral as far back as 1471. The present four-manual instrument, the largest in Ireland, was built by Henry Willis in 1902 and contains some pipes from the Harris organ of 1693. This was 'Father' Willis's last piece of work. His earlier masterpieces included organs in St Paul's Cathedral, Salisbury Cathedral and the Royal Albert Hall in London. Special organ music can always be heard before and after Evensong on Sundays.

The Choir School

The Choir School, founded 1432, educates boys for the choir who, together with Lay Vicars Choral, sing two liturgical offices every day in the Cathedral. The Cathedral choir took part in the first ever performance of Handel's *Messiah* in Dublin (1742), conducted by Handel. He also gave an organ recital in St Patrick's.

St Patrick's Close
On the S.E. side of the Cathedral

This was built in 1864–69 as part of the restoration. The main entrance to the Cathedral is in the Close. Following the line of the graveyard where there is a statue to Benjamin Lee Guinness is the entrance to Marsh's Library,* built about 1701. The exterior of Marsh's Library was altered during the Guinness restoration but the interior remains intact. It is the oldest public library in Ireland.

St Patrick's Hospital
Steevens' Lane

Founded in 1745 according to the terms of the will of Jonathan Swift, Dean of St Patrick's Cathedral. It is the oldest psychiatric hospital in Ireland and, in these islands, the only foundation which ante-dates it is the Bethlem (Bedlam) Hospital in London. St Patrick's is on its original site and its original buildings are still in use. In Swift's time, the mentally ill were chained, manacled and even whipped to subdue violence. Medical treatment when given consisted of bleeding, emetics or violent purging. The hospital was designed to hold 54 patients in accordance with the original plan drawn up by Semple in 1748. In 1778, parliament voted money to double the size of the building, and this was carried out by the architect Cooley. With further additions there were nearly 200 patients in 1815. As the original bequest could no longer finance the hospital, a charter was granted in 1888, enabling fees to be charged on a non-profit-making basis.

In recent years, there has been a considerable increase in the number of patients accommodated. This has been made possible by the provision of a Nurses' Home as well as by new buildings.

St Patrick's Well Lane
See **Nassau Street.**

St Paul's (C of I)
North King Street
Created a parish from part of St Michan's in 1697. This church had become ruinous by 1821 and was rebuilt and completed in 1824 in the Gothic style. It was closed for public worship in November 1987 and handed over to a community-based Trust for conversion into an enterprise centre.

St Paul's (RC)
Arran Quay
Part of an old parish created at the beginning of the eighteenth century. The present church was designed by Patrick Byrne with four Ionic columns supporting a portico. Built in 1835–37. The bell turret was added in 1843 and, at the beginning of this century, the bells of St Paul's echoed along the quays. A replica of the Lourdes grotto was erected in the 1930s in front of the presbytery and adjoining the church. The church is at present closed for public worship.

St Peter's (C of I)
Aungier Street
The parish dates from about the time of the Anglo-Norman invasion. The first church stood in Stephen Street. A new church was built at Aungier Street in 1680. Between 1863 and 1867, it was rebuilt in the Gothic manner, the old walls of the nave being retained but refaced. The Duke of Wellington and Robert Emmet* were baptised in the church. The new YMCA building stands on the site of the demolished church.

St Saviour's (RC)
Dominick Street Lower
The twelfth-century Dominican priory was suppressed at the dissolution of the monasteries under Henry VIII. It stood near the Four Courts. Dominicans were in Denmark Street from 1772 until 1860. The foundation stone of the present church was laid in 1852 and the church, designed by J. J. McCarthy, was opened for public worship in 1861. Impressive interior with well-carved vaulted arches and large rose window. The priory at the side of the church at nos. 5–11 Dorset Street was opened early in the twentieth century.
See also **Dominick Street.**

St Stephen's (C of I)
Mount Street Crescent
Since 1790, the residents of the squares and streets of the rapidly expanding Fitzwilliam Estate had asked for a church to be erected in their neighbourhood, but it was not until 1821 that plans were prepared for a chapel of ease of St Peter's union. The church was designed by John Bowden and completed after his death by Joseph Welland at a cost of £5,169. The building was consecrated on Sunday, 5 December 1824. It was built on a site given free by the Pembroke Estate which also made a contribution of £700 towards the building. The portico is of Ionic order. Over the pediment rises a belfry tower which is of octagonal form. The tower and dome are copies from Athenian models and rise to 100 feet. The body of the church measures 111 feet by 49 feet. Internally the church is Victorian Renaissance in style with spacious galleries and a flat timber ceiling. An apse and vestry were added in 1852. The church, known affectionately to generations of citizens as the Pepper Canister, is one of Dublin's familiar landmarks.

St Stephen's Green. The park in its present format was opened in 1880. Sir Arthur Guinness bore the cost of laying it out.

St Stephen's Green

Originally it formed part of a considerable tract of ground east of the old city, extending as far as the River Dodder. It is marked without boundaries on Sir William Petty's 'Down Survey' map of Dublin in 1655. Towards the end of the seventeenth century, it consisted of about 60 acres, with no streets nearer to it than Patrick's Well Lane and Stephen's Street. It was approached from the city by a lane which afterwards became Grafton Street. The road to Baggotrath Castle was on the north side, from the south west a lane which is now Cuffe Street led to Kevin Street and on the south east was the road to Donnybrook, which is now Leeson Street. In 1664, the Corporation marked out an area of about 27 acres to be preserved as an open space for the use of citizens and around this about 30 acres were divided into strips and sold as lots for building. About 1666, William Harvey was employed in 'plowing up and levelling St Stephen's Green' and, in 1669, the area was

surrounded by a stone wall about 4½ feet high, built by Edward Briscoe and Patrick Henderson. The following year, Richard Buxton and Thomas Jones, gardeners, were paid £50 for planting trees. A ditch was dug inside the wall to carry water and, between this and the wall, a gravel walk was laid and planted on each side with elm or lime trees. In 1671, the way from Hoggen Green to St Stephen's Green, what is now Grafton Street, 'being so foule and out of repaire that persons cannot passe to the said Green for the benefit of the walks therein', the Corporation ordered it to be repaired and put in order.

In the eighteenth century, the north side of the Green was a fashionable promenade known as Beaux' Walk. The principal entrance to the Green was opposite York Street, with a gateway of four piers of black stone, each surmounted by a granite globe, and seats were in place as early as 1753 for the convenience of 'cripples, weary people and children'. Under an act of 1814, Commissioners were appointed to improve the Square and enclose it with railings and locked gates, and only householders who paid a guinea a year had access, thus depriving the ordinary citizens of Dublin of the right to enter. This arrangement continued until 1877 when Sir Arthur Guinness (later Lord Ardilaun), MP for the city, put through an Act of Parliament placing the area in the care of the Board of Works and re-opening it to the public. He himself bore the cost of laying out the present park which was opened in 1880. A statue of him was erected on the west side of the Green in 1892.

The main entrance facing Grafton Street is a memorial arch commemorating the Dublin Fusiliers who served in the Boer War. There is also a granite memorial to O'Donovan Rossa. Other monuments are a 'Three Fates' fountain, a gift from the German people in acknowledgment of Ireland's share in relieving distress after the Second World War. Busts include James Clarence Mangan, Thomas Kettle, Countess Markievicz and James Joyce. A statue of Robert Emmet stands opposite the house (now demolished) in which he was born. Wolfe Tone and a group depicting the famine face Merrion Row.

On the north side, no. 8, the United Services Club, was built in 1754 and closed as a club in 2003, when it was sold to Clubko Ltd, for over €10 million. Clubko proposes to turn it into an exclusive venue for professional people, with a restaurant and gymnasium. Number 9, built in 1756, houses the Stephen's Green Club, founded as a club in 1840 by Daniel O'Connell; parts of the building may date to 1730. The front was redesigned in 1905 and another floor added. A major refurbishment took place in 2004/5 with the architect T. Austin Dumpy. Numbers 14 and 15 on the corner of Dawson Street were completely restored by Dublin City Council in 2003 and let as offices. The architect was David Slattery, a historic buildings consultant, with Neil Donnellan as project architect, and main contractor Michael Glennon (Moate) Ltd. Number 16 was built in 1776 by Gustavus Hume,* with the plasterwork by Michael Stapleton. Next door, Milltown House, built for the Leeson family, dates from the same period and also has plasterwork by Michael Stapleton. From 1850, it was the home of Dublin University Club, which merged with the Kildare Street Club in 1976 to form the Kildare Street and

St Stephen's Green showing the massive shopping centre which opened in 1988, and the terminus of the Luas.

St Stephen's Green. Shelbourne Hotel.

University Club. Number 22 was until recently the home of the Friendly Brothers of St Patrick and is now occupied by Brown's Restaurant. The impressive Shelbourne Hotel stands on the site of Kerry or Shelbourne House. In 1842, Thackeray stayed at the hotel where he paid 6s.8d. for full board. While there, he did a sketch of his hotel window, which he included in his *Irish Sketch Book*, published in 1843.

On the south side, Iveagh House* incorporates nos. 80 and 81; no. 80 was built in 1730 by Richard Cassels; nos. 82–87 were part of the Catholic University; no. 84 is late nineteenth century; no. 85 is also by Richard Cassels and the ceilings are by the Francini brothers. Number 86, Newman House built 1760–65, is attributed to Robert West and named after John Henry Newman, the first Rector of the Catholic University of Ireland which occupied this premises and no. 85 from 1853. When Newman came to Ireland, it was part of the agreement with Cardinal Cullen that a university church should be built. Professor John Hungerford Pollen, like Newman a convert to Roman Catholicism, helped to design the Romanesque building, which opened in 1856. It became a parish church in 1974. The Methodist Centenary Church,* designed by Isaac Farrell in 1843, was sold in 1972 and is now a commercial bank. Wesley College* was built in 1879 to the design of Alfred Jones. A large office block now occupies the site.

On the west side, on the corner of Cuffe Street, the Winter Garden Palace stood at no. 106 but was demolished in 1975 for road widening. The Unitarian Church was built in 1863 and designed by the Belfast architects Lanyon, Lynn and Lanyon. It appears to be rather dwarfed by large office blocks on either side. Numbers 119 and 120 were built in 1761; the Royal College of Surgeons* was built in 1806 by Edward Parke and greatly extended over the years; nos. 124–125 were the house of Dr Robert Emmet, whose son's statue opposite points to the buildings now demolished. The massive Stephen's Green shopping centre was opened in 1988.

The east side is almost entirely a reconstruction of modern buildings. Two office blocks were erected in the 1970s (see Hume Street). Number 51 was purchased by the state in 1848 and housed the Museum of Irish Industry. The Office of Public Works has occupied it since 1913. At no. 55, the Loreto convent, founded in 1883, has recently been restored after a bad fire. The large Sean Lemass office complex corners onto Leeson Street Lower.

In 1965, on the south side, three eighteenth-century houses at 69–71 were demolished and a modern office block, Hainault House, was let to the Department of Justice for 75 years. Shelbourne developments bought the property in 2004 for €52.3 million and sought planning permission for a large extension and renovation of office space.

St Stephen's Street
See **Aungier Street.**

St Teresa's (RC)
Clarendon Street
The site was purchased by John Sweetman, a brewer, and the foundation stone was laid in 1793 for a church and monastery for the Carmelite fathers. After many setbacks, some caused by the 1798 rebellion, the church opened in 1810. It has been much extended, the eastern transept being added in 1863 and the western transept in 1876.

St Thomas's (C of I)
Marlborough Street
Separated from the parish of St Mary's in 1749. The church was built in 1758–62, the architect being John Smyth. Erected at the corner of Gregg's Lane, the church faced onto green fields, but with the building of Gloucester Street it appeared at the end of a long vista. The design was based on Palladio's Redentore in Venice. The building was extensively damaged in July 1922 when the area was occupied by the irregulars. Rather than being restored, the building was demolished, and Gloucester Street (now Sean MacDermott Street) was extended through to O'Connell Street. A new brick church, designed by Frederick Hicks, paid for by the state, was erected on an island on the north side of the new street in 1931–32.

St Tullock's Lane
The old name for part of Fishamble Street,* it is possibly a derivation of St Dúlach where a church allegedly stood prior to the building of St Olaf's or Olave's in the eleventh century. It may, however, be merely an Irish pronunciation of Óláfr.

St Werburgh's (C of I)
Werburgh Street
The original church was built in 1178 and named after the daughter of the King of Mercia. An act of 1715 which passed through the Irish parliament appointed commissioners for building a new church. A list, dated 17 June 1712, gives some 85 persons who made donations. In 1719, the church was sufficiently built to permit worship to be carried on but the tower was left unfinished, without either spire or dome. In 1728, James Southwell bequeathed £431 for a clock and peal of six bells on condition that the tower should be finished within three years of his death. Southwell's clock was erected in 1732 by Joseph Blundell, the vestry supplementing the bequest in order that it might have four dial plates. It is interesting to note that it took a friendly suit in chancery in 1747 against Southwell's executors to extract the money for the clock. On 9 November 1754, a fire broke out in the church, causing £4,000 worth of damage. Because of its importance as a church, George II granted £2,000 towards the cost of restoration. It was in this building that such people as the Viceroy were sworn into office, and seats were reserved for all sorts of people including members of Dublin Corporation. A restoration committee was set up and the congregation used St Mary's Chapel, Christ Church, until St Werburgh's could be re-opened for worship. Four years after the fire, only £500 had been raised in addition to the King's grant. The church was re-opened in 1759

without a tower and, for eight years, had no organ. In 1782, a plaque was erected to John Field,* the composer. The spire erected in 1768 was removed in 1810 and the tower supporting it in 1836 at the request of the Dublin Castle authorities. Sir James Ware and Lord Edward Fitzgerald are interred in the vaults.

Salvation Army
Lower Abbey Street
International Christian organisation and registered charity founded in London in 1865, the essential part of its ministry being to fight against poverty and social injustice. In 1888, the Army's work commenced in Dublin. The charity now provides 256 beds for homeless persons each night. Cedar House, Marlborough Place, opened in 1999, is managed on behalf of Dublin City Council by the Salvation Army, open 24 hours a day, providing accommodation for 50 men plus an emergency night shelter of 20 beds; users receive a cooked meal and breakfast. Granby Centre, 9–10 Granby Row, opened in 1994, provides accommodation for 107 single men and women who are homeless. It provides 55 places for service users with learning difficulties and mental health problems and an Alzheimer's society day centre. Lefroy House, 12–14 Eden Quay, caters for varied needs of young people under 18 years of age. The centre provides crisis and long-term accommodation, also Nightlight provides protection and care for young people 12–18 years, with access to showers, clean clothes and food. Seven beds offer crisis accommodation on a 1–2 night basis. York House, Longford Street Little, opened in May 2003 on the sale of a building in York Street to the Royal College of Surgeons.* Individual rooms accommodate 79 men with a maximum stay of 18 months. An intensive resettlement programme trains service users to be self-supporting, to seek employment and develop skills to resettle in the community. A ten-bed dry wing provides an alcohol- and drug-free environment with professional support from a substance-abuse worker.

Sandymount
At one time a maritime village 3 miles S.E. by E. from the General Post Office. Part of the lands of the Bagods and Fitzwilliams of Merrion, then through inheritance becoming part of the Pembroke urban district. Originally named Scallet Hill, the area had both a thriving herring fishery and a large brick works using local clay. A Martello Tower* was erected on Strand Road in 1804–06, at a cost of £1,800, to oppose a possible landing of Napoleonic troops.

The Church of St John the Evangelist (C of I) was built in 1850. It was erected at the sole expense of Lord Herbert and designed by Thomas Henry. The stone, imported from Caen in Normandy, has weathered badly. The Church of our Lady, Star of the Sea (RC) was opened in 1853 when a new parish was created from part of Donnybrook and Irishtown. The Presbyterian church, built about 1870, was used until the 1970s when the congregation united with that of the Methodist church, built in 1864, with a memorial porch being added in 1911. The attractive Sandymount Park was designed by James Gandon (1743–1823), architect of the Custom House. Brabazon House was built in 1902 at Gilford Road to provide sheltered accommodation for the elderly. A programme of development has seen the number of residents increased from 12 to 82. A further 20 apartments on Strand Road, backing onto the Brabazon complex, have been completed recently and named Northbrook House. This will replace the Old Men's Home on Northbrook Road.* W. B. Yeats (1865–1939) was born at his father's house, 'Georgeville', Sandymount Avenue, on 13 June 1865. Shortly after his birth, the family moved to London. Roslyn Park on Beach Road is a late eighteenth-century villa designed by James Gandon for the artist William Ashford, first president of the Royal Hibernian Academy. The villa has been restored and the interior furnished in eighteenth-century style by Brian Hogan and John O'Connell.
See **Newbridge Avenue.**

Saul's Court
An intersection off no. 8 Fishamble Street
Laurence Saul, a Roman Catholic distiller at the Sign of the Golden Key, was prosecuted in 1759 for shielding a lady Papist named Toole; he escaped and died in France in 1768. Rev. John Austin, a Dublin-born priest trained by the Jesuits at Champagne, returned to Dublin in 1750 and established a school here, where the majority of the inner-city Roman Catholic youth received their schooling. It was also a place for training priests before the foundation of seminaries. He is buried in St Kevin's churchyard,* Camden Row. Some tenements remained until the court disappeared with road widening at the time when Lord Edward Street was opened. The Gaelic Society, founded in 1806 for the preservation and publication of ancient Irish historical and literary documents, met at Saul's Court.

Schoolhouse Lane West
From High Street to Cook Street
Known in the fifteenth century as Le Ram Lane, probably from a building in the High Street named Le Ramme. The free school was erected here in the sixteenth century. The Court of the King's Bench was held here until 1745 in what was described as one of the narrowest lanes in the city. Speed's map of 1610 refers to Skipper's Alley as Rame Lane which is a continuation northwards to Merchant's Quay.
See **Bors Court.**

Scouting Ireland
In 1908, an organisation following the principles laid down by the English General Baden Powell was founded to help boys to develop their personalities. There was an emphasis on the outdoor life where various skills were achieved including a knowledge of first aid, camp cooking, map reading and signalling. Their motto, 'Be prepared', was meant to suit all aspects of their lives. The Boy Scout movement, as it was known, was meant from the start to be a non-denominational organisation. In 1927, the Catholic Boy Scouts of Ireland was founded by a Roman Catholic priest, Fr Farrell, with patronage from the diocesan bishopric, the organisation being divided on a regional or parish basis. Despite disapproval by the RC hierarchy, both organisations voted in 2003 to amalgamate under their new title Scouting Ireland.

Sean MacDermott Street
See **Gloucester Street.**

Sean O'Casey Avenue
See **Rutland Street Upper.**

Shamrock Cycle Syndicate Ltd
See **Brunswick and Shamrock Pneumatic Cycle Factory.**

Shelbourne Road
From Northumberland Road to Haddington Road
Originally Artichoke Road (1792). Named after the Earl of Shelbourne and Marquis of Lansdowne.
The Adoption Board at Shelbourne House is an independent statutory body, responsible for processing adoption applications from the registered adoption societies and Health Boards and for making domestic adoption orders.

Ship Street, Great
From Golden Lane to Ship Street, Little
Name comes from Sheep Street (le Shepes land), originally a grazing ground. Part of the old walled city, some of the stonework still visible. Originally a street of tenements and tradesmen, with the River Poddle flowing, now enclosed. Dr Ball had a school near the Castle Tower where Henry Grattan and Jonah Barrington attended. John Rocque's map of 1756 shows a terrace of houses with gardens and service buildings at the rere. In 1805, Robert Woodgate, the architect to the Board of Works, converted the early and mid-eighteenth-century houses on the south end of the street for use as accommodation for the military. In 1808, Francis Johnston

designed the Quarter Master General's building, now known as Block M. Houses on the north end of the terrace were replaced during the first half of the nineteenth century with new buildings for the military. During the 1990s, a complete refurbishment of all the buildings on the street was carried out by the Office of Public Works and these now house government departments. Two separate archways lead into Dublin Castle, the lower one being the Castle Gate which was a gate, portcullis and drawbridge which was rebuilt in 1617 and demolished during the eighteenth century. The remains of Stanihurst's tower may also be seen on the north side of Ship Street. A woodcut of 1577 shows the attack on Dublin Castle from Ship Street by Silken Thomas in 1534. Christianity was brought to Dublin in the sixth century by Aonghas, Bishop of Kilcullen, who founded a monastery on the banks of the Poddle in what is now Great Ship Street. The monastery mill was on the Poddle in what is now Little Ship Street and the Dam, a deep pool, was situated at the foot of the Castle steps. Gabriel Beranger made two water-colour sketches of the round tower which stood for 700 years in Great Ship Street; on each of them is written 'The old tower of Michael of Pole'. By the seventeenth century, 'pool' was spelt 'pole'.

Ship Street, Little
From Bride Street to Ship Street, Great
Originally a street of houses and shops including engravers, printers and wire works, all of which have been demolished. A new office block houses the Chief State Solicitor's office.

Sick and Indigent Roomkeepers Society
See **The Sick and Indigent Roomkeepers Society.**

Sign of the Three Candles
Fleet Street
A printing and publishing house owned by Colm Ó Lochlainn (1892–1972), it com-

menced business in 1916 as the Candle Press but was renamed after the Three Candlesticks (1730–50), printers and booksellers in the High Street. Ó Lochlainn renamed it the 'Sign of the Three Candles' in 1926. He specialised in the design of old Irish printing types and, in August 1967, the committee restoring Tailors' Hall* commissioned him to print the List of Delegates who attended the Catholic Convention in December 1792, using the original typeface. These were then sold as a fund-raising effort. The firm won many awards for high-quality book production and bookbinding.

Simpson's Hospital
Parnell Street
George Simpson, a merchant who lived at no. 24 Jervis Street, was a sufferer from gout and blindness. On one occasion, as he lay in pain, he was unable to reach the bell to communicate with others in the house. After consultation with his wife, he devised his estate with a view to founding an asylum for men suffering from similar disabilities, but in reduced circumstances. The arrangements, made in 1778 on Simpson's death, were found to be inadequate; a board of trustees was formed and the asylum was opened in Putland House in Parnell Street in 1781. This was eventually demolished and a new building was opened on the site in 1787. The inmates, who wore top hats and frock coats, were moved during the rebuilding to Judge Christopher Robinson's house in Jervis Street. Simpson's Hospital in Parnell Street cost £6,458 to build. A contemporary account states that, 'in the spring and summer the gay sound of the flute and violin is often heard from the benches of their little garden, and the whole institution has an air of cheerful content'. In 1925, the hospital transferred to the more airy and suitable country premises at Wyckham, Dundrum, and the building in Parnell Street became the offices of Williams and Woods who erected a factory at the rere. It was demolished in 1978.

Skinners' Row
See **Christchurch Place.**

Skipper's Alley
A laneway connecting Merchant's Quay with Cook Street
It was in line with Schoolhouse Lane on the opposite side of Cook Street. When the Franciscan church on Merchant's Quay, built in 1834, was reconstructed more than 60 years ago, it was built on the site of the Alley, and a new laneway was opened west of the original alignment. The name probably derives from Nicholas Skypper alias Bernes, a sea captain and master of his own barque, who lived and was actively involved in the area as early as 1575.

Slums—Slum Clearance
From the beginning of the eighteenth century and even earlier, Dublin had squalid overcrowded housing conditions inhabited by very poor people. Poverty and illness in the city were considered to be even worse than in London. Dr Hawkins, writing in his Medical Statistics, states, 'That Dublin appears to have suffered more continually from epidemic fever than any other great city of Europe. The causes of this calamitous state are attributed by the resident physicians to want of employment, poverty and sometimes famine amongst the lower classes'. Again, another contemporary Dr Rutty in 1772 observes, 'That those who know the situation of the poor here can be at no great loss to account for the frequency and the mortality, especially in fevers, several families being in one house, and not infrequently in one room, which must undoubtedly contribute not only to the propagation but also to the malignity of these diseases'.

Dublin has always been a city of violent contrasts: the inequalities of wealth and the social and sanitary conditions of the poor quarters of the city bore no resemblance to the style of living enjoyed by the affluent and ruling classes. The poor and working classes lived in tenements, usually large houses with multi-family occupancy and consistent overcrowding. The process of degeneration would continue into the nineteenth century in the wake of the 1798 rebellion and the Act of Union in 1801, with the dissolution of the Irish Parliament and the government of Ireland being conducted from Westminster. The Protestant Anglo-Irish ascendancy left their elegant houses and departed for England, leaving their properties in the hands of agents who packed the houses with families. A series of weekly detailed articles, entitled 'War on Slums', published in the *Irish Press* commencing 2 October 1936, described the landlords of the time as despotic and merciless.

In 1798, the year of the rebellion, the Rev. James Whitelaw, vicar of St Catherine's in Thomas Street, carried out a survey of the south city liberties and found the labouring poor and beggars crowded together 'to a degree distressing to humanity in truly wretched habitations with often 10 to 16 persons of all ages and sexes in a room not of fifteen feet square.' In Plunkett Street, he found 917 inhabitants in 32 houses and 108 inhabitants in one tenement in Braithwaite Street.* Whitelaw calculated the total population of Dublin at 172,091 plus a further 10,000 persons in the garrison, Trinity College and other institutions. In 1832, Asiatic cholera reached the Dublin slums and, within ten days, 500 burials in unmarked graves had taken place at Bully's Acre,* Kilmainham. According to E. A. Dalton in his history of County Dublin, 3,200 bodies had been interred there during the six months of the epidemic. The census of 1841 contained information on accommodation and the types of housing, which proved Whitelaw's survey to be reasonably accurate and showed multi-family house occupancy as the norm. By 1881, only 14,334 families, 26 per cent of the population, had exclusive occupancy of a house or cottage. This reflects the absence of rebuilding schemes in the nineteenth century.

The problem of overcrowding would increase after the great famine of 1845–49, caused by the failure of the potato crop through blight, with masses fleeing from starvation in rural areas entering the city. This resulted in the already overcrowded late eighteenth-century houses being divided into multi-small-room dwellings with often up to 80 persons in need of a roof over their head being accommodated in each house. By 1900, one third of Dublin's population lived in appalling and highly dangerous conditions in buildings where ruthless landlords had carried out no maintenance or repairs and where the most primitive of sanitary facilities prevailed. Very often, floorboards had been ripped out for use as firewood, and many houses had lost their stair banisters for the same reason. In 1902, two families died when their tenement on Townsend Street collapsed; and a house in Cumberland Street fell down in 1909, killing one person. A further seven persons died on 2 September 1913 when two houses at 66 and 67 Church Street collapsed. As a result of this, a housing inquiry was set up. This was published in 1914; having heard evidence from 76 people, it found that the housing problem was getting worse. In 1913, 87,000 Dubliners, 29 per cent of the city's population lived in slums, the majority of families occupying one room and very often 20 to 40 people sharing one closet. An alarming finding of the Housing Inquiry found that 14 members of Dublin Corporation were owners of tenements while three members between them held 61 properties. With the outbreak of the 1914–18 war, little was done in the way of building, due to shortage of materials and lack of grants from the Westminster parliament. *The Irish Times* of 4 September 1913, published during the Lockout of 1913,* attributed much of the unrest to the conditions in the Dublin slums. Following the 1916 Rising and the civil war of 1922, the centre of the city was in ruins and any financial effort was concentrated on the rebuilding of the city. Inflation also contributed to a slowdown in house building. A Church of Ireland clergyman, Rev. David Henry Hall, based in the parish of St Barnabas, East Wall, was living and

working in some of the worst slum conditions, with extreme poverty and severe overcrowding resulting in a high death rate. He founded the St Barnabas Public Utility Society on 9 January 1920 to build houses and improve the awful conditions in the area. The first ten houses were occupied on 24 June 1921 at St Barnabas Gardens and had a bath and other conveniences. Each dwelling had its own garden. A further 26 were built in Utility Gardens in April 1923. Further building by the society continued until 1926. As far back as 1875, Dublin Corporation under public health acts had started to clear areas in the Coombe and these were leased in 1876 to the Dublin Artisans' Dwelling Company* who built 216 cottages and houses. By 1907, they had constructed 2,961 dwellings housing 2,884 families in different parts of the city, the number of individuals housed being 13,330. By the end of the nineteenth century, the area between St Patrick's Cathedral and Werburgh Street had become one of the worst slums in Dublin. Starting with Sir Arthur Guinness and continued by Sir Benjamin Lee Guinness, then finished by his son, the 1st Earl of Iveagh, the entire area was cleared and a new park built beside a large complex of five-storey flats, designed by Joseph and Smithem with Parry and Ross, covering seven acres with a hostel for men, public baths and an impressive recreation centre, designed by McDonnell and Reid, opened on 15 December 1909. While these projects helped in a small way to ease the problem of overcrowding, in the 1930s it was estimated that 18,000 families were living in single-room tenements, more than in 1926, the date of the Civic Survey. New legislation on compulsory acquisition at this time resulted in impressive four-storey flats being erected in various parts of the city, with courtyards and play areas, including Mercer Street, Cook Street and Lower Bridge Street. These new housing acts of 1931 and 1932 stated that tenants in condemned buildings should be re-housed. This led to the demolition and refurbishment of

existing properties in certain areas of the city. In June 1963, two elderly occupants of a house in Bolton Street were killed when the building collapsed and, ten days later, two little girls were killed on the footpath when two tenements in Fenian Street fell down, burying them under the rubble. The ten years from 1948 saw an emphasis on moving people whose families had lived for generations in the inner city to developments in new suburbs of Ballyfermot, Crumlin, Drimnagh and Finglas. In the late 1950s, the trend of housing policy moved again from the supply of houses to flat development, with stair towers and balcony fronts. Ballymun, a scheme of seven 14-storey towers with 8-storey and additional 4-storey blocks, was completed in 1967. The early 1970s saw the commencement of housing estates in Tallaght and Darndale. Public housing policy has shown an enlightened shift in the past 20 years and a great many streetscapes have come to fruition with single-family houses replacing ugly apartment blocks. In the early years of this century, the Ballymun tower blocks were demolished and replaced with new housing models that would regenerate the area and retain the values of the community. In 2003, Derek Tynan Architects won the RIAI award for Best Accessible Project at Whiteacre Close, Ballymun. Dublin City Council in recent years has adopted a policy of upgrading inner-city apartment blocks especially where a serious drug culture had previously existed, a good example being the Hardwick Street flats, built in 1958 and housing approximately 500 persons. €11 million was spent upgrading this complex. Other examples are Fatima Mansions* and Killarney Street.* These refurbished areas are then managed by residents' associations. After hundreds of years, the term slum has disappeared.
See Liberties.

Smithfield
From Arran Quay to North King Street
Part of a Viking settlement including Oxmantown Green* which in 1635 was to be kept for the use of citizens to walk and take the open air. By 1665, this area was being divided up and sold by lots, nos. 87 and 88 being reserved for a school to be called 'The King's Hospital' or 'Blue (Blew) Coat School', apart from a convenient highway (Queen Street*) and a large market place which is now Smithfield. There were some fashionable houses built in the eighteenth century but it was frequently used for horse fairs, and country traders brought their cattle in for sale since 1541. Following its repaving in 1890, a new horse fair was established in 1900, to be held fortnightly with a toll on every horse, mare or gelding of 4d and each mule, ass, colt, filly or foal of 2d. There is a reference to Thomas Reynolds who at a sworn enquiry stated, 'I called at Leinster House upon Lord Edward Fitzgerald. I had a printed paper in my hand signed by Counsellor Saurin to the Lawyers' corps. These required them in case of riot or alarm to repair to Smithfield.' On 19 May 1798, Fitzgerald was arrested but the insurrection went ahead. A large corps of yeomanry was ordered to assemble at Smithfield but no fighting occurred. Work on a church commenced in 1697 and was completed in 1702, creating a new parish of St Paul's. In recent years, the former market place has been transformed with twelve brazier masts 26 m high, each with two curved wing-like shades, designed by McGarry Ní Éanaigh Architects. The granite sets have new pathways with flagstones, making walking more comfortable. The old Smithfield market was demolished in September 2002. The Jameson Distillery now houses the Irish Whiskey Visitor Centre and the chimney of the building has a glazed circular viewing platform for visitors. Two hundred and twenty new apartments, shops, restaurants and a hotel have given a new vibrant urban atmosphere to what was a run-down area and is now known as Smithfield Village. A new juvenile court, designed by John Tuomey, now sits in the area.

Smithfield. In recent years the former market place has been transformed, with twelve brazier masts, each 26 metres high, with two curved wing-like shades.

Smith's Buildings
See **Ely Place.**

Smock Alley Theatre
At the rere of Blind Quay, now Lower Exchange Street, stood Smock Alley Street. In 1661, John Ogilby, Master of Revels, opened a theatre near the present Essex Street West. The Puritans had closed his theatre in Werburgh Street in 1641. The Smock Alley Theatre enjoyed great popularity but in 1671, on St Stephen's Day, three people were killed when the gallery collapsed. In 1701, many members of the audience were killed or injured during the performance of Shadwell's *The Libertine*. A new theatre was built in 1735 which was at one time called the Theatre Royal. It continued to flourish but, towards the end of the eighteenth century, increased competition forced its closure in 1788. The building was demolished in 1815. The burial vaults of the church of St Michael and St John are allegedly the pit of the theatre.

Thomas Sheridan made his first appearance there in 1743. Margaret (Peg) Woffington was a regular performer as was Thomas Dogget who was one of the most celebrated actors of his day and author of *The Country Wake*, published in 1696. He subsequently became joint manager of Drury Lane Theatre. He died in 1721. John Lewis (fl. 1740–57) was an artist who worked as a scene painter at the theatre. He painted portraits of women and children, and his portrait of Thomas Sheridan is in the National Gallery of Ireland. In 1998, Horan Keogan Ryan, architects, designed Smock Alley Court, facing onto Essex Street, consisting of three buildings with 53 apartments and five shops around a courtyard. The apartments face onto the River Liffey and the Wood Quay city offices. Temple Bar Properties sold this to Dublin Corporation at cost; as social housing, it contains tenants who had agreed to vacate their corporation houses in the suburbs after their children had left home.

Smyly's Homes and Schools

About 1836, Mrs Smyly was concerned about the number of homeless and starving children on the streets. She hired a stable loft to act as a schoolroom and started to give a few of the children the first simplest steps in education. Then, with the help of friends, she hired an old forge in Harmony Row in Grand Canal Street, which would accommodate more children. A house at no. 52 Townsend Street was rented; it had a loft big enough to be turned into a dormitory for 40 boys. On 14 November 1861, a home was opened at Grand Canal Street and, about the same time, a dormitory for 50 girls was opened in Luke Street.

It soon became evident that a home for very young children was essential and a small cottage at Mounttown near Kingstown (now Dún Laoghaire), housing 40 youngsters, was founded and called The Birds' Nest. A larger house opposite became vacant and 81 children were packed in, using straw mattresses which could be stacked in day time. Then, on 11 April 1861, the foundation stone was laid in a nearby field for the new Birds' Nest. It was built at a cost of £4,000. In addition to these three houses, a new one was being built at Grand Canal Street to house 100 boys, and a home similar to it was started at the Coombe to hold a further 60, together with another home in Luke Street to act as a receiving station for extra-pressing cases.

In 1872, the widow of William Henry Elliott donated a large sum to provide another home, to be called the Elliott Home, at 165–169 Townsend Street, with accommodation for 100 girls and boys. From there, the Elliot Home moved to Bray and then to Charlemont Street.

On 16 May 1901, Mrs Smyly died at the age of 86. She left behind her seven homes and four day schools. Her five daughters had taken part in the work. Today the work continues at Glensilva, 95 Monkstown Road, and Racefield House, Mounttown.

Society of Artists

See **City Assembly House.**

Smyly's Homes and Schools. Subscription card c. 1910.

Society of Friends

The first settled meeting of the Quakers was at Lurgan in 1654, and in Dublin, the following year, at the Pole Gate, one of the city portals near St Werburgh's Church. It was in the home of George Latham. In St Audoen's Church,* in 1655, Elizabeth Fletcher and Elizabeth Smith, two Quaker missionaries, published their testimony of truth and were committed to Newgate by the Lord Mayor. In 1678, a house near Gormond's Gate was fitted out as a place of worship. About the middle of the summer of 1683, the government gave orders to the several sorts of dissenters in Dublin that they should forbear meeting publicly together in their worship houses.

On 1 June that year, the Marshal and several officers went to Wormwood Gate where John Burnyeat was speaking. He and others were committed to the Marshalsea jail.

In 1686, the Quakers relinquished the

house at Wormwood Gate which was found to be too small. In 1692, 'the meeting house of Bride Street being too little the Friends of Dublin built a large new meeting house at Sycamore Alley for keeping their afternoon meeting on the first day of the week; (it had) an entrance to Eustace Street; and a morning meeting on the sixth day of the week being held in Meath Street'. The Eustace Street house was sold in 1986. In the year 1696, the right of affirmation was granted to the Friends.

The present building in Eustace Street with its ornate stucco façade was built in 1728, with additional entrances in 1859 and 1877. They had a graveyard in Dolphin's Barn Lane, now Cork Street, and also in York Street on the site of the present College of Surgeons.

The library and meeting house in Meath Place moved to Swanbrook House, Morehampton Road, in 1986.

South City Markets
South Great George's Street
A site bounded by Exchequer Street, Drury Street and Fade Street was known as the Castle Market in 1704. A new Castle Market was opened in 1783, with butchers' stalls and slaughterhouses which extended to South William Street. In 1876, a group of business people, including the Pim family, had a Bill passed enabling them to acquire properties in George's Street, Exchequer Street, Drury Street and Fade Street. Messrs Lockwood and Mawson of

Bradford won an architectural competition for a new market with a large iron and glass central hall. The venture was not a success, possibly due to a boycott by the public because of the appointment of English architects and builders. The hall was eventually taken as a furniture warehouse by Pims. The markets and the hall were destroyed by fire in 1892 and were rebuilt with an arcade instead of a hall.

South Great George's Street
From Dame Street to Aungier Street
Formerly St George's Lane.
A church dedicated to St George stood here in 1181 and was rebuilt in 1213 on its incorporation with the Priory of All Hallows. To support the church, the parliament of the English Pale in 1457 enacted that, 'any person in the County of Dublin making prey upon the Irish enemys exceeding forty cows, should deliver one cow, or five shillings in money towards the repair of the church'. In 1586, the church was demolished and the stones used for a common oven.

In 1731, Madame Violante, a tightrope walker, opened her new booth or theatre (*see* Fownes Court) where she put on various entertainments and was supported 'in a splendid manner by principal persons of both parties'. The house was taken eventually by Bartholomew Mosse who, on 15 March 1745, opened the first Dublin Lying-in Hospital there (*see* Rotunda Hospital). When Mosse moved to new

Telephone 1451.

E. W. MILLS,
Creamery
Proprietor,

21 & 22, SOUTH CITY MARKETS,
Dublin.

FACTORIES:
Bulgaden—Kilmallock.
Commons—Thurles.

All quotations subject being unsold on receipt of reply and market fluctuations.

South City Markets. Trader's bill, 1902.

premises in 1757, it became a lock hospital for the treatment of venereal diseases until 1769. It stood opposite to Fade Street.

Today the street is dominated by the South City Markets,* opened in 1881 and designed by Lockwood and Mawson. Up to 1970, the lower end of the street housed Pim's large drapery store and warehouse, built about 1843 and refashioned about ten years later by Sandham Symes. This family of Quakers were the chief instigators of the South City Markets.* A modern office block used as government offices stands in place of the old Pim's building. There are several public houses including the Long Hall and a variety of shops, a supermarket and restaurants.

South Inner City Community Development Association

An umbrella group representing all of the organisations in the inner city interested in rejuvenating Dublin's medieval core and the Liberties. The group's document, 'Back to the People', suggests a mix of new housing, public, private and co-operative, and the use of the derelict church of St Nicholas Within as a tourist reception area.

Spire of Light (The)
O'Connell Street

A competition attracting over 200 entries was held for a suitable structure to replace Nelson Pillar,* which was seriously damaged by an explosion on the night of 7 March 1966 and removed two days later. The pillar, built between 1808 and 1809, had been a landmark where citizens met or congregated for over 150 years.

The successful winning entry was designed by Ian Ritchie, an English architect active in new structural technologies and with an interest in the theory of energy. The design concept of the spire is a breakaway from traditional monuments that commemorate a person or event; rather it heralds in the new millennium and guides and points into the future.

This striking slender spire is three metres in diameter at the base and rises to a height of 124.8 metres with a tip of 15 centimetres.

Spire of Light rises to a height of 124.8 metres. Designed by Ian Ritchie, it stands on the site of the former Nelson Pillar, damaged by an explosion in 1966. The lighting ceremony took place on 7 July 2003. In the foreground is the statue of James Larkin, erected in 1980.

Two internal cylinder pendulum-type weights, designed by Cormac Deavy, control and stabilise it against the wind factor by absorbing the motion and reducing sway. The construction and manufacture of this remarkable, stainless steel, engineering achievement of great precision and very fine tolerances was carried out by Radley Engineering Ltd, Dungarvan, Co. Waterford. The abstract satin finish on the lower sections was obtained by a method known as 'shot peening' where the surface of the steel is bombarded with small pieces of shot, while the top 12 metres have a patterned perforation of 11,844 holes lit from inside, giving it a luminous tip at night. The first part of the column left Waterford for Dublin on 18 December 2002, the second on 23 December and the third on 15 January 2003. All the pieces are bolted together internally but, because of high winds, the final two sections were not put into place until 21 January 2003. The large crane was supplied by McNally Crane Hire and the highly skilled operation of dropping each section into place was carried out by Davie Andrews, the crane operator. It has a total weight of 133.16 tonnes, which is carried on eight concrete piles, anchored to bedrock 20 metres below ground. The overall project manager was Michael O'Neill. The lighting ceremony did not take place until Monday, 7 July 2003, when the Lord Mayor, Cllr Dermot Lacey, led the ceremony with the burial of a time capsule, six metres below the pavement, which contained the front page and the property supplement of *The Irish Times* of 3 July, a packet of twenty cigarettes, receipts from the bar of the Shelbourne Hotel, Tesco and Dunnes Stores, copies of the RTÉ *Guide* and *VIP Magazine*, menus from Flanagan's, Domino's Pizza and Patrick Guilbaud's restaurants, a guide to Temple Bar and a Mont Blanc pen.

The Spire is twice the height of Liberty Hall* and seven times taller than the General Post Office.*

Sports Clubs

Cricket Civil Service, Clontarf, College of Surgeons, CYM, Dublin University, Garda, Leinster, Leprechauns, Malahide, Merrion, North County, Old Belvedere, Pembroke, Phoenix, Railway Union, Rush, Sandyford, Swagelok, The Hills, UCD, YMCA.

GAA Ballinteer St John's, Ballyboden St Edna's, Ballyboden Wanderers, Ballymun Kickhams, Castleknock, Civil Service, Clan na Gael Fontenoy, Clontarf, Colmcille, Commercials, Craobh Chiaráin, Crumlin Cuala, Cumann Barra Setanta, Donnybrook Davits, Erin's Isle, Faughs, Fingallians, Fingal Ravens, Garda, Garristown, Garristown Ladies, Good Counsel, Kevin's, Kilmacud Crokes, Lucan Sarsfields, Man-O-War, Mearnog, Na Fianna, Naomh Barrog, Naomh Fionbarra, Naomh Olaf, O'Dwyers, O'Tooles, Palmerstown, Parnells, Raheny, Round Towers–Clondalkin, Round Towers–Lusk, O'Connell's School–Dublin, Skerries Harps, St Anne's, St Brigid's, St Finian's, St James Gaels, St Jude's, St Margaret's, St Mark's, St Mary's, St Oliver Plunkett's Eoghan Ruadh, St Patrick's–Palmerstown, St Sylvester's, St Vincent's, Synge Street, Templeogue, Thomas Davis, Trinity Gaels, UCD, Whitehall.

Golf Balbriggan, Balcarrick, Ballinascorney, Beaverstown, Beech Park, Blanchardstown, Carrickmines, Castle, City West Hotel and Golf Course, Clontarf, Corballis Public Golf Links, Corrstown, Deer Park, Donabate, Dublin Mountain, Dún Laoghaire, Edmonstown, Elm Green, Elm Park, Finnstown Fairways, Forrest Little, Foxrock, Glencullen, Grange, Hazel Grove, Hermitage, Hollystown, Hollywood Lakes, Howth, Killiney, Kilternan, Lucan, Luttrelstown Castle, Malahide, Milltown, Newlands, Portmarnock, Portmarnock Hotel and Golf Club, Rathfarnham, Royal Dublin, Rush, Skerries, Slade Valley, St Anne's, St Margaret's, Stackstown, Sutton, Swords Open Golf Course, The Island, The Open Golf Centre, Turvey, Westmanstown, Woodbrook.

Hockey Aer Lingus, Ashton, Donabate and Portrane, Clontarf, Corinthian, Dublin City University, Dublin University, Dublin University Ladies, Norcal Youth, Pembroke Wanderers, St James's Gate, Skerries, Suttonians, Swords, UCD Men's, UCD Ladies'.

Rugby Bective Rangers FC, Blackrock College, Clontarf, De La Salle Palmerston, Dublin University, Landsdowne FC, Monkstown, Old Belvedere, Old Wesley,

Skerries RFC, St Mary's College, Suttonians, Terenure College, University College Dublin, Wanderers FC Rugby Club.

Soccer Shelbourne–Tolka Park, Bohemians –Dalymount Park, St Pat's–Richmond Park, Shamrock Rovers–RDS, UCD–Belfield.

Swimming and Waterpolo

DCU Swimming and Waterpolo, Dublin University Swimming Club, Half Moon Waterpolo and Swimming, Marian Waterpolo Club, North Dublin Waterpolo Swimming Club, UCD Swimming Club.

Standfast Dick

A large rock formation, extending from Dame Street, on which the Royal Exchange* (City Hall*) was built, extending beneath Parliament Street under Grattan Bridge to Liffey Street. At low tide, small ships very often ran aground while trying to reach the Custom House,* built in 1707, where the Clarence Hotel now stands.

State Paper Office

See **National Archives.**

Statues, Equestrian

Equestrian Statue George I A statue by John Van Nost the elder costing £1,500 was erected on a central buttress of Essex Bridge and unveiled on 1 August 1722. It was removed to Aungier Street on the rebuilding of the bridge in 1753. Rocque's map of 1756 shows the statue in Bedford Square* but this never materialised. It was erected in the garden of the Mansion House, at the expense of the Lord Mayor, on 1 August 1798. Various proposals for its re-erection came to nothing, including one to place it in Fitzwilliam Square. Professor Thomas Bodkin considered it to be one of the finest equestrian statues in the British Isles and bought it in 1937 on behalf of the Barber Institute of Birmingham (where he was director) for £500. Bodkin, on hearing that the equestrian statue of George II* had been blown up on coronation day, 1 May 1937, and fearing that George I might suffer

the same fate, travelled to Dublin and successfully negotiated its purchase. John P. Keane, city manager, acknowledged the cheque on 21 October 1937. It was in a bad state of repair and new parts were cast in England, including a foreleg. It now stands on a plinth in front of the Institute.

Equestrian Statue George II A bronze statue by John Van Nost the younger on a three-tier granite plinth was erected in St Stephen's Green in 1758. Van Nost may have been assisted in making the figure of the monarch in Roman habit by Patrick Cunningham, who was apprenticed to him through the Dublin Society. The Society records of 9 October 1760 state: 'Patrick Cunningham produced an equestrian statue on a marble base' and it was ordered that he should be paid ten guineas for his statue of 'our late glorious King George II'. Cunningham died in Paddington in 1774 and, according to Gilbert, 'was universally reputed the best wax modeller of his day in Europe'. The Royal Dublin Society made several requests for the statue but the Corporation refused. A bomb blew it to pieces in May 1937.

Equestrian Statue Field-Marshal Gough The statue by John Henry Foley was unveiled in the Phoenix Park in February 1880. It was erected by the friends and comrades of the hero of the Peninsular war, Field-Marshal Hugh Viscount Gough KP GCB, GCSI, and was cast from a cannon taken by the troops under his command. Foley received the commission but died on 27 August 1874 while working on the clay models for the O'Connell Monument. The horse was cast by Brock, Birch and Dewick from a mould used by Foley for a statue of Viscount Hardinge. The erection of the statue was originally proposed in 1869 but most of the sites suggested by the committee were turned down by Dublin Corporation. These included Carlisle Bridge, Foster Place and Westmoreland Street. On 24 December 1944, Gough's head and sword were sawn off. Following a tip-off, the head was recovered from the River Liffey near Kingsbridge. The horse's right hind leg was blown off in 1956 and, on 23 July 1957, an explosive placed in the belly of the horse blew the statue from its base. This was the last equestrian statue to be erected in Dublin. The city has no equestrian statues left to adorn its streets and parks.

Equestrian Statue William III The statue of William III by Grinling Gibbons was erected on College Green at the expense of the Corporation of Dublin on 1 July 1701, the anniversary of the battle of the Boyne, which was kept as a public holiday. (See Introduction for explanation of date.) At the unveiling, the Lord Mayor, with the full Council and representatives of the guilds,* marched from the Tholsel* preceded by a band and the grenadier companies of the Dublin Militia. Having marched twice around the statue, the Recorder delivered a eulogy on King William, after which the company marched a third time around the statue and returned to a reception in a house in College Green, which was attended by the Lords Justices, the Provost and Fellows of the university and many of the gentry. The large crowd outside was served with cakes, and several hogsheads of claret were opened. Because the King's back was turned towards the entrance of Trinity College, the students considered this to be an insult to their Alma Mater and often daubed the figure with mud or bedecked it in green ribbons. Sometimes a straw figure was placed astride behind the King. On 25 June 1710, the King's face was covered with mud and his sword and truncheon removed; three persons were caught and convicted. The statue was frequently mutilated and, in 1765, the lead statue was taken down and replaced on a much higher stone pedestal. In 1836, a bomb seriously damaged the figure of the King, which had to have a new head, left arm and leg, which were made by John Smyth. After other minor damage over the years, it was finally blown up in 1929 and removed.

Statues, Portrait

Albert Prince Consort, 1819–61. Bronze by Foley. Erected 1872 at centre of Leinster Lawn. Attempt made to blow it up, without success. Removed to south side of lawn when the Royal Dublin Society sold Leinster House to the State in 1924.

Ardilaun Lord, 1840–1915. Bronze by Farrell. Erected 1892 St Stephen's Green West in recognition of his bearing the cost of laying out the Green as a public park.

Blakeney General Sir William, Baron Blakeney 1672–1761. Metal gilt by Van Nost. Blakeney was known for his unsuccessful defence of Menorca in 1756. Erected 1759 in Gardiner's Mall. Paid for by the Friendly Brothers of St Patrick. Destroyed eight years later.

Burke Edmund, 1729–97. Bronze by Foley. Erected 1868 outside Trinity College.

Carlisle Seventh Earl of, George William Frederick Howard, 1802–64. Lord Lieutenant 1855–58, 1859–64. Bronze by Foley. Erected 1869 in People's Gardens, Phoenix Park. Blown up July 1958.

Dargan William, 1799–1867. Bronze by Farrell. Erected 1864 outside National Gallery of Ireland in recognition of Dargan underwriting the cost of the 1853 Exhibition on Leinster Lawn.

Davis Thomas, 1814–45. Marble by Hogan. Erected in City Hall — one of two, the other being in the mortuary chapel of Mount Jerome Cemetery having originally stood on the grave.

Drummond Thomas, 1797–1840. Under Secretary for Ireland. Marble by Hogan. Erected 1844 in Royal Exchange, now City Hall.

Eglinton and Winton 13th Earl of, Archibald William Montgomery, 1821–61, Lord Lieutenant 1852–53, 1858–59. Bronze by MacDowell. Erected 1866 St Stephen's Green North. Blown up 26 August 1958.

Emmet Robert, 1778–1803. Patriot. Bronze by Connor. Erected 13 April 1966 at St Stephen's Green West opposite his birth place. One of three castings. The others in Washington DC and San Francisco. This one was bought by Mr and Mrs Francis J. Kane of Washington, presidents of the Robert Emmet Statue committee of the USA. The committee included Ambassador Scott McCleod and six others and was presented to the Irish nation in 1966. This one was cast from the original statue in Washington. With the building of Luas the statue was placed inside the railings of St Stephen's Green West.

George II, King Lead and gilded by Rackstrow. Erected over entrance Weaver's Hall in the Coombe. Broken when being taken down in 1930. Head and feet in the Civic Museum.

George III, King Marble by Van Nost the younger. Presented to the Dublin merchants for the Royal Exchange by Earl of Northumberland, Lord Lieutenant 1763–65. Removed when statue of O'Connell was moved inside and placed on that site.

Goldsmith Oliver, 1728–84. Bronze by Foley. Erected 1864 outside Trinity College Dublin. Cost met from public subscription initiated by Earl of Carlisle.

Grattan Henry, 1746–1820. Patriot and orator born 3 July 1746 in Dublin. A Protestant, was a strong advocate of Catholic emancipation. The monument by John Henry Foley (1818–74) sited opposite the old Parliament House was erected in 1874 and shows Grattan in a dramatic stance with his hand raised, addressing the House where he had spoken so often. Bronze on a limestone base.

Grattan Henry. Marble by Chantrey. Erected City Hall.

Gray Sir John, 1816–75. Doctor, MP and newspaper proprietor. Sarravezza marble by Farrell. Erected 1879 on O'Connell Street. Commemorates his efforts in bringing Vartry water supply to Dublin in 1868.

Guinness Sir Benjamin Lee, 1798–1868. Bronze by Foley. Erected 1875 outside St Patrick's Cathedral in acknowledgment of his financing the restoration of the Cathedral.

Heuston Sean. Patriot executed 8 May 1916. Stone by Campbell. Erected People's Gardens, Phoenix Park.

Joyce James Augustine, 1882–1941. Poet, novelist and playwright, author of *Ulysses*. Bronze by Fitzgibbon. Unveiled at North Earl Street on Bloomsday, 16 June 1990.

Lucas Dr Charles, 1731–71. Marble by Smyth. Erected Royal Exchange 1773.

MacDonnell Sir Alexander, 1794–1875. Commissioner of National Education 1839–71. Marble by Farrell. Erected 1878 outside Model Schools in Marlborough Street. At present in storage with Office of Public Works.

Mathew Father Theobald, 1790–1856. Stone by Redmond. Erected 1893 in O'Connell Street. Stone of the base laid in 1890 to celebrate the centenary of the birth of the Father of Temperance.

Moore Thomas, 1779–1852. Born on 28 May 1779 at no. 12 Aungier Street, the son of a grocer and wine merchant. He is best remembered for his *Irish Melodies* published in parts between 1807 and 1834. A committee similar to that appointed for the O'Connell Monument commissioned Christopher Moore (1790–1863), sculptor, who was born in Dublin and lived at no. 2 Upper Gloucester Street until he departed for London about 1821, to make the Thomas Moore monument in College Street. His work largely consisted of portrait busts in which he was very successful but, according to Strickland, 'His powers were unequal to larger or more important works and in his statues and figure subjects he was not successful; his grotesque effigy of Thomas Moore in College Street, is an unfortunate memorial to the poet.' *The Irish Builder* described it as, 'that hideous importation from London the Moore Statue'. Erected in 1857, it depicts the poet in cast bronze wearing a voluminous cloak, poised on a square stone plinth. One of the people who was defeated in the competition for the monument was John Hogan (1800–58), one of the leading Irish sculptors of the nineteenth century. His plaster competition design depicting the bard holding a lyre stands in the National Gallery of Ireland.

O'Brien William Smith, 1803–64. Marble by Farrell. Erected 1870 at the southern end of Carlisle Bridge and moved 1929 to Lower O'Connell Street.

O'Connell Daniel, 1775–1847. First statue

to the Liberator. Marble by Hogan. Commissioned by the Repeal Association. Erected outside Royal Exchange but later moved inside and placed on a site where George III had previously stood.

O'Connell Monument, O'Connell Street Daniel O'Connell died in 1847 and a memorial in the form of a round tower was planned for Glasnevin Cemetery.* It was considered fitting that he should also have a monument in Dublin city. In 1862, a subscription list was opened and, two years later, in 1864, it was decided to hold a competition for a design. There were sixty entries none of which pleased the committee which included George Petrie, Frederick Burton and William Stokes. A second competition was held and, according to *The Irish Builder*, the designs were all 'wanting in grandeur and simplicity'. It was eventually decided to ask John Henry Foley (1818–74). Foley had received his education in the schools of the Royal Dublin Society* but had left Ireland in 1834 at the age of 16. He had become a leading monumental sculptor in England and was extremely busy as he was working on the Albert Memorial, as well as on statues of Lord Gough and Benjamin Lee Guinness. He died on 27 August 1874, before the O'Connell monument was finished, and the work was completed by his assistant, Thomas Brock.

The monument is in three parts. At the base there are four large winged figures representing victory through Patriotism, Fidelity, Courage and Eloquence. The base supports a drum surrounded by figures representing O'Connell's labours. The centre figure is Erin who holds the Act of Catholic Emancipation in her left hand while her right arm is raised pointing to O'Connell. The monument is topped by O'Connell wearing a draped cloak. *See* Glasnevin Cemetery.

Parke Surgeon Major Thomas Heazle, 1857–93. Bronze by Wood. Erected 1896 Leinster Lawn. He formed part of Stanley's expedition of 1887.

Parnell Charles Stewart, 1846–91. Bronze by Saint-Gaudens. Erected 1906–07.

Unveiled by John Redmond. The sculptor, Augustus Saint-Gaudens (1848–1907), was born at 35 Charlemont Street, son of a French father and Irish mother, but his parents emigrated to the United States six months after his birth. As most of the money for the monument was raised in the United States where Saint-Gaudens was well established, he was given the commission.

Plunket William Conyngham Baron Plunket, 1828–97. Archbishop of Dublin 1884–97. Bronze by Thornycroft. Erected 1901 in Kildare Place.

Shaw George Bernard, 1856–1950. Bronze by Prince Troubetzkoy. Entrance to National Gallery, a major beneficiary of the Shaw bequest. It was one of the few statues of himself that he liked. When he gave it to the Gallery, Shaw asked that it might stand outside because the Gallery had played such an important part in his education as a child.

Stewart Sir Robert Prescott, 1825–94. Musician. Bronze by Farrell. Erected 1898 on Leinster Lawn.

Victoria, Queen Marble by Hughes erected 1908 in front of Leinster House. Removed in 1948 to Royal Hospital, Kilmainham, and shipped to Australia, as a gift from the Irish Nation for Australia's Bicentenary in 1987.

Statues, Monuments, Sculptures
See:

Steevens' Lane
From Bow Lane to St John's Road West
Dr Richard Steevens (1653–1710) left his fortune to his twin sister Grizel for life and then to be applied to the building of a hospital. The street is sided by St Patrick's Hospital,* founded by Dean Swift, and Dr Steevens' Hospital.* On the opposite side of the street are various companies owned by Guinness, including the Camac Cask Company.

Stephen's Street
A meandering street from Golden Lane to Mercer Street
Name comes from the old church of St Stephen.
Mercer's Hospital* building stands on the site of the church at no. 36 and now houses Mercer's Health Centre, a general medical practice, a travel health centre and an international immunisation clinic. General trading street with two hotels, the Drury Court and the Grafton Capital. Leitrim House at nos. 68–69 named after William Sydney Clements, Earl of Leitrim (1806–78), murdered while journeying to Manorhamilton. At present occupied by Eircom solicitors' department. Numbers 70–74 are part of the old Ship Street barracks.
In 1889, John Boyd Dunlop (1840–1921), veterinary surgeon and inventor, made the first pneumatic tyre in Belfast in 1889 and later that year opened the first factory making these tyres at no. 75.

Stoneybatter
From Church Street to the North Circular Road
Stoneybatter, originally *Bóthar-na-gcloch*, the Road of Stones. At one time it was a village bordering Oxmantown Green* and was on a main artery from Tara to Wicklow. By the Middle Ages the name became Stoney-Bothar, Stoney Road. Today, under the 1985 development plan, it covers an area from Church Street, Smithfield, Prussia Street to the North Circular Road. In the 1660s, a large cattle market was opened and, throughout the eighteenth and nineteenth centuries, there was a concentration of dairies in the area, with cows being milked in back yards, and carts with large churns selling milk around the city. In the 1760s, fashionable houses were built in the area near Oxmantown Green as it still had a rural feel to it. During the eighteenth century, a festival was held on May Day when large crowds danced around a pole covered in garlands. This ceased in 1773 when unruly soldiers from the Royal Barracks, built in 1701–06, attempted to pull down the pole. Amid scuffles, shots were fired and the residents decided that it was no longer safe to hold a festival each year.

Store Street
From Beresford Place to Amiens Street
Designed by Gandon for the merchants to house their stores after the building of the new Custom House. One side of the street is now occupied by Busáras, one of the first major building projects started in the 1950s when building materials became more readily available after the emergency caused by the Second World War. Designed by Michael Scott, it was opened in 1953 as Dublin's first purpose-built modern office block and central bus station. Eight million passengers use the bus station each year. At no. 3 there is an entrance to the city morgue, and next door a Garda station. For many years, the city bakery of James Rourke was situated at nos. 6 and 7.

Stove Tenter House
Cork Street
A great many of the Huguenot weavers found that in the winter season 'when the rains, snows and frosts set in they are all thrown idle; neither the wool, warps nor cloths can then be dried'. Thomas Pleasants (1729–1818), a wealthy philanthropist, purchased a plot of ground on 10 March 1814 and, seven days later, the foundation stone was laid by his cousin, Joshua Pasley, for a suitable building. Stove Tenter House was officially opened for the use of the weavers on 20 October 1815. Built of brick, it was 215 feet long and 22

feet wide. The heat ascended from four stoves in the basement through pipes that passed through floors in the form of iron gratings. Built at a cost of £13,000. Over the years the weaving trade dwindled and, in 1855, the building was closed. In 1861, Fr Spratt rented the premises for St Joseph's Night Shelter and he purchased the building in 1872. Over 700 people a week visited the shelter. Any without homes were admitted free and given bread and cocoa at night and bread and tea in the morning. In 1872, the Sisters of Mercy agreed to take over and two sisters came from Baggot Street to take up residence. In 1873, the Sisters of Mercy built the present convent and schools on part of the gardens belonging to the original building.

Strangers Friends' Society
Established in 1790: 'An institution formed on the most disinterested principles, to lessen the calamities of life; to afford relief to the deserving objects; to snatch from the jaws of death the creature hurrying untimely to the tomb, the victim of cold, famine, and disease; for the relief of the sick and indigent of every description of religion, sect and party. No other recommendation is required than a sufficiency of evident distress. Any person may apply, or give notice of those that he knows or suspects to be in distress; a visitor is immediately appointed, who comes at an hour unexpected to be on his guard against imposition. He has ocular demonstration. If the distress is found to be real, present relief is afforded and continued to the extent necessary.' Today, the Strangers Friends' Society is run by the Dublin Central Mission.

Street Lighting
See **Public Lighting.**

Suffolk Street
From Grafton Street to St Andrew's Street
Possibly named after Sir Thomas Howard, Earl of Suffolk.
Contained part of the Thingmote,* an earthen terraced mound, possibly Norse in origin and levelled in 1685 by the City Recorder, Sir William Davis, in order to enlarge his estate near St Andrew's Church. While workmen were excavating in May 1857, they unearthed two copper axe-heads in a cyst burial (shallow stone-lined pit) which contained a crouched skeleton. The weapons, now in the National Museum of Ireland, date from c. 1800 BC. A street with public houses, a bank and general shops.
James Fitzgerald, Earl of Kildare, lived in the family home in Suffolk Street before moving to his new Leinster House.* Richard Cassels, the architect, also lived here. John Philpot Curran, the lawyer and advocate of Catholic Emancipation, had offices here. A tavern appears to have existed near the corner of Church Lane since the seventeenth century, where O'Neill's Pub now stands. From the middle of the eighteenth century, for more than 100 years, it was run by the Coleman family. The new Ulster Bank extension occupies the site of the Royal Arcade Hotel.
See **Royal Arcade.**

Summerhill
From Parnell Street to Ballybough Road
John Rocque's map of 1756 shows it as Summer Hill.
Nothing remains of this part of the Luke Gardiner estate. The (Royal) Dublin Society's Garden, established here in 1733, moved to Glasnevin in 1795 as the Botanic Gardens.* As far back as 1940, houses were being demolished or detenanted and, in 1989, a dual carriageway was opened. Some new red-brick Corporation housing backs onto the new road. An abstract female-form bronze sculpture on two cement plinths, by Cathy Carman, was erected in 1992. On Summerhill Parade, near the Royal Canal at Annesley Bridge, Bridgewater Hall, a five-storey apartment scheme over ground-floor retail units, designed by architects MacEoin Kelly, was built in 2003/2004.
See **Champion's Avenue, Rutland Street Upper.**

Sussex Road
From Mespil Road to Burlington Road
On the corner of Mespil Road, Dr Barry built Mespil House in 1751. This was demolished to make way for the Irish Life flats. In 1968, Wesley College sold Tullamaine, their junior girls' residence and preparatory school, to the P. V. Doyle Group. The 420-bedroom Burlington Hotel was built on the site and opened in May 1972.

Sutton
An area adjoining Howth and the suburb of Kilbarrack that was greatly developed since the opening of the coastal James Larkin Road. Sutton has a golf club divided by Burrow Road and Claremont Road and is served by the DART railway. St Fintan's (RC) Church was opened in 1973 to a design of Robinson, Keefe and Devane. It has an unusual split tower with interior furnishings by Christopher Ryan and Enda King. The Presbyterian church situated on Claremont Road and the Methodist church on the Dublin Road were both erected early in the twentieth century. The Marine Hotel is situated on the Dublin Road.

Swan Alley Exchange Court
Named after Richard Swan's Swan Tavern c. 1690. At the beginning of the eighteenth century, the Swan-tripe Club met there. In 1705, it was described at a Dublin Grand Jury as 'a seditious and unlawful assembly or club set up and continued at the swan tavern, with intent to create mis-understandings between Protestants . . . and to instill dangerous principals into the youth of the kingdom.' The Alley also contained several gambling dens frequented by characters of ill repute and was demolished in July 1768 to make way for the new Royal Exchange.*

Sweeney's Lane
Building lease from Lord Meath dated 1688. The lane was originally entered from Mill Street by a narrow gateway and terminated in the Tenter fields. The houses in the eighteenth century were occupied by persons working in the linen and weaving trade.

Swift's Alley
Between Francis Street and Meath Street
Named after a seventeenth-century merchant, Goodwin Swift.

Swift's Alley Church
A Baptist meeting house was built in 1653 in an alley between Francis Street and Meath Street, with a lease from Goodwin Swift after whom the Alley is named. The building was demolished and a new one built in 1738. In 1835, it was leased as a chapel of ease to St Catherine's Church, when £3,000 was spent on refurbishing the building. Swift's Alley church was closed in 1891.

Sycamore Street
From Dame Street to Essex Street
Known as Sycamore Alley until 1869. In 1846, Joshua Bewley, a Quaker from England, opened his first coffee house as a place for men to meet and discuss business without having to resort to a public house. He was soon to transfer to George's Street and, in 1916, opened another branch in Westmoreland Street. In 1926, he opened his third shop at no. 75 Grafton Street, where Samuel Whyte once ran his school and academy of drama. Bewley's coffee houses closed in December 2004. In 1993, the Olympia Theatre in Dame Street was granted permission to build a five-storey office and retail building with a floor area of 862 sq. m (9,278 sq. ft) with two entrances in the street. The glass canopy, a protected structure, was demolished by a lorry in 2004.

Synge Street
Crossing South Circular Road at Harrington Street
Number 33, built in 1795, was the birthplace of George Bernard Shaw. Born on 26 July 1856, he spent his formative years there. Shaw was one of Ireland's four Nobel Prize winners in literature. An appeal was

launched in 1988 to save the building which was in a grave state of disrepair. St Kevin's School, Synge Street, was founded by the Christian Brothers in 1864.

Synod Hall, Christ Church

John Roe junior, by whose generosity Christ Church Cathedral* had been restored, also offered to erect a synod hall for General and Diocesan Synods. The finished building was presented to the General Synod of the Church of Ireland in 1875. In 1981–82, it was calculated that it would cost £250,000 to put the fabric in order. It was decided to sell the building to a charitable trust set up by Dean Salmon, and the Church of Ireland ceased to have ownership of the hall in 1983. It was sold to Renaissance Projects Limited, which uses the hall to house a heritage centre, using the latest technology to present a chronicle of Irish culture from pre-history to the present day, called 'Dublinia'. The archway joining the cathedral to the hall remains the property of the Synod Hall Trust.

T

Tailors' Hall, The Dublin
Back Lane

The earliest mention of a Dublin Tailors' Hall is in 1539, situated in Winetavern Street, which hall was later leased to the Corporation. A wooden hall was erected in 1583–84, probably in Back Lane, and the cornerstone of the present building was laid in 1703, with work completed by 1707. It was considered the most fashionable venue in Dublin for balls, musical evenings and public meetings. This continued until after 1741 when the New Music Hall* in Fishamble Street attracted the society events. The hall was also used by other guilds as a meeting place, and the Grand Lodge of Freemasons met there from 1755 to 1818. Many other organisations used the Hall over the years and, from the start, religious sects including Baptists, Kilhamites and the New Jerusalem Society rented the building. The most important event to be held there was on 2 December 1792 when it was leased for the convention of the Catholic Committee, generally termed the 'Back Lane Parliament' organised by Theobald Wolfe Tone, Protestant leader of the United Irishmen. The convention used the hall for only a few days but the Dublin Society of the United Irishmen continued to meet there.

After the guild* system collapsed, the tailors used their monies to establish a school that would take up to 50 pupils, all of whom had to be members of the Church of Ireland or of the Presbyterian Church. In 1873, the school moved to the Merchant's Guild Hall,* 41 Merchant's Arch, now 46 Wellington Quay. Various religious groups then rented the Hall, the

Tailors' Hall. In 1966, Dublin Corporation handed over the hall to a committee of volunteers that had been formed to restore the building. The photograph taken on the day of the ceremony shows Daithi Hanly, Marie-Gabrielle (Mariga) Guinness, the author Douglas Bennett and Desmond Guinness.

last being the Legion of Mary. Eventually the Corporation architects declared the premises uninhabitable and in danger of collapsing. In 1966, a committee of volunteers was formed to restore Tailors' Hall by private enterprise, and many societies co-operated actively together with the citizens of Dublin to raise enough money to restore the building completely. In 1985, the hall was leased to An Taisce for use as its national headquarters.

Talbot Place

From Store Street to Talbot Street
Named after Charles Chetwynd, 3rd Earl of Talbot, Lord Lieutenant 1817–21.

Talbot Street

From Marlborough Street to Amiens Street
Named after Charles Chetwynd, 3rd Earl of Talbot, Lord Lieutenant 1817–21.
Formerly Cope Street, North.
In 1971, Irish Life bought the old Brooks Thomas warehouse in Lower Abbey Street and, within three months, had three acres stretching back as far as Talbot Street. Alfie Byrne, ten times Lord Mayor of Dublin, was a publican by trade and purchased The Vernon Bar in 1912. He served his apprenticeship in Cosgrave's, 1–2 Chancery Place. In 1989, Cosgrave's was renamed The Alfie Byrne.

Tallaght

A suburb 7 miles S.W. by W. from the General Post Office. Situated on the road to Blessington. On its southern side is Balrothery Hill on the River Dodder where a dam was built in 1244, creating a watercourse which passed through Templeogue and Dolphin's Barn, eventually ending at the city basin near James's Street. St Mael Ruain founded a monastery here. He died AD 792. The Stowe Missal was written in this monastery about AD 800. Students came from far afield to Tallaght and to Finglas at a time when these two centres of learning were known as the two eyes of Ireland. The Vikings burned the monastery AD 811 but it was later rebuilt.

The parish church of St Maelruain (C of I) is built on the site of Mael Ruain's monastery. It was commenced in 1829 to John Semple's design. Semple was at 13 College Green and was City Architect 1829–42. The old church, which had become a ruin by 1825, still remains with its high rectangular tower. St Mary's (RC) Church, opened in 1886 in memory of the Very Rev. Thomas Burke, stands on the site of the Dominican monastery which was opened in 1842 and incorporated a mansion built by Major Palmer c. 1826. An extension was built onto the church in 1969 which won a European Heritage award in 1975.

Sir William Howard Russell (1820–1907), a famous war correspondent, was born at Lily Vale on 28 March 1820. In 1854, he went to Gallipoli and his reports on the Crimean War made him a household name. Trinity College conferred an LL.D.

Tallaght. Over the past few years the area has greatly expanded with new shopping in the village quarter and with the arrival of Luas.

on him on his return. He was knighted in 1895. The Dublin and Blessington Steam Tramway Company* opened up this country district to the general public. The entire area is now covered with vast housing estates. The growing population exceeds 70,000, with 50 per cent under the age of nineteen.

At nearby Old Bawn, William Bulkeley, Archdeacon of Dublin, erected a house in 1635. It survived until 1914 when it was demolished. The impressive mantelpiece dating from the building of the house, was rescued and stands in the National Museum of Ireland.* Joseph McDonnell, a nineteenth-century occupier of the house, owned one of several paper mills in the district; another was operated at Boldbrook by Robert Boardman whose residence was at Airfield Cottage. The Federated Dublin Voluntary Hospitals group, established on 6 November 1961, moved to a new hospital complex at Tallaght. Over the past few years, the area has greatly expanded with new shopping in the village quarter and with the arrival of Luas. Section 23 tax-incentive apartments are being built, including the 50 one-, two- and three-bedroom apartments, designed by Henry J. Lyons and Partners at Belgard Square.

Tallaght Hospital

The hospital was planned in 1981 to house the Adelaide/Meath hospitals, and in-corporating the National Children's Hospital. Work commenced in 1993 and was completed in 1998. It was designed by Robinson, Keefe, Devane architects and at a cost of €140 million was the largest capital investment in health care ever undertaken by the state. It covers a 35-acre site with 513 beds including 56 for acute psychiatric services of St Loman's Hospital. A further 76-bed extension opened in 2001. The first 115 patients were installed on Sunday, 21 June 1998, when 12 Eastern Health Board ambulances transferred them from the three Dublin hospitals. It is a public voluntary teaching hospital and operates under a Charter agreed by Dáil Éireann on 1 August 1996.

Tara Street
From Pearse Street to George's Quay

A new street formed in 1885 on the site of the Shoe Lane and flea market. The entire street was widened with the reconstruction of Butt Bridge from a swing construction to the present cement bridge in 1932. The popular Tara Street public baths and wash houses are now closed, and Ashford House, an office block, stands on the site, erected by the developer, John Byrne, to a design of Brian O'Halloran and Associates. The William Richardson (lime, cement and plaster merchants) premises were demolished and a seven-storey office block, Liffey House, built on the site in 1982. The entire was let to Dublin Corporation's Building Control Bye–Law Section. This building was demolished in 2003 and a new seven-storey plus penthouse office block, also Liffey House, on the corner of Townsend Street and Tara Street, designed by Donnelly Turpin, was erected in its place and opened in 2004. *The Irish Times* moved into the building in 2005 from its head office at D'Olier Street/Fleet Street which the newspaper had occupied since 1895. Goldsmith's House on the corner with Pearse Street, built in the 1970s of precast concrete, had a face-lift in 2003 when an additional floor was added and the entire building cladded with black basalt.

Temple Bar
From Eustace Street to Fleet Street

Acquired its name from having been the site of the mansion and gardens of the family of William Temple, a fellow of King's College, Cambridge, and provost of Trinity College in 1609. After the building of the new Custom House in 1707, the entrance was from Temple Bar. CIÉ had been buying property in the area with a view to building a southern headquarters for buses; this was shelved and an EC report described the area as 'one of the last fragments of the central area which gives a picture of Dublin City before the Wide Streets Commissioners replaced its medieval street pattern with the spacious

Temple Bar, showing one side of a new curved street leading between Eustace Street and Temple Lane with the Arthouse designed by architects Shay Cleary and Brian McClean.

formality of Georgian streets and squares'. In 1991, a state agency, Temple Bar Properties, was set up to develop this designated quarter. A sister company, Temple Bar Renewal and Development, was also incorporated to advise on what projects would receive tax incentives. £41 million of public money, half of it from the EU, was given for the creation of ten cultural centres and new public spaces extending from Westmoreland Street to the Civic Offices at Wood Quay. The area now has approximately 2,000 residents but leans too heavily on pub/restaurant culture. Many interesting new buildings and conversions have taken place. In Eustace Street, the Film Institute* incorporating the Irish Film Theatre in the old Quaker Meeting House. The Ark – a cultural centre for children by Group

Architects Shane O'Toole and Michael Kelly retained part of the 1725 frontage, while on the other side, facing Meeting House Square, a large warehouse-type door opens to create a raised stage for outdoor performances. A flight of steps from Eustace Street leads to Meeting House Square where a thriving food market is held on Saturdays. This area includes the Gallery of Photography designed by Sheila O'Donnell and John Tuomey, architects. Its large window represents a camera lens, and a screen enables films to be projected on summer nights in an open-air cinema from the National Photographic Archive* opposite. This mixed-use building, with its delicate colours and textures, designed by Paul Keogh and Rachael Chidlow, architects, blends in well with the other buildings. The Arthouse forms one side of a new curved street leading between Eustace Street and Temple Lane, and was designed by architects Shay Cleary and Brian McClean. Much restoration has been carried out on existing buildings in the area.

A new concept was the ecologically friendly Green Building in Crow Street. Designed by the architects Murray Ó Laoire in collaboration with Conservation Engineering, a company run by Tim Cooper, with wind turbines and solar panels. At its launch in 1994, people queued all night to obtain apartments in the building. The wooden building by De Blacam and Meagher, on the corner of Lord Edward Street and Exchange Street, is a five-storey block, and a nine-storey tower, with 191 apartments over retail units, it has timber boarding and brick work. Many other buildings have been completed in Temple Bar including the Project Art Centre, 39 East Essex Street, designed by Shay Cleary; it houses Ireland's oldest arts centre with performance space at first-floor level and an exhibition gallery below. The Print Works by Derek Tynan, with a frontage onto two streets, has ten apartments and four studio retail units and a raised courtyard. The Temple Bar Gallery and Studios are housed in an early twentieth-century factory that was restored and extended with a new frontage to supply artists' studios and gallery space, to a design by McCullough Mulvin, architects. Many of the streets have cobblestones and there are extensive pedestrian ways.

See also **Contemporary Music Centre, Cow Lane, Essex Street, Exchange Street, Film Institute of Ireland, National Photographic Archive.**

Temple Lane South

From Dame Street to Temple Bar
Shown on Bernard de Gomme's map of 1673 and Charles Brooking's map of 1728 as Dirty Lane. Named after Sir William Temple. (*See* Temple Bar for details.)

Temple Street

From Hill Street to Hardwicke Place
Street laid out in the late eighteenth century. In 1886, the lower end of the street was renamed Hill Street as the moral character of the area had deteriorated so much. The Children's Hospital, founded in Buckingham Street in 1867, moved to the top end of Temple Street in 1872. A fine view of St George's Church* in Hardwicke Place may be seen from the street.

Templeogue Road

From Templeogue to Rathfarnham
In 1801 this road was opened, dividing the properties of Robert Shaw Junior, the well known banker, Lord Mayor 1815–16. He lived at Bushy Park* but, on the death of his father, he came into possession of Terenure House.* It was a turnpike road with the first gate near Fergus Road. This was discontinued after 1848 and the house was converted into a barracks for the Dublin Metropolitan Police in 1849.

Terenure

A townland containing 569 acres within the civil parish of Rathfarnham, Barony of Rathdown, Co. Dublin. The name first appears around the time of the Normans and is mentioned in various documents between 1212 and 1317, with various spellings as follows: Tyrinwer, Thirinuyr, Tyrnyuyr. This could suggest that the first syllable is the Irish word *Tír* meaning a district. As Terenure was neither a parish nor a village, it tended to be in private ownership.

The Barnwells came to England with William the Conqueror, and Hugo was given the lands of Terenure, Kimmage and Drimnagh by King John in 1215. In 1250, Hugo's brother, Reginald, gave portion of

Temple Street, looking towards St George's Church c. 1821.

the lands to the hospital of St John the Baptist* outside Newgate. When Edward died in 1590, he left Terenure and Kimmage to his son, Peter, who had a castle in Terenure near the present Carmelite college. Cromwell confiscated the lands of the Barnwells and, in 1671, Major Deane purchased the lands of Terenure and Kimmage from Richard Talbot, Earl of Tyrconnell, for £4,000. The Deane family was associated with the area until 1789 when the property was sold to Abraham Wilkinson of Dawson Street, who lived at Mount Jerome in Harold's Cross. The Shaw family came into ownership at the end of the eighteenth century and rebuilt part of what is now Terenure College with fine stucco-work ceilings. The house was eventually purchased from the Bourne family in 1860 by the Carmelite order, who opened it as a secondary school. The former AIB sports grounds on College Drive were sold in 2003 to Jackie Greene Construction who built 160 houses on the site, including three-, four- and five-bedroom houses, maisonettes, duplex units and 99 apartments, including 24 sheltered accommodation with a day room.

See also **Bushy Park, Kimmage Manor, Fortfield House *and* Templeogue.**

The Sick and Indigent Roomkeepers' Society

In 1790, five men met in a room in Charles Street West and passed the following resolution: 'As a charitable feeling for the distresses of our fellow creatures is highly pleasing to Almighty God, and He will take it as done to Himself: we therefore have resolved unanimously to form a society for relieving the sick and indigent roomkeepers in the City of Dublin.' It was decided that each member of the society subscribe not less than 2d per week or 8s 8d per annum for the relief of persons 'who had never begged abroad, industrious mechanics and indigent roomkeepers who, above all others, are the most pitiable objects of distress'.

In the early years, the activities of the Society were confined to the poor residing in Mountrath Street, Charles Street and in the neighbourhood of the Ormonde Market. Potatoes, meal, bread, straw and money were distributed. In the first year, 129 families benefited, and expenditure amounted to £17-9-6. By 1793, the number had risen to 2,157 and, in 1797, to 18,430, at a cost of £1,500. In 1800, 40,000 persons were given assistance. The Society had always met in taverns and other buildings but, in 1841, moved into no. 85 Dame Street. Its report of 1842 explains: 'The divisional meetings were held until within the last year in respectable taverns, but since the great temperance movement began, many with the best of intentions objected to such places of meeting.' In 1855, the Society moved to 2 Palace Street, having purchased the house for £355. The Society helps persons from all religious persuasions and its work continues to the present day. In 1992, the Palace Street premises were sold and, in order to make use of its limited funds, the Society changed its method of assistance and applications were no longer accepted from the general public. Instead, the trustees now consider only applications from hospital social workers, for those in special need due to illness, infirmity or severe difficulties, which are not covered by social welfare or other relief agencies. The Society receives no aid from the state or public bodies and is entirely dependent on voluntary donations.

Theatre Royal
Hawkins Street

The theatre opened on 18 January 1821 in premises that had been occupied by the Dublin Society.* Henry Harris, the lessee, took over the building gratis subject to ground rents of £610 per annum which the Society had been paying. It was completely refitted and designed by an English theatre architect, Samuel Beazley (1786–1851), and reputedly seated in excess of 2,000 people. An account of 1861 records that the theatre was packing in the crowds. Some paid 6d for a gallery seat or 3s 6d for the second circle. Others paid three guineas to sit in a box and be seen.

In 1880, the building was destroyed by fire. That night (9 February), Winston Churchill was in Dublin and decided to go to *Ali Baba* which was nearing the end of its run. On the way, he was stopped and told that the theatre was on fire. He recalled the incident in his memoirs written many years later. Only a few weeks previously, his mother, the Duchess of Marlborough, had been patron of a special charity matinée held in the Theatre Royal. It was thought that the fire was caused by a faulty gas jet in the Viceregal box. The owner, Michael Gunn, hired the London-based architect C. J. Phipps (1835–97) to design the Leinster Hall which opened to the public on 2 November 1886 and closed in 1897.

The building was then remodelled by architect Frank Matcham (1854–1920) and, in December 1897, the new Theatre Royal had its grand re-opening under the joint management of Frederick Mouillot and David Telford. This building was demolished in May 1934 and a new theatre, together with the adjoining Regal Rooms, was opened by Sean Lemass on 23 September 1935. The programme describing the interior stated: 'A richly lavish Moorish architectural scheme has been adopted for the decoration of the auditorium which is based on authentic details from the Alhambra at Granada in Spain.' The design was by L. C. Norton of London. A large Compton theatre organ was installed in the auditorium, with Tommy Dando appearing nightly at the great manuals. This, together with a cinema and variety show which included the Royalette chorus girls under Babs da Monte and Alice Dalgarno and the orchestra, under the baton of Jimmy Campbell, gave a programme of good value. The theatre, owned by the Rank Organisation, finally closed on the night of 30 June 1962, with many of the audience continuing the party in the street until early next morning. The building was completely demolished by November 1962

and an office block, Hawkins House, with 122,000 square feet of office space, was erected on the site to a design of Sir Thomas Bennett.

Actor Barry Sullivan portrayed as Hamlet; in one hand he holds the skull of Yorick. Statue by Sir Thomas Farrell RHA at Glasnevin.

Theatres

The city has a long tradition of theatre attendance, going back to 1637 when John Ogilby built a theatre in Werburgh Street. It was short lived, closed by the Puritans in 1641. After the restoration of the monarchy in 1661, the Smock Alley Playhouse or

Theatre Royal was founded, and survived until 1787. A sister theatre was opened in 1733 at Aungier Street but failed in 1746. The Crow Street Theatre, founded by Spranger Barry and Henry Woodward in 1758, continued until 1821. The Theatre Royal,* built in Hawkins Street, took over the patent of the Crow Street Enterprise. The Adelphi in Great Brunswick Street, which opened in 1823, later became the Queen's Theatre.* In 1896, the Grand Lyric Hall opened on Burgh Quay; it then became the Tivoli until the Irish Press bought the building in 1930. The Abbey Theatre* opened in 1909. The La Scala Theatre* and Opera House, later known as the Capitol, opened in 1919 and closed in 1972. The Gate Theatre Company was founded by Micheál MacLiammóir and Hilton Edwards in 1928. The Pike Theatre,* founded by Alan Simpson and Carolyn Swift, opened in 1953 and closed in 1960. The Gaiety* and Olympia theatres also survive. Present-day theatres include: The Abbey* and Peacock, Abbey Street; Andrew's Lane Theatre and Studio, 9–16 St Andrew's Lane; Civic Theatre, Tallaght; Focus, 6 Pembroke Place; Gaiety, South King Street; Gate, 1 Cavendish Row; The Helix,* Glasnevin; Lambert Puppet Theatre, Clifton Lane, Monkstown; Liberty Hall Centre, Eden Quay; New Theatre, 43 Essex Street; Olympia, 72 Dame Street; Project Arts Centre, 39 East Essex Street; Tivoli, Francis Street; St Francis Xavier Hall, Sherrard Street.

Present-day theatre companies include: Beg, Borrow and Steal, 35 Leinster Avenue, North Strand; Down to Earth, 61 Middle Abbey Street; Dublin Youth Theatre, 23 Gardiner Street; Iomha Ildanach Theatre Co., The Crypt, Dublin Castle; Opera Ireland, The School House, 1 Grantham Street; Opera Theatre Company, Temple Bar; Passion Machine, 27 Mountjoy Square; Rough Magic, 5 South Great George's Street; Team Theatre Company, 4 Marlborough Place; Temple Theatre, Temple Street.

See **Conciliation Hall.**

Thingmote

An earthen terraced mound estimated to have been 40 feet in height and 240 feet in circumference, bounded by College Green, Church Lane and Suffolk Street. Possibly Norse in origin, it appears in a grant of 1240 to John Thurgot, 'Thengmotha in parochia S. Andrea Thengmoth'. While workmen were excavating in Suffolk Street in May 1857, they unearthed two copper axe-heads in a cyst burial (shallow stone-lined pit) which contained a crouched skeleton. The weapons, now in the National Museum of Ireland, are dated c. 1800 BC. The Thingmote was levelled in 1685 by the City Recorder, Sir William Davis, in order to enlarge his estate near St Andrew's Church.

See **Nassau Street.**

Tholsel

About 1311, the Mayor and commonalty moved from the Guild Hall* in Winetavern Street to new premises in the High Street. There were six warehouses beneath the rooms reserved for the City Fathers. By 1676, this medieval building was in a dangerous state and had to be demolished. Additional adjoining sites were acquired with their old buildings, which were then demolished. These were at Skinners' Row near Ram Alley, and the new civic offices were built on the sites. The Tholsel survived until 1791 when it was considered to be in a dangerous state and was demolished. The Corporation then moved to the Assembly Rooms* in William Street. The premises at Skinners' Row had been considered unsuitable for some time because the court also sat there and attracted the most vicious of people, while the steam from the kitchens reeked with preparations for city entertainments. In 1765, the Corporation had petitioned parliament to instruct the Wide Streets Commissioners* to supply a plot of ground at Cork Hill* suitable for building a new City Hall.*

The Tholsel, from Charles Brooking's map of 1728.

Thomas Court

Named after the Liberty of Thomas Court and Donore which, in the 1830s, was divided into four wards: Upper Coombe Ward, Lower Coombe Ward, Thomas Court Ward and Pimlico Ward. Donore has been a separate unit since 1773.

Thomas Court was named after the Abbey of St Thomas the Martyr, founded in 1177 to perpetuate the name of Thomas à Becket, murdered at Canterbury. The following year, the King granted the lands of Dunower (Donore) to the order of the Canons of the Congregation of St Victor. When the monastery was suppressed on 25 July 1537 under Henry VIII, its lands had grown to enormous proportions and included four castles, fifty messuages, four mills, 16 acres of meadow, eight orchards, 30 acres of woods. Also included were the castle and lands of Kilruddery, Crumlin and Kilnamanagh together with St Catherine's and St James's churches. The lands passed to the Brabazon family who were to become Earls of Meath. Thomas

Court is clearly shown on John Speed's map of 1610, but by the time Brooking published his map, in 1728, only the name appears to have survived. The name still survives today in Thomas Street, Thomas Court and Thomas Court Bawn. The Abbey occupied the site between Hanbury Lane and South Earl Street.

See also **Liberties, Pimlico, Gray Street, Dublin Artisans' Dwellings Company.**

Thomas Street

From Francis Street to James's Street

Name comes from the Abbey of St Thomas founded in 1177 by order of King Henry II as atonement for the murder of Thomas à Becket. After the suppression of the monasteries under Henry VIII, the lands were granted to William Brabazon whose family became the Earls of Meath. The medieval church which was part of the Abbey stood at the top of the hill opposite Bridgefoot Street where St Catherine's Church* now stands. It was here that Robert Emmet was hanged on 20

September 1803. At the other end of the street is the nineteenth-century Church of St John the Baptist and St Augustine.*

In the seventeenth and eighteenth centuries, many trades flourished in the street, including a Huguenot settlement of wool and silk weavers. It also had a kerb-side market known as the Glib Market, shown on Rocque's map of 1756. In 1791, John Power owned a hostelry at no. 109 where he started distilling whiskey. Power's distillery was to spread eventually over six acres. The National College of Art and Design now occupies the site. William Jameson, another brewer, occupied 15 acres. Arthur Guinness founded his brewery in 1756 and built a large mansion for himself at no. 1. The Roe family took a site for a brewery in 1757 opposite no. 1, which would eventually spread over seventeen acres. On the site there are still the remains of the largest smock-windmill in Europe, used for grinding corn. Its giant sails were removed in 1860. The pear tree at its base dates from c. 1850. Henry Roe is remembered for restoring Christ Church Cathedral.* The Roe family, William Jameson and the Jones's Road distillery amalgamated in 1891 to form the Dublin Distillers' Company. With the introduction of prohibition in the US in 1920 and high tariffs into Great Britain, after Independence, whiskey distilling went into a decline. Today, Thomas Street is a busy shopping area with a few remaining kerb-side stalls. In 2003, Enterprise Ireland invested €2.3 million in the Print Depot, a 1930 landmark building in Thomas Street, which was refurbished and developed as a high-tech, broadband-enabled facility for established and high-potential start-up companies, working in the digital media sector as part of the Digital Hub.* The architects were the City Architect's Division, Dublin City Council, and the main contractor Duggan Brothers (Contractors) Ltd. Opposite, at 10–13, is the Project office of the Digital Hub.

Thom's Directory

In the eighteenth century, Dublin had several directories including *The Gentleman's & Citizen's Almanack*, compiled by Samuel Watson, and Peter Wilson's *Dublin Directory*, begun in 1751. William Corbett of no. 57 Parnell Street bought the copyright of Wilson's *Directory* in 1802 and this was purchased in 1843 by Alexander Thom whose name it bears to the present day. According to Thom, the aim of the compilers generally has been to make their work indispensable to all classes of the community as a library or office companion, by combining in one volume a ready book for reference about all subjects of public interest.

In 1999, *Thom's Directory* was bought by The Irish Press plc. In October 2002, Dublin Corporation Public Libraries published a directory for 1738 based on a bundle of eighteenth-century manuscript sheets discovered during reconstruction work at Green Street courthouse. These eventually passed to F. E. Dixon who produced a typescript of 800 names from various other sources, which were supplemented from further documents in the Gilbert Library.

Tighe Street
See Benburb Street.

Tivoli Theatre
See **Conciliation Hall.**

Townsend Street
From College Green to Hanover Street
From town's end, formerly Lazar's Hill,* because pilgrims and beggars gathered here from all over the country. The pilgrims were put up in a hostel here before embarking for Spain in crowded boats. Each one was given a rough cloak with a cross and, while in Spain, was given a medal that was supposed to have miraculous power. In Viking times, this area was under water as the River Steyne flowed into the sea at the junction of Hawkins Street and Townsend Street. A modern stone in College Street marks the spot. The land was reclaimed in 1663 when Mr Hawkins built a sea wall along the river

from Burgh Quay to Townsend Street. In the late seventeenth century, passenger boats had to disembark their passengers at Ringsend, from where they were taken by cart across the sand to Townsend Street. By 1770, the Roman Catholic Church had fifteen chapels in Dublin, one of which was in Townsend Street. In 1984, an eight-storey office block, College House, designed by Henry J. Lyons and Partners, was leased to the state. The Hospital for Incurables moved to Townsend Street in 1753 and then to Donnybrook in 1792, when it became the Royal Hospital.

In 1998, the central Dublin fire brigade station moved from Pearse Street to Townsend Street. A bronze sculpture of Countess Markievicz, with her dog, stands on a granite plinth outside College Gate, a modern apartment block and swimming pool, designed by Anthony Reddy and Associates for Treasury Holdings, on the site of the old, single-storey Markievicz' baths, built in the 1970s.

Trinity College
On east side of College Green

The foundation stone was laid on 13 March 1592 on the site of the suppressed Augustinian monastery of All Hallows. A charter was provided by Elizabeth I and, within two years, the college was receiving students. Today it stands on a 42-acre site and none of the original red-brick buildings surrounding a 120-square-foot courtyard have survived. The impressive Palladian frontage and Parliament Square are attributed to Theodore Jacobsen; Parliament Square was so called because much of the cost was defrayed by the Dublin parliament. It was completed in the late 1750s. On the south side of the square is the Theatre used for examinations and, according to Provost Hely Hutchinson in 1775, 'for publick exercises and exhibitions'; work commenced in 1777. The Chapel opposite was designed by the English architect, William Chambers, and was completed under the direction of Graham Myers, who altered Chambers' designs, excluding a proposed dome. The building

Trinity College, looking across Parliament Square to Charles Lanyon's campanile of 1852.

was consecrated on Sunday, 8 July 1798. In 1973, the chapel was opened to all the main Christian denominations. The Blessed Sacrament Oratory was opened for prayer in 1975. Other buildings include the Dining Hall, badly damaged by fire in 1984, carefully restored and re-opened in 1986. On the east side of Library Square are the red-brick Rubrics. The great long room of the Library on the south side is open to the public and houses one of the finest collections of books in Ireland, including the *Book of Kells*. It also contains the Brian Boru harp copied on our coinage. Nearby is the arts and social sciences block which incorporates the Douglas Hyde Gallery.

The impressive museum buildings and the printing house in the form of a Doric temple are also worth noting. A focal point is the campanile, built in 1852. There is also the Berkeley Library, the centrepiece of the college's library system, opened in 1967. The Ussher Library, opened in 2002 and designed by McCullough Mulvin and KMD Architecture, won the Downes Medal at the Architectural Association of Ireland awards in 2003. There are over 6,000 students in the college. Its past pupils and lecturers include Jonathan Swift, Edmund Burke, Theobald Wolfe Tone, Henry Grattan, Oscar Wilde, Douglas Hyde and Samuel Beckett.

Trinity Street
From St Andrew's Street to College Green
Trinity Lane until 1756.
Trinity Hall, a public free school, was erected about 1616 and demolished in the eighteenth century. It stood on the hill on which St Andrew's Church now stands; this hill was occasionally styled Trinity Mount. Offices and shops; the Moira Hotel stood on the corner of Dame Lane.

Tucker's Row
See Sackville Place.

Tur Gloine, An (The Tower of Glass)
A stained-glass workshop at no. 24 Pembroke Street Upper, founded in 1903 by Edward Martyn and Sarah Purser. Sarah Purser was the principal shareholder. It was run as a co-operative, each artist being expected to create a window from the cartoon stage to the finished product. Many of the artists working there had been either trained or influenced by Alfred Child. After his death in 1940, Catherine O'Brien took over as manager. Among the many commissions, one of the most important was for the windows for Loughrea Cathedral made by individual members of the group. Registered in 1940 as An Tur Gloine Stained Glass Works Ltd, it was dissolved on the death of Sarah Purser in 1944, although Catherine O'Brien continued to run a workshop there until her death in 1963.

U

Ulysses
See **Leopold Bloom Sculpture Trail,** *also*
Clanbrassil Street Upper *and* **Martello**
Towers.

University Church (RC)
St Stephen's Green
Built on the instructions of John Henry
Newman as a college chapel for his new
university. The church, which was opened
in 1856, is in the Romanesque style with
elaborate interior of marble walls and
reproductions of Raphael cartoons. Much
of the design was created by Professor John
Hungerford Pollen, including the altar
above which is a large semi-dome depicting
Our Lady, Seat of Wisdom. It is based on
the apse of the church of San Clemente in
Rome. University Church was made a
parish church in 1974.

University College Dublin
The Irish Universities Act of 1908 which
founded the National University of Ireland
incorporated the Catholic University of
Ireland,* founded by Archbishop Paul
Cullen in 1854 at 86 St Stephen's Green.
The exhibition buildings at Earlsfort
Terrace* were converted by the architect
Edward Kavanagh in 1886 to house the
examination halls of the Royal University

of Ireland. University College Dublin, part
of the National University of Ireland,
moved to this site when new buildings
were erected in 1914–19 to a design of
Rudolph Maximilian Butler. Some of the
exhibition buildings also remain as do the
boundary wall and gates.
Because of overcrowding at Earlsfort
Terrace and at the College of Science at
Merrion Street, Dáil Éireann ratified an
agreement in 1960 that UCD should transfer
to Belfield. Science was the first of the
faculties to move to the new campus
designed by Andrzej Wejchert and, in 1964,
occupied the Science Building, designed by
Joseph Downes, the professor of
architecture. Andrzej Wejchert's Arts and
Commerce Building was opened in 1970
and the administration offices were
completed two years later. Robin Walker's
Restaurant also opened in 1970. The first
section of the Library, by Scottish architect
Hardie Glover, opened in 1972 and the
second section in 1987. Patrick Rooney's
Agriculture Building was completed in
1980. More recent developments include
the Students' Bar, the Sports Centre, the
Engineering Building and the Industry
Centre, designed by Ronald Tallon; and
the opening in 1989 of the first on-campus
student residences.

V

Victoria Street
South Circular Road
See **Portobello Gardens.**

Violin Making
Thomas Molyneux (Molineux), George
Ward, John Ward, Thomas Perry and Mr
Peetrie represent the earliest Dublin makers
who introduced violin making into
Dublin.
Thomas Perry was the best-known maker
of violins and other stringed instruments in
Dublin at the end of the eighteenth and
beginning of the nineteenth century. He
produced his first instruments about 1760.
Perry probably learnt his trade from
George Ward whose business was at
Anglesea Street and whose violins are dated
from the late 1760s. Perry was there in 1771.
George Ward died in 1769–70. John Ward
died in 1778 and was buried in St Andrew's
Church.* John Ward's daughter was left a
house by her father in Aston Quay, which

she let in tenements. George Ward's
address in 1740 was Lee's Lane, Aston
Quay.
Thomas Molyneux, Christchurch Yard,
another well-known maker, died in 1757,
and Mr Peetrie, fiddle maker, Temple Bar,
died July 1771.
William Wilkinson was apprenticed to
Thomas Perry and later married Perry's
daughter, Elizabeth. In 1790, the firm
became Thomas Perry and William
Wilkinson of no. 6 and afterwards no. 4
Anglesea Street. Perry died in 1818 and the
business continued until 1828 or possibly
later. One of the last Irish master violin
makers was John McNeill, 140 Capel
Street, whose firm was founded about 1830
and who died in the latter half of the
nineteenth century. His two sons, John and
Thomas, together with their sister,
Elizabeth, carried on the business. Thomas
died in 1917, his brother in 1923 and sister
in 1929.

W

Walls, Towers and Gates of the City

It is not known for certain when the city was enclosed, but by the time of the Norman invasion in 1170, Dublin was a walled city. In 1585, a detailed report was prepared for the Lord Deputy, Sir John Perrott, of the wall and its gates which extended along the Liffey from Parliament Street to St Augustine Street then inland to the Castle, St Nicholas Place and Lambe Alley, enclosing an area of 44 acres.

Dublin Castle, which stood at the S.E. corner, was completely enclosed by a curtain wall and ditch. Starting at the N.W. corner of this stronghold, there was the Cork Tower, named after the Earl of Cork who had it rebuilt in 1629. It was demolished in the eighteenth century. The Castle Gate was where the present entrance is at Castle Street. Two circular towers enclosed the gate with a portcullis and drawbridge. This gate was rebuilt in 1617 and demolished in the eighteenth century. The Store Tower, or Powder Tower, was situated at the N.E. corner and was sometimes used as a residence as it contained several windows. It was taken down in 1711. The Record Tower (also known as the Black or Wardrobe Tower), which still stands at the S.E. corner, was built about 1215 by King John. The former Chapel Royal is close by. The battlements were added in 1819. The Middle Tower stood about halfway between the Record Tower and the Bermingham Tower. It was demolished about the middle of the eighteenth century and the present rectilinear-angled structure was erected in its place about 1760. The Bermingham Tower, built in the fourteenth century, was used as a prison and for storage of public records. It was partially demolished by an explosion in 1775 and was rebuilt two years later. At the gateway in Ship Street at the corner of the castle wall stood the small Turret. James Stanihurst's Tower also stood in Ship Street. The remains of this three-storey tower are set into the wall of the street.

At the corner of Ship Street near Werburgh Street stood the Pole Gate, named after the dam or deep pool on the River Poddle (*see* Ship Street Great). The guild of barber surgeons used it as a hall from 1661. Across Werburgh Street on what is now Ross Road, and 62 yards from Pole Gate, stood Genevel's Tower (three-storey). Continuing into Nicholas Street at Nicholas Place was the St Nicholas' Gate, with two round towers outside and two square ones within the portcullised gate.

The wall continued to Power's Square where, at the rere of John Dillon Street, stood the Round Tower. Continuing for about 113 yards along the present street was the two-storey Tower of Christopher Sedgrave who lived there in 1585. Thirty yards further on, at Lambe Alley, was the Watch Tower where a sentry kept watch over Newgate Gaol.* The wall followed along Lambe Alley to the corner of the present Cornmarket near the junction of Bridge Street. It was here that the Newgate stood with four circular towers and a portcullis. In 1285, it was established as the Newgate Gaol.* Between Bridge Street and St Augustine Street stood the Corner Tower or Brown's Castle. An engraving in Grose's *Antiquities of Ireland*, 1791, shows it as a four-storey building with two square

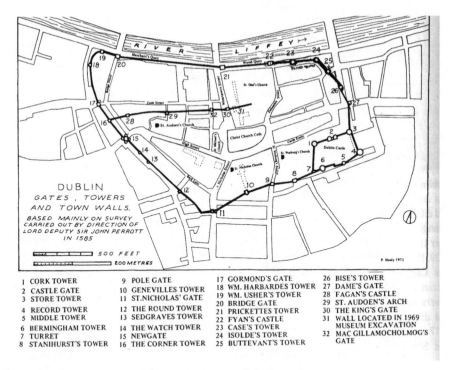

DUBLIN
GATES, TOWERS
AND TOWN WALLS.
BASED MAINLY ON SURVEY
CARRIED OUT BY DIRECTION OF
LORD DEPUTY SIR JOHN PERROTT
IN 1585

500 FEET
200 METRES

P. Healy 1973

1 CORK TOWER	9 POLE GATE	17 GORMOND'S GATE	26 BISE'S TOWER
2 CASTLE GATE	10 GENEVILLES TOWER	18 WM. HARBARDES TOWER	27 DAME'S GATE
3 STORE TOWER	11 ST.NICHOLAS' GATE	19 WM. USHER'S TOWER	28 FAGAN'S CASTLE
4 RECORD TOWER	12 THE ROUND TOWER	20 BRIDGE GATE	29 ST. AUDOEN'S ARCH
5 MIDDLE TOWER	13 SEDGRAVES TOWER	21 PRICKETTES TOWER	30 THE KING'S GATE
6 BERMINGHAM TOWER	14 THE WATCH TOWER	22 FYAN'S CASTLE	31 WALL LOCATED IN 1969
7 TURRET	15 NEWGATE	23 CASE'S TOWER	MUSEUM EXCAVATION
8 STANIHURST'S TOWER	16 THE CORNER TOWER	24 ISOLDE'S TOWER	32 MAC GILLAMOCHOLMOG'S
		25 BUTTEVANT'S TOWER	GATE

Walls, towers and gates of the city. The late Patrick Healy's 1973 map with corrections 1990.

towers and an arched gate at the side. Gormond's (Gormund's, Gudmond's) Gate was 47 yards further on at the corner of St Augustine Street (*see* Mullinahack), named after William Gudmund, 1233. In 1593, it was leased to the Corporation of Smiths.

At the rere of the Brazen Head hotel in Bridge Street there was William Harbard's Tower a two-storey building. Continuing towards the river was William Usher's Tower (*see* Usher's Quay). Bridge Gate was at the bridge across the Liffey at Bridge Street. Erected about 1200, it was rebuilt in 1598 and was sometimes called Ostman's Gate. Along Merchant's Quay at the bottom of Winetavern Street there was Prickett's Tower, a thirteenth-century house occupied by Mr Prickett in 1585.

Continuing along Wood Quay to the junction with Winetavern Street was Fyan's or Proudfoote's Castle. This was an early fourteenth-century castle granted to Richard Fyan in 1557 and appears to have

been rebuilt by him in 1571. Richard Proudfoote occupied it in 1605 but it was still referred to as Fyan's Castle on Speed's Map of 1610. Fitzsymon or Case's Tower on Blind Quay was restored by Robert Fitzsymon in 1471. Further along the Quay there was a round tower known as Isolde's Tower. It was occupied by the Corporation of Bakers in 1558, who were sued by Robert Newman in 1602 for excessively damaging the tower.

The Buttevant or Forward Tower was a thirteenth-century tower demolished in 1675 when the new Essex Gate was built at the street of the same name. Bise's Tower was granted to the Bise family in the sixteenth century. Standing halfway up Parliament Street, it was demolished when that street was laid out in 1763. Dame's or Damas Gate stood in Dame Street opposite Palace Street, with a narrow entrance between two towers and a portcullis. It was demolished in 1698. The wall then continued to the Store Tower, thus completely enclosing the city.

There was also an older and inner wall which ran from Brown's Castle along Cook Street and across Winetavern Street. In Page's Court, a passage between Cornmarket and Cook Street, there was Fagan's Castle. The only surviving gateway is St Audoen's Arch, together with a part of the wall in Cook Street. Due for demolition in 1880, it was unsympathetically restored by the Corporation following public protest. The King's Gate, or Winetavern Gate, was near the top of Winetavern Street. There was also an entrance gate at Macgiolla Mocholmóg Street, now St Michael's Close. It was called Porta Gillemeholmoc and is mentioned in a deed attested by Richard de Cogan, one of the original Anglo-Norman invaders of Ireland.

Ward's Hill
From New Row to Newmarket
Name comes from the Ward family who had a brewery here and in New Row. Richard Ward, a brewer, was living in New Row in 1680; John Ward, a brewer of Ward's Hill, died in 1738. Alexander Ward, of Read's Barn, Kilkenny, disposed of the brewery to Michael Reynolds of Newmarket. A lease of 1719 describes the houses on the west side of the street as 'lately built by James Edkins, late of Ropers Rest, Gentleman'.

In 1703, a Mr Rowe leased four acres for a market garden to an Englishman named Bullen. He was responsible for growing the first pineapples in Ireland. The Huguenots had introduced the art of topiary, that of cutting box hedges into animal shapes, and Mr Bullen had a display of hedges cut and shaped into designs representing animals and birds.

Warrenmount
Mill Street
Named after Nathaniel Warren, a Mill Street brewer. High Sheriff 1773, Lord Mayor 1782, MP 1784, one of three Commissioners of Police 1794, built a large residence here called Warrenmount. It

survived until 1894. It was built on the site of two double mills referred to in a grant of 1538 from King Henry VIII to William Brabazon. The area is occupied by the Presentation convent and schools.
See **Liberty of the Earl of Meath.**

Water Supply
The Poddle* river was the main supply to the city from earliest times. In 1244, the Dodder river was diverted at Firhouse and a canal known as the city watercourse was built linking the Dodder to the Poddle. The entire scheme was completed in 1248. This supply was extended in 1308 when two-thirds of the Poddle, augmented with the Dodder water, was channelled along Thomas Street and High Street to the city basin outside St Audoen's Church.* In 1600, the first wooden pipes were laid to carry water supplies. In 1660–71, lead pipes were also laid in the city. In 1721, the city basin was constructed at James's Street and this was supplied by the Poddle to provide 90 days' storage. At Mount Argus, an artificial tongue divided the stream, some going to the basin and the rest flowing by Harold's Cross. By 1735, water was being pumped from the Liffey to a basin at Islandbridge as the existing supply was insufficient to cater for a growing population. With the construction of the Grand Canal and the Royal Canal (1775 and 1789),* a new source of water supply became available to the Corporation. Reservoirs were built at Blessington Street, Portobello Harbour and James's Street to store water taken by agreement from the canals. The system is still in operation for supplying up to twelve million litres a day to Guinness's brewery. By the 1850s, the population of Dublin had reached 300,000 and the existing supplies were becoming inadequate. In 1853–54, cast-iron mains were laid to replace the wooden pipes, and negotiations were entered into with the canal companies for increased supplies of water, but agreement on price could not be reached.

As a result, the Corporation developed the Vartry river scheme in 1861, and its

Sir John Gray (1815–1875) owner of the Freeman's Journal, *knighted in 1863 for inaugurating the Vartry water scheme. Memorial at Glasnevin.*

completion in 1869 marked the beginning of today's water supply to the greater Dublin area. The project consisted of damming the Vartry river at Roundwood and building slow sand filters through which treated water is transported through 23¾ miles of tunnel to 17½ miles of 33-inch diameter pipe to a new 83,018,000-gallon reservoir at Stillorgan, and from there by two 27-inch mains to the city mains. In 1885, an additional 94,213,000 gallon reservoir was built at Stillorgan, bringing the total storage to 177,231,000 gallons. A new source of supply was developed when the Township of Rathmines and Rathgar dammed the Dodder river at Bohernabreena in 1886–88 and fed the water to slow sand filters at Ballyboden before supplying the township. Between 1919 and 1922, an additional reservoir was formed above the existing reservoir by damming the Vartry upstream of the first dam. This was to safeguard against drought such as happened in 1893.

The construction of a dam across the Liffey

at Poulaphouca, Co. Wicklow, in 1939 was the first step towards the completion of works begun under the Liffey Reservoir Act of 1936. The dam was built as a dual-purpose scheme for use jointly by Dublin Corporation and the Electricity Supply Board. Water from the impoundment is supplied by gravity to Dublin Corporation's water-treatment plant at Ballymore Eustace, Co. Kildare, which supplies half the daily requirements of the greater Dublin region which has a population of over 2 million people and includes Counties Dublin, Kildare and Wicklow, Dún Laoghaire Rathdown, Bray UDC and Dublin city. The rapid expansion of the suburbs in recent times has necessitated the development and expansion of the Ballymore Eustace scheme on the Liffey in 1945 and the Leixlip scheme, also on the Liffey, in 1966.

The present water consumption from all sources in the greater Dublin area is 500 million litres per day. The City Council produces 70 per cent of this water, with the balance being produced by Fingal County Council. Commencing in 2003, a 10 per cent increase in water pressure eliminated any need for rationing during the summer season. Water produced at the four major plants at Roundwood, Ballyboden, Ballymore Eustace and Leixlip is piped to a number of major service reservoirs nearer the built-up areas, and from there, several thousand kilometres of water mains, ranging from the cast-iron mains of the 1850s to PVC, asbestos cement, pre-stressed concrete and ductile iron, carry water to all users in the supply area.

Watling Street
From Thomas Street to Usher's Island

Prior to the Reformation, the parish of St James* was outside the wall of the city, starting at the junction of Thomas Street and Watling Street with an entrance at St James's Gate. In 1745, Fr Fitzsimons obtained a site at the east corner of the street and built a chapel that served until the present RC church was opened in James's Street. On the corner of the street joining Usher's Island is the night shelter and residential centre of the Dublin Simon Community, opened in June 1989. A street of Corporation flats and the Rupert Guinness Hall, named after the second Earl of Iveagh (1874–1967). The large tapering brick tower, with a copper dome surmounted by a figure of St Patrick, was built as a smock-windmill used for grinding corn in the early part of the nineteenth century for Roe's Distillery (*see* Christ Church Cathedral and Thomas Street). It was eventually incorporated into the Guinness brewery complex.

Weights and Measures Department
See **Harry Street.**

Wellington Monument, Phoenix Park. Foundation stone laid on 17 June 1817.

Wellington Monument
Phoenix Park
Named after Arthur Wellesley, Duke of Wellington (1769–1852), 'The Iron Duke'.
An entry in Faulkner's *Dublin Journal* of 20 July 1813 announced that a meeting of noblemen and gentlemen would take place this day at the Rotunda to arrange the plan and progress of a monument to Lord Wellington. A committee of 85 persons, including 35 peers, had raised £16,000 by 1814. They then advertised for suitable designs and a large number of these were submitted, out of which six were chosen.

From these, models of a uniform size were exhibited in the Dublin Society premises in Hawkins Street. Robert (later Sir Robert) Smirke's design in the form of an obelisk was chosen and, after a lot of controversy regarding location, the foundation stone was laid on 17 June 1817 by the Lord Lieutenant, Lord Whitworth, on a site in the Phoenix Park.

£22,000 had been raised for the monument but another £12,000 was needed to cast the bronze panels depicting the Duke's victories, to be made from cannon captured at the Peninsula. The monument stood unadorned for some years, as the Duke was to go through a period of unpopularity created by his opposition to parliamentary reform. In 1852, the Duke died and interest in the monument was revived. It was agreed that Joseph Robinson Kirk, Terence Farrell and John Hogan should each design a panel to be cast in bronze and erected on the obelisk at a cost of £1,500 per panel.

On 18 June 1861, 44 years after the laying of the foundation stone, the panels were exhibited in place. At the same time, pedestals that were originally designed to hold a statue of the Duke with lions were removed and replaced with sloping steps similar to ones on the opposite side.

Werburgh Street
From Castle Street to Bride Street
Name comes from St Werburgh's Church,* built on a site of 1178; the present church dates from 1759. Nothing remains of the

Wellington Monument. One of three panels erected in 1861 at a cost of £1,500 per panel, forty-four years after the laying of the foundation stone.

cage workhouses built in this area. The last remaining one on the corner of Castle Street was demolished in 1813. Dublin's first professional theatre was opened here in 1636 under the direction of John Ogilby. James Shirley, an Englishman, wrote *St Patrick for Ireland*, an Anglo-Irish play in the Irish tradition. The theatre appears to have survived until the outbreak of the 1641 rebellion.
See **Smock Alley Theatre.**

Wesley College
St Stephen's Green
Founded in 1845 at no. 79 as the Wesleyan Connexional School but moved in 1879 to a new building at the rear of the Methodist Centenary Church. The new school was designed by Alfred Jones and built at a cost of £20,000. During the centenary year of the school, a letter was sent to George Bernard Shaw, a past pupil, asking for a subscription. His reply said 'my curse on it'. He sent a donation instead to the High School. In 1969, the school moved to Ludford, Ballinteer. The nineteenth-century building was demolished and an office block now stands on the site.

Westland Row
From Pearse Street to Lincoln Place
Named after William Westland, property owner.
Royal Irish Academy of Music* (1856) at no. 36 is in the house of the Marquis of Conyngham. Oscar Wilde was born at no. 21. The Church of St Andrew or All Hallows was built 1832–37 to a design of

James Bolger (Boulger). The wooden crucifixion over the altar is by Oisín Kelly. Two paintings, *The Martyrdom of St Thomas à Becket* and *The Crucifixion*, were both presented by Daniel O'Connell who was involved in the building of the church. In 1859, a railway connection from Westland Row Station to Carlisle Pier at Kingstown (Dún Laoghaire) was opened, to take the mail to Holyhead and, in 1862, the station was extended, to a design of the architect George Wilkinson.
In 1989, Ronald Tallon designed the Innovation Centre for Trinity College, Dublin. Known as the O'Reilly Institute, the large glass structure completes a row of Victorian buildings owned by the college. The development was with the assistance of the IDA.

Westmoreland Street
From College Green to O'Connell Bridge
Named after John Fane, 10th Earl of Westmoreland, Lord Lieutenant 1790–94. Westmoreland Street and D'Olier Street were the last two major schemes to be carried out by the Wide Streets Commissioners.* Plans for the new street were sought in 1792 and, in 1799, one of three plans submitted by Henry Aaron Baker (1753–1836) was agreed, with four-storey brick buildings and shops at ground level. The street retains some of the original buildings together with some Victorian and twentieth-century constructions. Number 21, which corners onto Aston Quay, was built in 1802 by the Corporation, as the Ballast Office, for

O'CONNELL BRIDGE AND TRINITY COLLEGE, DUBLIN

Westmoreland Street and D'Olier Street were the last two major schemes to be carried out by the Wide Streets Commissioners, to a design of Henry Aaron Baker. Aerial photograph shows the two streets with the Ballast Office* on the corner of Aston Quay. The buildings of Trinity College are clearly visible.

preserving and improving the port of Dublin. It was remodelled in 1864 and, in 1866, following a fire at the next-door premises, it was extended to take in nos. 19 and 20. The clock which was installed in 1870 was connected to a time signal for mariners which was regulated from Dunsink Observatory. The building was demolished in 1979 when a new office block was erected. The Port and Docks Board had vacated the premises in 1974, having sold it to the Royal Liver Insurance for £250,000.

In 1960, the Paradiso restaurant, with one of the finest Art Nouveau designs in the city, was purchased, together with the *Irish Times'* office and Graham's Pharmacy, by the Educational Building Society. Two glass-fronted office blocks, to a design of Sam Stephenson, were erected with the façade only of the Paradiso left in the centre. The Westin Hotel, designed by Henry Lyons and Partners, opened in 1998 (*see* College Street). The Allied Irish Bank is in a new complex at 40/41.

Wexford Street
From Aungier Street to Camden Street
A gateway led from here into the Liberty of St Sepulchre. A nineteenth-century street in a busy shopping area with a variety of public houses and general trading.
See Liberties *and* Kevin Street Upper.

White Horse Yard
Off 12 Winetavern Street
Name comes from the White Horse House Inn, 1620. In 1568, known as the Chamberlain's Inns. The new Dublin Fire Brigade was formed under an act of 1862 and a new fire station was built in the yard, with Captain Ingram as superintendent. It received much press coverage at the time, as telegraphy was installed in order to liaise with its sister station in Coppinger Row. Dublin received its first fire engine in 1706 and two of these appliances may be seen in the porch of St Werburgh's Church.*

Whitefriar Street
From Stephen Street Lower to Peter Row
Possibly part of a Viking fort. The entrance to the Carmelite church was originally in the street. The White Friars monastery was built by Sir Robert Bagot in 1278 and was dissolved in 1539. The calced Carmelites were the only suppressed order to return to their original location. The church and monastery were rebuilt and extended between 1756 and 1816. The design for the present Church of Our Lady of Mount Carmel, by George Papworth, broke through the monastery with a main entrance into Aungier Street, with a large entrance porch and the interior greatly altered with high arches supported by columns. It was re-dedicated in 1827. Beneath the altar are the remains of St

Valentine, donated by Pope Gregory XVI to Fr Spratt in 1835. The remains were brought from Rome in a steel casket and arrived in Dublin on 10 November 1836. The custom of sending Valentine cards in all probability originates from the belief that 14 February, the saint's feast day, marks the beginning of spring and the mating season of birds in this part of the world. Opposite to what is now the side of the church are a few small shops including a long-established picture framer.
See **St Mary's Abbey.**

Wicklow Street
From Exchequer Street to Grafton Street
Originally, Exchequer Street extended to Grafton Street but the inhabitants in the part from South William Street petitioned the Wide Streets Commissioners to have the name changed to Wicklow Street as the street had a bad name which made it difficult to obtain respectable tenants for the properties. This was granted on 18 October 1837. General trading area with shops and offices. Weir and Sons, the jewellers, are at 1–3 and were established in 1869 by Thomas Weir, who arrived from Glasgow in 1865 to work for Wests, the jewellers in College Green. Brown Thomas, the general drapers, moved across the road from Grafton Street into the former premises of Switzer's. Switzer, a descendant of the Palatines, a group of Protestants who came to Ireland in the 1650s from a province in Germany called the Palatinate (Rheinland Pfalz), opened a drapery store in 1838 which eventually extended from 90–93 Grafton Street to 38–45 Wicklow Street.

Wide Streets Commissioners
Following the passing of an Act of Parliament in 1757, the city experienced the most enlightened period of planning in its history. The Wide Streets Commissioners were to transform narrow streets and laneways into the impressive streets that we know today. The Commissioners' first task was to make a wide and convenient way from Essex Bridge to the Castle of Dublin.

Under the direction of its secretary, Thomas Sherrard, Parliament Street was opened up in 1762. They then proceeded to widen Dame Street in 1769. By 1784, Sackville Street (Lower O'Connell Street) had been developed, also North Frederick Street and part of Cavendish Row. Westmoreland Street and D'Olier Street were under way at the beginning of the nineteenth century. Royal approval was given for a grant of £15,000 towards a new bridge across the Liffey in 1782, and it was decided to extend Sackville Street to the river and to continue it in the opposite direction to Dorset Street along East Rutland Square and North Frederick Street. The Commissioners had achieved their aims by 1800 and no further new major schemes were carried out after the Act of Union.

William Street North
From North Strand to Summerhill
The street is dominated by St Agatha's (RC) Church with a frontage onto Dunne Street. The church was opened in 1908 and designed by William H. Byrne in the classical style with Corinthian corner pilasters and a pediment having statues of Christ, St Patrick and St Agatha. Amid Corporation flats, St Agatha's Court and small dwellings is St Vincent's Boys' and Girls' Primary School and a large convent of the Daughters of Charity of St Vincent de Paul.

William Street South
Exchequer Street to Lower Stephen Street
Laid out by William Williams in 1676.
The street is dominated by Powerscourt House,* completed in 1774 for Richard, 3rd Viscount Powerscourt. In 1981, it was converted into a speciality shopping centre of 80 units. At no. 58 stands the City Assembly House,* which housed the Society of Artists in 1765 and, in 1791, housed the City Assembly. In the eighteenth century, it was a fashionable street inhabited by many personages of importance, including John Wainwright, Baron of the Exchequer (1732), Carew

Reynell, Bishop of Down (1739–42), and Henry Cope MD, Physician to the State. Today it is a general trading street with a variety of businesses and restaurants.

Wilton Place
Grand Canal to Lad Lane
From Wilton near Salisbury, the seat of the Earl of Pembroke and Montgomery. Row of brick and granite houses completed in 1844. Only nos. 1 to 6 remain. A modern block, Court Flats, completes one side of a triangle. Another side is taken up by three large office blocks all backing onto Lad Lane. Fitzwilton House, with 75,000 square feet of office space, was completed in 1969. This was followed by Wilton Park House and Gardiner House, with a large courtyard between them having an artificial lake and a bronze figure balancing on a trestle, completed by Carolyn Mulholland in 1987. Amidst all this at one time stood the Fitzwilliam Lawn Tennis Club which moved, in 1969, to a four-and-a-half-acre site bounded by Winton Road and Appian Way.

Wilton Terrace
Facing the Grand Canal at Baggot Street
From Wilton near Salisbury, the seat of the Earl of Pembroke and Montgomery. A fine row of red-brick and granite houses built between 1842 and 1844. The Pembroke Estate office was at one time housed at no. 7a. Four of the houses were demolished to make way for an office block which is now the headquarters of Bord Fáilte. The remainder were demolished and a red-brick office block constructed in their place. The original railed park remains, with a nineteenth-century cast fountain.

Winetavern Street
From St Michael's Hill to Wood Quay
Styled in old documents *Vicus Tabernariorum Vini*, was so called from having been originally occupied by keepers of wine taverns, usually described as taverners. There were a great many taverns in this area. In 1185, the Abbey of Thomas Court was granted a toll from ale and metheglin (a variety of mead), payable out of the taverns then existing in Dublin. In 1565, the increase of taverns in Dublin caused Nicholas Fitzsimons, then Mayor, to issue a proclamation that 'no woman nor maids should sell wine, ale or beer in the city unless such as should keep a sign at their doors under a penalty of forty shillings'. Originally the Guild Hall* or public court stood here but was disused after the transfer of its business to Skinners' Row early in the fourteenth century. In a deed of 1384, there is a notice of a vacant place where the Guild Hall stood. In 1597, 144 barrels of gun powder exploded in the street which, with adjoining streets, was razed to the ground with great loss of life. In 1539, the Tailors' Hall* was here. At the beginning of the nineteenth century, stepped red-brick houses were built. Second-hand clothes were sold here until the entire area was demolished. It has been rebuilt as part of the urban renewal scheme with a complex named Inns Court consisting of individual office units, office/residential units, three- to four-storey office block and lock-up garages. Designed by Aidan Powell.

Wood Street
Off Bridge Street
Name comes from Rev. Daniel Wood, curate of St Stephen's, 1634.
***See also* Huguenot Chapel of St Brigide's.**

Workhouse
James's Street
As well as caring for the sick poor, the charitable citizens of eighteenth-century Dublin were faced with the problem of providing for what had been termed the vagabond or sturdy beggar. The problem had persisted down the centuries and, about 1687, the city expended some £800 in laying foundations for a 'work house' where people could be dealt with as the authorities thought fit. Nothing further was done until 1703 when the City Fathers indicated their willingness to grant a piece of ground and an endowment valued at £100. On 12 October 1704, the foundation

stone was laid by the Duchess of Ormonde. In addition to receiving vagrants and able-bodied poor, the institution was also to provide for unwanted or destitute children. By 1729, the workhouse had been transformed entirely into a foundling hospital, and a turnstile was provided in the wall so that persons could leave unwanted children to be cared for by the authorities.

By 1773, the workhouse had been divided into two separate institutions, a House of Industry in Channel Row and the foundling hospital that had been rebuilt. Lady Arabella Denny, founder of the Magdalen Asylum,* was involved in the foundling hospital from 1759 and subscribed more than £4,000 towards the building costs and wages for the nurses.

In about 1800, Francis Johnston added battlements, a pair of modest wings and a cupola. He also added a chapel at the back. Later, a Church of Ireland chapel was added to the front, obscuring the fine doorcase. The bell from the workhouse, manufactured by Rudhall of Gloucester in 1802, together with the foundation stone, are retained by Dublin City Council.

While it was in use as a foundling hospital, the mortality rate of children was high and up to three-quarters of those admitted died each year. In the 1840s, the workhouse idea was again introduced, catering mainly for adults. Today, the large, modern St James's Hospital occupies the site.

See **House of Industry, Channel Row** *and* **Magdalen Asylum.**

Yarn Hall Street
Off North King Street
The Linen Hall was built here in 1716 to accommodate traders from Northern Ireland selling their wares. This was to develop into a multi-million pound industry. Part of the gateway survives. Adjoining streets, Coleraine, Lisburn, Lurgan, all bear N. Ireland place names.

York Street
From St Stephen's Green to Aungier Street
Name comes from Ernest Augustus, Duke of York and Albany, died 1728.
A fashionable eighteenth- and nineteenth-century street. Number 48 housed a school run by Mrs and Miss Knowles, relatives of Thomas Sheridan, the actor. All the original houses have been demolished and Corporation flats erected in their place. Entrance to the new extension of the Royal College of Surgeons.* Opposite was the headquarters of the Salvation Army* until the building was sold to the RCSI and demolished. A new building, designed by architects Brian O'Halloran and Associates, opened in 2004. A house was built in 1756 and on the garden Rev. Albert Nesbitt built York Street Congregational Church; part of the walls of this church were used in the building of the Salvation Army premises. In 2004, work commenced on a Dublin City Council development of 66 new apartments (15 three-bed, 31 two-bed and 20 one-bed) with basement car parking, community space at ground level and one commercial unit on the corner of Mercer Street. The Royal College of Surgeons is built on part of a Quaker burial ground, purchased in 1805 as a site for the new college.

Z

Zion Church

Zion Road, Rathgar

In 1860, John Gold (Goold), a rich stockbroker of Fownes Street, erected at his own expense a Protestant church and school for the parish of Rathgar. A site in Windmill Lane (Zion Road) was secured and the building, designed by Welland and Son, erected in the Medieval Gothic style. Established as an independent church, it was made a parish church in 1921.

Zoological Society of Dublin

See **Royal Zoological Society of Ireland.**

Zozimus

Michael Moran (c. 1794–1846), born in Faddle (Fattle, Foddle) Alley off Dowker's (Ducker's) Lane near New Street. A street balladeer and reciter, who became blind shortly after birth. He dressed in a scalloped cape and top hat and carried a blackthorn stick. The name Zozimus comes from one of his favourite metrical tales 'St Mary of Egypt' by Dr Coyle, Bishop of Raphoe, in which Mary is found in the desert by Bishop Zozimus. He sold his poems, many of which were political, on ballad sheets to whoever would buy them in the street. W. B. Yeats described him as the admitted rector of all the ballad mongers, in 'The Last Gleeman'. He died on 3 April 1846 at 14½ Patrick Street. He is buried in Glasnevin Cemetery; a limestone memorial was erected over his grave during the Dublin Millennium in 1988.

BIBLIOGRAPHY

Andrews, C. S., *Dublin Made Me*, Cork: Mercier Press, 1979.
Ball, F. E., *A History of County Dublin*, Dublin: Alex Thom, 1906.
Ballagh, R., *Dublin*, Dublin: Ward River Press, 1981.
Bence-Jones, M., *Burke's Guide to Country Houses*, London: Burke's Peerage, 1978.
Bence-Jones, M., *Twilight of the Ascendancy*, London: Constable, 1987.
Boylan, H., *A Dictionary of Irish Biography*, Dublin: Gill & Macmillan, 1978.
Boylan, H., *This Arrogant City*, Dublin: A. and A. Farmar, 1983.
Bradley, B., *James Joyce's Schooldays*, Dublin: Gill & Macmillan, 1982.
Bradley, J., ed., *Viking Dublin Exposed*, Dublin: O'Brien Press, 1984.
Byrne, M., *Dublin and Her People*, Dublin: Eason and Son, 1987.
Byrne, P., *Lord Edward Fitzgerald*, Dublin: Talbot Press, 1955.
Byrne, P., *The Wildes of Merrion Square*, London: Staples Press, 1953.
Chart, D. A., *Dublin*, London: J. M. Dent, 1907.
Church of Ireland Gazette, 8 July 1921, p. 423, and 8 February 1924, p. 87, St Barnabas Public Utility
   Society, 1921 and 1924.
Clarke, D., *Dublin*, London: Batsford Books, 1977.
Clarke, H. B., *Dublin c. 840–1540*, Dublin: Ordnance Survey Map, 1978.
Clarke, H. B., ed., *Medieval Dublin: The Living City*, Dublin: Irish Academic Press, 1990.
Clarke, H. B., ed., *Medieval Dublin: The Making of a Metropolis*, Dublin: Irish Academic Press,
   1990.
Clark, M. and Refausse, R., *Directory of Historic Dublin Guilds*, Dublin Public Libraries, 1993.
Comerford, M., *The First Dáil*, Dublin: Joe Clarke, 1969.
Conlin, S., *Historic Dublin*, Dublin: O'Brien Press, 1986.
Cosgrave E. MacD and Strangeways, L. R., *Illustrated Dictionary of Dublin*, Dublin: Sealy, Bryers
   and Walker, 1895.
Costello, P., *Dublin Churches*, Dublin: Gill & Macmillan, 1989.
Craig, M., *Architecture of Ireland from Earliest Times to 1880*, London: Batsford, 1982.
Craig, M., *Dublin 1660–1860*, second edition, Dublin: Allen Figgis, 1969.
Craig, M. and the Knight of Glin, *Ireland Observed*, Cork: Mercier Press, 1980.
Craig, M. and Wheeler, H. A., *Dublin City Churches*, Belfast and Dublin: APCK, 1948.
Cullen, F., *Cleansing Rural Dublin*, Irish Academic Press, 2001.
Culliton, J., *The City Hall*, Dublin: Eason and Son, 1982.
D'Alton, J., *The History of the County Dublin*, Dublin: Hodges and Smith, 1838.
de Breffny, B. and ffolliott, R., *The Houses of Ireland*, London: Thames and Hudson, 1975.
Delany, R., *The Grand Canal of Ireland*, Newton Abbot: David and Charles, 1973.
Delany, V. and D. R., *The Canals of the South of Ireland*, Newton Abbot: David and Charles, 1966.
de Vere White, T., *The Story of the Royal Dublin Society*, Tralee: The Kerryman, 1955.
Fagan, P., *The Second City, Portrait of Dublin 1700–60*, Dublin: Branar, 1986.
Fitzpatrick, S. A. O., *Dublin, A Historical and Topographical Account of the City*, London: Methuen,
   1907.

Geoghegan, P. M., *Robert Emmet*, Gill & Macmillan, 2002.

Georgian Society Records (5 Volumes), Dublin: Dublin University Press, 1909–13.

Gilbert, Sir J. T., *A History of the City of Dublin*, 3 Volumes, Dublin: Vol. 1 James McGlashan, 1854; vols 2 and 3 McGlashan and Gill, 1859.

Gilbert Sir, J. T. ed., and Gilbert, Lady, *Calendar of Ancient Records of Dublin* (19 Volumes), Dublin: Joseph Dollard, 1889–1944.

Gill M. H. and Son, ed., *Guide to Catholic Dublin*, Dublin: Gill and Son, 1932.

Gillespie, E., ed., *The Liberties of Dublin*, Dublin: O'Brien Press, 1973.

Gorham, M., *Dublin from Old Photographs*. London: Batsford, 1972.

Gorham, M., *Dublin Old and New*, Menston (Yorkshire): E. P. Publications, 1975.

Gorham, M., *Ireland from Old Photographs*, London: Batsford, 1971.

Gregory W., *Picture of Dublin. A Description of the City*, Dublin: Walter Gregory, 1815.

Guinness, D., *Georgian Dublin*, London: Batsford, 1979.

Guinness, D., *Portrait of Dublin*, London: Batsford, 1967.

Guinness, D. and Ryan, W., *Irish Houses and Castles*, London: Thames and Hudson, 1971.

Haliday, C., *The Scandinavian Kingdom of Ireland*, Dublin: Alex Thom, 1881.

Harbison, P., *National Monuments of Ireland*, Dublin: Gill & Macmillan, 1970.

Harbison, P., *The Shell Guide to Ireland (Revised)*, Dublin: Gill & Macmillan, 1989.

Harris, W., *History of Antiquities of the City of Dublin*, Dublin: L. Flynn, 1766.

Hobson, B. ed., *A Book of Dublin*, Dublin: Kevin J. Kenny, 1930.

Humphreys, A., *New Dubliners*, London: Routledge & Kegan Paul, 1965.

Hunt, H., *The Abbey, Ireland's National Theatre 1904–78*, Dublin: Gill & Macmillan, 1979.

Hyman, L., *The Jews of Ireland*, Shannon: Irish University Press, 1972.

Igoe, V., *Dublin Burial Grounds and Graveyards*, Dublin: Wolfhound Press, 2001.

Igoe, V., *A Literary Guide to Dublin*, London: Methuen, 1994.

Johnson, N., *Dublin, The People's City*, Dublin: Academy Press, 1981.

Johnston, M., *Around the Banks of Pimlico*, Dublin: Attic Press, 1985.

Kearns, K. C., *Dublin Pub Life and Lore*, Dublin: Gill & Macmillan, 1996.

Kearns, K. C., *Dublin Tenement Life*, Dublin: Gill & Macmillan, 1994.

Kearns, K. C., *Stoneybatter*, Dublin: Glendale Press, 1989.

Kelleher, D. L., *The Glamour of Dublin*, Dublin: Talbot Press, 1929.

Kelly, D., *Hands Off Dublin*, Dublin: O'Brien Press, 1976.

Kelly, F., *A History of Kilmainham Gaol*, Cork: Mercier Press, 1988.

Lalor, B., *Dublin*, London: Routledge & Kegan Paul, 1981.

Lewis, S., *A History and Topography of the City of Dublin*, Cork: Mercier Press, 1980.

Liddy P., *Dublin Today*, Dublin: Irish Times, 1984.

McCarthy, J., *Joyce's Dublin. A Walking Guide to Ulysses*, Dublin: Wolfhound Press, 1986.

McCready, C. T., *Dublin Street Names*, Dublin: Hodges Figgis, 1892.

McDonald, F., *The Construction of Dublin*, Cork: Gandon Editions, 2000.

McDonald, F., *The Destruction of Dublin*, Dublin: Gill & Macmillan, 1985.

McDonald, F., *Saving the City*, Dublin: Tomar, 1989.

McGregor, J. J., *New Picture of Dublin. Comprehending a History of the City*, Dublin: John Allen & John James McGregor, 1821.

McLoughlin, A., *A Guide to Historic Dublin*, Dublin: Gill & Macmillan, 1979.

McManus, R., *Dublin 1910–1940*, Dublin: Four Courts Press, 2002.

Malcolm, E., *Swift's Hospital*, Dublin: Gill & Macmillan, 1989.

Martin, F. X., ed., *A New History of Ireland* (10 volumes), Oxford: Clarendon Press, 1976–87.

Maxwell, C., *Dublin under the Georges*, London: George Harrap, 1946.

Maxwell, C., *A History of Trinity College Dublin 1591–1892*, Dublin: University Press, 1946.

Maxwell, C., *The Stranger in Ireland*, Dublin: Jonathan Cape, 1954.

Moody, T. W. and Martin, F. X., eds, *The Course of Irish History*, Cork: Mercier Press, 1967.

Norris, D., *Joyce's Dublin*, Dublin: Eason and Son, 1982.

O'Connell, D., *The Antique Pavement*, Dublin: An Taisce, 1975.

O'Donnell, E. E., *The Annals of Dublin, Fair City*, Dublin: Wolfhound Press, 1987.

O'Dwyer, F., *Lost Dublin*, Dublin: Gill & Macmillan, 1981.

Ó Raifeartaigh T., ed., *The Royal Irish Academy 1785–1985*, Dublin: Royal Irish Academy, 1985.

Otway-Ruthven, A. J., *A History of Medieval Ireland*, London: Ernest Benn, 1968.

Prunty, J., *Dublin Slums 1800–1925*, Irish Academic Studies, 1998.

Reynolds, M., *A History of the Irish Post Office*, Dublin: MacDonnell Whyte, 1983.

Robertson, O., *Dublin Phoenix*, London: Jonathan Cape, 1957.

Ryan, D., ed., *The Workers' Republic of James Connolly*, Dublin: Sign of the Three Candles, 1951.

Ryan, J., *Remembering How We Stood*, Dublin: Gill & Macmillan, 1975.

Shaw, H., *The Dublin Pictorial Guide & Directory 1850*, Dublin: Henry Shaw, 1850.

Somerville-Large, P., *Dublin*, London: Hamish Hamilton, 1979.

Somerville-Large, P., *Irish Eccentrics*, London: Hamish Hamilton, 1975.

Warburton, J., Whitelaw, J., and Walsh, R., *History of the City of Dublin* (2 volumes), London: Cadel & Davies, 1818.

Webb, J. J., *The Guilds of Dublin*, Dublin: Sign of the Three Candles, 1929.

Whitlock, N., *Picturesque Guide of Dublin*, Dublin, Liverpool and London: J. Cornish, 1846.

Wilson, W., *Post Chase Companion*, Dublin: Walter Wilson, 1786.

Wren, J., *The Villages of Dublin*, Dublin: Tomar, 1987.

Wright, G. N., *An Historical Guide to the City of Dublin*, London: Baldwin, Cradock & Joy, 1821.

Yeats, P., *Lockout 1913*, Dublin: Gill & Macmillan, 2003.

INDEX